CHRIST IN PROPHECY

Christ in Prophecy

Dr. Paul Heinisch
Author

William G. Heidt, O.S.B.
Translator

The Liturgical Press
Publisher

Christ in Prophecy, the third in a series on the Old Testament by Dr. Paul Heinisch, was translated from the author's manuscript. The two companion volumes are

THEOLOGY OF THE OLD TESTAMENT

HISTORY OF THE OLD TESTAMENT

Cover design and caligraphy by the Reverend John Domin. Index by Joseph W. Sprug.

Imprimi potest: ✠ Baldwin Dworschak, O.S.B., D.D., Abbot of St. John's Abbey. *Nihil obstat:* John Eidenschink, O.S.B., J.C.D., *Censor deputatus. Imprimatur:* ✠ Peter W. Bartholome, D.D., Bishop of St. Cloud. July 25, 1956.

Printed by The North Central Publishing Company, St. Paul.

CONTENTS

INTRODUCTION

PROPHECIES PRIOR TO THE EIGHTH CENTURY

THE PRE-EXILIAN LITERARY PROPHETS

PROPHETIC FORM AND FULFILLMENT

CHRIST IN TYPE

THE MESSIAH'S MOTHER

BIBLICAL MESSIANISM—A UNIQUE PHENOMENON

NON-JEWISH MESSIANIC HOPES

Christ

in Prophecy

Introduction

To wrest from the future its secrets has been one of man's most persistent endeavors. Curiosity is not the principal motive; the effort stems rather from the desire to arrange plans and programs in such a manner as to bypass the menace of misfortune or to obtain the knowledge needed to determine whether a given project be undertaken or abandoned. We are not referring here to such phenomena as happen by force of necessity or according to set laws as, for instance, an eclipse or a change of weather or the recovery from a common illness; nor do we have in mind a course of events that can be predicted with great probability by a wise and careful consideration of the whole situation as, at times, the policy of a statesman or a general. The problem here concerns such actions or events which in the last analysis rest upon the free will of man whose activity is not determined by any given set of circumstances or by some chain of interrelated conditions, and the course of which is beyond the human mind, known beforehand by God alone. Such knowledge comes to man only if God deigns to confer upon him a special supernatural gift, that of prophecy.[1]

Men have indeed always sought to lift the veil which is spread over the future in as much as it affects their own personal fortunes or that of their relatives and friends. Nevertheless, individuals as such do not ordinarily regard themselves as able to predict what the future holds in

[1] Cf. 1 Cor. 12:10; 13:2, 8.

3

store; therefore among all peoples, both in ancient and modern times, we find particular persons claiming to possess the special faculties needed to throw light upon the course of coming events.

1. THE BABYLONIANS. Goaded on by a belief that the gods at the beginning of each year decreed the course of events for the ensuing months, the Babylonians took as extremely serious the matter of unravelling the divine plans. They believed a divinely ordained relationship existed between that which men know about nature, the heavens and the earth, and the destiny of nations as well as of individuals; and of this relationship the gods leave certain indications which can be discerned by men. Accordingly, any departure from the usual in natural phenomena, whether in the skies above or in the activity of ants beneath the ground, was regarded as an omen of things to come. Only in a most exceptional case would the gods, in Babylonian theology, communicate with men in a direct, clear, and intelligible way, as for instance when through dreams they gave distinct directions for a certain mode of conduct.

Then too there existed the belief that human affairs ran in cycles, just as day and night, summer and winter, rain and sunshine. Therefore, when misfortune followed shortly upon a period of unusual prosperity, the inference came easily that similar good fortune would not be without its subsequent evil. But through prayer, offerings, incantations, the gods could be moved to ward off such accompanying evil; while the decision to proceed with a given project was rendered easier if some portent indicated that it would be crowned with success.

Interpreting the future required the experience of many years because an unlimited number of similar signs must first be studied and weighed. This knowledge was not easily acquired; it was a science reserved to a special class of priests, the *baru* — soothsayers. To them belonged "the mystery of the heavens and the earth," the wisdom of the Sun-god, Shamash, who illumined the universe, and of Adad, the god of storms and lightning. Nabu, too, was regarded as a giver of oracles. The work of these priests, who already formed a caste when Hammurabi's Code took form, can be traced to earliest times; in fact they attributed their knowledge to the prediluvian King Enmeduranki. Upon a foundation of practical experience and clever observation these soothsaying priests of Babylonia theorized and deduced complex systems embracing all possibilities. Their speculations and calculations filled countless volumes, sources which could be consulted when specific problems arose.

Because of the importance that a knowledge of future events has upon the plans and activity of individuals as well as upon the more weighty decisions in the field of politics, soothsaying priests became very important people. Before any civil project could be undertaken, the officials in charge were obliged to inform themselves of its outcome, and this applied not only to war and battles, but even to construction projects such as that of a temple, palace, or canal. With an eye on the costs involved, the common Babylonian would consult the priests only on special occasions, for example, at the birth of a child, before marriage, before beginning a journey to distant regions, in serious sickness, when some most unusual experience had occurred, or if he had had a very disturbing dream.

Many of the mediums used to discern the future were of a nature as to suggest such use, e.g., phenomena in the heavens and in the atmosphere, dreams, conduct of animals, unusual happenings at the time of birth. Other means employed were devised by human ingenuity, e.g., the examination of entrails, beaker divination, oracles.

Astrology played an important role in the work of predicting the future. Because the sky was regarded as the playboard of the gods, some significance was ascribed to every movement in the heavens, to the course and the appearance of the sun and the moon, to the arrangement and disposition of the stars. It was not for scientific purposes that men scrutinized the heavens, rather to deduce divine plans and purposes. Every major city in Babylonia and Assyria had its ziqqurat observatory at which astrologers watched the skies. As soon as a child was born its fortune was determined from the stars.

There existed omens too, whose meanings were plainly given in books, that pointed to disaster and misfortune, viz., a lunar eclipse would bring evils — on one's enemy, of course. When consulted about the significance of a dream, the soothsaying priest could open his "dream book" and find the answer. Among the domesticated animals the antics of dogs and sheep were of special value; among birds the falcon, eagle, raven, swallow, dove, chicken; among reptiles, snakes; among insects, ants. If some abnormality occurred at the birth of a child or of an animal, it was a certain sign either of good luck or the portent of coming evils — without too evident a reason for the difference; in this field especially did the interpreters allow full play to their imagination, magnifying the remotest similarity or proposing causes and reasons that were simply fantastic.

Of the internal organs highest importance was attributed to the liver, which was regarded as the seat of emotional life; it was common belief that through the liver of a sacrificed animal the gods revealed their plans. Ordinarily the liver of a sheep was selected for analysis, with each quarter telling its own story. Clay livers were made to enable apprentices to cover the fundamentals of their work more easily.[2] Ezechiel relates how Nabuchodonosor inquired of the gods whether he should first attack Jerusalem or the Ammonites who were in alliance with Judah: "He shakes the arrows, consults the teraphim (penates), inspects the liver."[3] Beaker divination consisted in pouring some oil into a vessel filled with water, or a few drops of water into a beaker filled with oil, and observing the interaction of the liquids — did they mix or remain separate; if the latter, in what particular form; and did tiny drops form? Widespread as liver divination was throughout Babylonia, the only passage concerning it in the Bible is that in Ezechiel quoted above.

Babylonian soothsayers and fortunetellers are mentioned in Dan. 2:2; 4:4; 5:7. In Is. 47:13 they are ridiculed because of their profession. Centuries later, after the Babylonian kingdom had long perished, "Chaldean" astrologers and diviners enjoyed a high reputation among the Romans.

An analysis of the *baru* methods for predicting the future shows that a) they are based upon an examination of visible phenomena; b) the interpretation of the future is inextricably bound up with some given present or past event; c) only a soothsaying priest definitely possessed the needed background for a pronouncement because he knew the technicalities and could refer to the pertinent sources; d) divination was a profession which featured and furthered its own ends; it could be learned, frequently was very lucrative, and was often transmitted from father to son as an inheritance.

2. THE EGYPTIANS. The Egyptians too were convinced that the future was no impenetrable mystery. Those who sought after this type of knowledge took as patrons Thot, god of wisdom or the "scribe-god," and the wise Amenhotep, the son of Hapu. Individuals to whom special insights were ascribed in this matter and who were credited with the ability of predicting future events on the basis of the sacred writings were called "those who know and write"; and they constituted a special class. Like their Babylonian colleagues they started with the movement of the stars and dreams. The art of predicting the future from dreams was as highly perfected in Egypt as in Babylon, and to the present day "Genuine Egyptian Dream Books" may be purchased at fairs and corner drug stores. One of the dream books composed in New Kingdom times has a remarkably modern table of contents, and certain interpretations have weathered the centuries.[4]

In the Joseph story the chief butler and chief baker became sorely

[2] See AOB No. 486 for an illustration. During the excavations at Mari on the middle Euphrates, 32 clay models of livers inscribed with texts were found.   Cf. E. Dhorme, *Les Religions de Babylonie et d'Assyrie*, 272.   [3] Ez. 21:21f.   [4] Ad. Erman, *Die Religion der Ägypter*, 312.

dejected upon having dreams that were quite similar, and therefore seemed to contain a message; but being in prison, they were unable to consult a skilled interpreter.[5] Upset by dreams, Pharaoh summoned the interpreters of dreams to his palace to learn what lay in store.[6] We find evidence for beaker divination among the Egyptians in the accusation of Joseph's house-steward against the sons of Jacob: "Why did you steal my silver cup? Is it not the one . . . he uses for divination?"[7] In Is. 19:3 the Egyptians are reproached for necromancy and the use of mediums.

3. THE CANAANITES. Canaanite interest in divination is attested by the Old Testament both in the Law and in the Prophets. We find strictures against practices which proved to be pitfalls for the Israelites, particularly the sin of necromancy.[8]

The Philistines subscribed to the same illusions.[9] Beelzebub of Ekron enjoyed special notoriety; to him King Ochozias of Samaria sent a delegation to discover whether he would recover.[10] Recent excavations at Ras Shamra have proven that the Phoenicians (Canaanites) did not neglect scrutinizing the heavens, the flight of birds, the entrails of animals; nor was the interpretation of dreams foreign to their everyday habits.

4. THE GREEKS. The Greeks regarded Apollo as the god who unveiled the future. Life without oracles from the gods seemed utterly unthinkable. Decisions on war and on peace, on legislation and on political organization depended upon the reply of some oracle. In this they differed little from the Orientals. Thunder and lightning, earthquakes, the leaping flame, the course of birds, dreams and the entrails of sacrificed animals all served as portents of coming events; nor was necromancy neglected. And there were diviners who by artificial means would transport themselves into states of trance in order to gaze into the future.

Of the various oracles none was more famous than that at Delphi. There upon a three-legged stool sat Pythia, inhaling the stupefying fumes which rose from a fissure in the rock, chewing benumbing laurel-berries, imbibing intoxicating liquids, and in this condition, when she could no longer think, uttering cries which the priests turned into oracles. Leaders of state, such as Lycurgus and Solon, accorded due attention to the Delphic oracles. The oracles at Dodona in Epirus and at Olympia likewise ranked high in popular esteem.

5. THE ROMANS. Although distinguished for sobriety in thought and action, the Romans showed little of their reputed conservatism toward

---

[5] Gen. 40:5f.   [6] Gen. 41.
[7] Gen. 44:4. The Coptic word *ref-šen-hin*, vessel-inquirer, may also point to beaker divination; cf. A. Sanda, AfO, 7, 287.
[8] Ex. 22:17; Lev. 19:26, 31; 20:6, 27; Deut. 18:9-14; 1 Sam. 28:3, 9; Os. 4:12; Is. 3:2; 8:19.
[9] 1 Sam. 6:2; Is. 2:6.
[10] 4 Kgs. 1:2f.

soothsayers and diviners. Listen to Livy's dictum: "Save through an auspice do nothing at home or on the battlefield." [11] No political move was considered, no military campaign begun without resort to augury to determine its outcome. The same held in private life. In his two books on divination Cicero tried to lay down principles for determining the divine impact on the course of future affairs. He distinguished two types of predictions, that by way of skill and art which follows definite rules and can be learned, and that through ecstacy which liberates the spirit from the weight of matter and bestows deeper insights.

The more ancient college of soothsayers at Rome were the augurs; their duty was to proclaim the will of the gods in civil and military actions. For this purpose they would observe the course of birds and the nature of lightning flashes; and from the habits of the holy hens that were taken along with the army, they could predict if victory would come. If, for instance, these hens ate greedily with portions of fodder falling from their beaks, it was a sign of good fortune. How the augur could slant the verdict can easily be seen; for if he put the hens on scanty rations and then prepared a goodly mash, they would eat hastily and bits would always fall from their beaks.

By the time of Cicero the augurs no longer enjoyed their previous high position; the *haruspices*, soothsayers, from Etruria were growing in importance. These formed a caste, and in the cities they held an important and highly lucrative office. Generals and civil officials sought their advice — Sulla, Caesar, as well as the later emperors employed them as prognosticators. And the common citizen did likewise. In giving answers they would consult the books in which they had recorded past observations. Alexander Severus even erected chairs for their "science" in the schools. They would note the course lightning took during a storm, and determine the god who was responsible. They interpreted the flight of birds, earthquakes, the appearance and antics of animals (the intrusion of predatory beasts and mice presaged misfortune). Of highest import, however, and their peculiar task was to read the future from the entrails of the sacrifices, particularly from the liver of a sheep. If disaster was in the offing, they presented themselves as able to pacify the gods and thus delay or avert fully the evil, because they would employ the proper methods and means of atonement — of which they alone possessed complete and definite knowledge. Only gradually were Christian emperors able to counteract this type of superstition and abolish it through imperial decrees.[12]

6. THE GERMANS. The Germanic peoples believed the future was discernible from the neighing of horses, the flight of birds, dreams, and

[11] I, 36.   [12] Regarding Vergil's prediction of the birth of a divine child, cf. p. 262.

the casting of lots. Priests had the right and the duty to interpret such signs. Female soothsayers were also found among them.

7. OUR MODERN AGE. Our "enlightened" age has in no way become less concerned about ways and means of discovering what the future holds in store; in fact, those very circles which proudly reject the tenets of Christian faith seem to cherish most avidly any type of superstitious belief. Procedures, indeed, have changed, at least in part—but the fundamentals have remained the same. Fortunetellers, especially female fortunetellers, are easily found; like their ancestors in antiquity their profession is a lucrative one and provides a life having few financial worries. They will predict your future by the lines on your palms, from a deck of cards, a dream. The beaker diviner of old has a descendant in the modern-day tea-cup reader; and while no professional soothsayer may be present as an onion is peeled and scrutinized on the last day of the civil year in your neighbor's cellar, it would seem that the last vestige of superstition remains to be uprooted. Fortunetellers have been responsible for the break-up of many a marriage, they have driven some to suicide.

Certain animals too seem to have retained their primitive ability of revealing the future. Does a cat cross your path, you will surely suffer some misfortune! Do you want good luck? Carry a rabbit's foot! And what hopes have been associated with drawing the better part of a chicken's wishbone!

Some 150 years ago a certain Madame Lenormand began to specialize in the use of cards as a medium for divining the future. She operated in Paris, then in Brussels, and with such skill as to become a millionaire. The leaders of the French Revolution, Robespierre and Marat, various generals, and at a later date the Empress Josephine, and the Emperor Alexander I of Russia eagerly sought her "predictions."

At the present time it is not too difficult to gain admittance to a seance where the spirits of the dead are said to be brought back to earth, shades of the witch of Endor some 3,000 years ago. By scanning the newspapers the credulous may discover how to have their horoscope read by astrologers plying a trade now some 5,000 years old. A late fad is the use of the term *clairvoyant*. Interesting cases are found even in the highest circles of political diplomacy of clairvoyant women prophesying a third World War, determining its beginning, its duration and its end, with exactitude! And they are not without a following.

8. ISRAEL. Many Israelites who had merely a superficial concept of God, one which did not touch the true nature of Yahwistic religion and recognized no fundamental difference between Yahweh and the pagan gods, attempted to discern the future by imitating the practices of

Canaanite neighbors and their soothsayers. The Law and the prophets took a very definite stand against soothsaying and necromancy. On Sinai, Yahweh had entered into a covenant with Israel; what Balaam proclaimed under the force of divine inspiration on the Plains of Moab should have always proven true:

> In Jacob there is no divination,
>   no soothsaying in Israel.
> When the occasion arises, it will be revealed to Jacob
>   what God will do, and to Israel.[13]

Because Israel possessed faith in the one true God, she must not resort to superstitious practices, as did other nations in their efforts to discern the future. Should it become truly necessary, Yahweh would reveal His will through divinely illumined men. Every attempt to determine future affairs on the basis of phenomena in the skies or from the acts of daily life implied a foray into the providence of God, who is Lord over the future and ordains all things according to His holy will. What a tremendous difference between Israel's revealed religion and the religions of neighboring nations, nations that in some regards stood on a higher cultural plane! Finally, in Messianic times, when Israel would actually be the holy people she should always have been, no diviner will be found in her midst.[14]

a) *Urim and Tummim.* In spite of all good will there remains within man the desire to know what the future holds in store in order to adjust his affairs accordingly. God took this weakness into account even as He first strove to make Israel worship Him alone without forcing her to regard the gods of other peoples as non-entities. At Sinai He gave them the Urim and Tummim, a medium through which the divine will could be ascertained on important matters. Nevertheless, resort to the Urim and Tummim could not be made at will but only through the high priest who formulated the query.[15] Very probably the Urim and Tummim were two stones of different colors or two different little rods; after wording the inquiry properly, the priest reached into the sack and drew out one of the stones or rods. The response would be affirmative or negative. At times, however, Yahweh gave no reply.[16] From this it seems that a third stone or a third rod was in the sack; when this third possibility was picked, it meant no answer was forthcoming. Or the two items may have been shaken before the sack was emptied and occasionally no stone or both would fall out.

This inquiry into the future by lot was permitted by God only because the people had not yet accepted the full import of Mosaic religion and

[13] Num. 23:23.   [14] Mich. 5:11.   [15] Ex. 28:24-30.   [16] 1 Sam. 14:37.

there was danger that they would adopt pagan practices, as did, in fact, frequently occur. As the people became more thoroughly imbued with the spirit of Yahwistic religion, the Urim and Tummim lost significance. David still resorted to its use,[17] but thereafter when difficult problems arose the matter was taken to the priests who settled the matter by reason of their knowledge of the Law; or a prophet was consulted. After the exile the Urim and Tummim no longer existed.[18] The Septuagint translation for these two words, revelation and truth, shows that at the time no clear concept was had of its nature and purpose.

b) *The prophets.* Balaam had declared that Yahweh would accompany Israel to reveal and direct her future. And after forbidding the consultation of pagan soothsayers Moses proclaimed that after him Yahweh would raise up prophets who, just as he had, would speak in God's Name to the people.[19] The word *nabi'*, speaker, underscores the mission of the prophets as heralds of God's holy will manifested to them through special revelation. The prophet was, as it were, the "mouth" of Yahweh.[20] The Greek word προφήτης (from προ before, and φημι to speak) also has the meaning of speaker, herald, particularly the herald of a revealed truth. It is not the usual connotation of the word to denote the manifestation of a future event.

A common obligation upon all the prophets was the task to keep the Chosen People from perishing in the universal paganism in spite of the popular tendency to worship false gods, in spite of the example of neighboring nations and the impact of world powers. They were, therefore, moral reformers. They did not proclaim a new concept of God but strove to counteract any and all deviation from the religion of Moses; they kept Israel conscious of the duties she had assumed when entering upon the covenant at Sinai. As credentials for His messengers and to effect a more ready acceptance of their teaching and admonitions, God endowed them with the power of working miracles or enabled them to prophesy the future.

When a prophecy was fulfilled during the prophet's life-time, the people had indisputable testimony for the divine mission of the person who had given the oracle. Thus Jeremias predicted the death of Hananias who had claimed that he was sent by God; two months later the false prophet was dead.[21] While Ezechiel was in Babylonia he saw in a vision that an important person in Jerusalem by the name of Pheltias suddenly died during a council of 25 men.[22] Immediately Ezechiel apprised his fellow exiles of the fact, and when the report was brought to Babylonia, the exiles could no longer doubt that Ezechiel had been enlightened by God at the time he had informed them.

[17] 1 Sam. 23:2, 11; 30:8; 2 Sam. 2:1; 5:19. [18] Esdr. 2:63; Neh. 7:65. [19] Deut. 18:15-22. [20] Ex. 4:12; Jer. 15:19. [21] Jer. 28:16, 17. [22] Ez. 11:13.

Before witnesses Isaias named one of his sons "Quick booty, speedy spoil"; these names, he explained, pointed to the imminent downfall of Damascus and Samaria. The fulfillment of his prediction should not take place without a unique, living memorial.[23] For the same reason Ezechiel put down in writing the date on which Nabuchodonosor invested Jerusalem.[24] Yahweh had revealed it to him in Babylonia, and the accomplished fact would serve as further vindication for his claims when the exiles heard the report through ordinary channels. When Jerusalem, the temple, and the kingdom perished, the contemporaries of Jeremias and Ezechiel realized that these men had received special insights from God; for they had prophesied the course of events to the last minute detail.

Most of the prophecies, however, were pointed to a distant future, and the prophets did not live to witness their fulfillment. The comminatory prophecies in which they foretold the punishment of God upon king and people in constantly severer terms — enemy attacks, decimation of the population, famine, the dissolution of the kingdom and the dynasty, exile — were meant to move sinful Israel to repentance. Prophecies of good fortune and national glory, of a new ruler on the throne of David, fertility of the land, divine blessings were given to imbue the pious with strength to persevere under the heavy visitations, to endure the sufferings which came upon them and not to grow despondent. Prophecies against foreign nations, proclaiming divine punishment as well as their final conversion to the one true God, provided further assurance to Israel that the God whom they adored was no weakling unable to protect His people. Although it seemed as if foreign gods were mightier than Yahweh, actually Yahweh was Lord of all the world and He determined the destinies of every nation. Prophecies, therefore, also filled the believing Israelite with confidence.

What an amazing difference between Israel's prophets and the fortunetellers of antiquity and modern times! These latter rely upon human techniques, they seek to unravel the future through natural mediums. Predicting future affairs is regarded as an art (to the ancient mind a science) which can be learned, which anyone can acquire by observation, book study, or by inducing a state of ecstasy. The soothsayer plied his trade whenever and wherever there were customers. Some stood in the service of the rulers, all of them gained status and advantages from their work, for theirs was a respected profession.

Israel's prophets became prophets upon being called by Yahweh through a unique and humanly inexplicable experience. It was not in response to their own desires for such an office, or even in response to

---

[23] Is. 8:1-4.   [24] Ez. 24:2.

personal zeal for God's honor, or to admonish the people to moral living. They spoke in God's Name only because God's call had come to them, a call that changed the course of their lives in a most extraordinary way. They did not predict the future upon request, but only when God had spoken to them.

Elias journeyed to Horeb to lay his problems before Yahweh because he had been granted no enlightenment from on High at a critical time.[25] When the Judeans inquired of Jeremias whether it was Yahweh's will that they betake themselves to Egypt, they were obliged to wait ten days before receiving an answer, while circumstances seemed to have demanded immediate action.[26] Ecstatic states, it is true, are related in the Old Testament accounts of the prophets, but these states did not occur as the result of personal wish or effort; they were due solely to the operation of divine power, and whatever God permitted them to see in that condition, they proclaimed in intelligible terms when the normal use of their faculties returned. As proof for this we have the discourses of the prophets, each showing a definite and distinct individuality even when the revelation itself had its source in a vision.

The exercise of their mission brought the prophets no notable compensation. When Samuel no longer was in a position to lead the people, he publicly avowed that he never had used his office to enrich himself.[27] Eliseus refused to accept any gift from Naaman whom he had cured.[28] Saul had in mind to bring some gift for the seer Samuel [29] and Jeroboam's wife wanted to show herself grateful to Ahias,[30] but neither the one nor the other was actually able to carry out such intentions.

In proclaiming the divine will the prophets took a position against the people, against the king and nobles, even against the priests. Consequently they were abused and persecuted, they were treated as traitors and blasphemers, some were imprisoned or even put to death. Against Moses the people made grave accusations and threatened him with death by stoning.[31] The burden of office oppressed him so heavily that he believed he would collapse, and on one occasion he asked God to "kill him." [32] During the persecution of Jezabel, Elias would have welcomed death.[33] Micheas was impounded by Achab and put on scantiest rations because he had predicted the king's defeat and death.[34] Amos was banished from the land by the high priest at Bethel for having prophesied the destruction of the Northern Kingdom.[35] For three years Isaias was obliged to wear the dress of a slave and go barefoot in order to impress his contemporaries with the fact that no aid would be forthcoming from Egypt.[36] Jeremias complained that "all cursed him" and

[25] 3 Kgs. 19.
[26] Jer. 42:7.
[27] 1 Sam: 12:3-5.
[28] 4 Kgs. 5:16.
[29] 1 Sam. 9:6.
[30] 3 Kgs. 14:3.
[31] Num. 14:10.
[32] Num. 11:15.
[33] 3 Kgs. 19:4.
[34] 3 Kgs. 22:27-28.
[35] Amos 7:10.
[36] Is. 20:2-3.

that "Yahweh's word brought him nothing but abuse and ridicule the whole day long"; [37] more than once he was in the danger of losing his life for heralding judgment upon Jerusalem and the dissolution of the royal dynasty. Joakim ordered the death of the prophet Urias after he had foretold the destruction of the temple and city.[38]

But the greatest cross that God imposed upon the prophets lay in that they were obliged to proclaim the sentence of rejection upon their own people, a people they loved so fervently! They were under constraint to preach penance and conversion while fully realizing that they were accomplishing nothing because the people remained obstinate, and that, in fact, their very work increased the guilt and the punishment of the people since they rebelled against their every word. Micheas groaned: "This is why I must moan and grieve, go barefoot and naked (as a sign of mourning), lament like jackals and mourn like ostriches, for there is no recovery from the blow with which Yahweh has struck Judah." [39]

Would any soothsayer have threatened his people and his king with destruction while predicting success and triumph for foreign, enemy nations? No nation produced men such as Israel did; nor did the religious leaders in any other nation proclaim ethical monotheism as the religion to which all were bound.

Another difference between Israel's prophets and the soothsayers. Like the modern fortuneteller the ancient soothsayer was ordinarily concerned with the material, earthly needs of individuals or groups. They never condemned the moral misdeeds of their neighbors, they did not bother about the religious and ethical improvement of those who came to them; rather they strove to confirm them in superstition.

Now the principal task of Israel's prophets was religious and moral in nature. Even when the occasion arose to issue pronouncements upon future affairs, they took into consideration the spiritual and moral state of the person who approached them. By informing Saul that the reason which had prompted his coming had been favorably resolved (the lost asses), Samuel sought to dispose him to accept with greater confidence the office of king.[40] Ahias revealed to Jeroboam's wife that the death of her son would follow as a punishment for introducing image worship into the Northern Kingdom and thereby made the king realize the seriousness of his sin.[41]

c) *False prophets.* When Moses promised the people that God would raise up prophets for them, he also warned them about men who would attempt speaking in Yahweh's Name without having received a divine

---

[37] Jer. 15:10 ; 20:7.
[38] Jer. 26:20-23.

[39] Mich. 1:8-9 ; cf. Jer. 8:21, 23 ; 13:17.
[40] 1 Sam. 9.
[41] 3 Kgs. 14.

commission.[42] From about the middle of the ninth century we meet
false prophets in Israel. Like those who were truly called by God, they
uttered pronouncements on the state of future affairs; but unlike Gentile
diviners they did not scan the skies, study the entrails of animals, or
artificially induce ecstatic states.

Nevertheless, such individuals had experienced no call from on High;
through their own prowess they purported to be divinely commissioned,
and they proclaimed as a message from God whatever pleased their own
phantasy and the wishes of king and people. They would recall how
Yahweh had entered into a covenant with Israel and therefore would
not abandon them or allow them to remain subject to pagan peoples for
any length of time. They urged resistance against oppressors and
painted the future in glowing colors: "Is Yahweh not in our midst? No
evil can come upon us." [43] They cried: "Prosperity . . . [44] The sword
and hunger will not be our lot." [45] Only of covenant rights did they
speak, not of covenant duties, and never a word concerning Israel's
obligation to live morally in order to enjoy Yahweh's protection. By their
preaching they confirmed the people in the illusion that Yahweh was
satisfied if fat sacrifices were brought to Him.

Some, perhaps, actually believed that their dreams, the illusions of
their fancies, and their hallucinations did come from Yahweh; most of
them consciously deceived the people, while all of them, like the pagan
diviners, regarded their activity as a profession, one that brought status
and material gain if only they spoke what their audience wished to
hear.[46] They loved to place themselves at the service of the king as
court prophets to confirm the wry royal policies against which the true
prophets inveighed. Achab retained 400 such creatures in his entourage.[47] Nor would these selfmade prophets utter any word of reproach
if the ruler allowed or furthered the cult of foreign gods.

The men who had been truly called by God experienced constant and
cruel opposition from the false prophets. Superficial as the masses are,
their inclination is to prefer messages of peace and prosperity to oracles
of defeat, famine, destruction, and exile; and of a fundamental change
of morals they do not like to hear. Israel should have been able to
distinguish God's genuine legates from the impostors. If a prophet lived
a morally upright life, if he was selfless, if he insisted upon the observance of God's commandments, if he inveighed against image worship
and idolatry, if he threatened sinners with divine wrath, if he even
suffered persecution in the discharge of his duties because he seared
the consciences of princes and people — then he had given proof that
he spoke in Yahweh's Name.

[42] Deut. 18:20. [44] Mich. 3:5. [46] Mich. 3:5-7, 11; Ez. 13:19.
[43] Mich. 3:11. [45] Jer. 5:12. [47] 3 Kgs. 22.

The false prophets were concerned over personal advantages, they spoke no harsh words against unfair rulers, they glossed over the popular lust for idolatry and would not condemn immorality. They proclaimed God's continued blessing without a need for inner conversion, while they themselves, after the example of Babylonians, employed charms to ensnare the innocent [48] and practiced adultery, even with the wives of their friends.[49] We could well apply the words of our divine Savior: "By their fruits you will know them." [50] The great majority of the people listened to these false prognosticators, regarding as genuine their predictions about a prosperous future; it seemed as if they wished to live under delusion until Yahweh came in judgment and catastrophe struck. This was actually the case. The Northern Kingdom perished first. Then the royal house of David fell, Jerusalem was destroyed, the temple burned, the people driven into exile. What had been described so often by the prophets whom God had sent had literally come to pass.

d) *Israel's religion and the Gentiles.* It was her religion that distinguished Israel from among all the nations on earth. There were nations with a greater population and more territory, nations that created world empires and nurtured amazing advances in science and art, nations that were illustrious for organization and world leadership or that engaged in business enterprises with lands far distant. It was her religion that saved Israel from appearing and then quickly vanishing from the Table of nations, as has been true of countless peoples both smaller and greater.

But the knowledge of God, Israel's peculiar glory, was not destined to remain solely with this little nation. In God's good Providence Israel's religion was to become the common heirloom of mankind, in time all peoples must turn to the God worshipped on Sion. It was for this mission that Israel was chosen, and for this same reason God raised up prophets in her midst. These men proclaimed that faith in one God with the willingness to live morally in His presence would result in forgiveness of the sins in which men were enmeshed, and that One, greater than Moses, would ultimately effect the salvation of the world and blot out its sin — the Redeemer Christ. Those passages which tell of the coming Messiah are the finest flowers in the beautiful, rich and full bouquet of Old Testament literature.

From the very beginning it was God's plan that Israel's religion become matured and deepened through a theology concerning her Messiah, and thus matured, become the religion of mankind. Israel's religion did not begin with Moses. Previously God had spoken with the patriarchs, and already in most primitive times He had planted within the

---

[48] Ez. 13:18.   [49] Jer. 29:23.   [50] Matth. 7:20.

human heart a desire to find its way back to God, freed from sin. That is why we meet prophecies of redemption and of a Redeemer already in the first pages of holy Scripture; and in the course of centuries the picture of redemption and of a personal Redeemer from sin became ever more clearly etched. Victory over sin and guilt could not have been realized save through God's love and mercy brought by a unique, personal Mediator whom God willed to send. This is the one central truth that received continual emphasis in the Old Testament prophecies.

Along with this objective redemption, the truth is clearly stated already in the first prophecies that individual men, even as Israel and the Gentiles, will share in the Messianic blessings if they refrain from sin. Another truth constantly stressed is that Israel and the nations will find the way back to God only after suffering a severe visitation that will make them realize the vanity of idolatry and the sinfulness of their mode of life. Judgment thus would become a preparation for redemption from sin.

e) *The Messiah*. Prophecies which concern man's redemption are called Messianic even when they do not treat directly of a personal Savior; for it is sufficient if they have some relationship to the work which the Redeemer would accomplish.

When Andrew sought to bring his brother Simon Peter to Jesus, he said: "We have found the Messiah (translated as: Christ)."[51] And at the well of Jacob the Samaritan woman said: "I know that the Messiah is coming (who is called Christ); when he comes, he will tell us all things."[52] Nevertheless, in the New Testament Jesus is called "Messiah" only in these two passages, otherwise He is called *Christos* (with or without the article). In the Old Testament we find the word used of our Redeemer only in Ps. 2:2.

The Hebrew word *mašiah* (*mešiha'* in Aramaic, and grecized μεσσιας) signifies *anointed*, even as does the Greek word *Christos*. Through anointing with oil persons and things were consecrated and separated from profane use; and a special efficacy accrued to them. The high priest was anointed,[53] kings were anointed.[54] In a figurative sense the prophets were called "anointed," because as organs of the divine will they were equipped in a special manner with God's spirit;[55] the same held for the patriarchs to whom God confided special tasks in His plan of salvation.[56] Even the Persian Cyrus is called "anointed", because he was destined to be God's instrument in destroying the Babylonian kingdom and granting freedom to the captive Judeans.[57]

Now since the spirit of God rests upon the coming Redeemer in all

---

[51] John 1:42.   [52] John 4:25.
[53] Ex. 29:7; Lev. 8:12.
[54] 1 Sam. 2:10, 35; 10:1; 12:3, etc.

[55] 3 Kgs. 19:16; Is. 61:1.
[56] Ps. 105:15.
[57] Is. 45:1.

fullness and more than upon any other individual commissioned by God,[58] and because God confided to Him the three offices of king, prophet, and priest, He is called "the anointed one" in an eminent sense. The Messiah expected by the Jews would come at some future day, "at the end of days" as the prophets expressed it. The Targum on Gen. 3:15 speaks of Him as *mešiha' malka'* "King Messiah." But Jesus did not adopt this title because the Jews had associated it too closely with earthly expectations and hopes.[59]

In the course of history certain rulers in various nations were lauded as saviors, and even at the present time there are persons who unashamedly style themselves "deliverers" of their own nation, if not of the whole world. Yet it should easily be seen that what oppresses man most is spiritual not material in nature, the consciousness of sin with all its concomitant evils. Now since a true concept of sin as an offense against God is possible only among monotheists, the hope in a "Savior" or a deliverer from the evils of sin can only be found in Old Testament religion. Here sin is present at the very beginning of man's history, but with it a protoevangel of hope in redemption, in forgiveness from an offended God; and the prophets, pointing to sin and guilt, proclaim redemption and a Redeemer who frees from the guilt of sin. Not only for the preservation of faith in the one true God are we indebted to the Old Testament, but there do we find planted and cultivated hope in a reconciliation with God from whom mankind had wandered away.

"Piecemeal and in many ways God spoke to the fathers through the prophets in times past." [60] In the following pages we shall endeavor to show how the expectation of a Messiah-Redeemer made its first appearance in primitive times, and how in the course of ages the picture of the Messiah-Redeemer became enriched with new and varied lines until Christ Jesus came to earth and began the mission which the eternal Father had allotted Him.

[58] Is. 11:2.
[59] Although the word Messiah is etymologically identical with Christ, we need not restrict the Christ picture to that of king, prophet, and priest, but may well include, e.g., the work of the Suffering Servant of Yahweh who carries and blots out the sins of the world.
[60] Heb. 1:1.

Prophecies Prior to the Eighth Century

~~~~~~~~~~

§1. THE FIRST GOOD TIDINGS
Gen. 3:14-15

"Yahweh, God, imposed this obligation upon man: Of every tree of the garden you may eat, but of the tree of the knowledge of good and evil you may not eat. For on the day when you eat of it, you must die." [61]

In His goodness God had granted the first man and woman the blessings of paradise, blessings which included, first of all, a most intimate and loving communion with their creator and benefactor; then bodily immortality together with a freedom from suffering, sorrow, pain and disease. These blessings were theirs directly and immediately without any merit on their part, granted through the sheer mercy of God as a permanent endowment. Nevertheless, they were to show themselves worthy of so great favors.

Good and evil, as referred to in the paradise commandment, imply moral concepts, because God added the sentence of death as sanction and later inflicted it. Moreover, after the deed conscience began to stir. The tree was meant as a test. Did man obey, then would he experience

[61] Gen. 2:16-17.

how good it was to fulfill God's will. Should he disobey, then he would discover how dreadful it is to rise up against God. Through obedience to God's decree man should merit for himself the blessings of paradise and of eternal life. At the tree it should become clear whether man willed to be obedient, i.e., morally good, or disobedient, i.e., morally bad. If he would not forego the fruit, he must die, must suffer physical death, and that "on the day" when he sinned. It is true that Adam did not die at the moment, but his destiny was decided; he had forfeited his right to life.

It was not a knowledge concerning the differences between the sexes that the tree would give. Already before their sin Adam and Eve knew these fundamentals; for the man called the creature that Yahweh brought to him *'iššah*, woman, and in Hebrew the ending *ah* is a sign of the feminine. Moreover, the Biblical writer adds: "Therefore does a man leave his father and mother and cling to his wife; and the two become one flesh." Surely the reason for Eve's creation was marriage.[62]

Nor is the message that with the violation of the commandment reason awoke; for then the distinction between "good and evil" previously made would have been unintelligible. Already before the fall our first parents knew how to act in a reasonable manner — Adam was enjoined to care for the garden, he gave names to animals, understood that animals were not on the same plane as himself, and recognized the woman as having the same nature that he possessed.

The expression "to know good and evil," however, could have implied the knowledge of "all things"; for in Gen. 3:22 God ascribes to Himself the ability of "knowing good and evil." It was to this meaning that the tempter alluded. The serpent, the third figure in the paradise drama, dazzled the woman's eyes by saying: "God knows that when you eat of it, your eyes will be opened and you will be like God, knowing good and evil"[63] — you will obtain preternatural and supernatural knowledge, and secret things which are now unknown to you, you will experience; you will be like God Himself. The woman lent a receptive ear to the serpent's insinuations, she reached for the forbidden fruit and inveigled her partner into the act. The sin in paradise was one of disobedience proceeding from pride: they strove to resemble God.

When brought to give an account, our first parents did not deny that they had been disobedient, but neither did they plead for forgiveness. As a mitigating circumstance the man noted that his wife had induced him to violate the divine command; the woman sought to throw the greater part of the guilt upon the serpent, but nevertheless they incurred the punishment God had threatened. It had been possible for them to

[62] Gen. 2:23-24.   [63] Gen. 3:5.

live forever, now they were doomed to die. "Through sin death has come into the world." [64] By delaying the execution of the death sentence, however, God granted our first parents a respite, and by expelling them from paradise afforded them an opportunity to do penance and to regain His favor through suffering. Thereupon man began his battle for daily bread. He sought to be like God; now by hard toil he must wring his livelihood from the earth: "Through sweat on your face you shall eat bread till you return to the ground from which you were taken." [65] A great burden would likewise rest upon the woman; children would be a source of much care and sorrow, and only through pain would she bring them into existence. She who had attempted to be like God now found herself subject to man. [66]

But would God remain angry against mankind forever? Driven from the bliss of paradise, conscious of having forfeited the love of their God, would they not despair? God did not abandon them to utter despondency, and the tempter through whom the divine plan had come to nought, must not revel in a lasting triumph. God permitted a ray of consolation to shine upon the road of human suffering, the single beam of light that appears in the judgment pronounced against the serpent:

Genesis

3:14
> Because you have done this, cursed shall you be
>> among all cattle and all beasts of the field.
> Crawl you shall upon your belly,
>> eating dust your whole life through.

3:15
> I will cause enmity between you and the woman,
>> between your seed and her seed;
> it (Eve's descendants) shall crush your head,
>> though you may wound its heel.

Some present day exegetes hold that the curse imposed upon the serpent explains why snakes have no feet, why they eat dust (according to ancient Oriental ideology), and why men have such a natural aversion for them. But it would be highly improbable that the sacred author would, at this point in the narrative, introduce a parenthesis on the peculiarities of the reptile world and account for the aversion men have for snakes by a special divine ordinance. The passage comes as the climax to a highly integrated account which shows how happily our first parents had at first lived in communion with God; how the woman permitted herself to be tempted and in turn tempted her husband; how both disobeyed; how they became conscious of their transgression and found it necessary to cover their nakedness, not daring to appear before God; how they were brought before God to give an account and be made conscious of the gravity of their deed. Had the author had in mind

---

[64] Rom. 5:12.   [65] Gen. 3:19.   [66] Gen. 3:16.

an animal endowed with the ability to speak, he certainly would have included the loss of this skill in the condemnation. Never in the Old Testament do we find the offspring of animals called *zera'*, seed. It was, therefore, a demonaical being hostile to God that appears in the Genesis story.

The author described this being as "more cunning than any wild beast that Yahweh, God, had made." The serpent, then, was a creature of God. Not only was it more cunning than other beasts, but even more crafty than Adam and Eve whom it deceived. It possessed more than natural knowledge for it knew the secret of the tree whose fruit was forbidden to man. The serpent realized that men possessed the love of God and enjoyed bodily immortality as long as they did His will; he envied their good fortune and sought to despoil them of it.

With genuine diabolical cunning he proceeded to gain the woman's confidence, knowing full well how to sow seeds of doubt in God's sincerity in her heart, how to lessen her fear of divine judgment — "Of course you will not die" — how to stir the desire for hidden secrets, while insinuating that God does not bear a true love toward men since He withheld such knowledge from them. Nor does he directly urge the woman to reach for the fruit because such action might have caused her to hesitate. The tempter knew that the poison he had injected into the woman's heart would accomplish its purpose. It was his plan to destroy the peace reigning in paradise and to frustrate God's purposes with man by bringing man into opposition with God.

Because of these considerations the serpent must not be regarded simply as a symbol of a growing inclination to sin within man's heart. If the first two characters in the paradise story, the man and the woman, are real persons and not allegorical figures, then the third character too, the serpent, possessed real existence.

The exegesis that the serpent represents a being hostile to God has support in Sacred Scripture itself. Referring to the sin in paradise the author of the Book of Wisdom writes: "Through the envy of the devil death has come into the world."[67] The apostle John brands the devil as a "murderer from the beginning"[68] and as "the old serpent who betrayed the whole world."[69] To which we might add the opinion of the author of the Fourth Book of Machabees who identified the tempter to impurity with the serpent of paradise.[70]

Because of the role assigned to snakes in the folk lore of neighboring peoples, an Israelitic reader would spontaneously have thought of an evil agent upon reading about the serpent in the paradise story. In the Babylonian Gilgamesh epic a serpent steals the "herb of life" from

[67] Wis. 2:24.   [68] John 8:44.   [69] Apoc. 12:9.   [70] 18:8.

the hero and thereby renders it impossible for him to attain immortality, an end for which he had strenuously striven.[71] Demons frequently appear in the form of snakes in Babylonian mythology and act in hostile fashion against the gods. Among the seven evil demons which harassed the Moon-god was one called "the Dreadful (serpent)." Meeting a snake was interpreted by the diviners as an inauspicious omen. The Arabians did not regard demons or jinnies as pure spirits but ascribed to them animal forms, usually that of serpents or snakes, with the result that every such reptile was looked upon as the habitat of a jinny. Among the present day inhabitants of Palestine certain snakes are considered to be the abode of good spirits, others of evil spirits who perform their impure acts in ruins and in abandoned places, a view not unlike that found in many prophetic passages.

The ancient Egyptians, who worshipped snakes and pictured gods as serpents, linked the snake with the evil being that created obstacles for the dead in the netherworld. The Pyramid texts provide us with pertinent incantations from the earliest period, and in the Book of the Dead there are spells and charms to be used against the power of evil serpents. Even the father of the gods, Re, was subject to their attack, being bitten by a serpent. In India and China the serpent represents a demonic power which brought misfortune upon mankind at the beginning of human history.[72]

In the sentence of condemnation passed upon our first parents we find confirmed the view that the Biblical writer presented as a snake the demonic being that brought them into opposition with God. For upon it rested God's curse. In the Bible the serpent always appears as an agent of evil, of malice, and of wickedness — lurking in the background, then stealthily striking in attack. Creeping on the belly was regarded as something contemptible.[73] The expression "to eat dust" originally meant "to die," to "descend into the underworld"; in the Babylonian mind the inhabitants of the underworld nourished themselves on ground, "earth is their food, clay their nourishment."[74] A secondary meaning for the expression would be to crouch in abject humiliation. In Messianic times the Gentiles will do homage before the Israelites "with their faces upon the ground, kissing the dust upon their feet."[75] Prophetically the psalmist describes how "enemies will lick the dust" in the Messiah's presence.[76] Micheas begs God to make the pagan nations

[71] 11, 304f.

[72] M. Jastrow, Die Religion Babyloniens und Assyriens, I, 166, 195, II, 776f. M. Witzel, Der Drachenkämpfer Ninib, 136, 156, 189. K. Frank, Studien zur babylonischen Religion, 249f. A. Deimel, VD 4, 1924, 342–349. Al. Musil, Arabia Petraea, III, 320. T. Canaan, Dämonenglaube im Lande der Bibel. A. Erman, Die Religion der Ägypter, 45. G. Roeder, Urkunden zur Religion des alten Ägypten, XXIX, 140, 255, 256.

[73] Gen. 49:17; Is. 59:5; Mich. 7:17; Job 20:14, 16; Ps. 140:4.

[74] Descent of Ishtar, V 8.

[75] Is. 49:23.

[76] Ps. 72:9.

"lick the dust like snakes, like worms in the ground"; literally he simply wanted all men to be made subject to the Messiah.[77] The same phraseology may be found in the Amarna letters: "while our enemies look on and eat dust." [78] In the Genesis text the sacred writer's judgment consisted in that the tempter would be despised by all and at all times — "all the days of your life."

The curse implied a total rejection, without hope for foregiveness or return to favor. The fate of the first man and woman was quite different, they were not cursed. At a later date Cain, as an individual, was cursed because he had hardened himself against every merciful advance on the part of God.[79] Among the Fathers of the Church who held that God cursed Satan may be numbered Augustine, Gregory the Great, Bede, Hupert, etc.[80]

After our first parents had heard God inflicting an eternal curse upon the tempter who by ruse had incited them to disobey, there came a pronouncement that contained much consolation and comfort for them: God would maintain a state of enmity between the tempter and the "woman," by whom Eve is meant in the context. She had associated with the serpent, had lent a ready ear to his solicitations, had believed him rather than the divine warning: "the day when you eat of it, you must die." This friendly relationship with Satan was now replaced by a state of hostility. The woman need not fear that she would remain permanently under the influence of the tempter because of her error; in the future she would have the strength to withstand his enticements. And if thenceforth she refused to listen to his whisperings, she could regain God's friendship; for Yahweh and the serpent stood opposed to each other as good against evil. Hostility toward the serpent was certainly not directed against an animal, but against the tempter; it arose from ethical and moral considerations, not from repugnance or physical appearance. The woman is addressed directly because it was she who had first given ear to the tempter; indirectly the encouraging words apply to the man too, who also sinned.

Our first parents need not then despair; for alongside God's justice they would experience His mercy, His hands lovingly outstretched to embrace the sinner who looks up to Him and strives to approach Him. God punishes, but does not remain angry forever. The tempter had brought misfortune upon them, but he could not keep them away from God eternally. All that was necessary was a determination to withstand temptation and act accordingly. This bit of comfort was desperately

[77] Mich. 7:17.
[78] Knudtzon, *Die El-Amarna-Tafeln*, no. 100, 36, p. 452.
[79] Gen. 4:11.
[80] Passages are given in L. Reinke, *Beiträge zur Erklärung des AT*, II, 286f.

needed by our first parents as they were driven from paradise; without it despair would have overpowered them.

God's words also describe a state of hostility that would be lasting — between the seed or followers of the serpent and the seed or descendants of the woman. In the verse following, which contains the sentence of punishment upon the woman, there is direct reference to the children she would bear; while after the account of the creation of the woman the author had pointed out that man and wife should be bound together in a most intimate oneness with each other. The seed of the woman, accordingly, are those to be born of her — in fact, the whole human race. Not only were the first man and woman tempted by the enemy, it will be the lot of everyone. Every person must stand the test whether he wishes to listen to God and obey His commands, or whether in the pride of his heart he decides to rise up against God, as happened in paradise.

Since the "serpent" is the devil, the seed of the serpent includes the whole host of evil spirits. Nor was this unintelligible to the Israelitic reader; for to the Oriental mind devils were not extreme individualists, they sought companionship.[81] A "brood of vipers," they gloat over the work of leading men into evil, just as their chieftain in the garden. The same means are employed, viz., enticement, deception, pleasures which prove empty as soon as man has touched them. Every one feels "another law in his members which wars against the law of his mind";[82] and if he resists, the tempter will try to win by brute force, through a flood of suffering, to make him despair of God and His love.

The hope to win in the struggle against Satan was not restricted to our first parents: "It (the seed or descendants of the woman) shall crush your (the serpent's) head."[83] In describing the battle that will rage between men and temptation, the author continues in the same vein. If one chances upon a snake coiled to strike, the natural reaction is to eliminate further danger by crushing the creature's head. The meaning of the picture is: *man will win out over the tempter if he but act courageously and not surrender himself to the devil.* The battle will not be an easy one, quickly over. The serpent will seek to wound him.[84] The wound may be painful, but will not result in death if properly attended to. To put it more plainly: the tempter will harm those who resist his allurements as much as he can — their goods, honor, health, and perhaps he may deprive them even of physical life.

---

[81] Matth. 8:28f; 12:45. [82] Rom. 7:23.
[83] The pronoun is that of the third person masculine in the Hebrew text and refers to *zera'*, seed. Textually this reading is supported by Sam G It, and the following forms of the verb and suffixes. The Vulgate's *ipsa* refers to the woman, but of the Vulgate manuscripts some have *ipse*, some *ipsa*.

[84] The Hebrew text (M) contains the same verb *šuph*, crush, in both clauses; but since a snake cannot "crush" a man's foot, the word may be given an approximate meaning, viz., to wound, to bite at, harm; accordingly it is not necessary to resort to the form *ša'aph*, to snap at.

An example of such a battle, and of how man may finally triumph over the tempter is given in the Book of Job. Job feared God. Satan sought to make him unfaithful, even as he had succeeded with Adam and Eve. Attack followed attack; all that Job possessed was taken away; then his children; lastly health. His honor too was questioned, as friends interpreted his suffering as punishment for secret sins. Job knew that he was innocent, but he could not understand how God was using such means to prove and purify him. Though Job complains and even challenges God to judgment, he always remains faithful; only after begging repeatedly for recovery does he finally place his lot humbly in God's hand and merges his will with that of His creator. This constitutes the finest triumph that man can obtain in his struggle with Satan.

We could also point to the martyrs of ancient and modern times who suffered and even died because they willed to obey God rather than Satan's agents. God has promised us that we will triumph if we remain loyal; the tempter may rob us of all earthly goods but he can never snatch away our love and friendship toward God.

But if the descendants of the woman have victory in prospect, it is only for those who struggle. God's words are a promise, not an unconditional assurance. Many succumb, abandoning themselves to the tempter. This was the case already in the first generation. Cain hated his brother Abel because he was loved by God. God warned Cain to overcome his evil dispositions: "If you do not act uprightly, will not sin lurk (demon-wise) at the door and its demands pursue you, over which you ought to be master?" [85] Just as in Gen. 3:1 an evil spirit set a trap for the first men, so sin appears in this passage as a living agent, a demon, seeking to waylead Cain (and every man) into evil. Cain rejected God's warning, yielded to temptation, and murdered his brother.

While in the previous sentence the message concerned the perpetual conflict between the seed of the serpent and the woman's seed, God now speaks of the struggle as between the seed of the woman and Satan himself; for whatever the temptations or whoever the tempter, it is ultimately the serpent of paradise who is battling — these are his instruments; and if their leader and master is conquered, they too are vanquished. The seed of the woman is the subject because all Eve's children, not only Eve herself, were destined to fight and triumph. The serpent never dies, even when man wins the victory; the struggle will continue on to the end of time. Each individual must fight, he may and should win. Of course, this developed exposition is only obscurely contained in the judgment upon the serpent, later revelations and his-

---

[85] Gen. 4:7. The word *robes,* crouch, brings to mind the demon Rabisu. The Babylonians held that demons lay in wait at each door, ready to pounce upon men. M. Jastrow, *Die Religion Babyloniens und Assyriens,* I, 280, 356, 359, 360, 376.

tory have cast light upon it. But our first parents and their descendants through them were taught at least this much by God: a) they did not need to despair; b) the tempter would indeed return again and again to vex them; c) he was in no position to separate them from God if they but stood firm against his advances.

The judgment passed upon the serpent in paradise with its message of the struggle man will have against the diabolical enemy as well as the victory that may and should be gained is the first "good news" which God granted to our first parents and to all their descendants. It is the *protoevangel*, the first joyful message of forgiveness from sin, and therefore the first instance of a Messianic prophecy.

It is indeed the lot of every individual to contend against the serpent and perhaps be bitten in the encounter; yet from the New Testament we know that a certain descendant of the woman entered the struggle in a unique way and won such a definitive triumph that we all may share in it, although our personal struggle may continue. He, whom St. Paul refers to as *factus ex muliere*, made of a woman,[86] was tempted by Satan in the desert.[87] Then a "generation of vipers"[88] beset Him, the Pharisees who had "the devil as their father."[89] Betrayed by Judas into whose heart Satan had planted the act,[90] Jesus surrendered Himself to His enemies; and "the power of darkness" seemed to triumph.[91] As Jesus made the way of the Cross, as He hung and died upon the gibbet, He received the bite of the serpent. But by surrendering His human nature to death, He crushed the serpent's head and broke its power with the result that *qui in ligno vincebat, in ligno quoque vinceretur* — the serpent *who triumphed on the tree* (of paradise) *was vanquished on the tree* (of the Cross).[92]

Now that we have attempted to determine the sense of the protoevangel, there remains one other problem: Did God in paradise speak the words as we now find them in Genesis, and did they remain unaltered through countless millenia of human history until they were committed to writing in relatively recent times?

One may assume that at the core of the various accounts found among ancient peoples concerning a blessed life of the first man and woman that came to an end through sin prompted by the machinations of a serpent, there lies a vestige of primitive tradition.[93] Nevertheless, the Biblical account does not reflect any such tradition in detail; for in that case Abraham must have brought it along from Mesopotamia, and some

86 Gal. 4:4.
87 Matth. 4.
88 Matth. 3:7.
89 John 8:44.
90 Luke 22:3 ; John 13:2, 27.
91 Luke 22:53.

92 Preface of the Holy Cross. Regarding the interpretation of "the woman" as Mary, cf. ch. 8, "The Messiah's Mother."
93 P. Heinisch, *Probleme der biblischen Urgeschichte*, 101f.

story would necessarily exist that would agree at least along the major lines. But such is not the case. If the Biblical account does have points in common with primitive revelation, it seems best to maintain that Moses was not only under the influence of divine inspiration as he wrote, receiving the impulse to commit such tradition to writing (*impulsus ad scribendum*) together with the divine assistance in the act of composition needed to preserve him from error, but that in addition a unique divine revelation was simultaneously granted him. For the subject matter treated in the opening chapters of the Old Testament has decisive importance upon the knowledge of God and the moral standards for men of all ages. Here is explained how suffering and death came into the world after God had made all things good; here we are given hope in God's mercy and goodness; truths that affect all are clearly stated; and Christianity's doctrine of the redemption finds here its ultimate reason.

In comparison with attempts by other nations to explain the origin of sin and evil, the Genesis account shows forth a sublimity of conception that could never be accounted for adequately by the personal reflections of a merely human author. The protoevangel depends upon a very special divine revelation accorded to Moses. This by no means jeopardizes the fact that God addressed words of consolation and admonition to our first parents in paradise. They and their descendants were to face life not with gloomy resignation but with trust in God's mercy and faith to meet the problems before them. Laocoon, bound by serpents and powerless against an unalterable destiny, was not to be their symbol; rather Dürer's Christian soldier battling and triumphing over death and Satan.

§2. SALVATION THROUGH SEM
Gen. 9:24-27

Cain already disregarded the warning to resist the promptings of the evil one who had brought misfortune upon his parents, and this despite a special appeal by God. His descendants became increasingly earthly-minded; and Seth's children too apostatized from God: "The wickedness of man on the earth was great; his every thought, his every bent of heart was nought but evil." [94] For this reason God caused a great flood to come upon the earth. From its waters only Noe was saved, for he alone had found grace with Yahweh, he and his family.

But even the horrors of this dreadful judgment made no lasting impression upon one of the few who survived. Overcome by wine, Noe lay naked in his tent. Ham, the youngest of his sons, saw his father's condition, took evil pleasure in the sight, and sought out his brothers to lead them into the same sins against piety and purity. Sem and Japheth, however, took another course of action and covered their father. When Noe discovered how his sons had acted, he uttered a curse upon Ham and a blessing over Sem and Japheth:

Genesis

9:25	Cursed be Canaan;
	meanest of servants shall he be to his brothers!
9:26	Blessed be Yahweh, the God of Sem!
	Canaan shall be his servant.
9:27	A wide expanse may God give Japheth;
	he shall dwell in the tents of Sem,
	and Canaan shall be his servant.

In any discussion of curses and blessings one must remember that in ancient times the spoken word was not regarded simply as a sound but as the beginning of the act itself; to the words of a blessing or a curse common estimation attached the power to effect what had been uttered.[95] In the text under consideration there is question of a curse and of a blessing pronounced by a father after his honor had been seriously impaired; and, moreover, a curse and a blessing spoken by a just man whom God had chosen in preference to all others upon earth.

According to some exegetes the political conditions current at the time are reflected in Noe's pronouncement; but history knows of no situation in which Canaan was subject to Sem and Japheth. If Sem is identified with the Israelites, Ham with the Canaanites, and Japheth with the Phoenicians, there arises the difficulty that the Canaanites never were dominated by the Phoenicians — in fact ethnically the Phoenicians were Canaanites. If one attempts to align Japheth with the Arian "Sea Peoples" who invaded Asia Minor and Syria around the year 1200 and to whom the Philistines who then occupied the coastland of Palestine likewise belonged, it becomes impossible to show how the Philistines exercised sovereignty over the Canaanites. If Japheth is regarded as the Arian element among the Hittites, similar difficulties arise.

According to the Genesis story the three brothers are the recipients

[94] Gen. 6:5.
[95] P. Heinisch, Das "Wort" in Alten Testament und im alten Orient, BZF X

7, 8. J. Hempel, Die israelitischen Anschauungen von Segen und Fluch im Lichte altor. Parallelen, ZdmG 79, 20-110.

of curse and blessing in such a way that one is cursed for his miscon-
duct, while the other two are blessed for their virtue. Since the blessing
accorded to Japheth was to be fulfilled only in his children, it may be
assumed that the other two utterances would likewise become effective
only at some later date. Accordingly, Noe's words were a prophecy.
Moreover, there is a religious tone to the words spoken to Sem, and we
may assume the same for the other two.

The blessing pronounced upon Sem takes the form of praise to God.
Yahweh is called the God of Sem. Sem, viz., his children, therefore
would enjoy a peculiar relationship to Yahweh. Some of them, perhaps
the greater number, might prove unfaithful to the true God, but the
knowledge of the true God and of how to worship Him worthily would
never be utterly lost in the family. The sacred writer uses the name
Yahweh because this name designates the true God, and the Israelites,
who belonged to Sem's descendants, worshipped Him under this name.

Japheth would receive from God a wide expanse of land.[96] His descendants would spread themselves over large areas, be very numerous.
It may be noted that the sacred writer does not use the name Yahweh as
he did for Sem, but Elohim. "He shall dwell in the tents of Sem." The
subject of this sentence is not Elohim, for in that case the blessing that
had already been pronounced over Sem would merely be repeated; and
the blessing upon Japheth would be interrupted. Rather, Japheth should
dwell in the tents of Sem, but not in the sense that he would dislodge
his brother or reduce him to servitude — for this would have implied a
curse upon the pious Sem who was destined to stand under Yahweh's
special protection. The meaning simply is that Japheth would enjoy
friendly relations with Sem; not as an enemy would he come to Sem's
tent but as a guest to share in his good fortune. Now Sem's special
distinction was the knowledge and worship of the one true God. The
blessing, therefore, implied that Japheth would some day come into the
possession of the true religion through the mediation of Sem. This interpretation was given to the text by the Jerusalem Targum: "His
(Japheth's) sons shall be proselytes and live in the schools of Sem."

One difficulty that cannot be wholly resolved lies in the fact that
the curse was directed against Canaan while it was Ham who was
guilty. Some authors refer to the Table of Nations where Canaan is
mentioned as Ham's last son[97] and say that Ham, since he was Noe's
youngest son, should be punished in his youngest son. Canaan, others
say, took part in the sins of his father; of this, however, there is no indication in the text. Moreover, in the Table of Nations the "sons" of Ham

[96] In Hebrew there is a word play on
the name: *yapht-yaphet*.

[97] Gen. 10:6.

are lands and the inhabitants nations, viz., Cush (Ethiopia, and that part of Arabia bordering the Red Sea), Misraim (Egypt), Put (or Punt, along the Red Sea and the Gulf of Aden). Canaan is mentioned in the fourth place and in the following verses (10:15–18) those begotten by Canaan are the Phoenicians (Sidon), the Hittites, and a series of smaller tribes inhabiting Canaan. The author of the Table of Nations had in mind cultural and political norms for classification, and for this reason he made Canaan a "brother" of Egypt and the "father" of Sidon. Still other exegetes regard Noe's oracle as a separate tradition according to which the three sons in question were called Sem, Japheth, and Canaan. Copyists of the Greek versions, aware of our difficulty, substituted Ham for Canaan.

Most probably, however, the curse was originally pronounced upon Ham. Because of his sin his descendants should serve the descendants of Sem and Japheth. In the time of David and Solomon the Canaanites did come under the sway of Israel, and since they were in close contact with Ham (as witnessed by the Table of Nations), the Israelites believed that the curse upon Ham was fulfilled by this political development. It was an easy conclusion for the Israelites who abhorred the Canaanites because of their immorality and therein found the reason why they were obliged to purify the land.[98] In the course of time some editor substituted Canaan for Ham in Noe's curse, and as a clarifying gloss in v. 18 and 22 added that Ham was the father of Canaan.

Ham's descendants were destined to live in subjection to Sem and Japheth. Would they be under this curse forever? The servant will learn about the God of his master, and pray to Him. Thus servitude opens the way to true faith. Accordingly, Ham's children were not excluded from the blessings of salvation; in fact, they were to become sharers in it through the agency of Sem and Japheth.

The protoevangel had made it plain a) that every person would be tempted by the devil yet would have the power to withstand his enticements; b) that God's plan for the salvation of mankind would not be sabotaged by Satan. Before the flood a great portion of mankind had become unfaithful to God, but then, as Noe's prophecy shows, God provided in a different way that mankind should not forfeit salvation. He indeed permitted "the nations to walk in their own ways." [99] He narrowed the circle of those to whom He would give special guidance but only to this end that they would become instruments of salvation unto those who stood afar off. The true religion would remain among the descendants of Sem; through Sem it would become firstly the heritage of the descendants of Japheth, and then through Sem and Japheth

<hr/>

[98] Gen. 19 ; Lev. 18:24-30 ; 22-24.   [99] Apoc. 14:15.

the heritage of the children of Ham. As in paradise, the evil spirit would at first be victorious, but in the end would fall vanquished. Noe's oracle prepared the historical background for Jesus' words to the Samaritan woman: "Salvation comes from the Jews." [1]

§3. ABRAHAM, A BLESSING FOR ALL NATIONS
Gen. 12:1-3

Millenia had passed since Noe uttered his prophecy. His descendants were countless, had spread themselves over vast regions. Nations and kingdoms arose, but men refused to acknowledge God; of which the story of the tower of Babel serves as one example.[2] Would the knowledge of God disappear utterly? On a previous occasion when godlessness and immorality defaced the earth, God destroyed mankind through a great flood; only Noe escaped, because he kept himself undefiled. From the religious and moral viewpoint conditions now seemed equally depraved — everywhere polytheism and its usual sequel, immorality. Again God intervened. This time it was not some dire catastrophe inflicted as punishment — He had promised: "Never again will I destroy every living creature, as I have done." [3] Rather He now proceeds to execute the plan revealed in Noe's prophecy, viz., from a descendant of Sem, as witnessed by Sem's genealogy,[4] He chooses the man divinely destined to act in a role of greatest importance for the preservation of true religion:

Genesis

12:1   And Yahweh said to Abram:
        Leave your country, your relatives and your father's house,
        for the land that I will show you.

12:2   I will make a great nation of you.
        I will bless you, and make your name great,
        and you shall symbolize blessing.

12:3   I will bless those who bless you,
        and curse those who curse you.
        In you shall all families on earth be blessed.

It was at Haran in Mesopotamia, a center of cult to the moon-god, where Abram received God's call. From Ur of the Chaldees, likewise

[1] John 4:22.   [2] Gen. 11:1-9.   [3] Gen. 8:21.   [4] Gen. 11:10-26.

a center of moon worship, he had come with his father Thare. We do not know the reasons why Thare decided to leave Ur and journey northwards toward Canaan, nor why he tarried at Haran.

Thare and his family were not monotheists although their religious ideas may have been purer and more refined than those of the Canaanites.[5] Laban, Thare's grandson, kept idols of certain gods in his house, the teraphim which he consulted; [6] he knew that the god worshipped by his father Nahor was not the God to whom Abraham prayed.[7] At a later date Josue reminded the Israelites of this fact: "Your fathers, down to Thare, the father of Abraham and Nahor, dwelt beyond the River and worshipped alien gods." [8] Abraham himself could not have remained untouched by the religious ideology approved by his own family and permeating his whole environment. Even though we may not regard him as a polytheist, nevertheless his monotheism left much to be desired. God's call preserved him from perishing in the current polytheism and purified his concept of the divinity, a concept which became more and more profound by subsequent revelations and trials.

God's call constituted an extraordinary grace for Abram, it also implied great sacrifices. He must leave his family which provided protection; he must abandon the country which had become a fatherland to him and where he lived in security; he should depart into the unknown. Nor did God give him the specific reason why He was requiring this act of renunciation. God simply demanded faith and obedience. Indeed the decision was made easier and sweeter for him by the divine promise that a great people would stem from him. But this very promise called for a heroic act of faith, because Abram was childless and his wife, Sarai, sterile. Abram should abandon what was certain — home and relatives — to plunge into what, humanly speaking, seemed most uncertain.

God's promise continued: "I will make your name great!" Such prestige would come to him that his name would be a formula used in benediction. Not only would he personally be the recipient of many favors, through him all who honored him would be blessed. And if anyone cursed him, Yahweh would cause the curse to return and rest upon his own head. This would hold true not merely during his lifetime. Abram's significance would be such as to affect all subsequent human history. All families on earth would be blessed in him, would share in the good fortune with which he had been favored.[9]

[5] Gen. 24:3 ; 28:2. [7] Gen. 31:53.
[6] Gen. 31:19-30. [8] Jos. 24:2.
[9] The passive interpretation of the Niphal of *barakh*, to bless, is supported by G V Targ and in Sir. 44:21; Apoc. 3:25 ; Gal. 3:8. If the Niphal be taken in a reflexive sense, "in you all the nations of the earth shall bless themselves," the sense would be that the nations would strive to share in Abram's good fortune. The Niphal is found in Gen. 12:3; 18:18; 28:14; the Hithpael in Gen. 22:18; 26:4.

Abram, mediator of divine blessings! The greatest distinction and prerogative accorded him, that which elevated him above all his fellow men consisted in being divinely preserved from perishing in polytheism and in gradually deepening true religious concepts. Therefore the blessing that through him would accrue to all nations is *faith in the one true God.*

While the disbelief and disobedience of our first parents brought misfortune upon mankind, the faith and obedience of Abraham served as the source of salvation and redemption for all men. This is why God demanded so exacting a sacrifice from him. He must play a role in the redemption of the human race, and grace was accorded him not primarily for his personal advantage but for the sake of the human race. He was an instrument in God's hand in the execution of the divine plan of redemption. Abram's call did not imply that God was abandoning the peoples of earth but that He was preparing for them the way to salvation. As under a veil this thought lies hidden in the promises given to Abram, but later prophecies render it clearer and clearer.

It was to the future, then, that Abram must direct his gaze. It was not too long before he gained wealth and respectability. But that which he desired most — and the essential point in the promises, children — was not granted. Again God promised that his descendants would be as numerous as the stars of the heavens — another act of faith.[10] Agar, Sarai's handmaid, bears him a son, Ismael,[11] but this child is not destined as the heir to the promises. For if the preservation of the true faith depended upon a special intervention of God, then the people to whom God would accord the mission of preserving and transmitting this faith to the world should also owe its origin directly to God. Sarai, at ninety years of age, should bear a son, and over the descendants of this son Yahweh willed "to be God," i.e., to act in a special relationship to them, for they were destined to keep intact the true religion.[12]

To show that this was a special act of divine favor, God changed Abram's name to Abraham and Sarai's name to Sara.[13] Because it was Isaac who was destined to inherit the promises, Abraham was obliged to dismiss Ismael from his tent.[14] Then Yahweh demanded that the patriarch sacrifice Isaac with his own hand! The individual whom God had selected to be a model in the religious history of mankind should overcome natural love toward a son in the performance of duty. Again Abraham's obedience and faith triumphed. And in return God assured him that through his descendants salvation should be transmitted "to all the nations in the world."[15]

---

[10] Gen 15:5.　　　　[11] Gen. 16.
[13] The change in both instances is ortho-
graphical rather than etymological.

[12] Gen. 17:18.
[14] Gen. 21:14f.
[15] Gen. 22:18.

The promises made to Abraham were renewed to his son Isaac.[16] Isaac had two sons, Esau and Jacob. Because Esau, the elder, proved himself unworthy by trading the rights of the first-born for a mass of lentils,[17] he forfeited the inheritance to his younger brother Jacob. The blessing that Isaac conferred upon Jacob [18] was confirmed during the dream of the ladder reaching to the heavens granted him at Bethel.[19] Thus the promise that mankind would receive salvation through Abraham and his descendants was repeated five times.

§4. THE DESCENDANT OF JUDA
Gen. 49:8-12

God had revealed to Abraham that his descendants, among whom the true faith would always be preserved, would become a nation in a foreign land.[20] Obedient to a divine directive, Jacob migrated with his family to Egypt.[21] There, upon his deathbed, he saw with prophetic eyes what fortunes were awaiting his children, foretold events which came to pass during the following centuries, and was granted a glance into the dim, distant future when mankind would again find its way back to God. After words of reproach against Ruben who had sinned with Bala, his father's concubine, and against Simeon and Levi who had shown themselves wily and revengeful, he addressed Juda, who as Lia's fourth son would obtain the rights and privileges of the first-born:

Genesis

49:8	Juda,
	you your brothers shall praise!
	Your hand shall rest heavy on the neck of your enemies;
	your father's sons shall prostrate before you.
49:9	A lion's whelp is Juda;
	with prey, my son, you go forth.
	He crouches and couches as a lion,
	as a lioness — who dare rouse him!
49:10	The sceptre shall not depart from Juda,
	nor the staff from between his feet,
	Until he comes to whom it (the sceptre) belongs
	and whom the nations shall obey.

[16] Gen. 26:4.
[17] Gen. 25:33.
[18] Gen. 27:27-29.
[19] Gen. 28:14.
[20] Gen. 15:13.
[21] Gen. 46:3-4.

49:11   To the vine he tethers his ass,
              his ass's colt to the choicest vine.
          He washes his clothing in wine,
              his garments in the blood of grapes.
49:12   His eyes sparkle from wine,
              his teeth are white with milk.

In the various oracles over his sons, Jacob makes allusions to their future habitats and occupations (Zabulon, Issachar); or to the difficult struggles in store for them (Dan, Gad, Benjamin); or to the good fortune that would be theirs to enjoy (Aser); or to their love of liberty (Nephtali). In addressing his beloved Joseph, he recalls the past — how the lad grew up protected and guarded in his parents' house until becoming the object of his brothers' hatred — and then accords to him the blessings of fertility of land and countless children that had been given to himself. But of all the blessings the choicest was reserved for Juda.

Over all his enemies Juda would triumph. And he would become the leader of the other tribes: "Your father's sons shall prostrate before you" — not only the sons of his mother. This blessing was realized when David united the tribes under his sceptre and subjugated the Moabites, Edomites, and Aramean city states after throwing off the Philistine yoke. Because sovereignty would rest with Juda, Jacob compared him to a lion, the king of beasts and the symbol of strength and invincible courage. After the lion has taken prey, he retreats to his lair in the mountains to feast in peace. Would any creature be so foolhardy as to disturb him there? Equally dangerous is the lioness, especially when with young.

The pre-eminence Juda enjoyed over his brothers and the status which will be his as conqueror over enemies is indicated by the sceptre and the staff, symbols which rulers placed between their feet when enthroned. In themselves these signs do not necessarily imply kingship, but merely superiority over related tribes and neighboring peoples.

Juda's sovereignty would not cease "until *shiloh* comes." In a 500 page volume Posnanski has collected the various interpretations which were attached to this enigmatic word in antiquity and during the Middle Ages. Nor has any of the numerous explanations advanced in more recent times been universally accepted. There are no reasons for regarding verse 10, or even vv. 8c–11, as an interpolation. The translation, "till he (Juda) or till one comes to Shiloh," understanding Shiloh as a site in Ephraim where a celebrated sanctuary was situated, is now supported by very few. This sanctuary had been destroyed by the Philistines long before David; and, moreover, there existed no connection between Judah's pre-eminence and the Shiloh sanctuary.

Others have tried to deduce a meaning through text emendation, e.g., *še'elah*, petition, or the granting of a petition — the word is regarded as a prophetic name for the Messiah, suggested by the name of Juda's third son, Sela; *mošeloh*, his Ruler; *še'iloh*, the one for whom he prayed; *šilloh*, from *šalal*, to draw out, viz., his newborn son; [22] *šalew*, the peaceful one or peacemaker; [23] *šiloh*, till peace arrives; Accadian *šelu*, *šilu*, the shining one, prince, ruler. Gematria, the technique of later Jewish exegetes who equated the words of Sacred Scripture with numbers and numbers with words and thereby obtained most astonishing answers, has likewise been exploited to find a suitable signification for the expression. Together with the previous word *yabo'*, *šiloh* gives a numerical value of 358, the same numerical value that has been assigned to *mašiah* — Messiah.

Along with these efforts to wring some significance from the text, the question arises how the ancient and venerable versions, those witnesses to earliest Jewish tradition, understood the term. The Septuagint reads: "until that which belongs to him comes," or "that which is reserved for him." [24] Like many Septuagint manuscripts Theodotion, the Coptic (Bohairic) version, and many patristic writers give: "to whom it (the sceptre) belongs," also witnessing to *šelloh*. The same reading is wit- nessed by 40 Hebrew manuscripts, and by manuscripts of the Samaritan Bible; moreover, it is the source for the Itala version (*quae reposita sunt ei*, with *cui repositum est* as a variant); the Syriac version ("him whose it is"); as well as the Vulgate (*qui mittendus est*). [25]

The ancient versions understood the passage in a Messianic sense. Similarly the Targum of Aquila (Onkelos): "until the Messiah comes, to whom the kingdom belongs," and Pseudo-Jonathan: "Till the time when the King, the Messiah, the last of his sons, has come when all nations will subject themselves to him." In Bereshith rabba 98 we read: "till Shiloh comes, viz., the Messianic king." The Talmud too identifies Shiloh with the Messiah. [26] Upon this passage Ez. 21:32 depends: "Till he comes, who has the right to it, and to him will I give it," viz., the kingship which then had come to an end. It is also very natural to ascribe a personal subject to that part of a couplet which has a second member: "and him the nations will obey." In the Gospel genealogy of

---

[22] Cf. Accadian *sallu*, new-born.

[23] From *šalah* — a name for the Prince of peace who would form the counterpart to Judah's rule through might, and thus serve as a transition to verses 11–12 where the blessings of the Messianic age are described.

[24] *šelloh*, i.e., *'ašer lo*.

[25] Probably as a result of an ocular er- ror Jerome read *šlh* as *šlḥ*; or the word was misspelled in his copy, and he trans- lated it as *šaluaḥ*.

[26] Sanh. 98.

Jesus, Matthew lists Juda as a forefather of Christ,[27] and John alludes to Jesus when he speaks of "the lion of the tribe of Judah" in the Apocalypse.[28] Gen. 49:10, accordingly, is the oldest passage in Sacred Scripture that tells of a *personal* Messiah.

The words, "till he comes to whom it belongs," are often given the following interpretation. When Herod the Idumean became the king of the Jews, the sceptre vanished from Judah; the time, therefore, had come for the Redeemer to appear whom Jacob had prophesied.

This interpretation lacks foundation. Actually the sceptre vanished from Judah in 587 when Nabuchodonosor deposed Sedecias, the last king from the house of David, and forced him into captivity together with the greater part of his people. After that Judea was a province, first of Babylon, then of Persia, of Alexander the Great, the Egyptians, the Syrians. The Hasmonean princes who ruled after the Machabean revolt were not descendants of Juda. Judea then became a province of the Romans until Herod maneuvered his installation as king. Moreover, if the passage were to be understood in this manner, viz., that with the appearance of the Messiah Judah's sovereignty would cease, Jacob's prophecy would not actually entail a blessing for Juda — a resolution that in no way can be harmonized with its solemn introduction.

Rather, according to Semitic idiom the expression "till" designates some definite segment of history, a preparatory period and not a termination, a phase in the evolution of an action. When Jacob was fleeing to Mesopotamia, Yahweh promised him: "I will not abandon you till I have fulfilled my promise."[29] In a foreign land God would guard him and finally bring him back to Canaan. Would God withdraw His protection then? In Psalm 110 Yahweh addresses His anointed One: "Sit at my right until I make your enemies a footstool for your feet." Certainly the Messiah's rule continues *after* his enemies have been humbled. "The just man shall not fear till he looks down upon his foes"[30] — will he begin to fear *after* he has triumphed? In the Infancy Account we read: Joseph did not know his wife Mary "till she had brought forth her firstborn son."[31] With this passage compare one from Samuel: "Michol, Saul's daughter, bore no child till the day of her death."[32] After the birth of Jesus Mary remained a virgin, and Michol did not become pregnant when she died.

The expression, consequently, simply implies that the appearance of the Messiah would constitute a new and important phase in the history of the tribe of Judah. Whether or not other tribes and neighbor-

[27] Matth. 1:3.
[28] Apoc. 5:5.
[29] Gen. 28:15.
[30] Ps. 112:8.
[31] Matth. 1:25.
[32] 2 Sam. 6:23.

ing nations continued subject to Judah in the course of history, a day would come when a particular descendant of Juda would wield the sceptre in a most unique way: Him the nations will obey.[33] His kingship would extend over all the Gentile nations. Yahweh had promised Abraham that in him, viz., in his descendants, all the nations of the earth would be blessed.

The blessing of the dying Jacob revealed a) that it would be a specific person who would bring mankind the blessing of true religion, b) this person would stem from the tribe of Judah. The Messiah did not appear until long after Judah had lost the actual exercise of royal power. But prophetic vision scans long periods of time; in one picture the prophets beheld facts between which centuries might lie, passing over in silence countless events filling the intervening period.[34] In this way Jacob foretold that sovereignty rested with Judah till the Messiah would assume the sceptre.

With prophetic insight Jacob described the Messiah's rule: his kingdom is a kingdom of peace and brings a superabundance of material blessings to the land. He rides upon an ass (as in Zach. 9:9), not upon a war horse, and the vineyards become so productive that they no longer need to be protected from animals: "He tethers his ass to the vine." There will be so much wine that little attention will be paid to its use — one could, in fact, take it to wash clothes! Later prophets continued in this vein when describing the fertility of the land, a fertility beyond measure.[35] Milk too would flow in superabundance.[36] Of course, teeth will not change color and become white because of milk, but a striking picture must not be judged according to physical reality. The Septuagint and Vulgate render the passage as a comparison: "darker than wine his eyes, and whiter than milk his teeth." In such figurative descriptions the prophets portrayed a supernatural, spiritual fruitfulness that becomes fully intelligible only in the light of fulfillment.

The words of Jacob to his sons can be interpreted as *vaticinia post eventum*, hindsight prophecy, only by such persons who deny God the power to grant privileged individuals the ability to know the future. With our "shiloh prophecy" this position cannot be reasonably maintained. That Genesis chapter 49 represents a single literary unit is shown by the play on words characteristic of the whole composition, e.g., on Juda — *yoduka*, your brothers praise you;[37] Issachar, laborer;[38] Dan — *din*, to judge; Gad — *gedud*, raiders; Aser, blessed;[39] Benjamin, son of

---

[33] G S V: for him the nations are waiting.
[34] Cf. p. 206: "Prophetic Form and Fulfillment."
[35] Am. 9:13; Joel 4:18.
[36] Cf. Joel 4:18.
[37] Perhaps, too, *yadekha*, your hand
[38] Cf. Gen. 30:18.
[39] Gen. 30:13.

fortune; Zabulon — *zabal*, dwell.[40] In favor of the unity of the whole passage we may point to the repeated comparisons with animals: Juda — lion; Issachar — ass; Dan — snake; Nephtali — deer; Benjamin — wolf; while Joseph is compared to a fruit tree. Nor would the tribes of Ruben, Simeon, Levi have been pleased to keep alive the unfavorable dictums given against them.

Certain points in the prophecy were fulfilled already during the time of the Judges when the tribes occupied and settled Canaan, e.g., aspects in the histories of Dan, Gad, Benjamin, and Issachar too. There is no allusion to the fact that the tribe of Benjamin provided Israel's first king. The words to Joseph give no indication of the separatist tendencies shown by the tribe of Ephraim already during the period of the Judges. In the Song of Debora [41] the tribes of Zabulon and Issachar are praised for their valor against a common enemy. This reflects a mentality quite different from that in Jacob's blessing where Zabulon simply dwells by the sea, and Issachar controls the trade routes between Phoenicia and the south. The predictions, then, must have been made before the period of the Judges.

During the wilderness wanderings the tribe of Levi distinguished itself for fidelity toward God and was entrusted by Moses with the execution of sacred cult; the dictum against Levi would accordingly point to a pre-Mosaic period. And in the address to Ruben the grief of a father whose honor has been wounded is expressed so poignantly that it can hardly be ascribed to some later invention. Some of the prophecies do not point out any specific characteristic of the tribe in question, although subsequent history provided ample material — Zabulon, Issachar, Aser, Nephtali; this too needs no explanation on the assumption that the chapter dates from a period prior to the occupation of Canaan. With reference to Jacob's oracle over Juda, it came easy to promise him the leadership after the three older sons of Lia had forfeited their rights; and Jacob knew that his children would return to Canaan and occupy the land. Now since the Egyptians and most other smaller nations were governed by a king, he could presume that his descendants too would in time become a kingdom. Yahweh had already promised Abraham that kings would proceed from his loins.[42]

At first Jacob's words were handed down orally, and during this stage they took poetic form. Jacob and Israel could not have been used as names for the nation until a nation existed, certainly not in the patriarch's own day. Moses may well have been the final redactor.

[40] Cf. 30:20.
[41] Judg. 5.
[42] Gen. 17:6, 16.

§5. THE STAR OUT OF JACOB
Num. 24:15-19

Jacob had begun his prophecy with the words: "Come together so that I may inform you what shall happen in the days to come." With an eye to the future he brought the patriarchal story to a worthy conclusion and set the stage for the history of the nation. Centuries passed, families coalesced into tribes, the tribes were oppressed by the Egyptians. Under Moses' leadership Israel regained liberty and journeyed toward the land Yahweh had promised their forefathers. In due time the desert wanderings had come to an end, and Jacob's descendants were encamped on the eastern side of Jordan over against Jericho.[43]

This territory, called the Plains of Moab because it previously had belonged to the Moabites, was still inhabited by Moabites although the Amorites had shortly before taken control. Here Israel prepared to enter Palestine proper, the land of the patriarchs, and thus begin another important segment of her history. At this juncture the prophecy of Jacob concerning the ruler from the tribe of Judah was, in God's providential plan, developed further; and that in a way in which Israel would never have anticipated — by a pagan soothsayer, Balaam.

When the Israelites were approaching the sources of the Arnon and were heading for Cisjordania, they approached Sihon, king of the Amorites, with a request for passage through his domain. Sihon refused. An encounter ensued, Israel won and deprived the Amorites of a part of Transjordania. Balac, king of the Moabites, now hoped to regain the land that belonged to his predecessors before the Amorite expansion southward. Nevertheless, Israel was showing no signs of continuing the march. Perhaps he even feared that they would expand their holdings to the south of the Arnon and make him subject. Nor would it be wise to declare war on Israel after they had triumphed so gloriously over the more powerful Amorites.

Balac resolved to try another means to induce Israel to leave the land over which he made claim. To the ancient mind the spoken word was no empty sound, but contained in itself a certain inherent power; it would produce results, whether as a blessing or a curse, as noted above in the explanation of Gen. 9:24-27. Balac recalled that in the territory about the upper Euphrates there was a man, Balaam by name, with the reputation of pronouncing a peculiarly effective curse. Soon messengers were on the way to invite him to come and curse Israel. Balaam knew, or perhaps he discovered through the messengers, what wonders Yahweh, Israel's God, had already accomplished for His people

[43] Very probably in the great oasis of Kefren, er-Rame and Suweme (Num. 22:1).

— how He had forced the Egyptians to give slaves liberty, how the power of Pharaoh was ineffective in restraining them, how Egypt's gods became unable to aid their devotees when Yahweh decreed to destroy them in the Reed Sea. Then at Sinai Yahweh revealed Himself in lightning and thunder; and the nations through whose lands the Israelites willed to march could not prevent them, not even the Amorites. To the Oriental mind this was a clear indication that Yahweh was more powerful than the gods worshipped by the nations Israel encountered, gods powerless even in their own domains!

Balaam was deeply impressed. And now Moab wanted him to curse this people who evidently enjoyed the protection of an irresistible divinity, and thus come to grips with Yahweh Himself! When his apprehensions were divinely confirmed in a dream, he obeyed without delay and gave the messengers a negative reply. Balaam was no monotheist; to him Yahweh was Israel's God just as other peoples had their gods. But he realized that Yahweh was stronger than other gods and thus he easily could have decided to worship Yahweh as his God. Had he cooperated with divine grace he would have attained, thanks to the revelation granted him, an ever deeper understanding of Israel's monotheism.

Yahweh chose Balaam as an instrument in the unfolding of His plan of salvation. It must have made a great impression upon Israel when this illustrious soothsayer, whom their enemies were employing to do them evil, pronounced a blessing upon them in Yahweh's Name. It should have filled them with confidence that Yahweh would render easy their entrance into Canaan. In the fourth or final blessing that Balaam uttered, Jacob's prophecy concerning the coming ruler who would bring salvation was renewed and confirmed.

Balac did not meekly accept Balaam's initial refusal. Greater promises of reward were proffered, and now Yahweh permitted the soothsayer to journey to Moab: "But that only shall you do what I will show you." [44] While Balac had demanded and was awaiting a curse upon Israel, Balaam pronounced a triple blessing, faithful to Yahweh's command. According to his first blessing, Israel would become as numerous as the dust upon the earth. According to the second Israel would be preserved from every evil, would enjoy the protection of her God, her king; Yahweh would reveal to her the future, and in battle would accord her victory. In the third prophecy Balaam beheld Israel living in Canaan, possessing fruitful fields, and victorious over any and every attack.

Chagrined, Balac ordered the soothsayer to return home in sharpest words. He derided him for having forfeited the promised reward by

[44] Num. 22:20.

following Yahweh's promptings. Balaam prepared to leave, but not before announcing to Balac what Israel would do to Moab "in the days to come" (a formula we already met in the introduction to Jacob's prophecy):

Numbers

24:15   Thus speaks Balaam, Beor's son,
           thus speaks the man with the closed eye.

24:16   Thus speaks the one who hears the words of God
           and knows the thoughts of the Most High;
    Of one who sees what the Almighty sees,
           prostrate but with unimpaired vision.

24:17   I see him, though not already now;
           I behold him, though not yet near.
    A star rises from Jacob,
           a sceptre from Israel.
    It shatters the brows of Moab,
           destroys all the sons of warmongers.

24:18   Edom becomes subject (and Seir too, his enemies)
           while Israel grows in power.

24:19   One from Jacob rules (over his foes)
           and destroys the remnant of Seir.

Evidence that Balaam realized he was enlightened by God to utter a prophecy is had in the introduction, which distinguishes this fourth oracle from the preceding ones.[45] He sees a person who in the distant future will arise in Israel and speaks of him as a "star" and as a "sceptre." In the ancient Orient, in Egypt, and among the Hittites, rulers were often compared to stars, at times to the sun. In the Amarna letters the Canaanite vassals called Pharaoh "my sun," because Pharaoh was regarded as the incarnation of Re, the sun-god.[46] In Is. 42:6; 49:6, the Messiah is called "light."[47] And the sceptre symbolized the power of ruling.[48]

While in the previous oracles Balaam had pronounced words of blessing and good fortune upon Israel, the protection of her God and victory over enemies, he now speaks of a king who will appear when the other prophecies have been fulfilled, when Israel will have been victorious over her enemies. This Israelitic king will crush the skulls of the Moabites. A crushed skull implies death; Balaam's oracle therefore implied Moab's fall. In the following line, "all the sons of *šeth*," read *še'eth*, which may well be translated as "all the sons of warmongers,"[49] for just as Moab, so all opponents of the "star that rises from Jacob"

[45] V. 15-16.
[46] L. Dürr, *Ursprung und Ausbau der isr.-jüd. Heilandserwartung*, 107f. F. J. Dölger, *Sol Salutis*, 336f.
[47] Cf. Is. 9:1.
[48] Gen. 49:10 ; Ps. 110:2.

[49] *še'eth* from *ša'ah*, to make an uproar; cf. Jer. 48:45 *ša'on*, turmoil. Other scholars read *še'eth*, exaltation, from *naša'*, to lift up, i.e., the proud, by which the Moabites are meant, will be brought low ; Is. 16:6 ; 25:11.

will be humbled. Closely associated with the Moabites were the Edomites, who dwelt in the hills of Seir.[50] The latter had denied passage to
Israel on the wilderness journey, forcing them to make a long and weary
march.[51]

Under David Moab became tributary to Israel, and a governor was
placed in Edom. But the defeat inflicted upon these nations was not as
thorough as seemingly indicated in our prophecy. Both nations were
able to throw off the yoke and at times create difficulties for Israel; during the Babylonian exile the Edomites even occupied a part of Jewish
territory of which they never again were dispossessed. Repeatedly the
prophets inveighed against Edom and Moab, and eventually these two
nations became types of the enemies of God's people in Messianic
times.[52] It is as such that they appear already in Balaam's oracle. In his
vision Balaam had no better perspective of the future than any of Israel's
prophets. In one dimension-less picture he beheld the chastisement of
Moab and Edom in his day because they had shown themselves hostile
to Israel, their subjugation by David, and the subjection of powers
hostile to God by the Messiah.

While Jacob's prophecy proclaimed the coming ruler as a peaceful
prince to whom the nations would eagerly and joyfully submit, Balaam's
oracle described him as a warrior king who crushes his enemies by sheer
power. The difference is explicable from the circumstances occasioning
the oracles. At the time of Jacob's death an indefinite period of peace
was in prospect; but when Balaam appeared, the Israelites were on the
brink of long years of conflict with the Canaanites. Still Balaam's prophecy does not lack all thought of the spiritual. Nor does it consist only in
that Israel will have a ruler destined to lead God's people in triumph
over enemies and thereby reveal the omnipotence of her God and fill
her with trust in His protection. Would not Israel's foes after their unprecedented defeat recognize Yahweh as mightier than the gods they
had served? Would not the catastrophe that had overwhelmed them
prove to be a blessing — like Ham's servitude in Noe's oracle? In their
comminatory prophecies against foreign nations later prophets developed this theme.

We have the Targum of Onkelos to show that the Jews attributed to
Balaam's oracle Messianic import: "The king from the house of Jacob
will arise, the Messiah from the house of Israel will be great. He will
slay the potentates of Moab and rule over all the children of men." The
Targum of Jonathan and the Midrash Bamidbar Rabbah likewise give
a Messianic meaning to our text.[53] When at the time of Hadrian (132

---

[50] Read *še'ir* instead of *me'ir*, out of
the city.
[52] Is. 25:9-11; 34:5-15; 63:1; Ez. 35;
Abd. 18.

[51] Num. 20:14-21.
[53] Brierre - Narbonne, *L e s prophéties
messianiques*, 10f.

A.D.) the Jews revolted against the Roman yoke, they called their leader Barkochba, "The Son of the Star." For they believed that Balaam's oracle on the star from Jacob was then being fulfilled and that through him God would utterly destroy the Romans.

Moses could easily have learned about the affair between Balac and Balaam as well as Balaam's oracles from the Moabites in whose neighborhood the Israelites had encamped, and with whom, despite their hostility, a certain amount of communication existed. In fact, so intimate were these contacts that the Moabites invited the Israelites to their sacred festivities and tempted them to participate in their immoral rites.[54] And the Midianites, too, who entered Israel's encampment,[55] could have recounted Balaam's story.[56]

The external literary form of the prophecies is due to Moses; in consigning them to writing he kept in mind the prophetic oracles from primitive and patriarchal times.[57] As in Jacob's blessing over Juda,[58] we again meet the picture of the crouching lion.[59] Jacob spoke of a *sceptre* that would belong to one of Juda's descendants,[60] — in Num. 24:17 we find mention of a sceptre rising out of Israel. Yahweh had said to Abram: "I will bless those who bless you, and I will curse those who curse you";[61] and Isaac used a similar invocation over Jacob: "Who curses you, let him be cursed; and who blesses you, let him be blessed."[62] Almost identical expressions are found on Balaam's lips: "Who blesses you, let him be blessed; and who curses you, let him be cursed."[63]

In blessing Israel, Balaam was acting in the service of the true God, and of this fact he was conscious. It is likewise certain from the Bible that he uttered his prophetic message under divine illumination and in Yahweh's Name. Nevertheless, he proved unworthy of this high privilege. 2 Pet. 2:15 tells us that he went astray because he loved the wages of wrongdoing, and St. Jude[64] speaks of the "error of Balaam for the sake of gain." He had been well paid for all his previous predictions and soothsaying, and Balac had promised rich gifts. At the moment when he was under the influx of divine light, the thought of pay had receded, but it soon revived, and in the end his lust for money caused his utter ruin. He was not a man of strong character.

The return journey took Balaam through Midian territory. Through Balac he had come to know the Midianites and now he acceded to their request to remain with them.[65] He counselled them to tempt Israel into worshipping Baal-Phogor and to have them participate in the licentious

---

[54] Num. 25:1–2.
[57] To which also he gave the final written form.
[62] Gen. 27:29.
[63] Num. 24:9.

[55] Num. 25:6.
[58] Gen. 49:9.
[60] Gen. 49:10.
[64] V. 11.

[56] Cf. Num. 31:12, 18.
[59] Num. 24:9a.
[61] Gen. 12:3.
[65] Num. 22:7.

rites practiced there; [66] for he was aware that Yahweh would not support His people if they sinned. Midian hastened to bring this scheme to Moab's attention, and at Shittim [67] many Israelites did, in fact, fall victim to the wiles of Moabite and Midianite women.[68] Yahweh punished His people by inflicting a plague; but He did not abandon Israel or deliver her over to defeat as Balaam had wished. Rather, Yahweh ordained that the wickedness of Midian be avenged, and in the slaughter Balaam himself perished.[69]

Did the Midianites perhaps promise to remunerate the soothsayer, and did he, to compensate for his loss in Moab, seek other ways to harm Israel, realizing that Yahweh would prevent any curse? Did he hope that Balac would re-consider when he saw that Israel was actually being weakened through his advice? Balaam's conduct and character bring to mind the traitor Judas. Judas was taken into Jesus' inner circle of apostles, he preached and worked miracles in Jesus' Name.[70] And yet, goaded on by love for money, he betrayed his Lord and Master and came to a miserable end.

§6. A PROPHET LIKE MOSES
Deut. 18:15, 18

The purpose for which Yahweh gave Moses his mission in Egypt was not merely to free a people from servitude and to lead them back to the land promised their forefathers. Rather, the principal reason was to establish firmly faith and knowledge in the true God in the midst of a pagan world and to guarantee its continuance in the future. On the basis of revelations he had received, Moses deepened the concept of God that had been handed down from the patriarchs. He taught the Israelites how to lead moral lives reflecting God's holy will; he ordained how they could worship God in a worthy manner; he was the mediator of the covenant Yahweh made with Israel at Sinai. Would Israel stand in no further need of supernatural guidance and help after his death? Her proneness to idolatry and immorality had been shown so often, even

---

[66] Num. 31:16.
[67] I.e., in the oasis of Kefren.
[68] Num. 25:1-3.

[69] Num. 31:8.
[70] Matth. 10 ; Luke 10:1-17.

in the face of the countless miracles wrought by her leader Moses. Nor was Israel only involved, mankind at large was affected because the true faith should be preserved for all.

Before his death Moses assured his fellow men that Yahweh would continue to espouse their cause:

Deuteronomy
18:15   A prophet like me Yahweh, your God, will raise up from among
18:18   your own brethren. To him you must listen . . . my words I will put into his mouth, and he will tell them all that I command him.

The words, "a prophet like me," do not refer to any specific individual; the singular is to be understood collectively and signifies that in the future God will raise up a prophet as often as it becomes necessary — hence a series of prophets. This is shown by vv. 20–22 in which "the prophet" (singular) is condemned who presents himself as a herald of the divine will without having received a special call from God, or who speaks in the name of strange gods — "such a prophet must die." The term, "prophet," therefore, includes each and every false seer.

Verses 10 and 11 of the same chapter forbid the presence in Israel of any "fortuneteller, soothsayer, augur, diviner, charmer, one who consults ghosts and spirits, one who calls forth oracles from the dead." [71] All these terms are in the singular. The Fertile Crescent never lacked individuals proficient in these immoral practices. To them the Gentile nations loved to listen, but in opposition to such God would place His "prophet" (singular) in Israel, and to him Israel should lend a willing ear. We may regard a verse from Jeremias as a commentary to our text: "From the day when I led your fathers out of Egypt until the present moment have I sent to you my servants the prophets, early and late." [72]

Hence it was part of the divine plan that after Moses' death God would commission others as heralds of His will. They were to speak to Israel in His Name, teach her, admonish her. Finally when the time had arrived for the sprout of Juda whom the nations would obey, would not he as the last and greatest prophet give them the final word on God and God's plan for man? As God's mouthpiece would he not bring prophecy to its climax by addressing, not a small people, but all nations? After the example of Moses would he not arrange a lasting covenant between God and mankind?

When the Pharisees wished to ascertain whether John the Baptist was justified to preach and baptize, they directed to him the question: "Are you the prophet?" [73] Relying upon the words of Moses, some Jews,

[71] Deut. 18:10-11.   [72] Jer. 7:25.   [73] John 1:21.

accordingly, were expecting a prophet in connection with the Messianic era. They believed that this prophet and the Messiah would be two distinct persons; and the Baptist had previously denied that he was "the Christ." This double interpretation was also assumed by the populace when Jesus appeared; some regarded Him as "the prophet," others as "the Christ." [74] After the miraculous multiplication of the loaves, the people exclaimed: "This is indeed the prophet who is to come into the world"; [75] for they believed that the promised prophet had appeared in the person of Jesus.

The Samaritan woman at the well of Jacob gave expression to the same conviction: "I see that you are the prophet . . . the Messiah is coming . . . when he appears, he will tell us all things." [76] Now since the Samaritans acknowledged only the Pentateuch as inspired, they rested their hopes upon this statement of Moses in Deuteronomy. Jesus applied the passage to Himself when He challenged the Jews: "If you had believed Moses, you would have believed me; for he wrote of me." [77] Peter too regarded the prophecy as fulfilled in Jesus,[78] and likewise Stephen.[79]

According to Hebrews 1:1-2, God spoke in times past through the prophets, and finally "in these days through his Son." He was to be the last and greatest of the prophets.

Although Deut. 18:15, 18 cannot be interpreted as directly Messianic, i.e., as a text that has its fulfillment solely in Christ, the passage nevertheless has contributed significantly to the picture Israel was drawing of the coming Deliverer. To that picture later prophecies added new lines and greater depth.

§7. THE ETERNAL DURATION OF DAVID'S HOUSE
2 Sam. 7:16

When Israel had taken control of Canaan after long and difficult struggles, God's promise to the patriarchs as well as Balaam's prophecy was fulfilled in so far as the occupation of the Promised Land was con-

[74] John 7:40-41.
[75] John 6:14.
[76] John 4:25.
[77] John 5:46.
[78] Acts 3:22.
[79] Acts 7:37.

cerned. But it was not an easy matter for the tribes to act as a unit — they were scattered over a large area, Canaanite enclaves made union difficult, petty jealousies arose as each tribe preferred its own advantages. The Canaanites continued their opposition and neighboring nations made inroads upon Hebrew settlements. Moreover, many Israelites worshipped alien gods alongside Yahweh; they participated in the cult of Canaanite Baals, and by indulging in sacred prostitution yielded to the temptation to do honor to Astarte.

In this period of political and religious turmoil, Yahweh raised up "Judges" or local chieftains who courageously exhorted the Israelites to resist oppression, and their idealism resulted in a bettering of religious conditions. Israel's "Judges" directed the soldiers of only one or two, or at most three tribes, and having accomplished a specific mission, e.g., the defeat of a foreign oppressor, they returned again to private life.

In the course of time, however, there arose an enemy far more dangerous than those previously encountered. The Philistines were not as numerous as the Israelites, but they were united, had definite aims and able leadership. Without extraordinary effort they succeeded in bringing under their control the various tribes occupying central Palestine, including Judah. It now no longer sufficed for a few tribes to unite temporarily. Israel must again develop a sense of national solidarity as in the days of Moses and Josue, and their military forces must be held together in spite of some momentary success. Realizing this, the Israelites asked Samuel to give them a king after the manner of neighboring nations.[80]

But even among zealous patriots this was a course of action not to be pursued hastily. Under the leadership of Moses and Josue the Chosen People had accomplished marvels, and these leaders never wore a crown. Nor should Israel on principle resemble other nations. According to the notions of the time, a nation's god was its king; this attitude we find expressed at the time of Moses already. In his second blessing over Israel, Balaam proclaimed: "Yahweh, his God, is with him; and with him is the victory of his King." [81] And in his third blessing: "Mightier than Agag is his King." [82] While imparting his last blessing Moses praised Yahweh: "He became King of Yeshurun (a term of endearment for Israel)." [83] The Song of Triumph at the Reed Sea, as later expanded, ends with the exclamation: "Yahweh is King forever and ever." [84] True to this tradition Gedeon renounced the honors of kingship proffered to him and his children.[85]

Although political conditions had changed greatly in the meantime,

[80] 1 Sam. 8:5.   [82] Num. 24:7.   [84] Ex. 15:18.
[81] Num. 23:21.   [83] Deut. 33:5.   [85] Judg. 8:88-23.

Samuel was unwilling to inaugurate the change from theocracy to monarchy. Only when convinced that God approved the appointment of a king to lead the people, did he yield. The king, however, must always act in the best interests of Yahwistic religion; he must remain conscious of being "the anointed of Yahweh." [86] His most important duty was to promote the rule of God among the people, and even military campaigns must somehow serve this purpose. It was precisely on this point that Saul, Israel's first king, failed. He regarded war as his most important work; he resisted the directives of Samuel, and therefore the prophet, at Yahweh's command, anointed David, Jesse's youngest son. David responded and proved himself truly the "servant of Yahweh." [87]

When David united the twelve tribes, Jacob's prophecy came true: Judah attained the hegemony in Israel. To this fulfillment of God's plan David alluded: "He has chosen Judah as prince; and from the tribe of Judah, the house of my father; and from among the sons of my father he chose me to rule as king over all Israel." [88] Deeply concerned about furthering the worship of Yahweh, David was considering the construction of a temple. At first Nathan, the prophet, commended his noble resolve, but soon returned to the king with the divine communiqué that the execution of the plan, as pleasing as it was to Yahweh, should be reserved for his son.[89] David would indeed have grown greatly in prestige if he had been permitted to carry through his heart's cherished wish; but obedient to God's will he desisted, cost what it may. In reward for his spirit of submission, Nathan brought to him, on God's request, the message:

2 Samuel
7:16   Your house and your kingship will exist forever before me; [90]
      your throne will remain firm forever.

This guarantee applied to the whole house of David. In a special manner it held for Solomon who was destined to build the temple David was planning: "I shall make a natural son of yours your successor and shall confirm him in his kingdom. He will build a house to my Name . . ." [91] "I shall set him over my house and over my kingdom forever, and his throne will remain firm forever." [92] Of course, all of David's descendants would not remain faithful to Yahweh. These He would punish, but His good favor He would never recall wholly from the Davidic family.[93]

David understood the prophet's words as indicating the creation of a dynasty as shown in his thanksgiving prayer [94] and in the hymn in

[86] 1 Sam. 12:5 ; 2 Sam. 1:14.
[87] 2 Sam. 3:18 ; 7:5, 8 ; 3 Kgs. 3:6.
[88] 1 Chr. 28:4.
[89] 2 Sam. 7:3f.

[90] Read thus with G ; M: "before you."
[91] 2 Sam. 7:12.
[92] 1 Chr. 17:14.   [93] 2 Sam. 7:14-15.
[94] 2 Sam. 7:29 ; 1 Chr. 17:27.

which he praised Yahweh "who shows mercy to his Anointed, to David and his descendants forever."[95] Mention might also be made of David's "last words" when, certain of being divinely enlightened, he said: "The oracle of David. Yes, the oracle of a man who was granted high privileges.[96] The spirit of Yahweh has spoken to me, and his word is upon my tongue." After pointing out a king's duties and implying that his own rule was one of justice and fear of God, David continued: "Indeed, my house stands firm before God; because he made an eternal covenant with me, one that is firm on all points, and guaranteed."[97] He regarded himself and his descendants as linked to God forever in a very special manner.

In Biblical usage *forever* often connotes only a relatively long period of time. To Josue, Abram's ancestors, his father Thare, and his brother Nachor, lived *forever* beyond the Euphrates,[98] viz., in the long distant past. Anna dedicated Samuel to Yahweh's service *forever*, viz., for his whole life.[99] The exile lasted forever,[1] and at its end the devastated cities of Judah had become "eternal ruins."[2] A man can become a servant *forever*, viz., for his entire lifetime.[3] Royal acclamations always contained the wish that the king reign *forever*.[4]

Actually, however, the Davidic dynasty did come to an end with the dethronement of Sedecias and his exile to Babylon in 587. Before this catastrophe one of the psalmists had recalled the glorious epoch of David and the promise given him by Nathan at a time when Judah was sorely humbled, oppressed by foes, its king powerless for the moment. Nevertheless, while meditating upon the promise made to the great king, he does not hesitate to say that David's throne would continue "as long as the heavens, as the sun before me, as the moon that abides forever."[5]

The literary prophets, Amos, Osee, Isaias, Jeremias, Ezechiel, related Nathan's oracle to the Messiah whom they were proclaiming, and saw how in this descendant of David the prophecy would be fulfilled in fullest sense — in him David's throne would be firmly established. When the dying Mattathias recalled to his sons illustrious personages from the past and said of David, "He received the royal throne for all ages because of his piety,"[6] it was at a time when the family of David had been dethroned for centuries. Mattathias must have had in mind that promised Son of David who would inherit the sceptre of His ancestors. The Psalms of Solomon[7] also witness to the common expectation that a son of David should rule as king over Israel.

[95] 2 Sam. 22:51.
[96] ne'um, as in the "oracle of Balaam," Num. 24:3, 15.
[98] Jos. 24:2.
[1] Is. 42:14; 57:11.
[97] 2 Sam. 23:5.
[99] 1 Sam. 1:22.
[2] Is. 58:12; 61:4.
[3] Ex. 21:6; Deut. 15:17.
[4] 3 Kgs. 1:31; Dan. 2:4; Neh. 2:3; Ps. 21:5.
[5] Ps. 89:30, 37, 38.   [6] 1 Mach. 2:57.
[7] 17; 21; composed between 63 and 48 B.C.

Just as Jacob promised leadership to Juda after his sons had multiplied into tribes, and beheld a Redeemer from the tribe of Judah; just as when Israel was on the threshold of Canaan a pagan seer described the Messiah as a victorious warrior; just as Moses before his death heralded the future Deliverer as a prophet; so now, when Israel was becoming sovereign throughout Syria, the awaited Savior was proclaimed as a descendant of the founder of the dynasty, though details remained obscure.

When Jesus appeared, it was a common belief among the Jews that the Messiah would belong to the family of David. Without delay the Pharisees replied, "David's," [8] when Jesus asked them: "What do you hold concerning the Messiah, whose son is he?" The Scribes too called Him the son of David.[9] After Jesus had healed a possessed man, the astonished crowd exclaimed: "Is this not the son of David?" [10] Those who sought aid turned to Him as to the Son of David.[11] "Hosanna to the son of David" the multitude sang as He triumphantly entered Jerusalem.[12] When the angel Gabriel brought to Mary the good news that God had chosen her to be the Mother of our Saviour, he said: "The Lord God will give him the throne of David his father, and he will rule in the house of Jacob forever, and of his kingdom there will be no end." [13] The angel proclaimed that Nathan's prophecy would be fulfilled in Mary's Son, a Son of David. Matthew gives the genealogy of Jesus from Abraham to Juda to David; Luke from David to Juda to Abraham and Sem. And St. Paul reminded the Romans that Jesus "was an offspring of David, according to the flesh." [14]

Surely the kingdom destined for this Child of David would not be an earthly but a spiritual one. It would not be restricted to Israel but would embrace the whole world. On this point God's plan and Jewish aspirations were diametrically opposed.

THE PSALMS OF DAVID

Because of his musical talents David was called to the court of Saul. By playing on the harp he should soothe the king's melancholic moods, a task in which he often succeeded.[15] That he wrote inspired poetry is

[8] Matth. 22:42.
[9] Mark 12:35 ; cf. Luke 20:41.
[10] Matth. 12:23.

[11] Matth. 9:27 ; 15:22, 20:30.
[12] Matth. 21:9, 15.   [13] Luke 1:32-33.
[14] Rom. 1:3.   [15] 1 Sam. 16:23.

shown by the dirges in which he poured forth his sorrow at the death of Saul and Jonathan, and after Abner's assassination.[16] He was the "pious king" whose chief concern was to celebrate the services of God in a solemn manner. He brought the ark of the covenant to Jerusalem and danced before it.[17] He ordained that the Levites accompany the sacred liturgy with music and chant.[18] The tradition which regards David as the composer of sacred hymns has everything in its favor. That he was conscious of being divinely enlightened on special occasions is expressly noted in his "final oracle."[19] He was destined by God to enrich the picture of the Redeemer, the greatest of his children, with new lines. Using psalms in which David described the Awaited One, the Israelites gave expression in prayer to their longing for a Savior.

§8. SON OF GOD AND RULER OF THE WORLD
Ps. 2

1 strophe 2:1   Why do the nations rage
      and the peoples devise vain things?
    2:2   The kings of the earth band together,
      and the princes take counsel in common
      against Yahweh and against his Anointed:
    2:3   "Let us rend their bonds asunder,
      and cast away their yoke!"

2 strophe 2:4   He who is enthroned in heaven, laughs,
      the Lord scoffs at them.
    2:5   Then in anger he addresses them,
      in his wrath he frightens them:
    2:6   "Have I not established my King
      upon Sion, my holy mountain!"

3 strophe 2:7   A decree from Yahweh I will proclaim.
      He said to me: "You are my son,
      today have I begotten you.
    2:8   Petition me, and I will give you the nations as an inheritance,
      the ends of the earth as your possession.
    2:9   With an iron bludgeon you will crush them,
      shatter them like a vessel of clay."

4 strophe 2:10 Now, you kings, be wise;
      take warning, you rulers of the earth.

---

[16] 2 Sam. 1:17-27 ; 3:33-34.
[17] 2 Sam. 6.
[18] 1 Chr. 6:16-32 ; 15:16-32 ; 23:3—25:7.
[19] 2 Sam. 23:1-2.

2:11   In fear serve Yahweh,
                with trembling feet approach to kiss him
2:12   lest he become angry and you perish on the way
                for his wrath may blaze forth quite soon.
                Blessed are all who seek refuge in him.

The sacred poet, under the influence of prophetic spirit, opens before us in dramatic fashion a vista of the conduct of the nations and their rulers. Dark clouds of rebellion cover the horizon, the whole world is in revolt. Nations and their princes refuse submission to Yahweh and to a descendant of David's family. Certainly there is room for earthly kings under the Messiah's sceptre, as the prophet Isaias proclaimed.[20] But whereas Isaias saw our king standing as the standard-bearer to whom the nations make their way,[21] in this prophecy they take a position against him. They had accepted his law, but now no longer are inclined to obey it.

The "Anointed One" against whom their revolt is directed cannot be one of Israel's historical rulers. The kings of Babylonia and Assyria and Egypt's Pharaohs strove for world sovereignty, and later the Persian kings; their expanded realms and the power at their command flattered their ambitions. No king in Israel, however, not even David or Solomon, entertained similar dreams; it would have been utopian, considering the tiny area actually theirs. It is the Messiah, according to the oracle over Juda, to whom the nations would listen. Our psalm, therefore, does not refer to conditions current at the time of David, or shortly thereafter. The ever expanding sway of "the Anointed One" over the world is not a mere wish of the poet, but a fact which he beholds as realized, even though that fact pertains to the distant future.

In the second strophe the sacred writer directs our attention to the heavens. Against God men are helpless, it is futile to withdraw from what He enjoins. In majestic repose God watches the mad antics of men as, for example, when they constructed the tower of Babel. But when the proper moment has arrived, He intervenes: how could their moves prove successful since He Himself had established His Anointed One as King! From Sion Yahweh rules. Thither the nations journey,[22] and from there He will hold judgment.[23]

In the third strophe the Anointed One begins to speak. Yahweh had said to him: "You are my son." Israel as a people and, later, individual virtuous persons were called "sons of God."[24] The descendants of David

---

[20] Is. 11:10-12.
[21] Is. 11:10; 2:2-4.
[22] Is. 2:2-4.
[23] Is. 31:9; Abd. 16; Ez. 38—39; Joel 4:2.

[24] Ex. 4:22; Deut. 8:5; 14:1; Os. 11:1; Jer. 3:19-20; Sir. 23:1, 4; 51:10; Wis. 2:12-20; 5:5; 9:7; 12:21; 14:3; 16:21; 18:4.

upon the throne were "sons of God." [25] David "became" God's first-born son.[26] The angels are sons of God.[27] In all these passages, however, there is question of sonship in a transferred sense, of adoption. But to express adoption the Old Testament never used the formula, "You are my son." Moreover, in the passage under consideration Yahweh continues speaking to the Anointed: "Today have I begotten you." The word "begotten" is also used in a transferred sense; Yahweh begot Israel.[28]

In our psalm, however, there is question of an individual person.[29] A comparison of Ps. 2 with Ps. 110, a directly Messianic psalm, occasions the conclusion that the two contain similar prophecies. Accordingly, the Anointed is God's son in a most unique manner, and as such he is accorded sovereignty over the entire world. The word "today" has reference to the solemn proclamation of the Messiah as God's son. Such a message would not have been beyond the grasp of an Old Testament reader. He would not be confused; there was no divinization of royalty in Israel as there was in Mesopotamia and in Egypt.[30]

In favor of a Messianic interpretation we find verse nine used in the seventeenth Psalm of Solomon.[31] St. Paul believed the prophecy fulfilled in Jesus. His resurrection proved that He was truly the Son of God. In the opening chapter of the Letter to the Hebrews support is drawn for the divinity of Christ and His transcendency over all creation from the fact that God never addressed an angel with: "You are my Son, I have begotten you." [32] Jewish interpreters too understood the Anointed as the Messianic King.[33] Only an adoptive relationship is assumed in the Midrash Tehillim.[34]

In the fourth strophe the poet himself speaks. Every revolt against Yahweh must result in the defeat of the rebels. A day of judgment will come. Princes and people therefore should desist in good time from their perverse designs. The expression, kiss the son, *naššequ-bar* (v. 11), is unusual. The only Aramaic word in the psalm is *bar*, son, and in v. 7 the poet used *ben*. The Septuagint and Vulgate give "undergo correction"; Jerome: *adorate pure*. Taking into consideration the context and the consonantal text, the best textual emendation would seem to be *bire'adah naššequ beraglaw* (*gilu* and *bar* coalescing): "kiss him with trembling feet." [35] In the ancient Orient it was customary for vassals to

---

[25] 2 Sam. 7:14.
[26] Ps. 89:28.
[27] Job 1:6; 2:1; 38:7; Ps. 29:1; 89:7; Dan. 3:25.
[28] Deut. 32:18.
[29] On the "conception" of divine Wisdom, cf. Prov. 8:24-25.
[30] Cf. § 16, on Is. 9:5.
[31] Ps. Sol. 17:23-24.
[32] Heb. 1:5; 5:5. Augustine, Cassiodorus, and others interpret v. 7 of the eternal generation of the Son; Justin, Methodius, Hilary apply it to the solemn proclamation of Jesus as God's Son at His Baptism; Hilary, Ambrose, Chrysostom relate the passage to the resurrection; Cyprian, Ambrose, Chrysostom, Augustine of His birth. Passages may be found in Calmet, *In Psalmum secundum*.
[33] Cf. Strack-Billerbeck, *Kommentar zum NT*, III, 675f.
[34] Brierre-Narbonne, 12.
[35] Cf. Closen, Bb 21, 288-309; Köbert, *ibid.*, 426-428.

cast themselves before their sovereign and kiss their feet as a sign of loyalty. In the Old Testament there is reference to such action in Ps. 72:9; Mich. 7:17; Is. 49:23. The new Roman version of the Psalms has *exultate ei; cum tremore praestate obsequium illi.* The psalmist concludes with the prayerful hope that Messianic salvation may be the portion of all men of good will.

Already in apostolic times the opposition against Jesus on the part of Herod and Pilate was regarded as the beginning of the revolt described in Ps. 2.[36] Down through the ages the Church of Christ has stood firm against the attacks of godless governments and peoples. Often she experiences trying times, but is never overcome. Her struggles end only in victory.[37]

Date of composition. According to a prayer in the Acts of the Apostles, Ps. 2, which has no superscription, was composed "by the Holy Spirit through the mouth of our father David." [38] Now this statement may be understood simply in the sense that David is *the* psalmist *par excellence*, as Moses was *the* Lawgiver; accordingly, this text, strictly speaking, would not prove that David personally composed the second psalm.

But its content points to a period before the time of the literary prophets, in fact, to David himself. For according to the prophets the Messiah inaugurates an era of peace, and the nations approach him of their own accord; while Ps. 2 pictures an open revolt which the Messiah suppresses by force if the rebels fail to desist in time. It is a scene that recalls the prophecy of Balaam — the sceptre that will crush the skulls of Moab and destroy the sons of warmongers.[39] Repeatedly David had been involved in the insurrections of subjugated neighboring nations; nor is there any point against Davidic authorship in the observation that he described the Messiah as the sovereign ruler of the world after Jacob had beheld him as the king of nations and Balaam had proclaimed him as the victorious warrior. David would have found it extremely easy to speak of the Messiah as God's Anointed, since he himself was anointed king by the prophet Samuel upon God's command; and in his last address David called himself the "anointed of the God of Jacob." [40] Moreover, as he was approaching death, he enjoined the solemn anointing of his son Solomon as king.[41]

---

[36] Acts 4:25.

[37] In accord with current efforts to explain many of the psalms as poems celebrating the king's enthronement on the feast of New Year, Bentzen, leaning upon Mowinckel, interprets our psalm as follows: Israel's king is adopted by Yahweh; the foes over whom he is described as conquering were originally the forces of chaos. The theomachies of neighboring Oriental peoples were localized into wars between the various nations by the Israelites. Bentzen gives a similar interpretation to Ps. 110: "No theologian today holds that Ps. 110 is a prophecy of Jesus and His rule at the end of time."— Aage Bentzen, *Messias, Moses redivivus, Menschensohn*, 11f, 35.

[38] Acts 4:25.

[39] Num. 24:17.

[40] 2 Sam. 23:1.

[41] 3 Kgs. 1:34.

§9. KING AND PRIEST
Ps. 110

110:1   A psalm of David.
Yahweh's oracle to my Lord: Sit at my right
until I make your enemies a footstool for your feet.

110:2   Your mighty sceptre Yahweh sends forth from Sion:
"Rule in the midst of your enemies!"

110:3   Sovereignty is yours on the day of your birth in holy splendor;
before the dawn, like dew, have I begotten you.

110:4   Yahweh has sworn, he will not retract:
A priest you are forever, according to the order of Melchisedech.

110:5   At your right
the Lord crushes kings on the day of his wrath.

110:6   He judges the nations, heaps up corpses,
crushes chieftains from field to field.

110:7   From a brook by the way he drinks,
and then again lifts up his head.

The introductory phrase, "Yahweh's oracle," specifies the psalm as a prophecy, which the content confirms. The "Lord," *'adon*, to whom Yahweh speaks, is not some earthly prince; for he participates in Yahweh's power, he sits at His right hand, is second only to God Himself.[42] In common with Yahweh he will rule the world, and to him Yahweh subjects all who might agitate against his sway. His foes are forced to lie at his feet as a sign of their deliverance into his power. The text reminds us of how Josue ordered the captains of his army to step upon the necks of captured kings.[43] It was a symbolic action, to which Rib-Addi, for instance, referred in the Amarna letters as he wrote to Pharaoh: Behold, I am the footstool for the feet of the king, my lord, and his loyal servant.[44]

David is speaking as the psalm begins, but Solomon is not the lord he had in mind. David did not greet him in this manner after his enthronement,[45] and even during his regency Solomon remained David's son. Moreover, Israel was enjoying a period of unprecedented peace with her neighbors when David installed his successor. Nor can there be question of any other Israelitic king at whose installation some court poet sang of royal victories. For which of Israel's kings sat at God's right hand, and upon Yahweh's own throne? And was any of them "priest forever" by divine design? Without doing violence to the text, no interpretation of the psalm as portraying one or the other of Israel's kings has as yet appeared.

[42] Cf. Ps. 45:10.
[43] Jos. 10:25. Cf. Is. 51:23.
[44] Knudtzon, *Die El-Amarna-Tafeln* 84, 4.
[45] 3 Kgs. 2:1.

As in Ps. 2:8–9, the poet describes the bestowal of royal power upon the Messiah. 'adoni, "my lord," was a common form of address to a superior, particularly to a king. In spirit David heard how Yahweh spoke. The one whom He was addressing was, therefore, more exalted than David himself — he was David's lord. Such a one could only be the promised Messiah. The words, "until I make your enemies a footstool for your feet," do not indicate a given moment at which the dominion of the Messiah-King will come to an end; for 'ad, until, as in Gen. 49:10, only indicates some significant phase in the given course of action, not a conclusion or an end of the entire affair. The Messiah will rule forever, whether his foes are in revolt against him or whether they lie crushed at his feet.

Then Yahweh takes the sceptre from the Messiah's hand, as it were, and holds it out before him: all enemies will fall before him. The center of the Messianic kingdom is Sion; from there the Messiah will govern the whole world.[46]

The text of v. 3 is uncertain. According to the Hebrew the poet addresses the Messiah: Your people are full of willingness to follow on the day of your march in holy array — from the womb of the dawn comes the dew of your manhood, i.e., in the battles which the Messiah must wage to maintain his sway over insurrectionists, he will not stand alone; youths will join him, well equipped and as fresh as the dew that sparkles in the meadows at the break of day. The Messiah is beloved by his followers, they are ready joyfully to sacrifice themselves for him and his noble purposes. "In holy array": war in Israel was a sacred undertaking, especially the conflict in question, since it was under the banner of the Messianic king.

In the Septuagint and Vulgate, Yahweh speaks: Sovereignty is yours on the day of your power in the splendor of the saints; from my womb before the dawn I have begotten you. This reading would declare the eternal generation of the Son from the Father. The Messiah is God's son by nature, and therefore he may sit at God's right hand. But it would be very strong anthropomorphism if the psalmist had ascribed a womb (rehem) to God; and the New Testament, which leans so heavily upon Septuagint readings, never cites this verse when there is question of Christ's divinity. One may doubt whether this reading of the Septuagint and Vulgate is entirely independent of Ps. 2:7. A translation of the new Roman Latin version is given above. This reading rests upon certain emendations in the Hebrew consonantal and vocalic text made according to the Septuagint.[47] Before the dawn — before time began God had

---

[46] Ps. 2:8–9.

[47] Read: 'immekha nediboth beyom hilekha . . . beterem šaḥar ketal jelidtikha.

begotten the coming ruler, he is truly God's Son, not only an adopted son. The way in which he proceeded forth from God is wrapped in mystery, just as the dew which God causes to fall upon the earth during the night is wrapped in mystery. While instructing Job, God reminded him of the deficient character of his knowledge in matters concerning nature: "Does rain have a father? and who begets the dewdrops?" [48]

Yahweh continues to speak in verse 4. Upon the Lord, the Messiah-King, He bestows the dignity of priesthood, and that forever. As mediators between the Godhead and man, priests among all peoples have as their principal task to offer sacrifice, to consecrate gifts, the gifts with which individual persons or the people as a whole thank God, petition forgiveness for sins, or seek to assure themselves of divine aid. In Sumeria as well as in Assyria, kings also functioned as priests in the early periods. In Egypt the Pharaoh at all times was the only priest, and priests who served at the various sanctuaries performed their duties at his bidding. According to the covenant made at Sinai, priesthood in Israel was restricted to the family of Aaron, and cult was regulated by law in its principal phases. Kings could introduce no essential changes, and under no pretext could they deprive the family of Aaron of traditional rights. Because of political reasons Solomon deposed the aged Abiathar. But Sadoc, who then became the sole high priest, was a descendant of Aaron from the older line of Eleazar. [49] When Israel's kings concerned themselves with religious affairs, as David did when he regulated the ceremonial for the transfer of the ark of the covenant and the cult at the tabernacle, or as Solomon in the building of the temple, they did not act in virtue of any priestly power, but as rulers.

At first, it is true, the kings of Israel claimed the right to offer sacrifices on the basis of ancient custom. Before the Sinai covenant, the father of the family acted as priest for his household, and the leader of a tribe for his kinsmen. For some time the exercise of this right, which was restricted to the priests by the Law, was tolerated. Saul offered sacrifice. [50] On the first occasion he was censured by Samuel, not because the Law had been gravely violated, but because he had not waited for the prophet; on the second his sin did not consist in offering sacrifice, but in not inflicting the ban as Samuel had enjoined. David sacrificed at the transfer of the ark [51] and after the cessation of the plague. [52] Soon after becoming king, Solomon offered sacrifice at Gibeon [53] and before the ark; [54] again on the last day of the dedication of the temple, [55] and regularly three times a year on the principal feasts — at these he even

[48] Job 38:28.
[49] Abiathar belonged to the younger line of Ithamar.
[50] 1 Sam. 13:9-12 ; 15:15.
[51] 2 Sam. 6:13, 17.
[52] 2 Sam. 24:15.
[53] 3 Kgs. 3:4.
[54] 3 Kgs. 3:15.
[55] 3 Kgs. 8:62-64.

officiated at the incense offering in the sanctuary.[56] Jeroboam likewise offered sacrifices.[57] Although still serving strange gods, Achaz personally dedicated with sacrifice the new altar which he had ordered to be erected in the temple.[58]

Only gradually could the priests insist upon all the particulars granted them by the Law. In offering sacrifices some of the kings acted out of motives of piety, others out of motives of political expediency, believing they would gain prestige if they ascended the altar before the eyes of the people. But no king received the title "priest," nor made any claim thereto. A passage in Second Samuel mentions that David's sons were priests [59] and that a certain Ira was a priest.[60] Nevertheless, it is uncertain as to what extent these individuals performed priestly duties; it may be assumed that only in a few cases did they offer sacrifice in David's name, or perhaps certain priestly allotments were assigned to them.[61] 3 Kgs. 4:5 calls Zabud, the son of Nathan "a priest, a friend of the king," but the word priest is probably a gloss. In any event these were exceptional cases.

In Ps. 110 Yahweh solemnly conferred the office of priest upon him whom David recognized as his Lord. This person was not a priest by descent from Aaron, but by virtue of a special divine ordinance. His priesthood, moreover, would continue forever, resembling that of Melchisedech; like the patriarch he would combine the royal with the priestly dignity.[62] Melchisedech's ancestors are not given in Sacred Scripture because he did not owe his priesthood to them; but Israel's priests did owe their dignity to descent from Aaron. These ideas are developed further in the Letter to the Hebrews: [63] since Abraham gave tithes to Melchisedech, the priest-king of Salem was superior to the patriarch and consequently to the descendants of Levi and the priests descended from them. Therefore the Priest according to the order of Melchisedech is higher in dignity than any priest of the Old Law.

In the Melchisedech account we read that he went out to meet Abraham after the latter was returning from a successful encounter against the kings from the east and that he "brought out bread and wine." These words do not imply sacrifice, yet it is very probable that, being a priest, he offered a sacrifice at this victory celebration; and the matter used would naturally have been bread and wine. The Babylonians and Egyptians used bread and wine as objects of sacrifice although always in connection with other items.[64] Would the Messiah offer a sacrifice similar to that unbloody sacrifice of Melchisedech but still far superior

[56] 3 Kgs. 9:25.
[58] 4 Kgs. 16:12.
[60] 2 Sam. 20:26.
[61] 1 Chr. 18:17: "they were the first at the king's side."
[57] 3 Kgs. 12:32-33.
[59] 2 Sam. 8:18.
[62] Gen. 14:17-20.
[63] Heb. 5:4-6 ; 7:1-12.
[64] Fr. Blome, *Die Opfermaterie in Babylonien und Israel*. Erman-Ranke, *Ägypten und ägyptisches Leben*, 316.

to it, even as he himself stood far above Salem's king? That Melchisedech's offering actually was a type of the Last Supper and the Mass, its continuation to the end of time, is due to subsequent revelation.

Beginning with Clement of Alexandria, the Fathers of the Church and patristic writers have no doubts about Melchisedech's sacrifice and that this sacrifice prefigured the oblation of the true Melchisedech, Christ. Citations could be multiplied; here we must restrict ourselves to St. Cyprian: "In the priest Melchisedech we see prefigured the mystery of the Lord's sacrifice. Melchisedech was 'priest of the most high God' because he offered bread and wine, because he blessed Abraham; for who is more a priest of God most high than our Lord Jesus Christ who offered to God, His Father, the same offering Melchisedech made, bread and wine, His Flesh and Blood." [65] This interpretation of the text has found an expression in the canon of the Mass where the priest is mindful of the offering "of the high priest Melchisedech."

Verses 5 and 6 describe how Yahweh accomplishes the oracle given in verse 1. In verse 1 the Messiah-King took his place at God's right hand; now Yahweh is at his side to accomplish the mission entrusted to him. He inflicts judgment upon those who oppose His representative upon earth. The psalmist painted this judgment in colors appropriate to the age, even as the prophets did at a later date. On a field of slaughter the forces hostile to God are vanquished, rebellious kings are liquidated, mounds of corpses cover the plains.

The Messiah-King is the subject in verse 7. Through him Yahweh executes judgment. A change of person — from Yahweh in verse 6 to the Messiah in verse 7 — is not unusual in prophetic compositions. Now that the Messiah has won the battle, he capitalizes on it, giving himself no rest. He stops only for a draught of water to revive his strength and immediately continues on in hot pursuit to complete the enemy's destruction. He crushes them with an iron cudgel, batters them like a vessel of clay.[66] As in the prophecy of Balaam, the Messiah is pictured as a warrior.

At the time of Christ it was universally believed that the Messiah would be a descendant of David. Jesus was aware of this when, with our psalm in mind, He asked the Pharisees: "How does David in spirit (i.e., by prophetic illumination) call him Lord when he says: The Lord (Yahweh) says to my Lord . . . If David calls him Lord, how is he his son?" [67] These words not only guarantee the Messianic character of the psalm, but by inference Jesus claims to stand in a much closer relation-

[65] Ep. ad Caecil. 63, 4. Numerous quotations are given in Bellarmine, De Missa, I, 6. Cf. E. J. Jerome, Das geschichtliche Melchisedech-Bild und seine Bedeutung im Hebräerbrief. G. Wuttke, Melchisedech der Priesterkönig von Salem, ZntW Beih. 5. M. de la Taille, Mysterium fidei de augustissimo corporis et sanguinis Christi sacrificio, 68f.   [66] Ps. 2:9.   [67] Matth. 22:42-46.

ship to God than David. He implies being God's Son by nature. Davidic authorship of the psalm is also implied in the words of Jesus, a point witnessed by its inscription.

It is mere fancy to apply the psalm to an Israelitic king serving as a type for the Messiah. After the time of Jonathan, the Hasmoneans united the dignity of prince and high priest in themselves, but they were in no sense world rulers, and their priesthood rested upon descent from Aaron; no solemn investiture was needed on Yahweh's part to make them priests in Jerusalem, nor did they fulfill the requirements of Israel's Messianic expectations because they belonged to the tribe of Levi, not Judah.

The ancient Greek translators understood the psalm as referring to the Messiah; for according to their version the Son of David is begotten by God, evidently with reference to the interpretation common at least among the Jews of the diaspora during the second century before Christ. Nor did the Scribes and Pharisees question the psalm's Messianic character. Speaking on the first Pentecost, Peter referred to the psalm's opening verses and saw them fulfilled in Christ's ascension to a seat at God's right hand.[68] St. Paul likewise spoke of Jesus sitting at God's right hand after His resurrection.[69] According to the Letter to the Hebrews Jesus as a priest offered a sacrifice for the sins of men and now is enthroned at the right hand of God.[70]

§10. THE INNOCENT SUFFERER
Ps. 22

22:1 For the music director: after "Does of the Dawn." A psalm of David.
22:2 My God, my God, why have you forsaken me,
    keeping my deliverance far from the words that I groan?
22:3 My God! by day I cry to you, and you do not answer;
    and by night, and get no rest.

Pursued by enemies, broken in body, abandoned by all and with death staring him in the eyes, the psalmist turns to God. He realizes that previously he had been on most intimate terms with God, happy in

[68] Acts 2:34-35.
[69] Rom. 8:34; 1 Chr. 15:25; Eph. 1:20-22.
[70] Heb. 1:3; 4:14; 10:12-13. Concerning

Jewish tradition on this subject, cf. Strack-Billerbeck, IV, 252f; Brierre-Narbonne, 29.

His love, and with God always answering him and granting his requests; but now it appears as if the Almighty had abandoned him. Like Job, our psalmist is certain of being innocent. He can see no explanation for God's way of acting. This is his most bitter trial, to feel deserted by God and to be without sensible consolation. In this dark night of the soul, however, he does not despair, he does not tire calling upon God unceasingly for assistance. Indeed, God is now his only refuge.

22:4   Yet you are the Holy One,
              enthroned above Israel's hymns of praise.

God is and ever remains the Holy One. His justice prevents Him from abandoning a man who needs His aid and who asks for it, and has done nothing evil. Daily indeed He is praised by the Israelites as the Holy One in the sanctuary. The history of the Chosen People was a veritable chain of favors since the days of the patriarchs:

22:5   Our fathers put their trust in you,
              they put their trust in you, and you delivered them.
22:6   They called to you and were set free,
              they put their trust in you and were not put to shame.

Abraham and Isaac, Jacob and Joseph found themselves in great distress, but God espoused their cause. The distressed psalmist, therefore, has good reason to look up to God with trust and confidence. He might find himself in a far greater plight than his forefathers, three times he repeats how they trusted in Him — a good indication that he himself was not lacking in this virtue. The sufferer continues to describe his desperate state in various pictures. It is not with words of cold logic that he speaks, his cry comes from a heart that is sorely tried:

22:7   But I am a worm, not a man,
              the scorn of men, despised by the people.
22:8   All who see me scoff at me,
              they mock me with parted lips and wagging heads.

No one has a word of comfort toward him. His distress is regarded as due punishment inflicted by God. His fellow men even ridicule him for having dared to abandon himself to Yahweh's help:

22:9   He relied upon Yahweh.[71] Let Yahweh save him;
              Yahweh will help him, if he is pleased with him."

These bitterest words, spoken in ridicule of his trust in God, serve to give the sufferer courage. What his enemies say is true:

22:10   Indeed, you did bring me forth from my mother's womb,
              at my mother's breast you made me safe.

71 With G It V read *gal* instead of *gol*.

22:11 I was yours since the moment of my birth,
    since I left my mother's womb you have been my God.

From the day of his birth throughout his early childhood he experienced God's kindly guidance.[72] Why should he despair now? Though he finds no aid from men, God will surely remember him:

22:12   Stay not distant from me, for I am in distress;
      be at my side, for no one is here to help.
22:13   Many bulls are encircling me,
      the fattened beasts of Bashan are surrounding me.
22:14   Against me they open wide their jaws
      like a lion ravening and roaring.

The enemies opposing him he compares to bulls that find excellent pasturage in Bashan, the land east of the sea of Galilee. The ancient Oriental regarded the bull as a symbol of might and power, a power made effective through the animal's horns (v. 22), even as the lion (v. 14 collective) through his teeth. As a result of such afflictions, the psalmist lost all strength:

22:15   I am poured out like water,
       disjointed are all my bones.
     My heart has become like wax,
       melting away within me.
22:16   Dry as a potsherd is my throat,
       my tongue is glued to my palate,
       in the dust of death you seek to place me.

Water, poured out upon dry earth, flows away and is lost in the ground; and wax, upon becoming warm, can offer no resistance — two metaphors for a hopeless condition. The poet, moreover, was stricken by a tormenting thirst. It appeared as if God had delivered him over to death. How desperate his condition was is indicated by the following lines:

22:17   Dogs close in upon me,
      a horde of scamps encircle me,
      they pierce my hands and feet.

The mention of dogs brings to mind the savage hounds of Oriental alleys. Verse 17 is a *crux interpretum*. The Masoretic text has *ka' ari* "as a lion my hands and feet" — his enemies are mangling him as lions do their prey; but the verb is lacking. The versions attempt to supply a verb form. The Septuagint read *ka' ru* or *ka' aru*, they pierced. This was

---

[72] One may recall the custom among certain peoples of putting the new-born child upon the father's knee for him to acknowledge as his own; cf. Job 3:12.

followed in the Vulgate and the new Roman Psalter giving *foderunt.* To "pierce" would not imply to pierce through as with a lance or nails; it simply means "to dig a hole." The idea would be: his enemies are preparing great suffering for him in his hands and feet. The textual difficulties inherent in the passage undoubtedly explain why the evangelists do not cite these verses in their narrative of Christ's passion. Punishment by crucifixion was unknown to the Israelites, it was introduced into Palestine by the Romans.

22:18   I can count all my bones,
               they gape at me, they stare scoffingly.
22:19   They divide my clothes among them
               and for my robe they cast lots.

On his very body he bears the marks of persecution. Near death, he sees how the foe will divide his clothing, like impatient heirs who cannot await their benefactor's dying breath. The sufferer again turns to God as his refuge:

22:20   O Yahweh, do not remain distant,
               my strength, hasten to aid me.
22:21   Deliver my soul from the sword,
               my only (life) from the power of the dog.
22:22   Help me escape from the jaws of the lions,
               from the horns of the wild oxen that surround me.

This wringing cry brings his pleading to an end, and the situation suddenly changes. In high spirits the psalmist is grateful for the aid that has come to him from on High. Such a change of mood is found in many of the penitential and petition psalms, as well as in certain Babylonian hymns; consequently there is no reason for assigning our psalm to two different authors. How deliverance actually came is not stated.

22:23   I will proclaim your Name to my brethren,
               in the midst of the assembly I will praise you.
22:24   You who fear Yahweh, praise him,
               you descendants of Jacob, honor him.
               revere him, all you descendants of Israel.
22:25   For he did not spurn or despise the sufferer in his misery,
               he did not hide his face from him;
               and when he cried to him, he listened.

The sufferer knows that God delivered him from death. He is grateful, and exhorts the pious Israelite to join him in praising Yahweh who has worked a miracle of mercy by responding to his plea for aid. At the point of death the sufferer had made a vow: in case he recovered he would bring a peace offering, and to the meal following the sacrifice he promised to extend the first invitations to those in need, as directed by the Law: [73]

22:26   Upon you will I center my praise in the great assembly.
         I will fulfill my vow in the presence of those who revere him.
22:27   The needy shall eat and be filled,
         those who fear Yahweh shall praise him;
         May your heart live forever!

Now he scans greater horizons as he bids others besides the pious Israelites who cling to Yahweh and had no part in afflicting him to rejoice over his deliverance. For the effects of the miracle extend to the whole world:

22:28   All the ends of the earth
         shall remember and turn to Yahweh.
         All families of the nations
         shall worship him.
22:29   Because dominion belongs to Yahweh,
         He is the ruler of every nation.

All nations on earth learn how the sufferer was saved from mortal danger. It makes them realize the power and goodness of his God, and they turn to Him. His rule is acknowledged by all, including the princes of the earth. The following verses too have suffered textually; emendations are according to the Septuagint and Vulgate:

22:30   Before him alone shall the mighty ones of earth fall prostrate,
         before him shall all those in the dust bend the knee.
         To him my soul shall live,
22:31   my descendants shall serve him.
         The coming generation shall be told about the Lord,
22:32   they shall proclaim his justice to people still unborn.
         Yahweh has accomplished this!

The innocent sufferer, the speaker throughout the psalm, is not the people of Israel. He is despised by the people (v. 7), a mother gave him birth (v. 10–11), he has bones, heart, palate, tongue (v. 15–16), clothes (v. 19) and a soul (v. 21). Israelites oppose him and mock him for his trust in God, and Israelites are exhorted to rejoice in his deliverance; they are invited to the sacrificial banquet made in thanksgiving for aid received. Neither David nor any other prophet or saintly person of old was subjected to the mistreatment described, nor could any person have imagined that his personal deliverance from death could be the occasion for the world's conversion. Such a sequel and such a hope must be restricted to the future Redeemer.

[73] Deut. 12:12.

The psalm reads as if it were composed at the foot of the Cross. This interpretation was held already by the evangelists who allude to its fulfillment in the passion of Christ. St. Matthew had, in fact, our psalm in mind throughout the whole passion story. Jesus Himself uttered its first words (in Aramaic form), "My God, my God, why have you forsaken me," [74] during His three hours of torment on the Cross. In His soul it was night, the darkness covering the earth a picture of His interior anguish. He felt as a crushed worm, not as a man, as He was mocked by His own people, blasphemed by them, derided by wagging heads.[75] The high priests, Scribes and elders scoffed at Him for His trust in God: "He trusted in God; let God deliver him now, if he cares for him."[76] His enemies rushed upon Him like wild beasts, and He was unable to ward them off. His tongue clove to His palate, and He lamented "so that the Scriptures might be fulfilled: I thirst."[77] The soldiers divided His garments among themselves, and because they did not want to cut a robe woven in one piece, they cast lots for it "so that the Scriptures might be fulfilled."[78] The nails in His hands and feet caused indescribable agony.[79]

And finally His lifeless body was consigned to the dust of the tomb. The eternal Father permitted this extreme. The climax of His suffering was not the physical pain and derision, but His state of soul — the feeling of utter abandonment and the absence of all consolation when God seemingly had forsaken Him to the spite of enemies.

Nevertheless, just as the Man of Sorrows in our psalm exhorts those of good will to praise God for the deliverance accorded him, just as he directs the attention of all peoples to the marvellous act which "Yahweh had accomplished," so too Jesus concluded His passion with the loud cry of triumph: "It is consummated!"[80] With the death of Jesus began the conversion of Jews who were not influenced by the delusions of the chief priests and Pharisees. In preaching to the Gentiles the apostles stressed both the suffering and the wonderful deliverance of the Crucified on the third day. In the light of fulfillment the vow mentioned in verse 26 may be applied to the Eucharistic banquet.[81]

According to the Masoretic text and the Septuagint, Psalm 22 was composed by David. When citing verses, the evangelists say that Scripture or the prophet said.[82] There is no evident reason for denying Davidic authorship. In Pss. 2 and 110 the Messiah is, indeed, described as a glorious king triumphant over all his enemies, while in Ps. 22 he

[74] Matth. 27:46 ; v. 2.
[75] Matth. 27:39 ; v. 8.
[76] Matth. 27:43 ; v. 9.
[77] John 19:28 ; v. 16.
[78] Matth. 27:35 ; John 19:23-24 ; v. 19.
[79] V. 17.
[80] John 19:30.

[81] Every detail of a prophecy must not be pressed in its fulfillment — v. 3 says that the Man of Suffering called "day and night" to God; our Savior's passion, however, did begin already the night before on Mount Olivet.
[82] Matth. 27:35; John 19:24.

appears as the Man of Sorrows. David was a successful ruler and a brave soldier, nevertheless he experienced much opposition during his lifetime and more than once was at the point of death. We need but recall the period during which Saul was in continual pursuit, or later when Absolom was stirring up rebellion. Through many trials his trust in God never faltered, and when it appeared as though there were no escape from the hopeless situation into which his enemies had maneuvered affairs, God effected deliverance in most remarkable ways. When David, under prophetic inspiration, composed Pss. 2 and 110, he pictured one of his descendants ruling over a far more glorious kingdom than his own, a kingdom that embraced the entire world; and likewise when writing Ps. 22 under divine illumination, he saw his descendant resembling himself in suffering. Both as king and as sufferer his descendant would far surpass him, and his deliverance would have meaning for all mankind.

The similarities between certain expressions in our psalm and the prophecy in Is. 53 concerning the suffering and dying Servant of Yahweh may be explained on the basis of background. But in Is. 53 the Servant dies and is buried, while Ps. 22 only says he is near to death. In Is. 53 his marvellous deliverance from death and afterlife is the reason why the pagan world is converted, in Ps. 22 the deliverance from the brink of death is the occasion — conversion is hoped for through the happy termination of the matter, but is not effected by it. Is. 53 therefore constitutes a further development in the Messianic picture.

Jewish commentators related the psalm to David, to Jeremias, or to Esther. Only the Midrash Pesiqta Rabba from the ninth century interpreted it of the Messiah.[83]

§11. FREED FROM THE BANDS OF DEATH
Ps. 16:9-11

There can be no doubt regarding the monotheism of the author of Ps. 16. He clings to Yahweh, his God; Yahweh is his portion. He abhors pagan gods, and the sacrifices offered to them. According to the superscription David is speaking, and this too is the view of Sts. Peter [84] and Paul.[85] The occasion for its composition, implied in the text itself, may well be a time when David, persecuted by Saul, found himself forced to live in a pagan land. Now anyone who left the confines of Canaan, fell into the danger of worshipping the gods of the country where he was sojourning; for according to the ancient Oriental way of thinking, the gods exercised special power in their own land and had a right to be worshipped. Because of this ideology David's persecutors remarked: "Go, worship strange gods." [86] It was advice our psalmist indignantly rejected. Yahweh had been at his side in all adversity, and under His protection he was being sheltered:

Psalm

16:8   Steadily do I have Yahweh before my eyes;
     because he is at my right side, I shall not waver.

Then the psalmist lifts his gaze beyond the present:

16:9   Therefore my heart rejoices and my spirit is glad.
     My body too shall rest in confidence;
16:10   because you will not abandon my soul to the nether world,
     nor allow your faithful one to undergo corruption.
16:11   You will show me the way to life,
     the fullness of joys in your presence,
     delights in your right hand forever.

The psalmist is speaking of actual death and bodily decomposition, the lot of every mortal. Now, like every other person, David was destined to die. His body decayed, his soul went to limbo and remained there. There was no alternative. But in verses 9-11 the psalmist voices his conviction that death would have no lasting power over him; his soul would not stay in sheol, and his body would not decompose. He awaits resurrection, and resurrection before the body would have been destroyed through the natural processes of decomposition. Moreover, he is confident that his soul would enjoy heavenly delights in intimacy with God.

David was in no position to ascribe the fulfillment of such privileges to himself. At his time the nature of life after death was extremely vague and undeveloped, no one awaited beatitude in eternity or bodily resurrection. Accordingly it is not a private meditation that David is giving, he is speaking under the guidance of prophetic illumination. He is pointing his words of confident expectation not at himself but at one whose ancestor he was, one in whom his oracle would find fulfillment. Jesus died and was buried. He did not undergo corruption. On the third day He arose gloriously, and His human soul was accorded heavenly delights after its departure from the body.

[84] Acts 2:25-28.   [85] Acts 13:35-36.   [86] 1 Sam. 26:19.

Speaking of Christ's resurrection in his Pentecost address, St. Peter referred to our psalm: David died and was buried, and his tomb is with us unto the present day. But since he was a prophet, he, foreseeing it, spoke of the resurrection of the Christ — for neither was He abandoned to the nether world, nor did His flesh undergo corruption.[87]

The apostle Paul too quoted our prophecy: "David, after he had in his own generation served God's purposes, fell asleep and was laid among his fathers and did undergo decay; but he whom God raised to life did not undergo it."[88] According to the decision of the Biblical Commission of July 1, 1933, Psalm 16 is Messianic and heralds the resurrection of Christ. The Midrash Tehillim finds Christ's suffering in the psalm but not His resurrection.[89]

[87] Acts 2:25-32.   [88] Acts 13:35-37.   [89] Brierre-Narbonne, 14.

The Pre-Exilian Literary Prophets

The most important prophecies concerning the future Redeemer are found in the writings of the literary prophets. Not only did they foretell that Israel and the nations would turn to God, but that God would effect this conversion through punishment inflicted upon them because of sin. This approach is a development of earlier prophecies beginning with that of Noe over Ham. In sketching the figure of the future Redeemer prophetic preaching attained its zenith.

The claim of the Wellhausen school that the passages in the writings of the pre-exilian prophets which portray a glorious future for Israel were added in postexilian times has no support either in the text tradition or in the activity of the prophets themselves. The prophets were commissioned to arouse sinful Israel in every compartment of life, and to make her conscious of her desperate lot; as God's messengers they were forced to speak of punishment, of death, of exile. But they were not merely doomsday prophets, they were not sent to destroy but to build. For them judgment was not the finale upon the nation, still less the end of Yahwistic religion. Judgment was intended as a means to make prince and people realize their sinfulness, and repent their error.

71

Judgment would attain its purpose if it effected the nation's purification, not its dissolution. The penitent people Yahweh would pardon and take back into His good graces. Salvation follows judgment. This theology lies at the bottom of the constantly recurring admonitions to turn from evil.

The rays of hope which the prophets repeatedly added to their comminatory oracles should not have lessened their force — in fact, only a few, a very few in Israel would escape with their lives. Amos made this comparison: "Just as the shepherd saves two bones from the jaws of the lion or a tip of the ear, so shall the Israelites save themselves . . ."[90] The city that musters a thousand shall have a hundred left, and the city that musters a hundred shall have ten left . . .[91] If ten men remain in a house, they shall die."[92] The assurance that Yahweh would have mercy on the remnant of Israel after He had inflicted judgment must have been a consolation for the upright and an inspiration to remain loyal to the demands of Mosaic religion during the visitations in store for them. Had they not been able to think of God's mercy when the prophets spoke of the suffering which they then personally experienced, they would have fallen victim to despair. Psychologically, if for no other reason, the oracles of Messianic blessings were a necessity.

§12. THE DELAPIDATED TENT OF DAVID
Amos 9:11-15

When Nathan at Yahweh's behest announced to David the eternal duration of his dynasty, he made it abundantly clear that God's promise was not a license permitting the king's descendants to sin as they wished. If they disobeyed the divine will, God would punish them. In the second half of his reign Solomon already became unfaithful to Yahweh and supported the false worship of his foreign wives in spite of the special graces accorded him at the beginning of his rule and at the dedication of the temple. In punishment there were rebellions,[93] and the prophet Ahias announced the division of the kingdom after his death;

---

[90] Amos 3:12.   [91] Amos 5:3.   [92] Amos 6:9.

postponement of punishment was due to David's sake.[94] David's descendants were not exempted from judgment because the awaited Savior would come from their family.

The division of the kingdom effected no change of heart in Israel. In the North as well as in the South, religion and morality went from bad to worse. Mention a command of God, and Israel had violated it. Canaanite practices were introduced in Yahweh's sanctuaries on the high places — religious prostitution, Canaanite gods, and finally with the support of Queen Jezabel in the North and Queen Athalia in the South, Baal of Tyre found countless worshippers. Feasting and immorality, oppression of the poor and unjust legal decisions were the order of the day; and the kings set the bad example for the people.

True, a few rulers appeared in the Southern Kingdom who fostered religious reforms — Asa, Josaphat, Joas; but in the Northern Kingdom Yahweh was worshipped under the image of a bull since the days of Jeroboam, nor did any king always act worthy of the high office he held. In vain the prophets raised their voices — Elias, Eliseus, Micheas, the son of Jimla. And there were no few instances in which loyal Yahwists were persecuted unto death. For a time the prophets in the Northern Kingdom believed a change of dynasty would effect an amelioration of religious conditions; but they were deceived in the candidates they favored and aided to the throne. Then the menacing clouds of a mighty world power began to gather on the horizon. The Assyrians were seizing the ports on the Great Sea, destroying kingdoms and leading whole nations into captivity. Would a halt be made at the confines of Israel? Was not her guilt too great?

Jeroboam II (783–732), a descendant of Jehu whom the prophet Eliseus assisted to the throne, came to power at a most favorable period in international relations. The Aramean kingdom of Damascus, which till then had been causing serious trouble for Samaria, was suffering from the campaigns of Salmanassar IV (782–772) and Assurdan (772–754). Jeroboam guided successful military expeditions and extended the borders of his kingdom from Hamath in the north to the Sea of the Plains (Dead Sea),[95] giving Israel control over practically the same territory she had in the time of David. The Northern Kingdom exercised sway over the whole of Transjordania and the land north of Moab. Commerce flourished, the people were prosperous, some even lived in luxury.[96] A sense of security came over the nation. Although in religious and moral matters they were sinning gravely, they believed Yahweh's good pleasure was theirs to the highest degree because they made offer-

---

[93] 3 Kgs. 11:25.
[94] 3 Kgs. 11:9-13, 31-40.

[95] 4 Kgs. 14:25 ; Amos 6:14.
[96] Amos 3:10 ; 6:4-6.

ings of fat sacrifices. They regarded themselves as "the first of the nations"[97] and eagerly desired the "Day of Yahweh," the visible intervention of God that would bring all enemies to their feet. Had not Balaam predicted that God would batter the skulls of Moab and destroy all the sons of warmongers?[98]

Then about the year 760 before Christ there appeared at Bethel in the midst of a festive gathering a certain Amos from Tekoa, a town southeast of Bethlehem. To him Yahweh's call had come while he had been quietly engaged in cattle raising and the care of mulberry trees. He was to be God's prophet in the neighboring kingdom of Samaria, proclaiming destruction to a people certain of divine protection and love. So sure was Amos of heavenly enlightenment that he voiced a dirge over the Northern Kingdom at a time when it stood at the pinnacle of power:

> O house of Israel, hear this word
>   that I am raising against you, this dirge:
> She is fallen, never shall she rise again,
>   the virgin Israel.
> She lies prostrate upon her own lands
>   and there is no one to lift her up![99]

Amos voiced his oracle to the rhythm of a dirge, and the hearers were reminded of those most sorrowful moments when they stood near the bier of a loved one. How such a dreadful prediction must have rung in the ears of those who foresaw no dangers, who during the decades of war and woe had but the one wish — that the Day of Yahweh come soon, very soon! True, they had heard David's last words: "The wicked — like chaff they shall be scattered; one shall not seize them with his hand. Whoever meets them will arm himself with iron and spearshaft, and with fire shall they be completely destroyed wherever they rest."[1] But if they recalled this prophecy, they would refer it to the pagan nations who had oppressed them. And now a prophet was proclaiming: "Woe to those who desire the Day of Yahweh! What shall the Day of Yahweh bring to you? Darkness, not light."[2]

The Day of Yahweh would certainly come, a day of judgment. On these points the Israelites were right. But they themselves would be the first to be judged, they who precipitated God's wrath by their sins. Yahweh's eyes were directed against them unto evil and not unto good,[3] to destroy their wicked kingdom from the face of the earth.[4] No one would escape the ordeal. "It shall be as if some one escapes from a lion and is attacked by a bear; or as if one enters his house and puts his hand against the wall, and a snake strikes him!"[5] The Israelites should not feel themselves safe because they continued making offerings: "I hate,

[97] Amos 6:1. [99] Amos 5:1-2. [2] Amos 5:18. [4] Amos 9:8.
[98] Num. 24:17. [1] 2 Sam. 23:6-7. [3] Amos 9:4. [5] Amos 5:19.

I despise how you act at your festal gatherings. Bring me burnt-offerings if you so wish; your cereal-offerings do not please me, and upon the peace-offerings of your fatted calves I will not look."[6] Their worship exhausted itself in mere external rites, it was not accompanied by a moral life.

Therefore their high places would be destroyed,[7] their cities and their proud palaces would go to ruins,[8] whole families would die out[9] and whatever would escape the sword of the enemy would be herded off to captivity.[10] "I will change your feasts into mourning, and all your songs into dirges. Sackcloth I will put upon all loins and baldness upon every head. It shall be like the mourning over an only son, and its end like a bitter day."[11] It will be impossible to escape judgment: "If they break into sheol, from thence my hand will bring them out; if they hide on the summit of Carmel, I shall hunt them out and take them away from thence; if they conceal themselves from my eyes on the ocean floor, there shall I bid my serpent to bite them. If they go into captivity before their enemies, I shall there command the sword and it will slay them."[12]

Judgment will also come upon Judah, the prophet's homeland. Jerusalem will go up in flames, the dynasty will be dethroned, the inhabitants exiled.[13] Nor would the neighboring nations escape punishment — Damascus, the Philistines, Edom, Ammon, Moab; for there exists a natural moral law which they had gravely violated. In a most cruel manner Damascus had executed prisoners from Transjordania; Ammon had tortured captured women in an inhuman way; Moab had burned the bones of the kings of Edom into lime, not even allowing their enemies the peace of the grave; like the Edomites the Philistines too had sold Judeans into slavery.[14]

But if Yahweh brings such disaster upon His people in both kingdoms, what about the prophecies and promises He had made? Will there still be a sprout of Judah, David's Messianic descendant? Will there still be an outpouring of blessings upon Israel when Judah takes the sceptre in fulfillment of Jacob's oracle?

At the end of his book Amos draws a picture of Messianic times.[15] Judgment is not the end. It will effect conversion, and thereby a change in the fortune of the people:

Amos
9:11   On that day I will raise up the fallen hut of David,
        I will wall up its breaches, repair its ruins
        and rebuild it as in the days of old.

[6] Amos 5:21-22.
[7] Amos 7:9.
[8] Amos 6:8, 11.
[9] Amos 6:9.
[10] Amos 7:11, 17.
[11] Amos 8:10.
[12] Amos 9:2-4.
[13] Amos 2:4-5 ; 9:11-14.
[14] Amos 1:3—2:3.
[15] Amos 9:11-15.

9:12 Then they will occupy the remnant of Edom
     and of all nations in which my Name is invoked.
     It is the oracle of Yahweh, and he will accomplish it.

9:13 Behold, days are coming (it is the oracle of Yahweh)
     when the reaper follows the plowman
     and the treader of grapes the sower;
     the mountains drip with new wine and all the hills melt away.

9:14 Then will I change the fortunes of my people Israel:
     they will rebuild and dwell in the ruined cities,
     they will plant vineyards and drink wine,
     they will make gardens and eat their fruit.

9:15 I will settle them upon their own land,
     and they will never again be torn from the soil that I will give
     Thus speaks Yahweh, your God.   [to them.

The dynasty of David will fall under divine judgment, even as the common man in both kingdoms. Prophetically inspired, Amos beheld the magnificent royal palace as a hut in ruins, a heap of stones. Or more simply: the dynasty had already fallen from its high prestige, and now Amos sees how she forfeited power and reputation, and shared the lot of the people. Kingship had come to an end in Israel. Thereupon follows a transformation — Yahweh did not forget the promise He made centuries before. He rebuilds the ruins into a palace as in the days of old, a new age of David and Solomon. And as Israel during that golden era extended her sway over neighboring nations, so too the new kingdom of David embraces Edom, of which only a remnant remains because Edom too had fallen under judgment, and, in addition, "all the nations in which my Name is invoked." According to Deut. 28:10 Yahweh's Name is invoked in Israel, she is His peculiar possession. Joab refused to take Rabbath Ammon personally, preferring to give the honor to David "so that my name will not be mentioned in her." [16] The glory of having captured the city should be the king's.

On the same argument the Davidic kingdom of the future would embrace all nations that invoke Yahweh, that acknowledge Him as Lord. Now since acceptance of the true faith is equivalent to membership in the Messianic kingdom, salvation is detached from nationality; the Messianic kingdom would not be political — earthly, but spiritual — heavenly. Amos contents himself with the intimation that the Gentiles would convert and find a place in the Messianic kingdom. It is an echo of Jacob's oracle foretelling how the "nations would obey" a descendant of Judah.[17]

Amos makes no reference to the person of the coming king, but the allusions to Nathan's prophecy are so clear that his audience knew he

[16] 2 Sam. 12:28.   [17] Gen. 49:10.

was speaking of the expected sprout from David's family. He was not awaiting salvation from Jeroboam II or his dynasty, but from a descendant of David. And since he announced that the house of David will be restored as in the days of the great king, a divided kingdom will then no longer exist; the Northern tribes will come under the sceptre of David's son. What the prophet foretells will surely come to pass: It is Yahweh who is speaking, and Yahweh accomplishes His word.

In the next verses Amos describes the blessings of Messianic times after the method in Jacob's prophecy. Under the Messiah's sceptre there will be wine and milk in undreamed of quantity.[18] Sowing and harvesting, winepressing and plowing follow one another without interruption. Upon the slopes there is a superabundance of grapes, the hills are luxuriant with grasses and the cattle find easy feeding. This implies a time of peace. So that Israel may enjoy these blessings fully, Yahweh will bring the exile to an end, and never again will His people be forced to leave their homes — the Messianic kingdom endures forever. The implication is that the Israel of the future will never offend God or force Him to intervene with a chastising hand.

To older prophecies Amos adds a) that Israel will lose political independence, b) that she will be led away into exile, and c) that the Davidic dynasty will perish before the Messiah appears. With the coming of the Redeemer there will be a change in the hearts of men, the tribes will again unite, and the family of David will resume the throne of power.

When the question was raised at the meeting of the apostles as to whether converts from paganism would be bound by circumcision and the observance of Mosaic Law, St. James quoted the prophecy in Amos 9:11-12 in favor of Christian liberty.

§13. ISRAEL BLESSED UNDER KING DAVID
Osee 1–3

Beginning with the paradise story, God's love and mercy is easily seen throughout the Old Testament. Not only words but striking examples show how God forgives the most miserable of sinners as soon as he recognizes and regrets his evil deeds. Nevertheless, it is the Book

[18] Gen. 49:11-12.

of Osee that describes most touchingly how Yahweh loved Israel despite the fact that she was continually offending Him.

About the year 750, after Amos had been active for a considerable time, Osee received from Yahweh the command: "Go, marry a harlotrous woman and (beget) harlotrous children; for the land has prostituted itself by turning away from Yahweh." [19] On God's bidding, the prophet was obliged to take in marriage a woman of ill repute, knowing full well that such an individual would never remain faithful. The marriage was a great sacrifice for the prophet, but he entered upon it in obedience to God who had called him, convinced that God had a very specific purpose in mind, one closely linked to his prophetic work. Among the people the union of a respected person, one who stood in a special relation to God, with a notorious woman must have caused considerable comment. The lesson divinely intended was this: just as Osee loved his wife despite her evil conduct, so Yahweh loved Israel with whom He had entered into a (marriage) bond at Sinai despite the fact that she so often had proven unfaithful, had lusted after strange gods, and was giving no signs of a change in heart.

How intensely God loved Israel is shown, for instance, in the passage: "How could I deliver you over to oppression, Ephraim, abandon you, Israel? My heart turns against me, my mercy too is flaming up. I do not want to act according to my fierce wrath." [20] And to prove that He would not reject Israel definitely but would show mercy as soon as she repented, Osee was compelled to receive back the woman who had disgracefully left him. "And Yahweh said to me: Continue to love the wife that lusts for a paramour and breaks the marriage bond — even as Yahweh loves the children of Israel although they turn to other gods." [21]

Nevertheless God's mercy is not weakness: "Yahweh must bring to judgment the inhabitants of the land because there is no more fidelity, no more love, no more knowledge of God in the land." [22] Osee should make his wife realize her evil ways, while preventing her from again wandering off into sin: "And I (Osee) said to her: Many days shall you remain quiet before me; you shall not play the harlot, nor belong to a man; neither will I myself approach you." [23] The significance of this action toward an unfaithful wife forced to live as a solitary is then explained: "Because for many days the children of Israel shall remain without king and without princes, without sacrifices and without boundary stones, without ephod and without teraphim." [24] For a long period Israel would have no civil leaders, would perform no acts of sacred cult. She would be deprived of the things forbidden by the Law but to which she was deeply attached, e.g., masseboth, large stones set next to the

<hr>

[19] Os. 1:2.   [20] Os. 11:8-9.   [21] Os. 3:1.   [22] Os. 4:1 ; 7:2.   [23] Os. 3:3.   [24] Os. 3:4.

altar as symbols of Baal; the ephod, a means reserved to the high priest for ascertaining the divine mind; teraphim, household gods. Israel would no longer be politically independent. Exile was implied.

But in captivity the people would return to reason: "Then shall the children of Israel repent and seek Yahweh their God, and David their king; and they shall hasten to him in the fear of Yahweh, and to his blesssings at the end of days." [25] For Osee too judgment was a preparation for salvation and its prerequisite. Punishment will cause Israel to amend her ways and to honor Yahweh; then she again would have a king in David, the sprout from the Davidic dynasty "at the end of days." As a descendant of David he is called David, and later prophets retained this name.[26]

The lesson that Israel who resembled an unfaithful wife would amend in exile and thereupon would be re-admitted into Yahweh's good graces, is developed in another form in chapter two:

Osee

2:15 She ran after her paramours, forgetting me —
   is the oracle of Yahweh.

2:16 Therefore, behold, I will entice her and lead her into the wilderness
   and speak to her heart.

2:17 There she shall answer me as in the days of her youth,
   as on the day that she came up from the land of Egypt.

2:19 I will take away the names of the Baals from her mouth
   so that they shall no longer be mentioned by name.

2:20 On that day I will enter into a covenant for her
   with the beasts of the field and with the birds of the heavens
   and the creeping things on earth;
   the bow, sword, and war I will obliterate from the land,
   and I will make her dwell in security.

2:21 Then I will betroth you to myself forever,
   I will betroth you to myself in righteousness and justice,
   in grace and mercy.

2:22 And I will betroth you to myself in fidelity
   so that you may (truly) know Yahweh.

Messianic salvation, which will last forever, consists primarily in God's love toward a humbled and purified people. He makes a new covenant with them after the covenant on Sinai is voided because of sin. Conversion is final, Israel does not return to her former Baal. She worships Yahweh as the only God, "Men shall address Israel: Children of the living God." [27] The two kingdoms, divided by the sin of Solomon, are re-

---

[25] Os. 3:5.
[26] There is no reason to eliminate the passage as a later interpolation, because *daraš*, to seek, is used with spiritual connotations. Also in Is: 11:10 the nations "seek" the Messiah, and according to Jer. 30:9 the Israelites "serve Yahweh their God, and David their king." — Jewish exegesis recognized the Messiah in David in Os. 3:4. (Brierre-Narbonne, 61).
[27] Os. 2:1.
[28] Os. 2:2.

united under the Messiah's sceptre: "And the children of Judah and the children of Israel will unite themselves together, and they will place at their head a single leader and come up out of the land." [28] In that era of salvation Yahweh will make a covenant with the beasts forbidding them to harm His people; war will be no more since the new Israel is divinely protected. The people will increase by leaps and bounds: "The number of the children of Israel will be as the sand of the sea which cannot be measured or counted." [29] And as Jacob and Amos had previously prophesied, the land will become wondrously fertile.[30]

To make more concrete and vivid Israel's exile and liberation, Osee employed the following picture. Deprived of independence, the nation resembled a corpse, and the land of exile, sheol. But this was not the end: "From the power of sheol I shall free them, from death I shall redeem them. Where are your plagues, O death? Where is your pestilence, O sheol?" [31] Israel rises to a new life, thanks to the omnipotence and mercy of her God. "Yahweh heals her backsliding, Yahweh loves her freely."[32]

Continuing Amos' message, Osee added the note of God's truly infinite love toward Israel. Moved by love, He enters into a new covenant with her. Osee speaks more clearly of the ultimate union of the two kingdoms, and calls the Savior "David." He makes no references to pagan nations; his whole attention was directed toward Israel's sinfulness and her ultimate restoration in divine love.

§14. THE VIRGIN'S SON
Is. 7:13-14

In the year that King (Azarias-Uzziah) Ozias of Judah died (789–738), Isaias was favored with a magnificent vision and called to the office of prophet. Yahweh appeared to him sitting upon a throne, while Seraphim were praising His holiness. Isaias belonged to a prominent family. This gave him easy entrance to the court and enabled him to make his influence felt upon political decisions; it would have been fortunate for Judah if her kings and high officials would have listened to him more frequently.

[29] Os. 2:1. [30] Os. 2:23-24; 14:7-8. [31] Os. 13:14. [32] Os. 14:5.

During the long and happy reign of Ozias the country had prospered. But there arose in the Northern Kingdom as well as in the Southern a spirit of self-sufficiency and luxury which tended to make men forgetful of their duties toward God and neighbor. The very fact that Yahweh raised up a prophet is an indication that religion and morality needed attention. Hardly had the prophet accepted the call when he was told: "Harden the heart of this people, close their ears and blind their eyes so that they will not see with their eyes nor hear with their hearts, and thereby find salvation."[33] The people were unwilling to listen to the preaching of the prophet, and their obstinacy cried to heaven for judgment. Soothsaying and necromancy, idolatry and all types of superstition were flourishing, while righteousness and justice had fled. The officials gave evil example, the poor found no redress at the courts.[34] What good were sacrifices and feast days? Yahweh demanded virtue.[35]

When Joatham ascended the throne, political conditions took an ominous turn. In God's providence it was a fitting occasion for Isaias to herald the appearance of the Redeemer from sin. Tiglath-pileser III (745–727), one of Assyria's most illustrious monarchs and after 729 king of Babylonia under the name Pulu (in the Bible Phul), was pursuing an energetic political policy in the West. In 740, by three military campaigns against Arpad in northern Syria, he reduced the region to an Assyrian province, and by 738 the land of Azrija'u of Ja'udi in northwestern Syria likewise was under his control. Syrian and Phoenician princes made speedy obeisance, including Rasin of Damascus, Manahem of Samaria, and a certain Arabian queen.[36]

The death of Jeroboam II was followed by revolution and dynastic changes in the Northern Kingdom, while political policy wavered aimlessly between Damascus and Assyria. Jeroboam's son Zacharias was assassinated by Sellum after six months of rule. Sellum, a friend to the Aramean party, was displaced by Manahem (742–737) within a month; to gain protection from Assyria, Manahem sent a tribute of 1000 talents of silver — about 9 million gold francs. His son Phaceia was murdered by one of his officers, Phacee (736–732), who because of the common dissatisfaction over the tribute paid to Assyria, changed the course of politics and sided with Aramean party. Already a plan for forming a coalition of the small principalities in the West to regain or preserve independence from Assyria was being considered. Rasin of Damascus was the leader of the league. In addition to Damascus and the Northern Kingdom membership included Sidon, Tyre, certain cities of Philistia, and the Arabian Queen Samsi.

[33] Is. 6:10.   [34] Is. 1:23 ; 3:14-15.   [35] Ch. 1—4.   [36] AOT 345f.

It was necessary, however, to gain the support of Egypt, and this occasioned an invitation to Joatham to join the league. And if Judah joined, there was hope that the small principalities of Moab, Ammon, and Edom would cooperate. If Judah remained aloof, the undertaking· was destined to disintegrate. Joatham refused. Rasin and Phacee intended to force Judah's entry, they already had selected a candidate for the throne in the person of a certain Tabeel whom they knew was hostile to the Assyrian party.

While preparing for the campaign Joatham died, and his son Achaz succeeded him (736–721). He was 20 years old and inexperienced. Achaz' stand on Mosaic religion is shown by the judgment given in the Book of Kings: "He did not do that which was right in the eyes of Yahweh, his God, as his father David had done. He walked in the ways of the kings of Israel; he made his son pass through the fire [37] according to the abominations of the Gentiles whom Yahweh had driven from before the sons of Israel, and he sacrificed and burnt incense upon the high places and upon the mounds and under every green tree (he furthered the cult of Baal)." [38] It was to be expected that one of such a spirit would oppose every effort of God's prophets to influence the court and people.

Achaz was determined to continue the political policies of his father and accordingly refused to act against the interests of the Assyrian party. Soon it came to war. Defeated in battle against the Northern Kingdom, Achaz was forced to retreat to Jerusalem.[39] When the report came that the Aramean army too was approaching and was already in the land of Ephraim, "the heart of Achaz trembled and the heart of his people as the trees of the forest shake before the wind." [40] In this crisis God wished to assure the king, and prevent him from acting imprudently. A siege was imminent and as Achaz proceeded to inspect the water supply, Isaias met him. At Yahweh's direction the prophet had brought along his son Shear-Yashub, "a remnant will return." The boy's name reminded the king of the comminatory sermons the prophet had given without apparent success — only a remnant had listened! A dramatic climax! But the child's name also contained a note of consolation, viz., a remnant at least would return to God and find salvation. Would Achaz be included in this Messianic remnant?

The prophet speaks encouragingly to the king: Be calm, do not fear. The two kings you fear are like stumps of firebrands — they do indeed smoke, but can cause no great damage. What they are plotting against Judah will not stand, it will not come to pass. Yahweh, indeed, de-

[37] Offered him to Moloch.   [38] 4 Kgs. 16:2-4.   [39] 2 Chr. 28:8-15.   [40] Is. 7:2.

mands unconditional confidence from His people; therefore if they "do not believe, they will not abide." [41]

Achaz refused, he had his own plan ready. His trust was not in Yahweh, but in intervention by Assyria; this he must not jeopardize, rather promote. His decision had been to solicit aid from Tiglath-pileser.

Isaias was not ignorant of the resolve taken in the royal council. Yet he believed it possible to restrain the king from executing the plan, one that he knew would prove to be a political mistake and fatal to the religious life of Judah. He offered to work a miracle as an indication of Yahweh's power and His willingness to intervene in Judah's behalf: "Ask for a sign from Yahweh, your God. It may be either from the depths of sheol or from the heights of heaven!" Achaz was given a wide field to choose from. What human strength could not accomplish, God's omnipotence would bring to pass whether the king asked for an earthquake, a resurrection from the dead, or a flash of lightning out of the clear sky.

Although Achaz was not ardently devoted to religion, he did not deny Yahweh's existence. Polytheism acknowledged the rights of any god in his own domain, and Yahweh remained the God who had led Israel from Egypt to Canaan. Nor did he consider it impossible for Isaias to work a miracle; otherwise he would have asked for one and when nothing happened, the prophet would have discredited himself. But if Yahweh worked the miracle, the king would have been obliged by popular pressure to desist from his cherished political strategy; and here he refused. He rejected the proffered miracle, quoting in hypocritical piety a verse from Deuteronomy: "I will ask for nothing and will not tempt Yahweh." [42] According to his resolve, he sent legates to Tiglath-pileser with the message: "I am your servant and your son. Come and save me." [43] And to give weight to his request, Achaz added rich gifts from the treasury of the temple and palace. Now he had openly shown his apostasy from Yahweh, an apostasy that had already taken place within his heart.

But God will not permit his servants to be mocked. Achaz' refusal of the sign from God did not proceed from humility but from a spirit of obstinacy and pride, and could not remain unpunished:

Isaias

7:13   Hear then, you of the house of David. Is it not enough for you to exhaust the patience of men that you likewise try the patience of

7:14   my God? Now Yahweh will give you a sign: Behold, the virgin will conceive and bear a son, and she will call his name Emmanuel.

Achaz had refused a miracle, God will work one nonetheless. Since Achaz had refused a miracle foreshadowing deliverance from present

[41] Is. 7:1–9.   [42] Deut. 6:16.   [43] 4 Kgs. 16:7.

danger, the sign God would work against his will would afford no consolation. It would indeed be a "sign," and would contain a message. The proffered miracle would have been an assurance of immediate help; the new sign pointed to assistance, not in Judah's present crisis, but an assistance which would come to the people in the distant future. And because Achaz had refused to believe, that which Isaias now prophesied required firm faith. At the beginning of the interview the prophet had said to Achaz: "Yahweh, your God." [44] Now he says: "Yahweh, my God." For Yahweh had abandoned Achaz. Moreover, Isaias now addressed his words to the "house of David." What he is about to say affects the royal family, not merely Achaz personally. The sign was Emmanuel, born of the virgin ('almah).

The name Emmanuel, "God with us," implied that God would help the people in a most extraordinary manner through the child. The prophet was thinking of the Messiah; this follows from 8:8 where he says that Emmanuel must be thanked if Judah does not perish utterly before the Assyrian onslaught, as well as from 9:5: "A child is born to us, a son is given to us; upon his shoulders rests the sovereignty." These prophecies certainly pertain to the Messiah; and they become fully intelligible only if the prophet had already spoken of the child — Emmanuel of 7:14. Moreover, we must not overlook the prophecy in Mich. 5:5 which, without doubt, is related to Is. 7:14.

Of peculiar import is the prophet's revelation concerning Emmanuel's mother. The very fact that she will be the mother of the Redeemer promised for centuries throws a veil of mystery about her. In Biblical usage 'almah means a young girl of marriageable age, presumably still a virgin. In Gen. 24:23 Rebecca, whom Abraham's servant recognizes as the future wife of Isaac, is called an 'almah, and in 24:16 she is praised as "a virgin (bethulah), one who had not yet had intercourse." According to Exod. 2:8 Miriam, Moses' sister, who watched the boy lying in the reed basket, was an 'almah; at the time she no longer was a child, although she was still living with her parents. The 'alamoth, walking in procession and striking timbrels in Ps. 68:26, undoubtedly were virgins, likewise the 'alamoth who in the Canticle of Canticles [45] tender their love to the bridegroom or as maidens wait upon the queens and concubines.[46] To the author of Prov. 30:19 "the way of a man toward an 'almah" appeared wonderful and beyond comprehension. That a strong man be irresistibly attracted by a gentle maiden seemed as inexplicable as the phenomenon of how the eagle soars into the sky despite its weight, how the snake glides over smooth surfaces despite a lack of feet, and how the heavily laden ship is borne by the waters as it hurries to port.

[44] Is. 7:11.   [45] 1:3.   [46] 6:8.

Nor may we overlook the fact that in the Isaian prophecy the virgin-mother names her child, although during Kingdom times this function and privilege was reserved to the father. The question spontaneously arises: will this child have no earthly father? Another indication of his miraculous conception and birth.[47]

The interpretation that the wife of Achaz or some woman of the royal entourage is meant by 'almah becomes impossible (apart from the idiom of the language) in the light of the context — the prophecy was directed *against* the king and his family. Nor can it refer to the prophet's own wife, for Isaias never imagined that a child of his would be the Messiah.[48] When he speaks of the conception and birth of his second son,[49] he uses no terms so full of mystery. Neither can the collective interpretation of the article with 'almah be regarded as exegetically sound: "Young wives, upon giving birth to infants, will cry out: Emmanuel — God with us — rejoicing over Judah's deliverance from the scourge of enemies." For Isaias knows of only one Emmanuel, one child-king,[50] and one 'almah. Nor would there be anything remarkable accompanying conception and birth in any of these false interpretations.

The miracle God promised to work, after Achaz had refused a miracle, was a sign for him and for the whole royal family. The coming Redeemer would hail, it is true, from the family of David, but he would be conceived without the agency of a father; the royal family would not be allowed to boast over having given him life. This marvel requires faith, faith which Achaz so miserably had lacked. Neither he nor his immediate successors would live to see the birth of this child; for Isaias looked forward to the Redeemer as coming from the *stump* of Jesse.[51]

Then Isaias added: "Curd and honey will he eat at the time when he will understand how to despise the evil and choose the good."[52] Never was curd and honey regarded as food for the gods. Yahweh had promised the Israelites a land flowing with milk and honey;[53] they would be blessed with a country having fertile meadows for cattle, blossoms and flowers for bees. Now when the prophet was speaking, Israel had become wholly agricultural, while a land of curd and honey is devastated grazing land where "one can keep only a young cow and a pair of goats," where instead of the vine only thistles and thorns sprout up, and where many wild animals lurk.[54] Emmanuel's youth would be marked by self-denial and privations. This agrees well with Amos' prophecy on the fallen hut of David and with the Isaian proclamation on the Savior's origin from the root of Jesse.[55]

---

[47] The Septuagint translation *parthenos*, virgin, is very significant. The Jews took no offense at this version until it was used by Christians as a Messianic text. The article refers to that Virgin through whom the marvel would be fulfilled. Isaias saw her in spirit; there was no need for her to be known to those present. (Gesenius-Kautzsch, 5 72).

[48] Cf. 9:5–6. [51] 11:1. [54] 8:21–25.
[49] 8:3. [52] Is. 7:15. [55] 11:1.
[50] 9:5–6. [53] Ex. 3:17; 13:5.

The prophet continued: "For before the child will understand to despise the evil and to choose the good, the land before whose two kings you stand in dread will be abandoned." [56] This devastation would come to pass within three or four years, before the child would have attained the age of reason. The verse is not without difficulties. It seems to say that Emmanuel would be reared in the kingdom of Samaria or Damascus. But in 8:8 Judah is the land of Emmanuel, while according to verse 18 Egypt (the gadfly) invades the land, an action more easily undertaken against the Southern Kingdom than the Northern. In verse 22 it is Judah that is devastated and whose inhabitants, including Emmanuel, are forced to live on curd and honey. In 7:18–25 the devastation of the Southern Kingdom is clearly described. This description is introduced by verse 17 which has no direct dependence on the preceding. The best solution may be that of Ceuppens who suggests that verse 16b, "before whose two kings you stand in dread," is a gloss added under the influence of 8:4 where the topic is the deportation of the inhabitants of Samaria and Damascus. The words of verse 16, "the land will be abandoned," would then refer to Judah.

With this supposition verse 17 follows logically (without a participle): "Yahweh will bring upon you and your people and the house of your fathers days such as have not occurred since the time when Ephraim seceded from Judah." In early boyhood the son of the virgin would be nourished by curd and wild honey, i.e., judgment upon Judah would come very soon.

Achaz sought to save his country from enemies; but Assyria, whom he was inviting as a savior, came as the destroyer. Achaz could have saved his kingdom from this calamity had he listened to Yahweh who spoke to him through the prophet. But since he refused, he brought misfortune upon himself and upon the whole land.

The Messiah, however, was born only after many centuries. Isaias himself had foretold this. In 9:5 he unites the happy event with the fall of Assyria, and Assyria was destined to destroy the Northern Kingdom, a development that did not occur till 721. He also announced that in the judgment upon Judah, Babylon would participate.[57] And one of his finest prophecies pointed out how the Messiah would be born from the stump of Jesse.[58] Many prophecies are set in an historical framework although details are not given in historical sequence.[59] Isaias saw events which came to pass at various epochs alongside one another; he had no time perspective. The prophecy of the virgin birth served to specify another event that he was expecting soon, the devastation of the Southern Kingdom. To his prophetic eyes the child was present ideally, he saw him

---

[56] v. 16.   [57] Is. 39:6-7.   [58] 11:1, 10.   [59] Cf. p. 206.

growing up before him. After three, or at most four years, when Assyria had thrown off the cloak of friendship and had become Judah's foe, Achaz would realize how unwisely he had acted.

Isaias, in attempting to restrain Achaz from seeking Assyrian aid, showed true political sagacity. Jerusalem could have withstood the siege for a time, while Tiglath could not have closed his eyes to a coalition which threatened his hold on the Mediterranean ports; moreover, he was planning the subjugation of Egypt. For his own interests he must intervene, Achaz' plea was entirely superfluous. When Phacee and Rasin discovered that Tiglath-pileser was preparing an expedition against the West, they retreated from Jerusalem. Achaz had requested help from Assyria and the Great King had responded, realizing how well such action accorded with his own plans. Achaz had bargained away independence, and Tiglath-pileser proceeded to "oppress him" [60] by imposing annual assessments; in the Assyrian inscriptions Jauhazi of Judah is mentioned among the princes paying tribute. Moreover, during his campaigns in the West there were occasions to plunder the territory of the Southern Kingdom.

True, Achaz could not have preserved full and absolute independence before the Assyrian advance, but without the overtures he made, Judah would have suffered less. Relations with Assyria would not have become too intimate with its concomitant dangers in the religious sphere — and it was exactly this development that Isaias sought to forestall. Two examples of the consequent evils are given in the historical books. When Achaz went to Damascus to do homage to Tiglath-pileser, the altar of the storm-god Hadad caught his fancy. Immediately he ordered the venerable bronze altar of Solomon in the temple at Jerusalem to be replaced by a stone altar made according to the model in Damascus — a move to flatter Assyrian officials.[61] Secondly, he "served the gods of Damascus," [62] i.e., the gods worshipped by the Arameans and the Assyrians. 2 Chr. 28:24 gives further evidence of Assyrian impact, "He shut up the doors of the temple of God, and made himself altars in all the corners of Jerusalem, and in all the cities of Judah he built altars (to false gods) to burn frankincense."

Our prophecy, therefore, teaches a) the oppression of Judah within a few years, principally by Assyria; b) the Savior's birth of a Virgin. The former Achaz lived to experience as a punishment for his evil deeds. The Messiah's birth of a Virgin would come to pass in the distant future.

When God called Abraham to preserve the true religion in one family and in the one nation stemming from him, He planned a new creation. That family should not owe its origin to purely natural generation. Abra-

[60] 2 Chr. 28:20.   [61] 4 Kgs. 16:10-20.   [62] 2 Chr. 28:23.

ham should receive a son from Sara when she was old and sterile, in the face of every physical disability: "Is anything too great for Yahweh?" [63] When the time came for the Savior to appear upon earth, God worked a similar miracle for Zacharias and Elizabeth, and they gave birth to the Messiah's precursor, John the Baptist.[64] A still greater marvel should mark the conception and birth of the One destined to lead mankind back to God: He would have no earthly father — He was God's own Son.

In the fullness of time the angel Gabriel was sent by God to a city in Galilee by the name of Nazareth, to a Virgin espoused to a man with the name Joseph of the house of David. And the Virgin's name was Mary. The angel said to her: Behold, you will conceive and bear a son, and you will call His Name Jesus. He will be great and will be called the son of the Most High. The Lord God will give Him the throne of David His father. He will rule over the house of Jacob forever, and of His kingdom there will be no end. Mary replied to the angel: How shall this happen? I know not man. The angel answered: The Holy Spirit will overshadow you and the power of the Most High will come upon you.[65]

After recounting the angel's mission to Joseph with the message that he should take Mary to wife since she had conceived of the Holy Spirit, St. Matthew introduces our passage in Isaias with the words: "All this came to pass that it might be fulfilled what was said by the Lord through the prophet." [66]

§15. EMMANUEL, JUDAH'S DELIVERER
Is. 8:8-10

Soon after the prediction of the Virgin birth, while Judah's political situation was still very critical, Isaias was instructed by God to write upon a tablet the words: "Quick booty, speedy spoil." He must do this before witnesses. For it was a divine prophecy soon to be fulfilled. The words should be the name of the baby who in the course of the year would be born to the "prophetess," his wife. Before the infant would be

[63] Gen. 17:15-31; 18:10-15.   [64] Luke 1.   [65] Luke 1:26-33.   [66] Matth. 1:22-24.

able to say "father" and "mother," the import of its name would be clear to all; for by then Assyria would have overcome the kings of Damascus and Samaria, who currently were threatening Judah.

But Judah too would be devastated by the Assyrians because she would not submit to Yahweh's kindly sway. The River Euphrates, a symbol of the Assyrian army, would inundate Judah. Nevertheless, Judah was and would remain the land of Emmanuel. Even if all the nations on earth rose up against her, Yahweh would protect her from utter destruction in view of the coming Redeemer. Her survival would be due not to the political astuteness Achaz believed he possessed, nor to the military might upon which he was relying and which was now turning against Judah, but to the Redeemer promised by God.

§16. THE NEW-BORN KING
Is. 8:23b—9:6

At the time when Isaias was proclaiming the conception and birth of the Virgin's son, the armies of Samaria and Damascus were marching upon Jerusalem. But the situation soon changed. In 733 Tiglath-pileser deported the inhabitants of the northern areas of the Kingdom of Israel. Only a parcel of the kingdom remained, and Phacee, whose political policies had proven worthless, was assassinated by Osee, whom Tiglath-pileser installed or confirmed upon the throne. In 732 Damascus was forced to surrender, and Rasin was put to death as an insurrectionist. Isaias had foreseen this turn of events and had proclaimed it loudly. Now it was his mission from on High to speak words of consolation to the oppressed and suffering in Israel as well as in Judah; for Judah too had been scourged by the evils of campaigning armies. For the moment Assyria appeared supreme, but the sprout of David would bring deliverance.

Isaias
8:23b   In past days he (Yahweh) brought disgrace
upon the land of Zabulon and the land of Nephtali,
but in the future he will make honorable the Way of the Sea,
Transjordania, and the region of the Gentiles.

9:1   The people who walk in darkness
          see a great Light,
      those who live in the land of the shadow of death —
          for them a Light has risen.
9:2   You have caused great jubilation,
          you have multiplied joy.
      The people rejoice before you, as men rejoice in harvest time,
          as persons exult when booty is divided.
9:3   For the burden of their yoke
          and the shaft upon their neck,
      the rod of their taskmaster
          you break as on the day of Midian.
9:4   For every boot inspiring terror
          and mantle drenched in blood
      is consigned to fire, is become food for flames.
9:5   For a child is born to us, a son is given to us!
          Sovereignty rests upon his shoulders,
          and his name is called:
      Wondrous-Counsellor, Mighty-God,
          Eternal-Father, Prince-of-Peace.
9:6   Great shall be his rule, there shall be no end of peace;
          (he shall sit) upon the throne of David and over his kingdom
          to establish and uphold it
          through righteousness and justice.
      The zeal of Yahweh, Lord of hosts, will accomplish this.

"In past days," viz., the period just over when Israel's enemies were victorious. The territory of the tribes of Zabulon and Nephtali west of the Sea of Galilee and the upper Jordan, as well as the northern section of Transjordania had been depopulated. Through this region passed the "Way of the Sea," the *Via Maris* of the Crusaders. Running from Damascus southwards, it crossed the Jordan and then took a westerly course to the Mediterranean. In this territory Gentiles from neighboring tribes and nations had settled. After the fall of Samaria and the deportation of its inhabitants, the area was systematically resettled with deportees from other parts of the Assyrian kingdom by Sargon, Ashurhaddon, and Ashurbanipal. This was done for political purposes; where a mixture of various peoples existed, rebellions proved more difficult. Foreigners would not make common cause with the natives, at least for a time.

As a punishment upon Israel for indulging in idolatry and having forgotten God's precepts in spite of prophetic admonitions, Yahweh "brought disgrace upon the land." Nevertheless, "in the last days," the Messianic future, He will again raise her to honor. Darkness, the shadow of death — death was reaping a rich harvest through the sword of the foe, famine, plague, and deportation — will be overcome by the Light.

Instead of mourning there will be happiness and rejoicing, freedom will displace servitude, peace the havoc of war.

Yahweh is called the Light of Israel in Is. 10:17 and Mich. 7:8, eternal Light in Wis. 7:26. The opening verse of Is. 60 consoles Jersualem with the words: "Rise! Be flooded with light; for your Light is come, and the glory of Yahweh is risen upon you!" But in our prophecy Isaias is referring to the Messiah whom Balaam likened to a star.[67] The joy Israel will experience when the Light of the Messiah begins to shine is compared to the happiness at harvest time, and to the loud jubilation of soldiers upon taking possession of the spoils after victory is won.

Once, in early days, the servitude to which Pharaoh had subjected Israel [68] came to an end through a miraculous intervention of Yahweh; the yoke fastened upon the nation by the Assyrians will likewise be smitten to pieces. The occasion will resemble the day when Gedeon with a small band routed the Midianites and crushed forever their lust for devastating Israel.[69] With Assyria's downfall, peace is assured. Never again will an enemy oppress God's people; soldiers' boots and soldiers' cloaks, symbols of war, are destroyed.

Who will bring this good fortune, while Israel moans griefstricken? A child whose birth the prophet, enlightened by God, sees as already having taken place, the child who will occupy David's throne. "To *us*" this child is born. He is destined not merely for the benefit of the Northern Kingdom whose visitation Isaias had recalled in the introduction to his prophecy, but for all the people. Upon the shoulders of the "sprout of David" will lie the royal mantle, the symbol of sovereignty.

Then the prophet delineates the child's peculiar attributes. The names given him reveal a mysterious union of divinity and humanity. "Wondrous-Counsellor": neither Moses nor Elias nor any other prophet who by the power of God wrought miracles and pointed out the way to God received a similar name. The child whom the prophet sees in spirit is greater than all God's previous messengers. Now God alone performs marvels.[70] If a man effects something beyond natural powers, it is done only through divine assistance. The child is called "wonderful" and "counsellor," i.e., he will possess extraordinary supernatural enlightenment to fulfill his duties as a ruler who leads men on the true road to God. Wisdom is, indeed, a king's most important asset; for it Solomon petitioned at his enthronement.[71] The Messianic ruler possesses this attribute in an eminent degree, more so than any king preceding him in Israel.

[67] Num. 24:17. Cf. also Is. 42:6 ; 49:6.
[68] Verse 3a portrays Israel as a beast of burden.
[69] Judg. 7:19-25.
[70] Gen. 18:14; Num. 11:23 ; Is. 25:1; 28:29.
[71] 3 Kgs. 3.

The "son given to us" is also called "Mighty-God," *'el-gibbor*. It is a phrase applied to Yahweh in Is. 10:21; Deut. 10:17; Jer. 32:18; Neh. 9:32. This would not have been a striking appellation for an Oriental king in ancient times. Pharaoh claimed to be the physical son of Re; the Sumerians and Babylonians divinized their rulers. Sacrifices were offered to Ur-nina, Gudea and other kings after their death. Certain monarchs arrogated the title of God and accepted divine worship from their subjects. Naramsin used the name "God of Agade." In the introduction to his Code, Hammurabi calls himself "God of kings" and "Sun-God of Babylon." A certain Babylonian took the name Hammurabi-ili, "Hammurabi is my God." After the age of Hammurabi the divinization of rulers in Babylon gradually ceased.[72]

In Israel, because kingship arose at a relatively late date and the power of the ruler was limited by Mosaic Law and many traditional norms of cult, movements to divinize the king never arose; and, moreover, the pious Israelite still believed that Yahweh only was Israel's true king. In addition Israel had prophets. Called immediately by God, the prophets did not hesitate to oppose kings when they strayed from the ways of justice and prudence. Incidents occurred with Israel's very first monarchs, Saul, David, Solomon. Saul was anointed by the prophet Samuel, and the Davidic dynasty owed its origin to him. To the prophets Nathan and Gad, David was obliged to give an account of his actions. Solomon could not escape words of reprimand and threat from the prophet Ahias. The accession of Jeroboam I to the throne of the Northern Kingdom was furthered by Ahias, who likewise contributed to the deposition of his son. The prophet Jehu, son of Hanania, opposed Baasa; Elias and Eliseus opposed Achab and Joram of Israel; and under Jeroboam II, Amos and Osee prophesied the destruction of the Northern Kingdom.

The name "Eternal-Father," one whose kindly care for his children never ceases, is easy to associate with the child's heavenly origin. Yahweh Himself "inhabits eternity,"[73] i.e., reigns forever, and was invoked as the "God of eternity."[74]

The word "peace" to an Israelite meant not merely a time without the fears of war, but the highest good fortune imaginable. What evils flourished in Judah when Isaias began his mission, and not only Isaias — every prophet was forced to oppose officials who misused their office and deprived the poor and helpless of their last possessions. Even the kings, who were purposely appointed to protect the weak against such tyranny, gravely violated their duty and themselves acted unjustly. The Messianic ruler, however, will not exploit his subjects, he will rule with

[72] J. Labat, *Le caractère religieuse de la royauté assyro-babylonienne.*

[73] Is. 57:15.
[74] Gen. 21:33.

justice and holiness. He will occupy the throne of David; he is David's son and in him God will fulfill the guarantee of his sceptre's eternal duration.

A perfect understanding of the deepest implications of this divine oracle was not possible until the second Person of the Blessed Trinity had become incarnate. To the reader of old there was much in the prophet's message that remained obscure. But he could gather that in the child seen by Isaias, God would reveal Himself in a most unique manner and bring to pass an unprecedented marvel. The prophecy's concluding words point the way: "The zeal of Yahweh, Lord of hosts, will accomplish this."

Did the prophet's oracle come true? St. John heralded the incarnate Son of God as "the Light that shines in the darkness but which the darkness did not comprehend" and as "the true Light that enlightens every man." [75] Simeon praised the Child Jesus as "a Light unto the illumination of the Gentiles." [76] Jesus referred to Himself as "the Light of the world." [77] After describing how Christ came to Galilee, the first evangelist introduces the prophecy in Is. 9:1 with the remark: "so that it be fulfilled what was said by the prophet Isaias." [78]

On the plains of Bethlehem angels announced the birth of the Prince of peace.[79] If men obeyed His bidding, if all were of good will to one another, surely war and enmity among nations would cease. Our prophecy of the Child has been called the "Silent Night" of the Old Covenant. Considered together, the attributes listed in Isaias find their fulfillment in Jesus, and in no other descendant of David. Only Jesus was God and man. Before Pilate He acknowledged being king of the Jews and then added: "My kingdom is not of this world." [80] The spiritual character of His kingdom had already been expressed in our oracle, a kingdom not founded or dependent upon the power of arms, but upon justice and righteousness, a kingdom of peace enduring forever. There likewise is a connection between the Light before which "darkness and the shadow of death" must flee and the name "Wondrous-Counsellor," for in the Messianic kingdom new doctrine and revelations are to be expected. Over this kingdom God is supreme. He rules through the Messiah who accomplishes His commands.

Like the prophecy concerning Emmanuel, this oracle is not unrelated to the age and the circumstances in which it was composed. In one picture the prophet saw the end of Assyrian world power and the birth of the child in a similar manner as he had alluded to Judah's partial survival because of Emmanuel.[81] Nowhere, however, does he say that the Redeemer himself will conquer Assyria. Actually, the history of

[75] John 1:5 ; 1:9. [76] Luke 2:32. [77] John 8:12 ; 9:5 ; cf. 12:35-36, 46.
[78] Matth. 4:12-16. [79] Luke 2:14. [80] John 18-36. [81] Is. 8:8-10.

Israel had been under the influence of special divine guidance from the moment she was chosen to maintain faith in the one true God for the whole world and constitute the people from whom the Messiah would arise.

But in the divine plan of redemption Assyria too had its divinely ordained role. Assyria was "the rod of his anger, the staff of his wrath;" [82] she was assigned the task of chastising Israel.[83] Nevertheless, it remained part of the same divine plan that a nation bent wholly on conquest and plunder, a nation proudly vaunting itself over all others and paying no heed to the natural law as a limit to its lusts would likewise perish.[84] Accordingly there is a relationship between the destruction of Assyria and the advent of the Messiah. Centuries might intervene between the two events, but to Isaias' prophetic spirit this interval had no existence.

§17. THE ROOT OUT OF JESSE
Is. 11:1-5

In the previous prophecy Isaias had related the coming of the Savior to the fall of Assyria. Now he adds some further details as to when the Messiah will appear on earth. Amos already had foretold that before the Messianic age would dawn, the Davidic dynasty would have been exceedingly humbled, no longer in possession of the throne. Isaias repeated the message; but while Amos spoke only of the house of David, Isaias placed the Messiah personally before the eyes of the reader and pointed out how God had equipped him for the Messianic mission.

Isaias

11:1   A twig will come forth from the stump of Jesse,
            from his roots a sprig will sprout.
11:2   The spirit of Yahweh will rest upon him:
            the spirit of wisdom and of understanding,
        the spirit of counsel and of fortitude,
            the spirit of knowledge and of the fear of Yahweh.
11:3   (And his delight will be in the fear of Yahweh).
        Not according to what his eyes see will he judge,
            nor according to what his ears hear will he decide;

[82] Is. 10:5.   [83] Is. 5:26; 7:18; 8:7; 28:1-4.   [84] Is. 10:7, 13; Nah. 3:1.

11:4 but with justice will he give judgment to the needy,
    and with equity render decisions for the poor in the land.
    The oppressor he will smite with the rod of his mouth,
    and with the breath of his lips he will slay the wicked.

11:5 Righteousness, indeed, will be the girdle round his loins,
    and fidelity the belt about his hips.

This prophecy follows a comminatory oracle against Assyria. Assyria's armies were advancing against Jerusalem. Yahweh intervenes. The foe suffers a disastrous defeat. As a hurricane cutting a path through woods and cracking the trees like stalks of corn, or as a corps of woodsmen felling a forest and leaving no tree standing, Yahweh obliterates the proud Assyrian. But while dead stumps only remain in the Assyrian fields, continues the prophet, out of the stump of Jesse a twig appears. Assyria had been a whole forest of mighty trees, the Savior will be a tiny sprig from a forgotten root! The illustrious empire is about to perish, while the Redeemer rises to found a new and lasting kingdom. In a previous chapter Isaias had used a similar picture: from the stump of the terebinth (after judgment had descended upon Israel and the mighty tree had fallen) a "holy seed" springs forth, the cleansed people, to whom the Messianic future belongs.[85]

Accordingly, the Messiah will appear at a time when the family of David will resemble a tree stump of no value or concern to any one. Long had the family fallen from its heights, robbed of its power and its importance; after having lost the throne, it had become one of the least in the land. When he appears upon the earth, the Messiah will resemble a twig. Humble though he be, he will be equipped with "spirit" enlightening him and enabling him to effect the salvation of Israel and all the world. The spirit of God came upon the Judges and filled them with courage and strength to accomplish remarkable deeds; they freed their people from oppressors — Othniel, Gedeon, Jephte.[86] God's spirit came upon Samson and gave him preternatural power.[87] By the spirit of God Saul was roused to muster Israel's warriors and smite the Ammonites.[88]

Far more significant was the spirit's mission when it filled the prophets — Moses,[89] Elias and Eliseus,[90] Micheas [91] — and enabled them to teach the people at Yahweh's bidding and to point out their duties. The spirit of God would be given to the Messiah not merely for a determined people or for certain prescribed actions, it would govern and inspire all his work — it would "rest" upon him, and his mission would endure forever.[92]

The prophet next indicates specifically what effect the spirit of God

[85] Is. 6:13.   [88] 1 Sam. 11:6. [91] Mich. 3:8; cf. Os. 9:7; Is. 48:16; 61:1.
[86] Judg. 3:10: 6:34; 11:29. [89] Num. 11:17. [92] Is. 9:6.
[87] Judg. 14:6, 19; 15:14. [90] 4 Kgs. 2:9.

would have upon the Messiah and upon his activity in behalf of the salvation of Israel and the world. Through the spirit of wisdom he would be enabled to know affairs as they actually are and their relationship to God; and he would likewise have the means to attain the ends divinely willed. The spirit of understanding would enable him to use these means properly. The spirit of counsel enables him to make correct decisions, for the Messiah is called the "Wondrous-Counsellor." [93] The spirit of fortitude confers the strength to carry out his decisions, he is the "Mighty-God." [94] Enlightened by the spirit of understanding, it becomes possible for him to plumb the depths of the mysteries of the Godhead. And the spirit of the fear of God prompts him to lead a life pleasing to God and to subject himself to the divine will.

Then we find added the words: "And his delight will be in the fear of Yahweh." The Septuagint and Vulgate have: "The fear of Yahweh will fill him." Now in the oracle proper the parallelism is so well observed that these words must be regarded as a gloss on the last member of the preceding verse, a repetition in a somewhat different form. The words "fear of Yahweh" were rendered twice in the Septuagint, by *eusebia* and *fobos theou*; the Vulgate followed with *pietas* and *timor*, piety and fear of the Lord. The Septuagint merely had tried to give different readings to the Hebrew phrase. St. Jerome and many patristic writers found the sacred number *seven* here, and interpreted it symbolically of the fullness of the Holy Spirit.

One of the Messiah's most important duties will be to supervise the administration of justice and righteousness.[95] The gifts of the spirit will enable him to accomplish this duty without yielding to opposition. He will render judgment not according to appearances or upon the evidence proffered, which might be fallacious, but with a perfect knowledge of the merits and demerits of each case. His impartiality will be of particular benefit to the weak and poor, those unable to bribe the judges. Moreover, such as win their cases contrary to the demands of justice will be summoned to judgment before him.

Opposition no longer will be between Israel and the Gentiles, but between the wicked and the virtuous. Sinners can expect no mercy, for with the rod of his mouth, with the breath of his lips he will slay them; a single word of condemnation is sufficient, he needs no material instrument. So important does this phase of the Messiah's activity appear to the prophet that he repeats the message. To an Oriental the girdle or broad belt was an important item of clothing, it held his garments in place and added greatly to appearance. It would have been impossible to picture a person without one, and it will be equally impossible to

[93] Is. 9:5.   [94] Is. 9:5.   [95] Is. 9:6.

think of the Messiah in any other role than that of a just and righteous ruler.

Is. 11 gives us another oracle in which the Messiah is not described as a warrior, the passage implies that his kingdom will be a spiritual one. We discover that in Messianic times the poor and needy will still exist, with places closest to their king. If with a mere word he destroys those who strive against his will, he must be more than human.

In summary, our passage describes the Redeemer as a king upon David's throne, exercising justice in his realm, and intolerant of the wicked. The spirit of God enables him to perform his duties. In Is. 42:1 Yahweh says: "Behold my servant, in whom I am highly pleased. I have put my spirit upon him, and he will bring justice to the nations." The Messiah who appears in this passage as the "Servant of Yahweh" is equipped with the spirit of God for the purpose of proclaiming true religion to the nations, hence of exercising the office of prophet. A few verses later in chapter 11, Isaias tells how in Messianic times "the earth will be full with the knowledge of Yahweh, as the waters cover the sea." [96] He is referring to the work of the Messiah, the one responsible for this tremendous blessing. The spirit of God will enable him to function also as a prophet.

§18. THE GENTILE WORLD

Isaias had seen the Messiah as the ruler upon David's throne and over David's kingdom.[97] David, however, extended his sway over Gentile nations whose lands touched Israel. Would not the new David, a far greater king than his illustrious forefather, likewise extend his might over Gentile nations? Certainly. And if for no other reason, than because he reigns as the "strong God"[98] and possesses full dominion over the entire world. Our prophet, moreover, had stated that the Redeemer would bring everlasting peace. Now the Gentile nations would cease afflicting Israel only if they were brought under the sceptre of the second David. This tallies with the prediction that Assyrian power would be broken before the Messiah appears.[99] The message contained obscurely in these passages is more clearly repeated in other Isaian

---

[96] Is. 11:9.   [97] Is. 9:6.   [98] Is. 9:5.   [99] Is. 9:3-4; 10:33-34.

texts — the Messianic kingdom includes the Gentile nations, to them the Messiah brings the knowledge of the true God. And this again implies a spiritual kingdom.

Already in connection with the prophecy of the twig from Jesse's stump, Isaias said: "On that day it will come to pass that the root of Jesse will stand as the standard for the nations. The nations will seek him and his residence will be magnificent." [1] Just as soldiers regard the flag as a rallying point, so the nations will gather around the root of Jesse. They will come willingly and joyfully, under no duress; and they will seek him in order to participate in the good fortune of the Messianic kingdom. Writing to the Romans, St. Paul quoted the passage rather freely: "There will be the root of Jesse, and he who will arise to rule the Gentiles . . . in him the Gentiles will hope." [2] By the word "residence" in Is. 11:10 is to be understood the Sion of Messianic times, the center of God's kingdom. The Vulgate renders the verse, *et erit sepulcrum eius gloriosum,* pointing to the tomb of Christ, since "the standard" was interpreted by some Fathers as the Cross about which the Gentiles gather.

How the Gentiles, inspired by the Messianic standard, proceed to enter the new kingdom of God, is described by Isaias:

Isaias

2:2   It shall come to pass at the end of days
           that the mountain of Yahweh's house will be firmly established
           upon the highest of mountains, lording it over the hills.
        All nations will flow toward it,

2:3   many peoples will ready themselves and say:
      "Come, let us ascend the mountain of Yahweh,
        the house of the God of Jacob,
      so that he may instruct us in his ways,
        and that we may walk in his paths."
      For the (true) doctrine will be proclaimed from Sion,
        and the word of Yahweh from Jerusalem.

2:4   He will render judgment among the nations
        and set aright many peoples.
      Then will they beat their swords into plowshares,
        and their spears into pruning-hooks.
      No longer will one nation raise the sword against another,
        no longer will they learn the art of war.

This prophecy may also be found in Mich. 4:1–3. In Micheas it stands in a better relation to the context than in Isaias, but this must be ascribed to subsequent redaction. Micheas was called to the prophetic office at a later date than Isaias. In his prophecy of the virgin birth [3] he relies upon Is. 7:14, and therefore we may reasonably assume that Isaias is the author of the prophecy given above. Micheas took the oracle and en-

---

[1] Is. 11:10.   [2] Rom. 15:12.   [3] Mich. 5:2.

larged it by adding: "Under his own vine each person will rest, and under his own fig-tree, without any one to frighten them." Micheas had been a simple man from the country and as such painted the era of Messianic peace in terms of the glorious epoch Israel had experienced under Solomon.[4] Nevertheless, it may also be possible that the prophecy represents an oracle from a more remote period which was preserved both by Micheas and Isaias.

At the end of days, in Messianic times, the mountain of Yahweh's house (the temple hill) will become firmly grounded. It will rise above all other hills and mountains. Did the prophet imagine that some tremendous miracle would completely change the physical geography of Palestine with the result that the temple hill would actually be higher than all other elevations? Hardly. To him the religious significance of the temple was the important thing, and the temple would become the only site at which the true God was worshipped. Because of this unique prerogative, Sion would constitute the center of the Messianic kingdom. Ethical monotheism cherished upon Mount Sion and proclaimed to all men, would be embraced by every nation. Till then Sion had been the religious center of God's faithful people Israel, now the nations of the whole earth journey thither. The Old Testament Chosen People broaden out to become the Church of the New Testament; and the latter is "catholic," embracing all peoples.

They will *stream* to Yahweh's house without letting themselves be deterred from their purpose by any kind of difficulty, just as a river finds its way past every obstacle. "Many nations," i.e., the whole Gentile world, willingly and with joyful hearts encourage each other to ascend the mountain of Yahweh. Since it would have been impossible for the prophet to imagine that the whole human race, including tribes from distant regions, would personally visit Mount Sion, he simply is implying that the religion, whose chief merit was the worship of the one true God, would draw the hearts and minds of mankind. Faith would influence and determine their manner of living; men would seek instruction in the commandments Yahweh puts before them — with faith in the true God, inner conversion always follows easily.

In verse 3 the prophet gives the reason why the nations long for Sion. It is to obtain light on the important problems which vex mankind; for in Sion true doctrine can be found, instruction on the nature of God, and the moral precepts of revealed religion. Men divinely enlightened will be at the service of all. The text does not say that the Gentiles will assume the burden of the Mosaic Law with all its prescriptions and rites. Doctrine, *torah*, has a very general connotation.

4 3 Kgs. 5:5.

Another point. Yahweh will render judgment among the nations. They will acknowledge Him as supreme Lord and master, and willingly accept His decisions. Mankind, so long estranged from God, finds its way back to God! No longer does sin exist, and consequently no dissension. Justice and love appear in the conduct of people to people, the sure guarantee of peace. Weapons of war are no longer needed, no nation seeks to enslave another, nor need any be ready to ward off attack. The implements of war are refashioned into the work tools of peace.

Has this prophecy been fulfilled? From Jerusalem the apostles set out to announce to every creature the good news of the Gospel. Salvation *did* come from the Jews,[5] and at the beginning Sion actually was the center of the Messianic kingdom. Over the fields of Bethlehem angels sang: "Peace to men of good will." [6] And Jesus told His disciples: "My peace I give to you." [7] Have wars ceased since the Gospel has been preached to the nations? Have spears and swords disappeared? Or have they only been displaced by more dreadful weapons of death, instruments with the potential of annihilating all life through vast areas! This question will be treated in a special chapter, along with similar problems.[8]

What in Isaias' mind was the relation between converted mankind and historical Israel as he spoke this prophecy? As he beheld the enthusiasm with which Gentile nations journeyed to Sion, he certainly would not have thought that they were coming to pay tribute or to become Israel's slaves. The relationship of the nations to Israel would be a purely spiritual one; they come, acknowledging that Israel possesses the true faith. However, and this too is significant, they do not take instruction from the Israelites on God's commandments, but await such teaching directly from Yahweh Himself.

The continuation of *political* independence among the various nations may be deduced from the fact that "Yahweh will render judgment among the nations." In the Messianic kingdom there will be room for earthly kings who rule their subjects under the sovereignty of God and His Messiah.[9]

Chapters later, at the end of a prophecy against Cush (Ethiopia), south of Egypt, the prophet again notes that in Messianic times the Gentiles will turn to Yahweh without thereby endangering their own political independence.[10] After subduing Egypt the government of Cush sent envoys to Ezechias of Judah (about the year 714) to arrange a common front against Assyria. Isaias bade the envoys return home. Then

---

[5] John 4:22.
[6] Luke 2:14.
[7] John 14:27.

[8] Cf. p. 198.
[9] Is. 32:1-2; Ps. 2.
[10] Is. 18:1-7.

addressing "all the inhabitants of the world and the dwellers on the earth," he proclaimed that Yahweh would intervene and destroy Assyria as soon as He decreed the time had come. What will happen after the destruction of Nineveh? "In that day gifts will be brought to Yahweh of hosts, by a nation tall and naked, by a nation dreaded now and always, a people mighty and victorious, whose land rivers divide, to the place where is found the Name of Yahweh of hosts, Mount Sion." [11] The sudden and unexpected fall of immoral Nineveh will strike fear into so distant and warlike a people as the Cushites. As representatives of the Gentile world, as witnesses to the dissolution of Assyria, they come to Sion, the center of the Messianic kingdom, to worship Yahweh. To Him they bring gifts, not to Israel.

The same ideas are found where the prophet discusses the lot of the Chosen People in Messianic times. After foretelling how the root of Jesse would be raised as the standard for the nations, and how the peoples would flock about it, he continued:

Isaias

11:11 And it will come to pass on that day
   that Yahweh will lift up his hand once more
  to redeem the remnant of his people
   that still remains — from Assyria and from Egypt,
  from Patros and from Cush and from Elam,
   from Shinar, from Hamath, and from the islands of the sea.

11:12 He will raise up a standard in the presence of the nations
   and will gather the dispersed of Israel
  and bring home the scattered of Judah
   from the four corners of the earth.

11:13 Jealousy toward Ephraim will then cease,
   and the enemies of Judah will be destroyed.
  Ephraim will no longer be jealous of Judah,
   nor will Judah be hostile toward Ephraim.

11:14 Down the Philistine slopes seawards they will fly,
   united they will plunder the sons of the east.
  Edom and Moab will become the property of their hands,
   and the sons of Ammon will obediently listen.

11:15 Yahweh will dry up the tongue of the sea of Egypt
   and shake his hand against the (Euphrates) river
  in the fury of his breath.
  He will scatter it into seven streamlets
   so that one may walk through with sandals.

11:16 Thus a highway will be made for the remnant of his people
   that still remains in Assyria —
  as existed for Israel
   on the day she came up out of Egypt.

Centuries before, Yahweh had led His people out of Egyptian servi-

[11] Is. 18:7.

tude "with uplifted hand" and brought them into the Promised Land.[12] The time will come when He will again raise His hand to lead back from exile the people he scattered over the whole earth in punishment for their sins. In this prediction Isaias repeated what the prophets Amos [13] and Osee [14] had already held out to the purified and cleansed people. When the Gentiles turn to Yahweh, Israel and Judah — the whole Chosen People — will come home from exile and enter the Messianic kingdom. The punishment inflicted because of her obstinacy will have terminated.

The prophet speaks first of the conversion of the Gentiles. Is this an indication that it will precede Israel's? Listen to what St. Paul said: "A partial blindness only has befallen Israel, until the full number of the Gentiles should enter (the Church), and thus all Israel should be saved." [15] After the Gentile world had found salvation, God would favor Israel; and then as a people she would enter Christ's kingdom. Moreover, the prophet notes that Yahweh will raise up a standard in the presence of the nations, i.e., they are to cooperate in gathering and re-settling the dispersed. Does this imply that through the preaching of Gentile missioners the conversion of the Jewish people will finally be effected, and that non-Jews will mediate the graces of salvation to the Chosen People of old?

After the two kingdoms of Israel are reunited,[16] dissension between the tribes will no longer exist. As in the days of David, they will advance in common against their enemies, against the Philistines to the west, and against Edom, Moab, and Ammon to the east. Here again the prophet uses history as a framework. As foes of God's Messianic people, he mentions those who in his day oppressed Israel. The message simply is: in Messianic times the enemies of God's kingdom will be annihilated. Although Isaias speaks of the conversion of the Gentile nations, he foresees and promises a day of reckoning not only for Assyria but for the Philistines, for Moab, Damascus, Cush, Egypt.[17] In fact, it is through the judgment Yahweh brings upon them that they begin to realize the vanity of their own deities and the omnipotence of Israel's God.

Again the prophet returns to his theme, the deliverance of the exiled Israelites. Their return from Egypt and Assyria will be accompanied by manifold marvels. Just as Yahweh prepared a road through the Reed Sea for their forefathers, so too when He brings them back from foreign lands, will He lead them with dry feet through the River of Egypt. And the Euphrates He will split into seven brooks, shallow and readily crossed. The message? After Yahweh has established the Messianic

[12] Ex. 6:6.
[13] 9:14.
[14] 2:17-25 ; 13:14.

[15] Rom. 11:25-26.
[16] Am. 9:11 ; Os. 2:2-3.
[17] Is. 14:28—20:6.

kingdom, He will bring the exiles home, even to the accompaniment of miracles if circumstances demand it. But a return of the Northern Kingdom from Assyria never occurred! It is another problem that has its solution in a consideration of the singular characteristics of prophetic pronouncements.[18]

In the days of Isaias, Assyria was Israel's foremost foe. And the prophet repeatedly threatened her with judgment. Israel's proverbial oppressor, however, had been Egypt, and in the comminatory prophecies Egypt and Assyria appear alongside one another; both are to experience Yahweh's power when He forces them to liberate the exiles. Will these nations perish utterly on the day of judgment, or will a remnant remain who, following the example of the other nations, accept the true faith? The answer to this question may be found in the concluding verses of one of the Isaian comminatory prophecies against Egypt:

Isaias

19:18	On that day there will be five cities in the land of Egypt where men speak the language of Canaan and swear by the Name of Yahweh of hosts; one of them will be called "Ghost-town." On
19:19	that day Yahweh will have an altar in the midst of the land of
19:20	Egypt, and a monument at its borders. It will be for a sign and a witness to Yahweh of hosts: When they cry to Yahweh in the face of their oppressors, he will send them a Savior who will intervene
19:21	and free them. Thus Yahweh will reveal himself to the Egyptians, and the Egyptians will accept Yahweh on that day and sacrifice to Yahweh victims and food offerings; they will make vows to
19:22	Yahweh and fulfill them. Yahweh will smite Egypt, smite in order to heal. When they turn to Yahweh, he will listen to their pleas
19:23	and heal them. On that day a road will stretch from Egypt to Assyria, and the Assyrians will travel to Egypt and the Egyptians to Assyria; both the Egyptians and the Assyrians will serve
19:24	(Yahweh). On that day Israel will be the third in a covenant with
19:25	Egypt and Assyria, a blessing in the midst of the earth, for Yahweh of hosts will bless it with the words: Blessed be my people, Egypt; and the work of my hands, Assyria; and my portion, Israel!

The prophet looks forward to a time when in the cities of Egypt [19] the language of Canaan, viz., Hebrew, will be spoken. The Egyptians will use this language in sacred worship because they have accepted Israel's religion. There will be an altar to Yahweh in their land, and upon it sacrifices will be offered to the true God. On the borders there will be a monument so that every one who enters the country will immediately know that the true God is worshipped in the land of the Nile. Not only in the temple at Jerusalem, which became the only legitimate site for

[18] Cf. p. 198ff.

[19] The five are representative, as the five brothers whom Joseph introduced to Pharaoh (Gen. 47:2) represented the family. The name given for one city in v. 18 is uncertain; some translations read "The City of the Sun" or "Sun-City."

cult after the reforms of Ezechias,[20] will sacrifices be offered to Yahweh, but likewise in foreign lands. There is no mention of the Aaronic priesthood; converted Gentiles surround the altar worshipping Yahweh.

Here Isaias is preparing for Malachy's prophecy, viz., Israelitic priests will forfeit their rights, and an oblation will be made to God in every place throughout the world.[21] But if the family of Aaron no longer retains its privilege after the conversion of the Gentiles, neither would the Mosaic ritual be binding upon the Gentile world. In their needs the Egyptians too may rely on Yahweh's love; He will aid them, and the evils He inflicts will only serve to make them realize their defects — He smites only to heal. In that mighty stream of Gentiles flowing toward Mount Sion,[22] the Egyptians, who for countless generations had worshipped the meanest of idols, will not be absent. Yahweh's mercy, however, does not end here, it extends to hated Assyria! Although the empires upon the Euphrates-Tigris and the Nile had frequently fought over the possession of Canaan, in the Messianic age of peace for mankind, they will no longer contend against each other. They will dwell in peace, united by faith in the true God and doing Him service. And Israel, the apple of discord, continually oppressed by one or the other and often seduced by them into idolatry, will no longer be an object of contention, rather a blessing. She is united with them in the worship of the true God; indeed, she now realizes her mission of being "a blessing in the midst of the earth." For by preserving the faith in the one true God, she had become the instrument of blessing for Egypt and Assyria, yes, for every nation — as Yahweh had promised Abraham.[23]

The Chosen People of Messianic times, therefore, consist of nations that have rejected their deities and honor the true God — represented by Assyria and Egypt — and the Israelites of old. All experience God's love. Egypt is called "my people" by Yahweh. A title that formerly had been strictly reserved to the Chosen People is now applied to Gentile nations. Assyria is called "the work of his hands" because God created her and spiritually transformed her; the same phrase is applied to Israel in Is. 60:21.

But Israel retains a primacy of honor, even though converted Gentile nations attain an equal status with her. Yahweh calls her "My portion"[24] because He chose her from among all the peoples on earth and constituted her the "first-born of the nations."[25] This privilege, which at no time implied a rejection of other nations, will not be taken away from Israel in the Messianic era. But the prophet expressly places Israel as the third member in the kingdom. May we perhaps interpret this (as in

[20] 2 Chr. 29—31.
[21] Mal. 1:10-11.
[22] Is. 2:2-4.

[23] Gen. 12:3.
[24] Deut. 32:9.
[25] Am. 6:1 ; Jer. 2:3.

11:12) as another indication of what actually occurred — that upon the Messiah's advent the Gentile nations responded first, and that the Jews, although salvation went forth from their midst, remained aloof from the Gospel message?

Another Isaian prophecy telling how the Gentiles will subject themselves to the sceptre of the Messiah-King is had in a discourse on the future lot of Moab.[26] First the prophet pronounces dire woe, then he adds words of consolation: Moab will send lambs to the ruler in Judah as a token of her submission.[27] Moab would find a refuge in Sion, for Sion stood under the protection of Yahweh; then Assyria could accomplish nothing against her. To the message of Moab's oppression and Jerusalem's preservation from enemy attack, the prophet adds a glance into the distant future: "When an end has come for the oppressor, when the destroyer has been destroyed and the marauder extirpated from the land, a throne will be erected through kindness; in David's tent will one sit in faithfulness, one who judges, who strives for justice and takes pains to do what is right." [28]

At the moment Assyria might enslave all the nations and destroy those who refused tribute, but her sway would end. Then the Messiah will appear. He will sit upon a throne which God in His goodness erects for him alone. And because he dwells in David's tent, he is a child of David. He is the ideal ruler, the one about whom the prophet had repeatedly spoken, the one who practices justice and righteousness.[29] Moab is taken under his protection, Moab, a people severely tried. It is a sign that the Messianic kingdom is not limited to Israel but embraces the Gentile nations of the entire world.

§19. THE BLESSINGS OF THE MESSIANIC AGE

The blessings which the Messiah will bestow upon all who embrace his rule are described by the prophets in boldest pictures. Of highest importance is the union of mankind with God, a union that will never

---

[26] Is. 15—16.
[27] Is. 16:1 is translated by Jerome: "Lord, send the Lamb, the Ruler of the earth, from Petra in the wilderness to the mountain, the daughter of Sion." He applies *petra deserti,* "the rock in the wilderness," to Ruth who came from Moab, was the great-grandmother of David, and thus an ancestor of the Messiah — Matth. 1:5 ; *In Is. Proph.* 5, 6, Migne 24:171. But as St. Jerome himself observes, this interpretation does not reflect the actual meaning of the passage ; the Messianic implication is injected into the text.
[28] Is. 16:4-5.
[29] Is. 9:6 ; 11:1-5.

again be broken. The followers of the Messiah are called saints;[30] they are the holy seed that grows out of the stump of the fallen terebinth, the remnant surviving the judgment whereby the filth of the daughters of Sion and blood-guilt of Jerusalem is sloughed away.[31] Sion finally becomes the "City of Righteousness," the "Faithful City."[32]

The moral conditions, proper to the Messianic age, are painted by Isaias in brightest colors:[33]

Isaias

32:1	Behold, a king who governs with righteousness,
	and princes ruling with justice.
32:2	Each will be as a shelter from the wind,
	as a covert from the weather,
	as brooks on barren slopes,
	as the shade of a mighty rock in an arid land.
32:3	Never again will eyes that see be plastered over,
	or the ears of those who hear be inattentive.
32:4	The rash of heart will learn discretion,
	and soon the tongue of stammerers will speak correctly.
32:5	Never will the fool be called noble,
	or the evildoer be regarded an honorable man.

What a contrast to the current state of affairs with injustice rampant, with rulers for whimsical reasons withholding from their subjects what was theirs by right! In the Messianic age the great and powerful will regard justice as the only norm of action; and to them the common man may appeal hopefully when conditions become oppressive. Every one will take to heart the admonition to live virtuously, every one will willingly acknowledge the wholesomeness of God's commands. No longer will there be a misuse of words; whoever is godless (foolish) will be called godless, no matter what his rank might be.

32:15	Then will the spirit from on High be poured out upon us.
	Then will the steppes become fertile gardens,
	and orchards regarded as woodland.
32:16	Then will justice dwell on the steppes,
	and righteousness tarry in the fields.
32:17	The result of righteousness will be peace,
	the produce of righteousness, rest and security forever.

The spirit of God will effect a transformation in nature as well as in men. The steppes, where the Bedouin lurk to rob the innocent traveller, are changed to fertile fields, and those who live there will never think of robbing or plundering. No one need worry any longer about war, for the sway of the Messiah means peace everlasting. He indeed is the Prince of peace.[34]

---

[30] Is. 4:3.　　[31] Is. 4:4; 6:13.　　[32] Is. 1:26.　　[33] Is. 32:1-20.　　[34] Is. 9:6; 2:4.

In this connection there may be mentioned a prophecy which occurs in the Book of Isaias, but which stems from a prophet in postexilian times. After this prophet had pronounced judgment against the nations of the earth,[35] particularly against Edom (to Israel the symbol of powers hostile to Yahweh), he described in chapter 35 the Messianic blessings consequent upon divine visitation. Palestine is changed into a paradise. Even in the desert there is water, wild animals have disappeared, with joy and exultation the redeemed return home to Sion. What blessings the redeemed may expect are listed in the following verses:

Isaias

35:4   Say to those with despondent hearts:
            Be firm! Never fear!
            See, your God! Vengeance is coming — it is God's requital.
            He himself will come to redeem you.
35:5   Then shall the eyes of the blind be opened,
            and the ears of the deaf shall function.
            Then the lame shall leap like a deer,
            and the tongue of the dumb shall cry out with joy.

Not only will the land become extremely fertile, men will experience in their very bodies the blessings of the Messianic age. While Isaias stressed the elimination of spiritual needs,[36] this prophet proclaims that physical infirmities too will cease. There will be no blind and deaf persons, none lame or dumb. Those who now suffer severely from bodily handicaps and disease will experience full healing.

35:10   Happiness and joy will be their portion,
                        grief and pain will vanish.

When John the Baptist sent disciples to Jesus to inquire whether He was the Messiah promised by the prophets, Jesus quoted this passage with reference to His miracles.[37] The Jews themselves recalled the prophecy in connection with the cures that Jesus had performed upon the sick.[38]

The remarkable fertility of the land that should characterize the Messianic age, a point already made in Jacob's oracle, is the burden of the verse:

4:2   On that day the Branch of Yahweh will be honorable and glorious,
            and the fruit of the land will be the pride and glory of Israel's saved.[39]

The blessings of the Messiah will not be limited to mankind, all creation will benefit. In paradise there was peace in nature. Through the sin of our first parents disorder came into the world. In the Messianic age, when sin will have been destroyed and all lead holy lives, wild beasts

[35] Is. 34.   [36] Is. 32:3, 4.   [38] Mark 7:37.
[37] Matth. 11:4-5; Luke 7:22.   [39] Cf. Is. 29:17; 30:23-26.

no longer will do harm, and poisonous snakes will cease to be dangerous.
Continuing the "Root of Jesse" prophecy, Isaias says:

Isaias

11:6   Then the wolf and the lamb will dwell together,
      and the panther will lie down with the kid.
     Calf and lion's cub will tarry with each other,
      and a little child will tend them.

11:7   Together, cow and bear will feed,
      their young lie down as friends.
     The lion will eat straw like an ox,

11:8   the suckling child will play at adder's hole;
     And against the lair of a viper
      one (hardly) weaned will place his hand.

11:9   They will do no evil, cause no ill
      on all my holy mount.
     For the earth will be full with the knowledge of Yahweh
      as the waters cover the sea.

The heavenly bodies too will undergo a transformation: "The light of the moon will be as strong as the light of the sun, and the light of the sun seven times greater." [40]

Whether the prophet actually *wished to teach* that animals would change their natures, that carnivorous beasts would be transformed into herbivorous ones, that children would be able to play with snakes without danger, and that the sun and moon would send out greater quantities of light and heat, these questions will be discussed in connection with other similar problems. [41]

To participate in the blessings of the Messianic age, faith and trust in God are absolute prerequisites. Isaias insisted upon these virtues on the occasion of his prophecy concerning the Virgin birth. Relying on aid from Assyria, Achaz rejected God's offer. Later, when conditions had changed and the officials in Judah were arranging an alliance with Egypt against Assyria, Isaias warned them: Not through self-confident politicians who scoff at a prophet's words of admonition will deliverance come, but through the intervention of Yahweh. "Therefore thus speaks Yahweh: Behold, I am placing a stone in Sion, a tested stone, a precious cornerstone. If one has faith, he will never falter." [42] Yahweh Himself cannot be this stone because it is He who lays it; nor is it a material stone that will form the foundation for Sion.

The Messiah, of course, is meant. It is he who will bring deliverance to the People of God, as the prophet repeatedly insists. The Messiah is the cornerstone that gives solidity to the structure Yahweh is erecting, viz., the Messianic kingdom centered at Sion. Only he who has faith,

---

[40] Is. 30:26.   [41] Cf. p. 204ff.   [42] Is. 28:16.

however, will gain its blessings.[43] Alluding to Ps. 118:12 Jesus called Himself the cornerstone of the kingdom that He was establishing.[44] St. Paul refers to the passage under consideration when he narrates how unfaithful Israel took offense at the Messiah.[45]

The prophet Isaias sketched a clearer and a more impressive picture of the Messiah and his kingdom than was granted to any of his predecessors. One might quote the statement of St. Jerome that Isaias was an evangelist rather than a prophet, that he seems to narrate past events rather than predict the future.[46] With what joy should his contemporaries, oppressed by Assyria and sorely tried by the horrors of war, have listened to his joyful message of the coming Redeemer and his glowing descriptions of the Messianic era; what comfort and courage should a later generation have derived from his words when under the successors of Ezechias the religious and moral conditions visibly deteriorated, when loyalty to Yahweh spelled persecution and death. To those who suffered but who retained faith and trust, the prophecies of Isaias afforded a sure footing and firm support.

§20. BETHLEHEM, THE MESSIAH'S BIRTHPLACE
Mich. 5:1-3

Like Isaias, Micheas experienced the evils brought upon Judah by the Assyrians, but the latter suffered personally to a much greater degree because he dwelt in the rural districts which bore the brunt of the invasion. The avaricious spirit of the higher circles that would have denied bare existence to the common man was a source of untold grief to him. He was the first of the prophets to foretell the destruction of Jerusalem and the temple,[47] a message that impressed the people so deeply as to be remembered more than a century later when Jeremias made the same prediction. Jeremias was threatened with death, but was saved by recalling that Micheas had uttered a similar comminatory prophecy; he reminded his opponents that Israel had then taken it to heart rather than rising against God's mouthpiece.

But although Micheas foretold the destruction of the city and the

43 Is. 7:9.   45 Rom. 9:33.   46 *Praef. in Is.*, Migne 28:771.
44 Cf. p. 212f for typical interpretations.   47 Mich. 3:12.

temple, he like Isaias saw in Sion the center of the Messianic kingdom to which the Gentile nations would journey.[48] When the Assyrians besieged Jerusalem in the year 701 and were sorely humbling King Ezechias,[49] when the situation seemed hopeless, Micheas feared as little as did Isaias.[50] Isaias betook himself to the king to encourage him,[51] since he belonged to the nobility and had access to the palace. Micheas consoled the common people. The Deliverer would come, the power of Assyria would cease. Then he enriched previous prophecies with a new line: David's illustrious son would be born at Bethlehem.

Micheas

5:1   And you, Bethlehem Ephrata — too small to be reckoned among the clans of Judah — from you will he come forth to me who will reign over Israel. His origins are from of old, from the days of eternity.

5:2   Therefore he will abandon them until the time when she who is with child has given birth; and those remaining of his brethren will return

5:3   home to the sons of Israel. He will appear and pasture his flock in the strength of Yahweh, in the majestic Name of Yahweh, his God. They will dwell in security, for then will he stand strong unto the ends of the earth.

David was a Bethlehemite,[52] his father an Ephratite.[53] Ephrata was the district in which Bethlehem was situated;[54] two names are used in order to distinguish the town from another Bethlehem in the territory of Zabulon.[55] According to common exegesis Micheas here designates the place where the Messiah would be born, an interpretation current among the Jews at the time of the evangelists. Jesus was born "in the city of David, called Bethlehem."[56] When the Magi from the East were inquiring about the new-born King of the Jews, the Scribes whom Herod called named Bethlehem as the birthplace of the awaited Deliverer and referred to our passage in Micheas.[57] When the Jews, impressed by the miracles and the preaching of Jesus, were arguing among themselves whether they should regard Him as the Savior foretold by the prophets, some objected because He was reared in Nazareth: "Can the Messiah come from Galilee? Does not the Scripture say that he will be of the offspring of David, and from Bethlehem, the village where David lived?"[58]

According to Micheas, therefore, it was not proud Jerusalem that would have the honor of first seeing the Light of the world heralded by the prophets, but small, unpretentious Bethlehem that ranked as a village rather than a city. "The weak things of the world has God chosen to put to shame the strong, and the base things of the world and the

---

[48] Mich. 4:1-4; cf. Is. 2:2-4.
[49] 4 Kgs. 18—19.
[50] Mich. 4:13.
[51] Is. 37.

[52] 1 Sam. 20:6.
[53] 1 Sam. 17:12.
[54] Ruth 1:2.
[55] Jos. 19:15.

[56] Luke 2:4.
[57] Matth. 2:4f.
[58] John 7:42.

despised has God chosen, and the things that are not, to bring to naught the things that are." [59] The Savior will be born in Bethlehem and not in Jerusalem, an indication that at the time of His advent, the Davidic dynasty will have fallen from power. Micheas is repeating what Amos had foretold concerning the fallen hut of David [60] and Isaias on the twig from the root of Jesse. [61]

Surely it was a special design of God that Micheas, the simple man from the farm, was privileged to foretell the Savior's birthplace. From the viewpoint of size and political influence, Bethlehem indeed was unimportant, but in the story of redemption it occupies a unique position. Therefore St. Matthew, who considered the prophecy fulfilled with the birth of Jesus, modified the text in his account to read: "You, Bethlehem Ephrata, are in no way the least among the princes of Judah!"

Yahweh continued: "From you will he come forth to me" who has been commissioned by Me to rule over Israel. The words, "His origins are from of old, from the days of eternity ('olam)," are interpreted by many of the Messiah's pre-mundane existence and consequently of his divinity — just as the surname, "Mighty-God," in Is. 9:5. But since the prophet was speaking of the "origin" of the Redeemer from Bethlehem, he intended to note that he, even if born in a tiny hamlet, was not without honor; for his origin, viz., the family from which he came, was ancient. In Am. 9:11 David ruled "in the days of eternity, 'olam;'" and according to Mich. 7:14 Israel governed Bashan and Gilead "in the days of eternity, 'olam," until Jehu's time, 842.

The prophet next writes of "one who is with child," [62] introducing the verse with "therefore." Yahweh's visitation of Israel will last until she who is with child has given birth; the child to whom she is giving life is the ruler who comes forth from Bethlehem, and who will free his people from the power of the enemy. The birth of the Deliverer is the reason why their affliction comes to an end. Now if the coming ruler is an historical person, so too "she who is with child," his mother. Light is thrown upon this passage by the Isaian prophecy of the Virgin birth; [63] like Isaias, Micheas makes no mention of a father. Contemporaries would have thought of the Emmanuel prophecy; the two oracles actually are closely related without supposing a literary dependency on the part of Micheas. The various prophets received their revelations independently of each other. Nevertheless, it is unusual that two prophets at about the same time proclaimed the same Messianic message.

It is not easy to interpret the words regarding "the remaining brethren" of the Redeemer who will "return home to the sons of Israel." Very

---

[59] 1 Cor. 1:27-28. [60] Am. 9:11. [61] Is. 11:1. [62] Verse 2. [63] 7:14.

likely Micheas was simply stating what other prophets before him had said, viz., the appearance of the Redeemer would effect a change in Israel's history. The tribes that had been separated so long will be united into one kingdom under the sceptre of the son of David. This Amos had proclaimed in his prophecy of the reconstruction of the fallen house of David.[64] Osee referred to the union of Israel and Judah under a descendant of David,[65] and Isaias spoke of harmony and cooperation between Ephraim and Judah.[66] Now since the division of the kingdom was equivalent to a defection of the Northern tribes from the Davidic dynasty, those who returned home could only be members of the Northern tribes, the remnant of those who had survived the exile dating to the days of Micheas. They are called brothers of the Savior because they belonged to him by right — David had once been their king — while by the "sons of Israel" is meant the Southern Kingdom, which always remained loyal to David.

V. 3. Equipped with the strength of God,[67] the Redeemer governs not only Israel but the entire world. Peace is his gift to mankind, the peace for which men long. As in Is. 9:6, 11:4, it is implied that the Messiah will not appear as a warrior; his kingdom is a spiritual one.

JEREMIAS

In the days of Isaias, Nineveh was the capital of the empire that subjugated the small city states of Syria. But under Ashurbanipal (668–626) the empire began to totter, she could not cope with continual rebellions, the rise of the Scythians, and particularly the onslaughts of the Medes. By 625 the Chaldean prince Nabopolassar had established the new-Babylonian kingdom. In alliance with the Medes he campaigned against Assyria. In 612 Nineveh was captured and destroyed. In 609 the remnants of the once proud empire perished dishonorably under its last ruler, Ashur-uballit II.

During the period when the fall of the Assyrian empire became evident to all, Jeremias received his mission from Yahweh to preach as a prophet. It was the year 626, the thirteenth of King Josias of Judah. Jeremias was obliged to approach a people who had worshipped Assyri-

---

[64] Am. 9:11.   [65] Os. 2:2-3.   [66] Is. 11:12-13.   [67] Cf. Is. 11:2.

an gods under Manasses (693–639) and Ammon (639–638), the son and grandson respectively of the pious Ezechias. Josias (638–609), who was as pious as his great-grandfather, began a reform in 627 that was primarily directed against Assyrian astral worship, but also involved the Canaanite high places. His efforts extended beyond Judah into the territory of the one time Northern Kingdom. Jeremias supported the king's noble work, but the core of the nation's festering wound was not touched — the reform went no deeper than the externals of cult. Note how under Josias' successor idolatry with all its accompanying immorality so easily returned, how little regard was given to morality and virtue.

Jeremias pleaded and threatened, and pointed out clearly the punishment which Babylon would inflict. He preached in vain; against him were leagued the princes, the priests, and the people. He spoke of the dissolution of the kingdom and the fall of the city, but to deaf ears. He was hated and persecuted, imprisoned and scourged, and more than once pursued to the very brink of death.

However, it was Jeremias' mission not merely to "pull down" but to build up, as Yahweh had indicated at his call.[68] He spoke not only of defeat and exile, but likewise of deliverance. The end of the kingdom and of the city with its temple did not imply annihilation for the people. By speaking of an exile lasting 70 years [69] — the number must not be taken mathematically — he foretold that few deportees would ever again see their homeland. But the nation as such would not disintegrate; the next generation would return to the land of their fathers. Jeremias' penitential sermons do not lack Messianic allusions. But because of the terrible sufferings he was obliged to endure and from which he seldom experienced an alleviation, his oracles are cast in sombre tones. The Messianic message of the prophet Jeremias does not ring loud and clear and joyous as does that of Isaias.

§21. THE HOLY TWIG
Jer. 23:5-6

Under the rule of Sedecias (597–587), whose lack of character and determination proved fatal for the kingdom, for the people, and for himself, Jeremias confronted the priests, who were gravely neglecting their

[68] Jer. 1:10.   [69] Jer. 25:11; 29:10.

flocks, and the king and the nobles, who were responsible for the manifold misfortunes burdening the people. Yahweh, he prophesied, would
gather together and lead home the dispersed in foreign lands and place
good shepherds over them. One of these oracles is of peculiar significance:

Jeremias

23:5   See, the days are coming, says Yahweh, when I will bring forth a
        holy twig for David. He will rule as king, he will act prudently and
23:6   bring justice and righteousness to the land. In his days Judah will
        experience salvation, and Israel will live in security. The Name
        they will give him is: Yahweh is our righteousness.

This prophecy of the twig, *ṣemaḥ*, proceeding from David, is not unrelated to Nathan's oracle,[70] and recalls the sprig from the Jesse's root
in Is. 11:1. Jeremias is not referring to the Davidic dynasty, but to a
particular son of David. This individual will rule as king, a true king,
not like the kings of David's family in the decades before the fall of
Jerusalem, who were dependent upon foreign powers and subservient
to a host of court attachés. Jeremias was not heralding a kingdom that
was political or secular in nature. Prudence, justice, righteousness would
characterize the rule of his king. Judah and Israel would again form a
single community under one sceptre, and because Yahweh would effect
justice and righteousness through His twig, the twig would be called:
"Yahweh is our righteousness." Upon him, as upon the root of Jesse,[71]
the spirit of God indeed rests, and therefore his activity in the last
analysis is the work of God Himself.

Isaias already had made important pronouncements on the righteousness of the Messiah.[72] Of itself this attribute does not imply divinity, for
the same name will be given to Jerusalem [73] when her inhabitants lead
holy lives in Messianic times. One could also cite the various names
given to altars: "God, the God of Israel," [74] or "Yahweh is my standard." [75] The name is symbolic, like the name Emmanuel.[76] By it Jeremias
sought to place the Messianic ruler in opposition to Sedecias, *My righteousness is Yahweh*, the name Nabuchodonosor had given to the last
occupant of David's throne. Sedecias should have practiced righteousness personally and as the ruler of Judah; but he did not, he made no
efforts to suppress idolatry and injustice and immorality. The Messianic
king, however, will truly further the cause of righteousness, complying
with Yahweh's demands.

The passage we have considered is repeated in Jer. 33:15–16: "In
those days and at that time I will cause a sprout of righteousness (*ṣemaḥ*

---

[70] 2 Sam. 7.   [71] Is. 11:2.   [72] Is. 9:6 ; 11:5.   [73] Jer. 33:16.
[74] Gen. 33:20.   [75] Ex. 17:15.   [76] Is. 7:14.

ṣedaqah) to grow up for David, and he will execute justice and righteousness in the land. In those days Judah will obtain salvation, and Jerusalem will dwell in security; and they will call her (the city): 'Yahweh is our righteousness'."

Moreover, looking forward to Messianic times, Jeremias beheld the conversion of Israel: "They will serve Yahweh their God, and David their king, whom I will raise up for them." [77]

Messianic blessings are likewise heralded in the prophet's words: "From her (Israel) will her prince arise. Her ruler will go forth from her midst; and I will accord him access to me, and he will approach me." [78] The Messianic king will enjoy Yahweh's love; at will he may appear before Yahweh, as once Moses was privileged to do. [79]

§22. THE MESSIANIC KINGDOM UNDER THE SON OF DAVID

In describing the blessings that the Messiah will bring, Jeremias leans upon preceding prophecies. The Babylonian exile will come to an end after attaining its purpose of bringing the sinful people to a realization of their guilt and to the performance of penance. The exiles both of the Southern and of the Northern Kingdom will return to the land of their fathers. The Northern tribes will again be united to Judah; like David, the Messiah will rule over all the children of Israel. "The days are coming, it is the word of Yahweh, when persons no longer will say: 'As Yahweh lives, Yahweh who led the Israelites out of the land of Egypt,' but rather: 'As Yahweh lives, Yahweh who guided and brought back the descendants of the house of Israel from the north land and from all lands whither I dispersed them, that they again may live on their soil'." [80]

In kindest words Jeremias urged the Northern Kingdom to desist striving against divine grace, reminding them of God's infinite mercies and long-suffering: "Return, faithless Israel, says Yahweh, for no longer am I directing my wrath against you. I am full of mercy, says Yahweh; I never remain angry forever — only acknowledge your guilt." [81] Chap-

---

[77] Jer. 30:9.   [78] Jer. 30:21.
[79] The interpretation that the Messiah is here presented as a priest because priests entered into Yahweh's presence to offer sacrifices, would read too much into the text.
[80] Jer. 23:7-8.
[81] Jer. 3: 12-13.

ters later another heartfelt plea is made to the exiles of the Northern Kingdom to return home:

Jeremias
31:22   How long are you going to refuse, faithless daughter?
          Yahweh, indeed, is doing a new thing on earth:
          A woman encloses (courts?) a man.

The whole context considered, this is a Messianic passage, but its interpretation is not devoid of serious difficulties.[82] Departing from the Masoretic text but still dependent upon it, the Septuagint reads: For the Lord makes salvation in a new planting; with salvation men shall walk about (*betobah* instead of *neqabah*); this the Itala rendered as: *in salute tua circumibunt homines.*

The prophets frequently represented Israel's relationship to Yahweh in terms of a marriage entered upon at Sinai. Apostasy from God was equivalent to adultery.[83] The Northern Kingdom became notorious for this sin. Would the meaning of the passage then be: The sinful Northern Kingdom, faithless through many generations, now returns to her God and strives for His love, as the adulterous wife returns to her husband in sorrow? And to express her love externally she covers Him with affectionate embraces?

Osee had developed this approach: "On that day, it is the oracle of Yahweh, you will again address me: My man! No longer will you cry out: My Baal!"[84] Is the new thing that Yahweh creates Israel's final return to her God after countless attempts to effect her conversion had failed? Is the new thing this miracle of grace? Is the woman (*neqabah*) Israel, and the man (*geber*) Yahweh? Can the conversion of Israel be termed something new?

In the Kal and Niphal the word *bara'*, to make, is used exclusively of divine activity and points the action in question as something marvellous, something new.[85] Our text expressly affirms that that which God does had never happened before. Would this apply to the conversion of Israel? The new thing which Yahweh does should effect conversion, it should influence Israel to mend her ways. The question therefore arises whether Jerome's interpretation, one which he alone among the ancients proposed,[86] is perhaps correct, viz., Jeremias is foretelling *the birth of the Messiah of a Virgin* in words full of mystery. This is a great marvel, it also is something new, unheard of. The Son of the Virgin

---

[82] For various explanations, see Al. Schaefer, *Die Gottesmutter in der Heiligen Schrift*[2], 54f; A. Condamin, *Le Livre de Jérémie*, 227; E. Tobac, *Les prophètes d'Israel*, 275.

[83] Cf. Heinisch-Heidt, *Theology of the Old Testament*, p. 251.

[84] Os. 2:16.

[85] Num. 16:30; Am. 5:14; Is. 40:26; 41:20; 48:7; 65:17; Ps. 51:12.

[86] The Greek and older Latin Fathers followed the Septuagint and Old Latin as a text and therefore did not treat the problem.

brings the great blessings which Israel's prophets describe. The Virgin birth is the reason why the people in exile prepare to return to their homeland. And it indeed was a work of God's omnipotence and love.

True, the usage of words would be unusual if these ideas were intended, but the usage of words is unusual with any of the many other interpretations proposed. The combination "the bearer bears" in Mich. 5:2 is unusual; [87] for readers who knew Is. 7:14 and Mich. 5:2 Jeremias' text was not unintelligible. Neqabah means woman, and the possibility of virginity is not excluded. When God created "man and woman — neqabah," [88] the woman at her creation was virginal. Geber, man, in the sense of the strong one, was perhaps chosen because Is. 9:7 heralded the Messiah as 'El Gibbor. Sabab in the Poel is used of one drowning in the engulfing floods, a picture of the enemies surrounding the psalmist. [89] In the Hiphil sabab refers to the changing of a name. [90] The possibility that by this term the prophet is poetically describing the formation of the child in the womb of the mother cannot be denied. The origin of a child in the womb ever remains a great mystery, one which cannot be fully understood. [91] Recall Job's reflection: "You clothed me with skin and flesh, with life and strength you endowed me." [92]

The capital of the kingdom where the tribes of the north and Judah in the south come together in brotherly unity and where the shoot of David reigns as king is Sion. [93] His rule will never end. [94]

In the Messianic age the soil will become unbelievably fertile, [95] the population will increase tremendously. [96] But what is most important in the preaching of our prophet is his *spiritual message*. Yahweh will dwell in the midst of His people, Jerusalem therefore will be called "Yahweh's throne." [97] He purifies them from all their sins, [98] and gives them a new heart and way of life. [99] They become His people, and He will be their God. [1] When the people are purified by divine grace, Yahweh makes a *new* covenant with them:

Jeremias

31:31   Behold, the days are coming, says Yahweh, when I will make a new covenant with the house of Israel (and with the house of

31:32   Judah), one unlike the covenant which I made with their fathers when I took them by the hand and led them out of the land of Egypt. That covenant they have broken in spite of the fact that

31:33   I was their Lord — says Yahweh. This is the covenant I will make with the house of Israel in those days, says Yahweh: My law I will put within them, I will write it upon their heart. I will be their

---

87 Here as in Jer. 31:22 the article is absent to emphasize the mystery.
88 Gen. 1:27; 5:1.
89 Ps. 55:11.
90 4 Kgs. 23:24; 24:17.
91 Qoh. 11:5; 2 Mach. 7:22.
92 Job 10:11-12.

93 Jer. 31:6.
94 Jer. 31:35-37.
95 Jer. 31:12.
96 Jer. 3:16; 30:19; 33:10-11.
97 Jer. 3:17.
98 Jer. 31:8.
99 Jer. 32:39.   1 Jer. 24:7; 32:38-39.

31:34   God, and they will be my people. No longer will each one tell his neighbor, 'Know Yahweh!', for all of them shall know me from the least to the greatest — it is the oracle of Yahweh. And I will forgive their guilt, and their sins I will remember no longer.

This covenant complements the covenant Yahweh made with Israel at Sinai.[2] While the latter was inscribed upon stone tablets to remind the people of their obligations, the new covenant is written directly upon the hearts of men; men will be interiorly convinced of owing obedience to God and with a willing spirit they will perform His precepts. How often Israel violated the Sinaitic covenant! The covenant of Messianic times is a permanent one, for it will transform the whole man. How often the prophets were obliged to preach God's oneness, justice, mercy — as Jeremias did — and the need for a virtuous life, without finding docile ears or pliant hearts. In the new covenant there will be no ignorance of religious matters, and men will act according to God's holy will. Because religion will be essentially a matter of the spirit, the ark of the covenant in which the tables of the Law were kept will lose its purpose. God will live in the midst of His people, and therefore it will be no great loss if that which was only a type of the divine presence in the temple would perish (as it did in the destruction of Jerusalem by Nabuchodonosor in 587). Then "men will no longer say: The ark of Yahweh's covenant. It will no longer come to any one's mind, no one will any longer think of it or miss it, nor will it be replaced by a new one."[3]

It is Yahweh who will initiate this new covenant with Israel. Then, as Jeremias proclaims, all the nations of the world will embrace the faith in the one true God. Jerusalem serves as "Yahweh's throne," not the ark of the covenant; and in Jerusalem "all the nations assemble, no longer following the promptings of their own stubborn and evil hearts."[4] Of course, Yahweh would first find it necessary to inflict judgment upon the nations, particularly upon Israel's wicked neighbors, and drive them from their lands. But this takes place in order that they should acknowledge Him as Lord and realize their guilt. Then their punishment will come to an end. Then "they will learn the ways of my people and swear by my Name, 'Truly as Yahweh lives!', just as they taught my people to swear by Baal. And thereupon they will be built up in the midst of my people."[5] Together with purified Israel the Gentile world will form the new people of God; for the nations will discover that the gods they worshipped till then were "only fraud, nothingness, and what was good for nought."[6]

While the expectation of the coming Redeemer represents the climax

[2] Ex. 19:6; 24:8.   [4] Jer. 3:17.   [6] Jer. 16:19.
[3] Jer. 3:16.   [5] Jer. 12:14-16.

in the prophecies of Isaias, this aspect does not occupy so great a place nor does it attain a similar profundity in the preaching of Jeremias. But the points he makes were sufficient to give strength to the few who at his time still remained loyal to the God of their fathers and obeyed His commandments; his comforting words enabled them to bear the suffering consequent upon the destruction of their country, city, and temple. With hope they could look forward to a better future which would follow the rise of the Savior from David's family. For the *massa perdita*, those who took to heart no admonition or threat, clearer insights into the Messianic mystery would have been futile; they would have thought that the prophet was retracting his comminations and would have become still more obstinate.

PSALMS FROM THE PERIOD OF THE PRE-EXILIAN PROPHETS

§23. THE MYSTICAL MARRIAGE FEAST
Ps. 45

45:2   My heart overflows with a lovely theme —
       my song I dedicate to my king.
       May my tongue be as the pen of a skillful scribe.
45:3   You are the fairest among the children of men;
       sweetness has been poured out upon your lips
       because Yahweh has blessed you forever.
45:4   Gird your sword upon your thigh, O hero,
       (it is) your majesty and your splendor.
45:5   Go forth triumphantly in the cause of truth and justice,
       and may your right hand show you awe-inspiring deeds.
45:6   Your arrows are sharp, nations fall before you,
       (they strike) the heart of the king's enemies.
45:7   Your throne, O God, stands forever and ever,
       a sceptre of justice is the sceptre of your kingdom.
45:8   You love justice and hate wickedness;
       therefore Yahweh, your God, has anointed you
       with the oil of gladness more than your fellow (kings).
45:9   With myrrh and aloes and cassia all your robes are fragrant,
       from ivory palaces string music brings you joy.

45:10   Kings' daughters are in your royal train,
           at your right stands the queen, in gold of Ophir.
45:11   Hear, daughter, and see; turn your ear,
           forget your people and your father's house.
45:12   The king is desirous of your beauty,
           for he is your lord, and you must reverence him.
45:13   The daughter Tyre comes with gifts,
           the wealthiest among the people court your favor.
45:14   Wholly magnificent is the king's daughter,
           her robes are of coral and spun gold.
45:15   In embroidered apparel she is borne in to the king;
           virgins follow her,
           her train is led in to you.
45:16   They are borne in with exultation and joy,
           they enter the place of the king.
45:17   Sons will replace your fathers —
           you will appoint them as princes in every land.
45:18   I shall make your name famous through all generations,
           therefore the nations will praise you forever and ever.

In this song, a noteworthy number among the psalms, the psalmist first praises the attributes of a king (vv. 2–10). Then he exhorts a royal daughter to give herself with all her love to the king, her bridegroom. In closing he glances forward into the future. Because the king is described as a great warrior, most commentators assume that the psalm was composed in pre-exilic times.

The composition has certain resemblances to the Canticle of Canticles. As with the latter, interpreters fall into three classes. Practically all the Protestant exegetes of the present time interpret the words very literally and find described the marriage solemnity of some Israelitic king. Those who are bold enough to point out some particular ruler mention Solomon; or Achab, because of his marriage with Jezabel, the princess of Sidon; or Joram of Judah, who was wedded to Athalia, Jezabel's daughter; or Jeroboam II; or even the Hasmonean prince Aristobul (104–103).

The ancient Church and the majority of present day Catholic commentators regard the psalm as an allegory.[7] Under the picture of a marriage feast the author describes the union of the Messiah with God's Chosen People of old, and because of the close relation between the Old and New Testaments, the union of Christ with the Church follows naturally. This interpretation has in its favor that a purely secular wedding song would hardly have been included in a collection of prayers used for spiritual purposes — the editor, at least, must have sensed a religious import in the composition, since for liturgical services an ordinary wedding song would not have been acceptable. Neverthe-

---

[7] *Sensus literalis improprius.*

less, it is not the judgment of the editor that is decisive. The religious values of a composition in the Canon derive from the author writing under the influence of divine inspiration. The question, therefore, concerns the ideas or judgments in the mind of the inspired author.

To portray Yahweh's love toward His people, the prophets frequently used the figure of marriage, the most intimate and strongest tie between two persons, and one which includes grave obligations. It was Osee, for instance, who developed this theme very beautifully and impressed its message upon the people by resigning himself to the woman God ordered him to marry. Jeremias regarded the days when God delivered Israel from Egyptian servitude and when the people were obedient to divine guidance in the wilderness as the nation's honeymoon, only to point out how their conduct in later times resembled adultery.[8] However, God's love was so immeasurably great that in spite of all He would forgive their infidelity.[9] Ezechiel too described God's relationship to Israel in terms of marriage disgracefully violated by the people;[10] and in exile a prophet spoke poignantly of God's re-acceptance of sinful Israel as "the wife of one's youth" after she had deplored her sins.[11] All this prepared minds to interpret our psalm of the Messiah and the ideal People of God, the sublimely perfect union realized in Christ and the Church.

Jewish interpreters saw the Messiah in the king of Ps. 45. The Targum, for instance, rendered verse 3a: "Your beauty, King Messiah, is greater than that of all the children of men"; and a similar treatment was given verse 8.[12]

Not without some reliance upon the Letter to the Hebrews, which deduced the Son's exaltation far above all the angels from Ps. 45:7,[13] Christian exegesis has consistently regarded Ps. 45 as Messianic. Jesus referred to Himself as the Bridegroom.[14] This unwavering tradition found an expression in the Vulgate rendition of verse 12: *Ipse est Dominus Deus tuus.*[15] Verse 8, in which the king is addressed as God, favors the traditional interpretation.[16] This exegesis would not, of course, exclude the psalmist's remembrance of some pompous, royal marriage celebration, Solomon's for example, which he himself may have witnessed or about which he had heard or read, a celebration that provided material for his imagination to form a magnificent picture. But from the very first line of his poem he intended to portray the relationship of God toward Israel with reference to the Messiah.

[8] Jer. 2:2. [9] Jer. 3:1-17.
[10] Ez. 16; 23.
[11] Is. 54:6-7.
[12] Other quotations from Jewish literature may be found in L. Reinke, *Mess. Psalmen* I, 353; Brierre-Narbonne, 22.

[13] Heb. 1:7-8.
[14] Cf. p. 237ff.
[15] For quotations from the Fathers, cf. Reinke, *Mess. Psalmen* I, 354.
[16] The deification of a royal sovereign was unheard of in Israel; cf. pp. 91-92.

A third approach to the interpretation of Ps. 45, one which likewise is advanced by some Catholic scholars, holds that the psalmist commemorates the actual marriage of some historical Israelitic king, but regards this marriage as typifying the relations between the Messiah and Israel.

Poetry abounds in figures, it is figurative language itself. When reading Ps. 45, a poetic composition, we must not investigate what every word refers to. For certain elements belong to the figure and bear no further theological meanings.

Verse 2. Full of enthusiasm for his subject, the psalmist in spirit sees the Messiah in all the glory of youth.[17] The first role expected of a king is leadership in war. The Messiah was presented as such in Balaam's oracle, and appears as a warrior in Pss. 2 and 110. Our poet prompts the king to gird himself with the sword and to mount the chariot. This was the practice not only in Assyria and Egypt but in Israel too. From a standing position in his chariot, the king drew the bow, as shown in Assyrian and Egyptian bas-reliefs. Similarly the Messiah-King will smite his adversaries (verses 5-7). His struggles, however, are for the cause of justice, for he is indeed the son of Yahweh; and victory is sure. He is the champion, *gibbor*, even as he had been heralded as *'el gibbor* by Isaias.[18]

Verses 8–10. On festive occasions the Israelites anointed themselves with oil, a symbol of joy. In the psalm this observation belongs to the allegory as such, just as the remarks on the queen's clothing and perfumes. Nevertheless, if one wishes, he may think of the graces proper to the human nature of the Messiah; and the queen-bride's apparel may be related to the virtues with which the People of God are clothed. At a marriage feast there must always be music and song to please the ears of the guests. In the bridal train there are a large number of attendants, maidens, virgins.[19] At a marriage in which the bridegroom was the king and the bride belonged to a royal family, only maidens of princely blood would be selected. The bride stands at the king's right, at the place of honor.[20] Her garments are magnificent.

Verse 11. The poet now addresses the bride and gives her fatherly advice, as the wisdom teachers would speak to a beloved pupil. She had come from a foreign country, but now she no longer should cast glances backwards toward homeland and relatives; with Ruth she should say: "Your people are my people; your God, my God."[21] Her renunciation of home and country will be richly repaid by the king's love; her new

---

[17] Because the psalm stands in an Elohim collection (Pss. 42-72), Yahweh is to be substituted for Elohim in v. 3 and 8.
[18] Is. 9:5.

[19] Matth. 25:1.
[20] 3 Kgs. 2:49.
[21] Ruth 1:16.

mission is to live for the king, her lord. The literal sense: if Israel is God's bride, she should make a clean break with the past. Till then she had given herself to the service of false gods, she resembled a foreigner; but now she is to belong heart and soul to the Messiah. This union implies an inner renovation, she must renounce certain things most dear to her, as, for instance, profane and pagan religious practices. In the light of the New Testament we see the Church of Christ as the bride from foreign lands, called from Gentile nations in the providence of God.

Verse 13. Gifts are never lacking at a marriage. For the nuptials here described, gifts come from distant peoples. "Daughter Tyre" [22]: nations are often referred to as daughters in the Old Testament.[23] Tyre represents all who manifested their devotion to the bride by gifts, because Tyre was exceptional for her wealth and farflung commercial enterprises.[24] The king's subjects, however, do not wish to be put to shame by foreigners; of these "the wealthiest" approach with gifts — the Gentile world accepts the Messiah and the Church though not all the Jews remain aloof.

Verse 14. The poet continues by describing how the wedding guests enter the royal palace. The bride, in shining apparel, leads the royal train; maidens, virgins, attendants follow. This procession is part of the marriage feast figure.

Verse 17. In a final word to the king the poet looks forward to his descendants. The words, "sons will replace your fathers," are difficult to explain in either the strictly verbal or the typical interpretations. If the king was Solomon, could it be that his sons would govern the various provinces from Hamath to the River of Egypt? Such policy, however, would have seriously endangered the unity of the kingdom. And a later Davidic king would never have divided tiny Judah into fractions. But taking the song as an extended metaphor, the passage does give meaning. The Messiah was a descendant of David, he followed the kings of the Davidic dynasty. These kings are the "fathers" of the Messiah. The sons of the Messiah will replace them in the new kingdom of God. If the "fathers" ruled over a small kingdom, the children from the Messiah's mystical marriage will rule over the whole earth in the Messiah's name.

Verse 18. The poet concludes by expressing the hope that with his song he may have aided the glorification of the Messiah-King. May his words of praise be proclaimed in all future ages and through the whole world — a *monumentum aere perennius*.[25]

[22] G V, "the Daughter of Tyre."
[23] E.g., the Daughter Sion.
[24] Ez. 27.
[25] Regarding the interpretation that sees Mary in the bride, cf. p. 240f.

§24. THE PRINCE OF PEACE AND HIS KINGDOM
Ps. 72

72:1 O God, endow the king with your judgment,
      the king's son with your justice.
72:2 He will judge your people justly,
      your afflicted ones with equity.
72:3 The mountains will yield peace for the people,
      and the hills justice.
72:4 He will secure justice for the oppressed among the people;
      he will help the children of the poor
      (while crushing the oppressor).
72:5 He will endure as long as the sun,
      as long as the moon, from generation to generation.
72:6 Like rain upon the newly mown meadow he will descend,
      like a shower that waters the earth.
72:7 In his days justice will flower,
      and the fullness of peace, till the moon be no more.
72:8 He will rule from sea to sea,
      from the river (Euphrates) to the ends of the earth.
72:9 Before him the desert dwellers will bow,
      and his enemies lick the dust.
72:10 The kings of Tarshish and the islands will bring gifts,
      the kings of Sheba and of Saba will bring tribute.
72:11 All kings will do him homage,
      all nations serve him.
72:12 For he will rescue the poor man who appeals for help,
      and the afflicted man who has none to aid him.
72:13 He will have pity on the weak and the needy,
      he will save the lives of the poor.
72:14 From oppression and violence he will redeem their souls,
      for their blood is precious in his eyes.
72:15 He (the poor man) will live,
      he (the king) will give him gold from Sheba;
      he (the poor man) will continually pray for him (the king),
      will beg blessing upon him at all times.
72:16 There will be a superabundance of grain throughout the land,
      even upon the mountain peaks;
      it will rustle like (the trees of) Lebanon,
      and the city (dwellers) will flourish like the verdure of the
72:17 May his Name endure forever —   [fields.
      as long as the sun shines, may his Name flourish.
      In him all the tribes on earth will bless themselves,
      all peoples will proclaim his praise.

There is no doubt that this psalm tells of a personal Messiah. The attributes and achievements predicated of him far surpass what may be legitimately ascribed to any human being; and the picture does harmonize well with acknowledged Messianic passages in the prophets. The king's domain is universal, it embraces all nations, it endures forever

(v. 7–11). The hope expressed in verse 8 is also found in Zach. 9:10. According to Is. 60:5–9 the wealth of Sheba and Tarshish will flow into Jerusalem in Messianic times. The Messianic king establishes a kingdom of peace, he rules in justice and is particularly concerned about the poor,[26] and his kingdom will never perish.[27] Moreover, he will make the earth unbelievably productive. The poet was thinking of the good days Israel enjoyed during the reign of Solomon, of the peace experienced during that era, of the ships that sailed to Tarshish or brought gold from Ophir, of the queen of Sheba coming gift-laden to Solomon, of the justice for which Solomon was famous, of the ambassadors from the East who began to reside in the Holy City. These past events the psalmist saw in a new setting, a foreshadowing or type of Messianic glory.

But the author was not merely presenting an historical king as a type of the Messiah. On the basis of the psalm's description of Messianic glory, attempts have been made to explain the (textually doubtful) superscription, "Of Solomon." Others interpret the phrase to mean "for Solomon," as if the psalm was dedicated to the celebrated king, particularly because he was the first to ascend the throne as "the king's son." Since there is no allusion to military activity, unlike Pss. 2 and 110, the hymn may have been written during the period of the pre-exilic prophets. The singular emphasis upon the justice of the Messiah in espousing the cause of the poor and the oppressed would point to this period. The emphasis on social problems allies the psalm to the preaching of the prophets.[28]

The Targum applied our psalm to the coming Redeemer, the "King-Messiah"; likewise the Midrash Tehillim, and the Talmud.[29]

V. 1. The king and the king's son for whom the psalmist is petitioning are one and the same person. The king is called the "king's son" because he ascended the throne legitimately, not by usurpation; he is not the "son of a nobody," as inscriptions designate a ruler who did not attain power through regular succession.[30] As a descendant of David, the Messiah is the "king's son."

V. 2–4. God should endow him with ability of governing the people wisely, not with the power of vanquishing all enemies. The great virtue that should grace this ruler is the ability to secure justice for Yahweh's poor and afflicted. How often these groaned for their rights, how often they were oppressed by those in power. The Messiah will inaugurate a new era! Upon hill and mountain — Palestine is prevailingly hilly — justice will prevail, and in its train Messianic peace.[31]

---

[26] Is. 9:6; 11:4-5. [27] Is. 9:6.
[28] Os. 6:6; Am. 2:6-8; Mich. 3:3; Is. 1:11; 10:1-3.
[29] Sanhedrin 98b, Bamidbar Rabba on Num. 7:13. Cf. Brierre-Narbonne, 24-25.

[30] Salmanassar III called Hasael of Damascus a "son of no one," i.e., a usurper.
[31] V. 4c is undoubtedly a later addition occasioned by Is. 11:4.

V. 5–6. This kingdom of peace will endure as long as the present order in the universe. Such cannot be predicated of any earthly ruler or earthly kingdom. Rain brings fertility. Mankind will long for the Messiah as for needed rain; and because rain "comes down" upon the earth, the poet uses the figure when he speaks of his advent. And as rain makes the meadows flourish, so the Messiah will cause justice to bud and prosper.

V. 7–11. There will be no limits, temporal or spatial, to the Messianic kingdom; it will extend to every part of the earth. In v. 9, *ṣiyyim*, desert dogs, undoubtedly refers to nomads. Everyone hostile to the Messiah will throw himself humbly in the dust before him. Tarshish is Tartessus on the Guadalquivir in Spain. The islands and the coasts of the Mediterranean join in giving homage to the Messiah. Sheba was a prosperous kingdom in southwestern Arabia.[32] According to Josephus[33] Sheba was the province Meroe between the White and the Blue Nile; Dillman places it along the coast of the Arabian sea. From the west, from the east, and from the south — from the whole world as the author says in v. 11 — kings and peoples come to acknowledge the Messiah as their leader and to be listed as members of his kingdom.

V. 12–14. Again the author speaks of the poor and the afflicted as the Messiah's principal concern, those who receive little sympathy. There are difficulties in v. 15. A change of subject must be presupposed. "He will live" refers to the poor man, although v. 14 uses a plural form. The poor man will receive gifts from the king who does not hoard up the treasures he receives from all the world, especially from Sheba, but distributes them to his needy subjects. The poor man shows himself grateful,[34] makes petition for the king, and wishes him God's blessing. This prayer becomes less striking upon recalling that the psalmist began his hymn with a prayer for the king. Its content is given in v. 16. After the sin in paradise God cursed the earth: "Thorns and thistles will it produce for you."[35] But in Messianic times the earth will become incomparably productive, and grain will grow even upon the tops of mountains where formerly goats and sheep could barely find sufficient fodder. The fertility of the fields will have a parallel in the fertility of women. Families will be large, and a man's descendants countless — just as the prophets too had described the Messianic era.[36]

The poet closes with wishing the Messiah-King an eternal rule in words which recall the blessing that was given Abraham at his call; all the nations on the earth will share in his blessing, viz., faith and love in the one true God.[37] Through the Messiah this blessing will become a reality.

---

[32] Ez. 27:22; cf. Gen. 10:7, 28.
[34] G V uses the plural: "They will pray for him."   [35] Gen. 3:17-18.
[33] Ant. II 10, 2 §249.
[36] Os. 2:7; 14:6-7; Jer. 30:19; Ez. 36:10-11.   [37] Gen. 12:3.

The Period
of the Exile

EZECHIEL

While Jeremias was proclaiming judgment upon the Jews in Palestine, another prophet raised his voice in distant Babylon to speak of sin and punishment. The visitation had already begun. A member of a priestly family, Ezechiel was taken into captivity in 597 with King Joachin and a goodly number from the higher classes. In 593 the fifth year of the exile, he was called to the office of prophet in a magnificent vision, Yahweh appearing to him sitting upon a throne carried by four cherubim.[38] The nature of his mission and its results were made abundantly clear. He was given to eat a scroll inscribed within and without with lamentations, mourning, and woe;[39] and he was informed that his preaching would be futile, for the exiles were a "perverse generation."[40] Such his mission for the years until the destruction of Jerusalem and the temple.

Nevertheless, shafts of light were not entirely absent from this first period of Ezechiel's activity. For the prophet also had the mission of comforting and encouraging the pious lest they become disconsolate through continuous pronouncements of judgment. He must likewise impress them with the mercy of God. By the symbolic act of lying motionless on one side of his body, he indicated that the exile would last forty years.[41] It was a sign that Yahweh would not be angry forever, but had decreed His people's deliverance from bondage. Moreover, the prophet's continued admonitions to repent and his stress on personal

[38] Ez. 1:1f.   [39] Ez. 2:10.   [40] Ez. 2:5.
[41] A symbolic number, like the number 70 in Jeremias (Ez. 4:6).

127

responsibility in matters of good and evil [42] proved a source of genuine comfort for the oppressed.

For six years Ezechiel warned and threatened in vain, and finally upon Yahweh's bidding he stopped preaching.[43] This occurred when the exiles heared the news of the catastrophe that had come upon Judah in 587. Thereafter it became the prophet's duty to counteract the waves of despair flooding in upon his fellow men by insisting that Israel still had a future, that the exile did not spell the nation's final doom. Yahweh would again accept them into His good favor if only they would acknowledge their sins and bear the visitation as a just punishment. Now too he could present the Messianic kingdom differently than during the first period of his mission, although in contradistinction to the oracles of Amos, Isaias, Micheas, and Jeremias, he devoted less space to the person of the Messiah and more to the glory of the Messianic kingdom, for the latter constituted an antithesis to the sorry condition in which the people then found themselves.

§25. THE TWIG FROM DAVID'S FAMILY
Ez. 17:22-24

By means of an allegory Ezechiel endeavored to show the exiles the deplorable condition of the royal house as it hastened to its end. A great eagle descended upon Lebanon, snatched off the tip of a cedar, plucked its topmost twig, carried it to a land of traders and set it in a city of merchants. From the land he also took seed and planted it in a field. It sprouted, and from a tiny bud there grew a mighty vine. Its tendrils turned toward him and its roots remained in solid earth; it became a vine with branches and foliage.

It was unnecessary to add explanatory comment, the exiles understood the allegory easily enough. Nevertheless, the prophet did extract the lesson so that they would have no excuse for remaining obstinate in the face of repeated pronouncements of approaching judgment. He recalled the events of the year 597 — how Joakim had refused obedience to the king of Babylon, how Nabuchodonosor appeared before the walls of Jerusalem, how the 18 year old Joachin capitulated after the death

---

[42] Ez. 18.   [43] Ez. 3:25-26.

of his father, and how he was taken captive to Babylon with his court and a large group from the upper classes. The great eagle was Nabuchodonosor, the cedar was the royal family of David, and Lebanon represented Jerusalem with its stately structures built of cedar.[44] The tip of the cedar or its topmost twig was Joachin, Judah's king at the moment. In his place Nabuchodonosor placed Sedecias, one from "the seed of the land," a born Judean, not a stranger. He was the third son of Josias, an uncle to Joachin. He is described as a vine, a noble plant; and it was Nabuchodonosor's hope that under his rule Judah would lead a peaceful existence.

But there was another great eagle, Egypt under the leadership of Psammetich II. Sedecias was not satisfied with his lot as a subject, and expected Egypt to liberate him from the yoke of Babylon — the vine stretched out to him its roots and drank more from him than from the bed in which it was planted. Then Yahweh asked: Will this succeed? Will he not tear out his roots and cut off his fruit? When the east wind strikes him (with its burning blasts), will he not be wholly burnt? In explaining the allegory the prophet emphasized how Sedecias had obligated himself to obedience by an oath, and Yahweh must avenge its violation. He foretold the siege of Jerusalem, and the king's capture and deportation to Babylon where a gruelling lot awaited him. Nabuchodonosor's planting, therefore, proved futile. The prophet continued with another story. In opposition to the king's efforts, Yahweh Himself would make a planting:

Ezechiel

17:22 I myself will take something from the tip of the tallest cedar and plant it. From its topmost branch I will pluck a tender twig and
17:23 transplant it myself upon a high and majestic mountain. Upon Israel's lofty heights will I plant it.

Again the cedar is the house of David, and the topmost twig, a person. It was Joachin, now it is the Messiah. This is evident not only from the phrase "a tender twig," an echo of the prophecy in Is. 11:1, but also from the description how this unpretentious bud will develop: "It will grow branches and produce fruit and become a stately cedar. In it birds of every feather will nestle, and in the shadow of its branches they will nest."[45]

The reference to the cedar-sprig transplanted from Palestine to Babylon proves that the prophet was speaking of the Messiah as a descendant of Joachin. The Messiah will appear in the Holy Land, upon Israel's lofty ridges. The high and majestic mountain is Sion; although actually not higher than other mountains, it certainly merits selection through

---

[44] Cf. Jer. 22:6–7, 23.   [45] Ez. 17:23.

its significance in sacred history as the place where true faith had its seat and from where it will radiate in the future.[46] Seemingly insignificant, the twig develops into a stately cedar in whose branches birds build their nests, "birds of every feather," i.e., the kingdom the Messiah will establish, embraces all nations, it is universal. The importance of this kingdom is stated in the following verse:

17:24   Then shall all the trees of the field know that I am Yahweh, that I have brought down the high tree, and have exalted the lowly tree; that I have caused the green tree to wither and the dry tree to bear foliage. I, Yahweh, have spoken, and I will accomplish my word.

The trees of the field alongside the cedar are the various governments throughout the world that will acknowledge the unique mission of the Messianic kingdom. The green tree that will wither is Sedecias; and here the prophet for the purpose of sharper contrast changes the metaphor — the dry tree which brings forth foliage is Joachin from whom the Redeemer proceeds. Note the progress in the delineation of the Messiah picture.

Joachin was kept in very mild custody because he was not responsible for his father's defection and had surrendered at an early moment. According to Bar. 1:3 he was allowed to attend divine services in the fifth year after the destruction of Jerusalem (583), an indication of very definite liberties. Babylonian clay tablets from the time of Nabuchodonosor record the quantity of oil allotted monthly to Ja'ukinu, king of the land of Ja'udi, and to his court; it would seem that he lived in a royal apartment and should have been satisfied with the arrangement. In 560 Nabuchodonosor's successor, Evil Merodach, granted Joachin full freedom, without, however, allowing him to return to Judah. His sons, whose names are given in 1 Chr. 3:17–18,[47] could not have been born after this event, for in 537 there appears an adult grandchild by the name Zorobabel as the leader of the exiles after the return to Palestine. Joachin's sons were born during the first period of his exile in Babylon, but it is not impossible that he had children already before the deportation who are not mentioned because they were not of age. Jeremias clarified Ezechiel's prophecy: Joachin would be "childless" because none of his descendants would occupy the throne of David.[48] Sedecias' children too were still quite small; they were put to death in the presence of their father before he himself was blinded.[49] In St. Matthew's genealogy Joachin appears as a forefather of Jesus.[50]

[46] Is. 2:2-4.
[47] Cf. Matth. 1:12.
[48] Jer. 22:30.
[49] 4 Kgs. 25:7.
[50] Matth. 1:12.

§26. DESTRUCTION OF THE DAVIDIC KINGDOM
Ez. 21:30-32

After the revolt of Sedecias, Nabuchodonosor did not delay long in punishing the king and his people. The Babylonian army was on the march, had come to Riblah on the Orontes. At this point Nabuchodonosor was obliged to decide whether he should attack Judah first, or Ammon for having joined the alliance with Judah. After consulting the oracle, he decided to proceed against Jerusalem.[51] He surmised that with the fall of the city, the Ammonites would quickly capitulate, and Egypt would be forced to intervene immediately if she wished to retain her allies.

What Ezechiel now told the exiles was, of course, "a fraudulent prophecy" in the eyes of those in Jerusalem who refused to be impressed by the seriousness of the situation; but the revolt and the violation of the royal oath called for punishment. If the Judeans were responsible for the impending evils, the primary responsibility lay upon Sedecias to whom the prophet addressed the words:

Ezechiel

21:30   You unholy, godless prince of Israel,
        your day is come, the time when sin brings the end.
21:31   For thus says Yahweh, the Lord:
        Off with the diadem! Away with the crown!
        It no longer has meaning.
        The lowly will be exalted and the high will be humbled.
21:32   Into ruins, ruins, ruins will I make it!
        No longer will it continue, until he comes who has a right to it,
        and to him will I give it.

The day had come when the king would receive the punishment deserved, the dissolution of the royal house of David and of the kingdom. The wicked ruler must put away the signs of kingly power. In other texts *misnephet*, diadem, signifies the head apparel worn by the high priest during official rites; in our passage the word is equivalent to *crown*. "It no longer has meaning": conditions will be radically altered, he will be stripped of the royal dignity. "The lowly will be exalted, the high will be put down": this refers primarily to Joachin from whom the Messiah would decend, and Sedecias who would lose the crown. Judah would come to an end, and to show how complete and final the dissolution would be, the prophet repeats three times the word *ruins*. Throne and kingdom would lie in ruins. But even if the Davidic family ceased to rule, if crown and sceptre sank into the dust, this was not the end. A Messiah would come. He possessed the right to the throne

[51] Ez. 21:21.

of David, he would take possession of it, and here the prophet echoes the *shiloh* prophecy of the dying Jacob.[52] Hope in the future must remain alive.

§27. A SHEPHERD AND A FLOCK
Ez. 34:23-24; 37:22-25

Judah perished as a nation. The royal house fell. Most of the people were deported to Babylon. Nevertheless, the exile did not mean the end. It did constitute a severe punishment divinely designed to humble and purify the Jews. Thereupon they experienced the mercy of their God, and the nation rose to new life. They returned to their fatherland to await the appearance of the Messiah whom the prophets had foretold.

Ezechiel

34:23   I shall appoint a single shepherd over them who will pasture them — my servant David. He will pasture them and he will be their
34:24   shepherd. I, Yahweh, shall be their God, and my servant David will be prince in their midst. I, Yahweh, have spoken.

Jeremias had called the Messiah David.[53] Here Ezechiel does likewise — Nathan already had designated the Messiah as a descendant of David.[54] He presents him as a shepherd, because David defended his sheep against lions and bears,[55] and as a shepherd was anointed king by Samuel.[56] As early as the prophet Micheas, the Messiah was called the good shepherd of his people.[57] The Messiah is the servant of Yahweh, because Yahweh established him in his office and because he does everything at the bidding and in the Name of Yahweh. He replaces the previous rulers in Israel who had been the ruin of their people. Under his leadership they will never again prove disloyal to Yahweh as had happened so frequently in spite of the many warnings and visitations. Yahweh will be their God, no longer will they seek strange idols. The Messianic age begins, an era the prophet then describes. Yahweh makes a covenant of peace with the people, for the Messiah had been heralded as the prince of peace [58] and his kingdom is a kingdom of peace.[59]

Not only in 17: 22–24 and 21: 30–32 but also in the present passage

---

[52] Gen. 49:10.   [54] 2 Sam 7:12.   [56] 1 Sam. 16:11.   [58] Is.9:4f.
[53] Jer. 30:9.   [55] 1 Sam. 17:34-36.   [57] Mich. 3:3.   [59] Is. 11:6f.

Ezechiel regards the Savior as a specific individual, following the lead of earlier prophets. There is no thought of a series of kings from the house of David. After the experience of Judah's last kings, he could hardly have seen the future's greatest good fortune in such an arrangement. Under the rule of the Messiah, the people would enjoy every blessing for which they longed. The wild beasts that prowled through the depopulated countryside [60] would be destroyed; the land, no longer visited by drought, but blessed with an abundance of water, becomes unbelievably productive; nor is there any further possibility of oppression by foreign nations.[61]

Frequently in the Old Testament Yahweh's love toward His people is portrayed by the relation of a shepherd to his flock.[62] In the New, Jesus too spoke poignantly of the Good Shepherd who lays down His life for His sheep.[63]

Ezechiel's teaching of the second David who would rule over all Israel is repeated and made more profound in a discourse which he clarified by a symbolic action. He took two pieces of wood in his hand. Upon one he wrote: "Judah, and the sons of Israel in alliance with her." And upon the other: "Joseph, and the whole house of Israel in alliance with her." [64] Then he held them in his hand in such a way they seemed to form one piece. The pieces represented the Northern and the Southern Kingdoms. Ezechiel then explained his act. Long had the tribes of Israel been divided, but the time would come when Yahweh would re-unite them.

Ezechiel

37:22   I shall make them into a single people in the land, upon the mountains of Israel; and a single king will rule over them. No longer will they form two nations nor be divided into two king-
37:23   doms . . . They will be my people, and I shall be their God. My
37:24   servant David will be king over them, and all of them will have
37:25   but one shepherd . . . They will dwell in the land that I have given to my servant David, in the land where your fathers lived they will live, both they and their children and their children's children forever. And David, my servant, will be their prince.

The prophet adds that Israel no longer will offend their God, and Yahweh will establish his sanctuary forever in their midst.

The end of the kingdom, the city, and the temple was a stultifying blow to the exiles simply because they had not believed Ezechiel's warnings. "Our transgressions and our sins lie heavily upon us, and because of them we waste away — how could we remain alive." [65] "Our bones

---

[60] Cf. 4 Kgs. 17:25.
[61] Ez. 34:25-32.
[62] Mich. 2:13; 4:6-7; Soph. 3:19; Jer. 23:3; 31:10.
[63] Matth. 18:12; Luke 15:4; John 10:10-16.
[64] Ez. 37:16-19.
[65] Ez. 33:10.

are dried up, our hope is gone, we have come to our end." [66] What could they expect from the future? Ezechiel's prophecies of woe and doom had been fulfilled, his credentials were proven authentic. His prophecies of salvation and blessings should also come true even though not in a crudely literal fashion. The kingdom would be restored; David's son would appear. And Israel's future would be far more glorious than her past.

THE SERVANT OF YAHWEH
Is. 40 — 55

In the second part of the Book of Isaias we find four poems on the "Ebed-Yahweh" or "Servant of Yahweh": Is. 42:1-7; 49:1-9a; 50:4-9 (10-11); 52:13-53:12.[67]

These poems or hymns are now given in a context which treats the return from the Babylonian exile, but the relation is so loose that originally they probably existed as independent compositions and only subsequently were put in their present position; and slight additions may have been made by the final redactor. Thus a number of repetitions can be explained, statements that could well have been made by the prophet himself, e.g., the Servant becomes a covenant with the people,[68] he is the Light of the nations,[69] he brings liberty to Israel,[70] kings and princes are filled with amazement in his presence.[71]

The expression "Servant of Yahweh" is used in the Old Testament of individuals and of groups devoted to the service of Yahweh or who had received from Him some special mission. Abraham is called the servant of Yahweh because of his role in mediating faith in the one true God to mankind; [72] likewise the patriarchs Isaac and Jacob as the forefathers of Israel, God's Chosen People; [73] Moses, as the greatest of the prophets; [74] Josue; [75] David, when God assured him of the throne; [76] Elias; [77] Isaias; [78] Job; [79] the promised Messiah.[80] Even Nabuchodononsor ap-

[66] Ez. 37:11.
[67] Scholars have disputed the exact length of some of these sections.
[68] Is. 42:6 and 49:8.
[69] Is. 42:6 and 49:6.
[70] Is. 42:7 and 49:9a.
[71] Is. 49:7 and 52:15.
[72] Gen. 26:24; Ps. 105:6, 42.
[73] Ex. 32:13; Deut. 9:27.
[74] Ex. 14:31; Num. 12:7.
[75] Jos. 24:29; Judg. 2:8.
[76] 2 Sam. 7:8, etc.; Is. 37:35; Ps. 18:1.
[77] 4 Kgs. 9:36; 10:10.
[78] Is. 20:3.
[79] Job. 1:8; 2:3; 42:7-8.
[80] Ez. 34:23-24; 37:24; Zach. 3-8.

pears as Yahweh's servant because he played a role in the fulfillment of the divine prophecies, even though unaware of it.[81] The phrase is used in a collective sense of the prophets,[82] of the angels,[83] of pious men,[84] of the people of Israel.[85]

The "Ebed-Yahweh" poems which we will now discuss in detail constitute a climax to Messianic prophecy, and from a theological or spiritual viewpoint belong to the most enlightening and consoling sections of the Old Testament. Among scholars, however, there seems to be no end to the disputes regarding the text and its interpretation.

§28. THE FIRST HYMN
Is. 42:1-7

42:1   Behold my servant, him do I support,
        my chosen one, in him do I delight!
    I have put my spirit upon him,
        he will bring justice to the nations.

42:2   He will not cry out or shout,
        in the streets his voice will not be heard.

42:3   He will not break the bruised reed,
        or crush out the flickering wick.
        Faithfully will he bring forth justice.

42:4   He will not weaken or collapse
        until he has established justice upon the earth;
        the islands, indeed, are awaiting his teaching.

42:5   Thus speaks Yahweh (who is) God,
        He who created the heavens and stretched them out,
        who produced the earth together with all its verdure,
        who gave breath to the people upon it
        and spirit to those who dwell in it:

42:6   I, Yahweh, have called you in justice,
        have grasped you by the hand and guarded you.
    I have made you a covenant with the people,
        a light for the (pagan) nations,

42:7   to open the eyes of the blind,
        to release captives from prison,
        from dungeons those who sit in darkness.

[81] Jer. 25:9 ; 27:6 ; 43:10.
[82] 4 Kgs. 9:7 ; Am. 3:7 ; Is. 44:26 ; Jer. 7:25.
[83] Job 4:18.
[84] Ps. 34:23, etc.
[85] Is. 63:17 ; 65:8-9, 13, 15 ; 66:14 ; Jer. 30:10 ; 46:27 ; Ez. 28:25 ; 37:35.

With the simple introduction, "Behold!," Yahweh presents His Servant to the world as though he were already well known — another instance of the mysterious methods of prophetic speech. The Servant, however, is not present; he will appear only at some future date. Upon him is put the spirit of God to enable him to perform his office, an action which brings to mind the prophecy of the twig from Jesse's root upon whom rests the spirit of Yahweh.[86] The very similarity already suggests a specific individual, not a community or series of persons. It will be his duty to bring "justice" to the nations, to teach the Gentiles their moral and religious duties, primarily the oneness of God.

He will work in a most unassuming way, not like Cyrus (whom the prophet mentions by name in his book), the conqueror who trod rulers under his foot like clay and for whom Yahweh cast down nations and broke to pieces doors of bronze and smashed iron bars.[87] Not by the force of arms will the Servant achieve his purposes, without fanfare he will begin his mission. Lovingly he will espouse the cause of the oppressed, not breaking the bruised reed or extinguishing the flickering wick.

V. 4. However difficult his duty to turn mankind back to God, he will never grow weary because the spirit of God strengthens him. His message will be eagerly awaited. In ages past Moses had brought a "teaching" destined for a small circle; the servant's teaching will be carried into the most distant regions, to the islands and coastlands of the Mediterranean. In different dress it was the same message that Isaias had expressed when he prophesied how the nations would journey to Sion to be instructed in what they must believe and do; for from Sion goes forth Torah, teaching. In Is. 2:2–4 the nations take pains to gain this teaching, in our Ebed-Yahweh poem, the Servant offers it to them.

V. 5. Now Yahweh proceeds to instruct His servant regarding his mission.[88] Yahweh, the omnipotent creator of the world and of men, equips him for an assignment far beyond human capabilities. He calls him "in justice," for it is a matter of the salvation of mankind, both of Israel and of the Gentiles. On Sinai Yahweh had entered into a covenant with Israel, but thereby He had not forsaken the pagan world; rather, Israel was to preserve the true religion and in due time to mediate it to them. Salvation itself was an expression of divine justice because God had promised it to Israel; and when He receives back into His favor a people purified by judgment, He acts justly. In as much as man can speak of a just claim over against God, Israel had a right to the Messiah; he was promised primarily to Israel. Jesus sent His apostles

[86] Is. 11:2.   [87] Is. 41:26 ; 45:12.   because the phrase "light for the (pagan)
[88] Verses 5-7 cannot be related to Cyrus   nations" refers back to verses 1 and 4.

first of all to "the lost sheep of the house of Israel," [89] and He healed the daughter of the Canaanite woman only after she had acknowledged Israel's primary claim.[90]

V. 6. In Babylon the king grasped the hands of Marduk during the New Year's celebration in token of having received the throne from him. After entering the capital city Cyrus clasped the hands of Marduk to show that he had gained victory and the kingdom through Babylon's principal god. In our hymn, however, it is Yahweh who grasps the Servant's hand and appoints him as His representative to Israel and the Gentile world. The Servant should vitalize the covenant Yahweh had made with Israel, a covenant Israel had violated so frequently through her transgressions. He is given the work of Moses, but he is far greater than Moses. He is the light of the Gentiles, as Emmanuel already was the great light rising upon those who sit in the shadow of death.[91]

V. 7. Chiastically the prophet speaks first of the Servant's mission to the pagan world. He will open the eyes of the blind, he will instruct the nations who do not possess the true religion. Then the prophet indicates the work the Servant will perform with regard to Israel. Prisoners he will free from chains. The prophet was referring not simply and solely to a spiritual deliverance, one from the bondage of sin. The exiles, longing for freedom, would think of their own sorry condition which at the time when Cyrus was winning victories and the Babylonian government was busy with rebellions had grown more deplorable; certain Jewish leaders may well have been imprisoned. The edict of Cyrus brought freedom to all political prisoners. The same thought occurs again in the second poem.[92]

The very fact that in describing the Servant the prophet alluded to previous Messianic oracles, noting how the spirit of God will rest upon him and how he will be a light to illumine the Gentiles, suggests that he identifies the promised Redeemer with the Servant. Actually the poem was fulfilled in Jesus, and only in Jesus. God singled Him out as His beloved Son in whom He was well pleased.[93] Upon Him the Divine Spirit descended visibly when baptized.[94] He did not wish His miracles to be publicized, a point the evangelist regarded as a fulfillment of our prophecy.[95] He who was meek and humble of heart lovingly interested Himself in the sick and the sinful, the afflicted and the oppressed. The bruised reed He did not break.[96] Just as Moses sealed the covenant between Yahweh and Israel with the blood of bulls,[97] so Jesus poured out His own blood, the blood of the new covenant.[98] His "torah," the

---

[89] Matth. 10:6. [90] Matth. 15:20.
[91] Is. 9:1.
[92] Is. 49:6.
[93] Matth. 3:16 ; Luke 9:35.
[94] Matth. 3:16.
[95] Matth. 12:17-21. [96] Matth. 11:28-30.
[97] Ex. 24:8.
[98] Matth. 26:28 ; Luke 24:8.

doctrine which He preached, outranked that of the Old Law: "But I say to you. . . !" As the Light for the enlightenment of the Gentiles Simeon heralded the infant Jesus,[99] and to the apostle John He was the Light of the world.[1] The verse that proclaimed how the Servant would open the eyes of the blind found literal fulfillment in the cures Jesus worked.[2]

§29. THE SECOND HYMN
Is. 49:1-9a

49:1   Listen to me, you islands,
        give heed, you peoples from afar.
    Yahweh called me from my mother's womb,
        at birth he gave me my name.

49:2   He made my mouth like a sharp sword,
        in the shadow of his hand he protected me;
    He made me a chosen arrow,
        in his quiver he concealed me.

49:3   And he said to me: You are my servant,
        (Israel), through whom I seek to glorify myself.

49:4   But I replied: In vain have I labored,
        I have spent my strength to no purpose, fruitlessly.
    Still before Yahweh I am in the right,
        and my reward will come from my God.

49:5c   Indeed, I am honorable in Yahweh's eyes,
        and my God is my strength.

49:5a   And now Yahweh speaks —
        (Yahweh) who fashioned me to be his servant from my mother's
49:5b   that I might lead Jacob back to him,   [womb
        that Israel be gathered together to him —

49:6   (He says:) Inconsequential is it that you are my servant,
        destined to raise up the tribes of Jacob,
        to bring back the preserved remnant of Israel?
    I shall make you the light of the nations
        that my salvation may reach to the very ends of the earth.

49:7   Thus speaks Yahweh,
        Israel's Redeemer, her Holy One,
        to him despised by every one, to him abhorred by men,
        to the servant of rulers:
    Kings will see, and rise,
        princes — and fall down for Yahweh's sake, who is faithful,
        the Holy One of Israel, who has chosen you.

[99] Luke 2:32.   [1] John 1:4-11; 8:12.   [2] Matth. 9:27; 11:5; 12:22; John 9:1.

49:8   Thus speaks Yahweh:
                In the time of favor I will listen to you,
                and in the day of salvation I will aid you.
            I have fashioned you
                and have made you for a covenant with the people,
                to raise up the land,
                to allot devastated areas,
49:9a   to say to the captives: Go forth!
                to those in darkness: Be free!

In the first Ebed-Yahweh poem God presented His Servant; in the second the Servant himself takes the leading role. He addresses the islands and shores of the Great Sea and the peoples inhabiting these regions. The whole world should heed his words; for his mission is worldwide. Just as at the call of Jeremias, Yahweh had said: "Before I formed you in your mother's womb I knew you, and before you left your mother's body I sanctified you and destined you as a prophet for the nations," [3] just as an angel announced to Zachary that his son would be filled with the Holy Spirit while still in his mother's womb,[4] so God imposed a name upon His Servant at birth, assigned him a special mission, and equipped him with the graces necessary for its performance.

With sword and arrow Cyrus conquered nations, executing God's design.[5] Our Servant, however, accomplishes his work by word of mouth — he is nabi', "God's spokesman." Yahweh makes his mouth resemble a sharp sword, he performs his task like a polished arrow. For God's word is like a mallet that crushes rocks,[6] keener than any two-edged sword.[7] According to Isaias the Messianic king will smite the oppressor with the "staff of his mouth," [8] i.e., through the power of a mere word. In Is. 11 it is the Messiah's word of command that destroys evildoers, in the present prophecy it is his preaching that no one can withstand. It resembles a sword that is kept secure, an arrow concealed in one's quiver until the time has arrived in which, according to God's plan, the Servant should begin his work.

The Servant, who will appear as a prophet, who will be sent by God to the nations, and who will glorify Yahweh by his work is called in verse 3, and only in this passage, "Israel." But according to verse 5 the Servant likewise has the task of restoring Israel. If the expression means an individual person, then it should be translated "contender with God," as in Gen. 32:29 and Os. 12:4. "Israel" in verse 3 is probably a gloss, introduced by some reader with the opinion that the same servant was referred to as in other passages where the term refers to the people of Israel. For Is. 42:1 the Septuagint gives, "Jacob, my servant, Israel, my chosen one." Perhaps the Septuagint translators found this reading in

[3] Jer. 1:5.   [4] Luke 1:15.   [5] Is. 41:2.   [6] Jer. 23:29.   [7] Heb. 4:12.   [8] Is. 11:4.

the text at their disposal; it would not constitute a proof for authenticity, but rather for the antiquity of a collective interpretation. It is also possible that the word Israel in verse 3 is simple dittography of the following word 'ašer. Even a considerable number of authors who advocate the collective interpretation admit that the word "Israel" in 49:3 is extraneous to the text.

V. 4. The Servant has begun his work and has been laboring for some time. He cannot but observe how futile the results. He does not, it is true, lose courage, for his trust in Yahweh is unshakable. If he accomplishes nothing, it is not a question merely of visible success but of the fruitless character of his mission. Nevertheless he receives a reward, one rendered the greater because his work in the face of obstinate, obdurate listeners had been truly selfless.

V. 5–6. Because he accomplished so little through no fault of his own, Yahweh adds a nobler mission to that which he had. Thereafter he must not limit his work to Israel — an indication of Israel's continued obstinacy — but his mission now embraces all the world. He should be a Light to the nations.[9] For this reason the Servant had invited peoples afar off to listen in the opening verses.

In the "return of Jacob to Yahweh" and the "gathering together of Israel," it was not merely a matter of conversion from sin. Certainly it was the purpose of the exile to make Israel aware of her guilt. Out of the crucible of suffering there should come a holy remnant, the beginning of a new people. This is why the prophets continued to speak of "the preserved of Israel." The exiles, therefore, looked forward hopefully to returning to Palestine as promised by Jeremias and Ezechiel. The phrases "to raise up the tribes of Jacob" and "to bring back the preserved of Israel" refer directly to the journey home from Babylon, a promise extended to all the Jews, the Northern tribes included. The Servant will have a task similar to that of Moses, he will lead the people out of captivity into the land of promise, and there assume the role Josue once held. But he is greater than Moses because his mission does not exclude the Gentile nations.

V. 7. The hymn proper comes to a conclusion with verse 6; what follows is commentary. First Yahweh points out the plight of His Servant. Not only is he unsuccessful, he encounters rugged opposition, is despised, abhorred. The Servant spoken of in the preceding verses is meant, not the people of Israel; this is shown by the use of the word *goy,* the people, and not *goyyim,* the Gentiles. He could be called the Servant of rulers since he was forced by virtue of his office to withstand the worldly great and powerful and make them feel his power; but a change

[9] Is. 42:6-7.

of fortunes was coming, he would not always be contemned as of little importance. Because of the success his preaching would have among the nations, kings and princes would stand amazed [10] and render God honor for raising up His Servant.

V. 8. Again Yahweh notes that the Servant's primary task was to work for Israel. Though the people might reject his teaching, the time would come when grace would prevail. Then the Servant would act as mediator of a new covenant with the people like a second Moses and Josue, and would lead them out of bondage back to Canaan.

The prophet does not distinguish between redemption from the Babylonian captivity and redemption from the slavery of sin. Israel's deliverance was a type and a preparation for the more universal deliverance of mankind from Satan's dominion to be accomplished by Yahweh's Servant. Zorobabel indeed was instrumental in the first deliverance, but he was not despised by the people, nor did he work in vain in the people's behalf for any length of time. Neither did Cyrus upon publishing the edict granting the Jews the right to return to Palestine enter into any covenant with the Jewish nation; and his directive pertained only to those exiled from the Southern Kingdom — not those from the Northern tribes to which verses 6 and 8 refer. The deliverance from the Babylonian captivity took place with the Servant in view. He was destined to accomplish his work in the Holy Land, just as in a previous prophecy the might of Assyria would come to an end with Emmanuel in view. Of course, the exiles should first learn to distinguish between reality and type, while the prophet himself only comprehended the profound implication of his words after the return from Babylon had taken place; similarly Ezechiel subsequently realized that his oracles against Tyre were not fulfilled in the manner he had thought; for Nabuchodonosor was unable to destroy the city or condemn her leaders to a miserable death.[11] That Nabuchodonosor was only partially successful, Ezechiel later admitted.[12]

The second Servant of Yahweh poem expresses more clearly than the first the Servant's role as a prophet and the impression his word would make upon Israel and upon the pagan world. In Israel his activity for a long time would be futile; in compensation he receives a mission to the Gentiles and is told that here his preaching would be fruitful. Israel's return from exile is stated more clearly in the second poem than in the first.

Is. 49:1-9a found its fulfillment in Jesus. From the womb of His mother He was destined for the service of the Father. His mouth was a sharp sword, as we read in the Apocalypse.[13] In His high-priestly prayer

---

[10] Is. 52:15.   [11] Ez. 26—28.   [12] Ez. 29:17-18.   [13] 19:15.

He thanked the Father: "I have glorified you upon the earth, I have finished the work that you gave me."[14] The apparently futile character of His mission prompted the complaint: "How often would I have gathered your children together as a hen her chicks under her wings and you would not."[15] He pronounced woe upon Corozain, Bethsaida, and Capharnaum because they disregarded His doctrine.[16] Falsely accused, He was brought before the "rulers," before Annas and Caiphas, before Herod Antipas and Pilate. His apostles He commissioned to go into the whole world. The kingdom of God was taken from Israel and given to a people that produced fruit.[17]

When the Jews at Antioch created difficulties for Paul and Barnabas, contradicting their message and blaspheming, the apostles quoted the text of our prophecy and turned to the Gentiles.[18]

§30. THE THIRD HYMN
Is. 50:4-9 (10-11)

50:4	The Lord, Yahweh, has given me a teacher's tongue
	that I might encourage the faint with (my) words.
	Each morning he awakens my ear
	that I might listen as disciples do.
50:5	The Lord, Yahweh, opened my ear
	and I did not refuse, did not turn backwards.
50:6	I gave my back to the strikers,
	my cheeks to the pluckers of hair.
	My face I did not hide
	from those who rebuke and spit.
50:7	But the Lord, Yahweh, stands at my side
	and I will not be put to shame.
	Therefore I make my face (hard) like flint,
	for I am certain I will not be confounded.
50:8	He is near who will do me justice.
	Who then will contend against me?
	Let us appear together!
	Who will be plaintiff against me?
	Let him approach.

[14] John 17:4. [16] Matth. 11:20-24. [18] Acts 13:47.
[15] Matth. 23:37. [17] Matth. 21:43.

50:9	See, the Lord, Yahweh, supports me.
	Now who is there who will condemn me?
	See, they all fall apart like a garment,
	the moth devours them.
50:10	Whoever among you fears Yahweh,
	let him listen to the voice of his servant.
	Whoever walks in darkness,
	whoever feels no gleam of light,
	let him trust in the Name of Yahweh
	and rely upon his God.
50:11	See, you all are persons who start fires
	and kindle brands.
	Walk, then, in the flames of your fires,
	and among the brands that you have kindled.
	Such will you experience at my hand,
	in torments you will lie.

V. 4–6. Again the Servant appears as sent by Yahweh. What he preaches, God inspires. For a long time Moses resisted God's call, but the Servant immediately accords obedience to the divine mission. Moses did not possess the gift of speech,[19] the Servant is well equipped in this regard. His mission is directed to the oppressed and disheartened,[20] to them he will bring consolation. Nevertheless Yahweh informs him how those to whom he is being sent will reject his doctrine,[21] how they will persecute him openly, will berate and torment him. The lot of all the prophets will be his, especially that of suffering like Jeremias. Plucking at one's beard is extremely painful, and to the Oriental, moreover, deeply insulting. Because the Ammonites offended David by cutting off the beards of his legates, war ensued between the two nations.[22] Spitting upon one was a grave offense.[23] The Servant, however, patiently bears all such insults and torments.

V. 7. Yahweh gives him strength, even as He made Jeremias like a well fortified city, an iron pillar, a strong wall;[24] or as He endowed Moses with courage to persevere when he longed for death in the midst of hostile attacks.[25]

V. 8. The Servant remains unshaken in his attachment to God. He challenges his opponents to bring their cases before Yahweh, conscious that his cause is just. Anyone who dares attack him falls into the judgment of God.

V. 9. In 49:6 the Servant received the mission to the Gentiles because Israel refused to listen; here too Israel acts most unfriendly. The Servant is certain of final triumph despite the action his foes take against him. They will come to nought as a garment eaten by moths.

[19] Ex. 4:10.   [20] Is. 42:3.   [23] Num. 12:14; Deut. 25:9; Job 30:10;
[21] Is. 49:4.   Matth. 26:30, 67.
[22] 2 Sam. 10:4; cf. Is. 7:20.   [24] Jer. 1:18.   [25] Num. 11:11.

Vv. 10–11 are a later addition by the prophet himself or by another hagiographer. The Servant, who pleads for a willing audience, is the same person as in the preceding lines. He encourages the goodhearted to greater trust and confidence in God, and then his exhortation changes into a divine threat. The obstinate, i.e., the greater part of Israel, are threatened by God with the fire of judgment. Those who had plotted the ruin of the Servant and his death by fiery tortures suffer the very fate they had prepared for him.

There is an advance in the thought content over the second hymn in that the Servant describes the insults and persecution he suffers, humiliations which he bears in greatest patience.

It was Jesus' "food to do the will of him, who sent him." [26] He openly declared: "I have not spoken on my own initiative, but he who sent me, the Father, he has enjoined upon me what I should say and what I should speak." [27] Only that which the Father had commanded did He will to preach. And for that reason was He persecuted, scourged, spit upon, blasphemed. Especially during the dark night of the sacred passion were the words of the third Song fulfilled in Him after He had pleaded with the Father: "Not my will be done but thine!" When the Great Council solemnly demanded a statement as to whether He was the Son of God, He did not flinch although He well knew that His answer would be regarded as blasphemy, and that it would occasion His death sentence.[28]

§31. THE FOURTH HYMN
Is. 52:13 — 53:12

52:13	Behold, my Servant will succeed,
	he will be great, he will advance and become illustrious.
52:14	How many have been startled over him —
	for disfigured, his appearance no longer was human,
	and his form no longer like the children of men —
52:15	thus will he amaze many nations;
	before him kings will shut their mouths,
	for they will see what had never been told them,
	and discover what they had never heard.

[26] John 4:34.   [27] John 12:49.   [28] Matth. 26:64.

53:1   Who would have believed the report made to us,
        and the arm of Yahweh — to whom was it revealed?

53:2   As a tender plant he grew before him,
        as a sprout on sterile ground.
    Neither appearance nor beauty did he have
        that we might have admired him,
        nothing noble that we might have rejoiced over him.

53:3   He was despised, he was the last among men,
        a man of sorrows, well-versed in suffering,
    as one before whom men cover their faces.
    He was despised, and we did not esteem him.

53:4   Yet it was our sufferings that he bore,
        and our sorrows that he took upon himself.
    And we regarded him as smitten,
        chastised by God and humbled.

53:5   But it was for our sins that he was pierced,
        stricken for our transgressions.
    He was bruised for our salvation,
        and through his stripes came our healing.

53:6   Like sheep we all had gone astray,
        each of us had wandered off on his own path,
    while against him Yahweh directed
        all our guilt.

53:7   Mistreated, he humbly complied,
        and did not open his mouth.
    Like a lamb led to slaughter,
        like a sheep dumb before her shearers,
        he did not open his mouth.

53:8   Through torment and judgment did he die.
        And his generation — was anyone concerned
    that he was cut off from the land of the living,
        stricken to death because of the sins of my people?

53:9   They allotted him a grave with the wicked,
        with evildoers, when he died;
    even though he had done nothing unjust,
        and no deceit could be found in his mouth.

53:10   For it was Yahweh's good pleasure to smite him
        and make him suffer.
    Upon sacrificing his life as a guilt-offering
        he will see posterity and live long,
        and through him Yahweh's plan will prosper.

53:11   (In reward) for the afflictions of his soul
        he will see (the light) and be filled.
    Through his knowledge my (just) Servant will justify many;
        and their guilt — that he will bear.

53:12   Therefore I will grant him many as his portion,
        countless will be his booty
    because he laid down his life in death,
        was counted among the wicked,
    while bearing the sins of many,
        and interceding for evildoers.

In the first song Yahweh presented His Servant as a prophet whose mission would embrace both Israel and all Gentile nations upon the earth. In the second the Servant complained over having accomplished so little. In the third he recounted the persecution he experienced because of his activity and confessed how he was relying wholly upon Yahweh. The fourth poem brings the series to a climax. We learn that the Servant not only suffered, but that he was unjustly put to death, that he voluntarily embraced suffering and death itself to atone for the sins of those who tormented him and those for whom he labored; moreover, that he rose from the abode of death to new life. The text in many instances is corrupt, emendations are difficult and doubtful, but the import of the passage is not uncertain. The prophet speaks as if death and resurrection were a matter of the past.

52:13. Yahweh speaks, as in the first poem. The Servant's passion and death are over, the time for reward has come. In the second and third poem the Servant's work seemed unsuccessful, but now the scene is one of unparalleled triumph. His work had not been in vain. Employing three different settings, Yahweh heralds the glory of His Servant so long despised and humiliated. The nations are amazed at the transformation, while kings place their hands over their mouths to indicate the failure of words to express their fear and homage.[29] What everyone believed impossible had taken place: the Servant arose from the grave, as the following verses show.

53:1. The Jews are speaking, not the Gentiles; and on their lips the prophet places a confession of guilt. It had been the Jews who opposed the Servant's preaching, had persecuted, and had put him to death. The scene before their eyes now, they had deemed impossible. They had not believed the oracles of the prophets, nor the words of the Servant. They had shunned the Man of Sorrows. As if to explain their conduct and excuse their guilt, they point out the unpretentious character of the Servant's origin and advent. For he indeed had been the sprout from Jesse's root, concerning whom Isaias long since had spoken.[30] He was a descendant of a family that no longer enjoyed status.

Before Him, viz., before Yahweh, he grew to manhood. That Yahweh would employ the lowly and unpretentious to accomplish His greatest work never entered their minds. Moreover, the afflictions, the sufferings, the ignominy which the Servant bore — these were certain signs in their estimation that God was venting His wrath. For they regarded suffering as due punishment for sin. It was a grave error, at least in the case of the Servant (53:4). He deserved no punishment, and what he bore, he suffered in behalf of those who persecuted him, to expiate their sins, to

---

[29] Cf. Mich. 7:16; Job 21:5; 29:9; 40:4.   [30] Is. 11:10.

obtain forgiveness for them from God. This they now realized. They themselves were the sinners, sheep that had strayed on devious ways while Yahweh apportioned to His Servant the judgment they had merited.

From verse 7 on the prophet speaks.[31] He begins a meditation upon the sufferings and expiatory death of the Servant. During his passion the Servant manifested indescribable patience. Moses, Elias, Job became impatient in the trials God sent them, and wished to die. No word of complaint crossed the Servant's lips. While his enemies resembled sheep that strayed from their divine Shepherd, the Servant was like an innocent lamb obedient to its shepherd even unto the altar of death. Twice the prophet notes: "He did not open his mouth." His death, as verse 8 tells us, was the result of a judicial sentence, an innocent man hurried off to death in atonement for the sins of mankind. The word *dor* in verse 8 is best explained as referring to the Servant's contemporaries; though responsible for the Servant's excruciating death, they remained indifferent, showed no sorrow. Such a base spirit the prophet could not overlook. Of the textual emendations suggested, the most acceptable would be *darko*, his portion, i.e., his death, which made no impression upon them. Patristic writers applied the Vulgate reading, *generationem eius quis enarrabit*, to the eternal generation of the Son from the Father, or to His human birth from Mary, or to the resurrection. But the word *dor* does not mean to beget.

V. 9. Jewish animosity and hatred did not cease with the death of their victim. They sought to deny the Servant an honorable burial, insisting that he remain among the evildoers with whom he had died. If verse 9 is translated, "And (but) he rested with the rich after death," it would imply that divine Providence had confounded the plans of the Servant's enemies and that he did obtain an honorable burial. Our thoughts would go to Joseph of Arimathea, the rich counsellor, who petitioned Pilate for the body of Jesus and interred it in his own new tomb where no one had previously been placed.[32] Because the reading did have so remarkable a fulfillment, the corrupt text has seemed very plausible. However, instead of *'ašir*, with a rich (man), read *'oše ra'*, with evildoers, as required by the parallelism.

V. 10. The interchange of the perfect with the imperfect consecutive and the imperfect points to some future person and to future events. The prophet regards the action as present or as already belonging to the past. The unparalleled suffering and patience of the Servant cannot remain unrewarded. It had been Yahweh who permitted his passion and death. Therefore, Yahweh now speaks again (verse 10c), as at the

---

[31] Cf. 8b.   [32] Matth. 27:57-60.

opening of the poem. The Servant had surrendered himself as a "guilt offering" for offenses against Yahweh's honor.[33] By this sacrifice he atoned for sin. As a reward he will not be denied posterity. Since the Servant had suffered a violent death and had been buried, "posterity" must necessarily be taken in a spiritual sense, i.e., the many who were saved by his death and were made sharers in the love of their God. He will "live long" after he died and was buried, i.e., he will rise to a new life which cannot be crushed out; and through him Yahweh's plan for the reconciliation of mankind will be realized. He suffered, and therefore must also see the light, i.e., life.[34]

This word too is best interpreted as referring to the resurrection. True, the eschatalogical ideas of the Jews during the exilic period were still undeveloped, but the final destiny of the Servant was exceptional, just as he stands unique in his call and in his suffering. "He will be filled" with the joys that are his portion. "Through his knowledge," viz., his suffering and his death which were required and accepted by God as a sacrifice for the sins of the world, he will justify "many," all, viz., for whom he suffered and died and with whom he shares this "knowledge," both Jews and Gentiles. The poem closes with a summary of the Servant's work, 1) he bears the guilt of mankind, 2) he vicariously atones for their sins, 3) in unparalleled patience he intercedes for those who tortured and put him to death in order that God would give to these evildoers the grace of conversion.

In all religious history we find but One who suffered and died to redeem mankind, and One who rose to new life from a grave — Jesus. He was "a sign that would be contradicted," as Simeon proclaimed.[35] In the Gospel account of Christ's passion we have the best commentary on the fourth Servant of Yahweh poem. Christ was the Lamb of God who takes away the sins of the world,[36] to quote the words with which John the Baptist presented Him to the people.[37] He came in order "to lay down his life as a ransom ($\lambda \acute{v} \tau \rho o \nu$, '$a\check{s}am$) for many."[38] Upbraiding the unbelief of the Jews, He referred to the prophet's words in Is. 53:1.[39] On the way to Mount Olivet Jesus reminded His disciples, "It must be fulfilled in me what was written: He will be classed with evildoers."[40] His innocence[41] was acknowledged by Pilate,[42] by Judas,[43] by the crucified thieves.[44] When Pilate led Jesus scourged and thorn-crowned before the crowd, he believed the mob would yield through sympathy: *Ecce homo!*[45] His blood was shed for many unto the forgiveness of

[33] Lev. 5:14.
[34] Cf. Ps. 49:20. The Septuagint reading, light, is confirmed by a Hebrew manuscript found in 1947 north of the Dead Sea from pre-Christian times which has '*or*, light.
[35] Luke 2:34. [36] Is. 53:7.

[37] John 1:29, 36.
[38] Is. 53:10; Matth. 20:28.
[39] John 12:38.
[40] Luke 22:37; Is. 53:12.
[41] Is. 53:4, 5, 8. [42] Matth. 27:24.
[43] Matth. 27:4. [44] Luke 23:41.
[45] John 19:5; Is. 52:14; 53:2-3.

sins.[46] Condemned by the religious and secular authorities as a malefactor,[47] He was "obedient to death on the Cross" [48] and while on the Cross He prayed for those who had plotted His death.[49]

The apostles believed the message of our poem fulfilled in Jesus. Peter reminded the faithful that they like sheep had wandered into devious ways,[50] but found healing through the stripes [51] of Him who had done no sin and in whose mouth no deceit was found.[52] It was Christ who arose from the dead to die now no more; [53] to Him God gave the Name that is above all names.[54] This fourth poem provided Philip with the opportunity to discuss Jesus and His work with the treasurer to the queen of Ethiopia.[55] The picture of the Lamb led to slaughter is not absent from the last book of the New Testament.[56]

The apostles, however, did have difficulty in accustoming themselves to the idea of a suffering and dying Messiah. When Jesus explained how it was His Father's will that the Jews should put Him to death but that He would rise again on the third day, Peter exclaimed: "This must not happen to you." Jesus strongly reprehended him for such an attitude.[57] When they finally realized that their Master must suffer and die they "became very sorrowful." [58] Even after the crucifixion, the disciples from Emmaus were greatly disturbed: "We had hoped that he would redeem Israel." [59] Only after our Savior's ascension and the descent of the Holy Spirit did it become clear how Jesus was obliged "to suffer in order to enter into his glory." [60] Then only did His followers understand how to distinguish the kingdom upon earth from the kingdom awaiting us in heaven.

§32. VARIOUS INTERPRETATIONS OF THE SERVANT OF YAHWEH POEMS

Patristic writers are unanimous in their conviction that the Servant of Yahweh poems sketch for us a picture of the Redeemer. Nor did the Protestant reformers make any change in the traditional interpretation of these prophecies. Only when higher criticism toward the end of the eighteenth century no longer regarded the second part of the Book of

[46] Matth. 26:28.
[47] Is. 53:8.
[48] Phil. 2:8.
[49] Is. 53:12 ; Luke 23:34.
[50] Is. 53:6.

[51] Is. 53:8.
[52] Is. 53:9 ; 1 Pet. 2:22-25.
[53] Is. 53:10 ; Rom. 6:9.
[54] Is. 52:13 ; Phil. 2:9.
[55] Acts 8:26-40.

[56] Apoc. 5:6.
[57] Matth. 16:21-26.
[58] Matth. 17:22.
[59] Luke 24:21.
[60] Luke 24:26.

Isaias as the composition of the prophet who lived in the eighth century, was the Messianic interpretation of the Ebed-Yahweh poems abandoned by many. New interpretations still appear at regular intervals, and the literature upon this problem is enormous.

a) *The Collective Interpretation.* Perhaps the most widely propounded interpretation is that which explains the phrase "Servant of Yahweh" in the Book of Isaias as referring to the people of Israel. Israel was beloved by Yahweh, and had been entrusted with a special spiritual mission.[61] She was under obligation to subject herself to God's will and to preserve Yahwistic monotheism for the nations of the whole earth.

This interpretation is not a new one.[62] Nevertheless, it is extremely difficult to prove the necessary organic relationship of these four poems to the remaining content of the book, a fact that militates notably against the collective interpretation. One immediately senses the great difference, even opposition, between Israel as Yahweh's servant and the Servant in our four poems. Israel suffered exile because she had deserved such visitation; it had been heralded as her punishment by Amos, Osee, Isaias, Jeremias, Ezechiel; and the author of Second Isaias himself portrayed the exile as a just chastisement.[63]

Israel had been addicted to sin from the very first years of her existence.[64] But the Servant of these poems is innocent and suffers for the sins of others.[65] Israel was obdurate in her suffering and wrangled over her lot;[66] the Servant is patient.[67] Israel was fainthearted, pusillanimous, and God was obliged to admonish perseverance;[68] the Servant loses himself wholly in the will of God.[69] Israel was blind and deaf to divine admonitions;[70] the Servant proclaims God's message with fullest enthusiasm.[71] Israel rejoiced in that vengeance would come upon her oppressors;[72] the Servant suffers willingly and intercedes for his oppressors.[73]

The Servant had the mission of conveying the divine will to Israel and of leading her to God as Moses once did.[74] In addition he received the mission to herald the consoling truth of monotheism to the Gentile world, while Israel's portion was to preserve the knowledge of the true God until the time for fulfillment came and the Messiah appeared. The Servant died and was buried. The exile was indeed regarded as the nation's grave and the liberation as her resurrection;[75] but the Servant was buried in the same tomb as evildoers. If the Gentiles are equated with the evildoers, where was their grave? They were not in exile.

---

[61] Is. 41:8-9; 42:19; 44:1-2, 21; 45:4; 48:20; cf. also Jer. 30:10; Ez. 28:25; 37:25.
[62] Cf. p. 139.
[63] Is. 40:2; 42:23-25; 43:22-28; 47:6; 50:1; 54:6.
[64] Is. 43:27. [65] Is. 53:4-5.
[66] Is. 40:27; 44:4; 49:14; 50:1-2.

[67] Is. 53:7.
[68] Is. 41:10; 44:2, 21.
[69] Is. 49:4. [70] Is. 42:19.
[71] Is. 42:3-4; 49:6.
[72] Is. 41:15-16; 42:13.
[73] Is. 53:12.
[74] Is. 42:3, 6-7; 49:6, 8-9a.
[75] Ez. 37.

Due to the difficulties which beset the collective interpretation of the Servant as the people of Israel, some scholars have pointed to an *ideal Israel*, the Israel which should have existed according to God's will, in contradistinction to the historical Israel or the Israel that actually existed. But how would this ideal Israel that never existed experience suffering and death, and how was this ideal Israel buried?

Others, accordingly, conjecture that the prophet is describing a *pious minority* in Israel, the better portion of the Chosen People; these could be viewed as a *type* of the Messiah. While in exile was this pious minority persecuted by the mass of people and put to death? Did they die for their fellow men? Did they celebrate a resurrection? Did they have a mission to the Gentiles?

Neither does the collective interpretation become more reasonable when applied to the prophets as a body, or to the teachers of the Law. True, the Servant is described as a prophet, and his duty included teaching the Torah or Law; but he is not presented as a group. The bands of prophets at the time of Samuel and Elias did not have the task and lot ascribed to the Servant; they were plain, ordinary prophets, each with some personal mission. And the teachers of the Law were obligated to instruct Israelites, not the Gentiles; they never received from God the duty of suffering and dying and thereby effect the nation's redemption. While to point to the mission of some single prophet or some individual scribe eliminates the hypothesis from the class of collective interpretation.

b) *The Individual Interpretation.* The realization that the poems concern an individual, not a community, has occasioned the assumption that some person is described who had lived prior to or at the time of the author. Various names have been proposed: Moses; Isaias; Jeremias; Ezechiel; Job; King Ozias, who suffered from leprosy; [76] Josias, who died a hero's death for his people; Joachin, who was led away into captivity but then was pardoned by Evil Merodach; Sassabasar, whom Cyrus installed as governor in Judah; Zorobabel, who led the exiles on their return to Palestine; Mosollam, the son of Zorobabel; [77] Eleazar, the martyr from the age of the Machabees; or some unknown person who suffered martyrdom in the exile and whom the prophet sought to glorify in his poems.

When the prophets speak of the future, they frequently use the perfect tense in Hebrew, hence the term *perfectum propheticum.* They see events scheduled to happen in the distant future as present, as current actualities. Note too how the perfect changes to the imperfect repeatedly in these poems.

[76] Suggested by *nagua'* in Is. 53:4, rendered in the Vulgate as *quasi leprosus*; the word, however, does not have this specialized meaning. [77] 1 Chr. 3:19.

The individuals listed above do bear certain similarities with the Servant described in the poems: Moses and the prophets were called to their mission by God and were obliged to undergo much suffering; Cyrus liberated the exiles. But all the points mentioned apply to no single person, and none had the mission of bringing the true religion to the Gentile nations. No one arose from the grave to a new life, and no one's lot changed so suddenly and wonderfully that nations and kings became amazed. Because of the difficulty in applying all the details to any specific historical personage, Sellin, a proponent of individual inter-pretation, changed his theory four times within forty years: in 1898 it was Zorobabel, in 1901 and 1908 it was Joachin, in 1922 Moses, in 1930 the author of Is. 40—55; and in 1937 he proposed that the author of Is. 56—66 commemorated the death of the author of Is. 40—55 in the Fourth Servant of Yahweh poem. Now if the Servant was some unknown in-dividual whom the prophet regarded as the Messiah and whom he therefore wished to glorify, he would have been the victim of a grand delusion when his hero died and did not rise again, and when his suf-fering and death obtained no significance for the Gentiles. Would any poet erect a monument in verse to such a hero?

According to Mowinckel's "autobiographical interpretation," which has had a considerable following,[78] the prophet to whom we owe Is. 40—55 speaks of himself in the Ebed-Yahweh poems. The treasurer from Ethiopia had just read Is. 53 when he asked Philip, "I pray you, of whom is the prophet saying this, of himself or of some one else?"[79] Any evaluation of authorship should grant the sacred writer a degree of humility and self-reserve. Would an inspired poet praise his own pa-tience in suffering, regard himself as a second Moses, ascribe to himself a mission to the nations of the whole world, believe he would amaze kings and peoples? That he spoke of a resurrection some critics ascribe to a high fever from which he must have suffered![80] Others, over-emphasizing the differences between the first three poems and the fourth, attribute the latter to one of the poet's disciples who hoped for the resurrection of his master.[81] If so, the disciple would have regarded his master superior to man or prophet — the Messiah, living already in exile times, without however accomplishing the Messianic mission!

c) *The Cultic-mythical Interpretation.* The trend of recent Oriental research and science to search out Biblical parallels to Babylonian myths has occasioned interpretations of the Ebed-Yahweh passages from this viewpoint. Some scholars point to Adonis[82] and Tammuz, for Adonis is a Phoenician divinity, Tammuz a Sumerian-Babylonian god,

---

[78] After ten years the author aban-doned his own interpretation.
[79] Acts 8:34.
[80] E. Balla, *Eucharisterion*; Gunkel, *Festschrift* I, 1923, 246.
[81] Sellin, in 1937.   [82] Cf. Is. 17:10.

the son of the beloved Ishtar; both are symbols of death and revival in the world of nature. This natural cycle, at least that of dying, was celebrated each year.[83] Imagination provided the incentive to invent the figure of the suffering servant. The "servant" consequently would be a savior imported from Babylon.

Indeed, Tammuz was honored to some extent among the Jews before the exile, but Ezechiel condemned the practice as idolatry and proclaimed the destruction of the city and the temple as punishment for this and similar aberrations; and the author of Is. 40–55 likewise took a strong stand against Babylonian idol worship. Consequently it is highly questionable whether the same sacred writer would have painted Israel's Savior in colors borrowed from the Babylonian pantheon. When he speaks of the death and resurrection of the Servant, he considers it an event that happens but once; the Servant's resurrection is a great marvel, while nature dies each year and each year rises with chronological monotony to new life. Tammuz descended into the netherworld as the grain was being harvested and vegetation was withering in the Oriental heat; there he remained until spring when refreshing, life-giving rains began to fall. Job expressly denied that man can be compared to a tree that sprouts again after it has been felled; [84] resurrection in nature, therefore, was not correlated with human destinies in Israel.

Nevertheless, the Israelite knew of a number of physical revivals effected by the prophets Elias and Eliseus [85] and the case of the dead man restored to life noted in 4 Kgs. 13:21. When Isaias promised to work a miracle for Achaz in the depths of the underworld,[86] he was offering to bring someone back from sheol. In Is. 53 the Servant dies in order to expiate the sins of mankind. This ethical consideration comes natural to the mission of the Servant, but it formed no part of the Babylonian myth.

Other writers have referred to a ceremony that took place in Babylon during the New Year's feast. On the fifth day of the twelve day celebration, the king removed the insignia of his royal dignity. The high priest brought him before Marduk, struck him on the cheek, pulled his ears, and ordered him to kneel down and recite a penitential prayer protesting his innocence. Thereupon the high priest restored the royal insignia to the king and struck him once more on the cheek.[87] This ceremony is said to have offered the inspiration for Is. 53, with the Babylonian king metamorphosed into a humble penitent for Israel!

No mention is made of the fact that the king never suffered death, that the ceremony was repeated year after year without causing any

[83] Ez. 8:14.
[84] Job 14:7-9.
[85] 3 Kgs. 17:17-24 ; 4 Kgs. 4:31-37.
[86] Is. 7:11.
[87] AOT 302.

consternation among nations or rulers, that the king's action blotted out no sins for any people. Neither did our Servant suffer as did Babylon's king. His humiliation was no mere ceremony, but a painful reality. He offered his blood and his life, dying as a prophet and as the herald of God's holy will. Moreover, there were many prophets in Israel who in consequence of performing their mission were tormented and persecuted, or even put to death. It would not have been necessary for our poet to borrow from some foreign source.

Finally, there are authors who link our Servant poems with the Babylonian "Sickness Psalms" in which the sufferer comes to the portals of the underworld and a divinity leads him back to life. How the Babylonians would describe the approach of death might be shown by a few quotations. A seriously ill king said: "The grave was already open; before I was dead the lamentations were made. My whole land said: How he has come to ill!" Of course, the sick king became well again; it was an instance of the danger of death, not of actual death; and this is evident to the reader throughout.

A similar approach is found in certain Old Testament texts where the author uses the occasion to praise God's power. Oppressed by enemies, one of the psalmists exclaimed: "The bands of the netherworld enmeshed me, the snares of death overtook me." [88] Another psalmist voiced his gratitude when delivered from the danger of death: "Yahweh, you have raised up my soul from the netherworld, you have led me back to life away from those who sink into the grave." [89] On the verge of despair we hear the complaint: "You have placed me in the bottommost pit, in thick darkness, in the darkest abyss." [90] In similar terms the Canticle of Anna describes God's power: "Yahweh puts to death and makes alive, he brings down to sheol and raises up again." [91] In all these passages it is clear that the individual did not actually die; there is present an element of hyperbole. But in Is. 53 the poet expressly says that the Servant died and was buried.

d) *The Messianic Interpretation.* We have noted serious objections against the interpretation that the Servant in the Ebed-Yahweh poems is a) the people of Israel, b) some historical person, c) an ideal figure, d) an adaptation from Babylonian mythology. There remains the interpretation of the apostles, of the Fathers of the Church, and of many exegetes down through the centuries that the Servant is the promised Messiah. Even here there have been aberrations; for the expectations of the prophet were fulfilled in the life and resurrection of Jesus not merely as a matter of "common faith"; nor can it only be established "historically" that Jesus made Is. 53 "the outline of His life's work and

[88] Ps. 18:6.   [89] Ps. 30:4.   [90] Ps. 85:7.   [91] 1 Sam. 2:6.

in this Old Testament passage saw God's plan for shaping His way of acting." [92]

Since in our explanation of the poems we noted their fulfillment in Jesus Christ, a summary suffices here. Jesus was sent to the people of Israel, but He likewise was commissioned by His heavenly Father to bring salvation and true religion to all men. He appeared as a prophet and was rewarded by His people with gross ingratitude. Innocent, He was persecuted, scourged, and condemned to death through a judicial sentence. In His life and in His death He prayed for His adversaries. He offered Himself as an atonement sacrifice for the sins of the world. And after He had risen from the dead, He gained a following from among Gentiles and kings.

One difficulty that may be adduced is that the poet seemingly orients much of what he says to the past, including the Servant's death and burial. Now keep constantly in mind the nature of Semitic idiom, and how, for example, the prophets propose future events as already accomplished because they were absolutely certain of their fulfillment. These texts present the Messiah not as the son of David or as a king as do the older prophecies, but rather as a prophet or a second Moses who suffers at the hands of his people,[93] who prays for his people,[94] who is ready to die for them,[95] who arranges a covenant between Yahweh and Israel and confirms it with sacrificial blood.[96] Just as Moses was called to the office of prophet while the people were languishing in slavery so that he could liberate them, so too the Servant should lead the exiles back home. The return from exile, however, and with it the Servant's appearance was expected momentarily. This is another peculiarity of prophetic vision, it does not distinguish sharply between events happening at some future date. Our prophet did not see too clearly how the return into the Promised Land was in itself a preparation and a type for a far more lofty deliverance from the bondage of sin. St. Paul's words, *ex parte cognoscimus et ex parte prophetamus*,[97] may be applied very profitably to the oracles found in the Old Testament.

The figure of the Servant of Yahweh was not an entirely new creation. True, he is not equated with the Messiah-King of pre-exilic times, yet he is alluded to as the "sprout," he is equipped with the spirit of God, he appears as "light," he brings justice to the nations. All these are familiar Messianic concepts. His suffering had already been insinuated in the prophecies describing the disintegration of the house of David,[98] the loss of the royal throne,[99] and the need of subsisting on curd and wild honey during his earliest years.[1] Moreover, there existed the prophecy

---

[92] Cf. Bentzen, 42.
[93] Deut. 1:37 ; 3:26 ; 4:11.
[94] Deut. 9:17-20.
[95] Ex. 32:32.
[96] Ex. 24.
[97] 1 Cor. 13:9.
[98] Am. 9:11.
[99] Is. 11:1.
[1] Is. 7:15.

of the Innocent Sufferer, the One abandoned by all the world and tortured to the point of death.[2]

Nor was the concept of vicarious atonement foreign to the Israelitic mind. Mosaic Law enjoined atonement sacrifices in which the blood of an animal was shed to obtain forgiveness from sin. On the Day of Atonement the scapegoat bore the guilt of the people away from the sanctuary.[3] Moses was willing to offer his life as a victim if God would pardon the sinful people.[4] The youngest of the Machabean brothers accepted suffering and death to atone for the sins of his fellow men.[5] The people who witnessed the fall of the Davidic dynasty and were marched away into exile would naturally think of the coming Redeemer as a man destined for suffering. Nevertheless, the prophet took this major step in the development of the Messianic picture not because of his own reflections but because of divine revelation.

Our prophet of exile times portrayed the Redeemer as a Man of Sorrows who, though innocent, dies for the people. He sought to give the exiles a model of innocence and patience so that they would realize their guilt and contritely accept their punishment. The Messiah should not only be the ruler from David's family, he would also be the humiliated and persecuted Servant *par excellence*. Easy as it should have been, the Jews found it extremely difficult to reconcile these two pictures of the Messiah. The Targum referred Is. 42:1 and 52:12 to the Messiah, the second Servant poem to Israel, the third to the prophets, while the passages treating of vicarious expiation were changed into petitions by the Servant. The Talmud Bab. Sanh. 98 understood Is. 53:4 of the Messiah. Since the twelfth century the Jews have favored the collective interpretation.[6]

---

[2] Ps. 22.
[3] Lev. 16.
[4] Ex. 32:32.
[5] 2 Mach. 7:38.
[6] Brierre-Narbonne, 41f. Strack-Billerbeck II, 282, 286, 290, 291. M. J. Lagrange, *Le Messianisme chez les Juifs*, 242-247. Ed. König, *Die mess. Weissagungen*, 321-337.

Postexilian Messianic Prophecy

§33. SION, THE CENTER OF THE MESSIANIC KINGDOM
Is. 60

With intense longing the exiles awaited the dissolution of Babylonian world power as foretold by the prophets. Jeremias long since had predicted the exile's end, if only after seventy years. When Cyrus became king of the Persians, prophets appeared among the Jews living in Babylonia who interpreted for them the signs of the times. In the past the Medes in alliance with the Chaldeans had administered the death blow to Assyria. Now the exiles heard: these same Medes will destroy the Babylonian regime, the tyrant oppressing God's people.[7] The very prophet who heralded the coming Redeemer as Yahweh's Servant proclaimed the joyous news: "Comfort, comfort my people! Finished is her time of service, cancelled is her guilt!"[8] The hour of deliverance had come, Babylon's sway soon would cease.[9]

In triumphant style Cyrus entered Babylon, greeted by the inhabitants as a deliverer. And upon grasping Marduk's hands, he publicly assumed the reins of government. One of his first official acts was to grant the Jews permission to return to their fatherland and rebuild the

[7] Is. 13:1—14:23.   [8] Is. 40:1.   [9] Is. 43:14; 46:1-2; 47:1; 48:14.

temple of their God.[10] For it was his policy to rehabilitate the nations displaced forcibly by previous regimes and to restore the cult of their gods.[11]

Nevertheless, not all the Jews availed themselves of the privilege. As long as they had been oppressed, the desire for freedom burned brightly, but now the change in government brought them equality and the opportunity of obtaining positions in the government itself. Already during the second half of the exile many Jews had settled in the larger cities, had developed a taste for business, had discovered how it was possible to obtain a goodly income with less effort than by cultivating fields. A new generation born in Babylon had grown up and had become acclimated to the environment. Should they now sell their lands and houses and businesses? Was it certain that they could reclaim the patrimony of their fathers in distant Canaan? Would those whose forefathers had been poor in Palestine find adequate income, equal to that now had in Babylon?

Those in financial difficulties found it easier to make the decision; and some were prompted by lofty ideals. Many remained, certainly more than half. Nor may we deduce from their action that religion meant little to them, for they believed the interests of their people would be better served if they made their influence felt in Babylon and financed those who departed.

The small group who left Babylon under the leadership of Zorobabel and the high priest Josue were convinced of being "the remnant, the holy seed" from which a new Israel would rise.[12] Hardly two centuries previously Isaias had proclaimed that the return of God's dispersed people would be accompanied by great marvels. Yahweh would dry up "the tongue of the sea of Egypt" as in the days when Moses led the people away from the land of servitude. He would smite the Euphrates "into seven streamlets so that one could pass over in sandals."[13]

During that very generation a prophet was describing how the return would take place amidst astounding miracles: "Every valley will be raised, every hill and mountain will be leveled; the rough will become plain, and the rugged heights a valley."[14] The returning caravans would cut a way directly across the desert wilderness, nor would they suffer any lack of water.[15] Trees would spring up, their fruits would delight the wayfarers, and their shade refresh them.[16] Yahweh would precede His people and protect their rearguard.[17] Far more marvellous would this march be than that which once was made from Egypt.

Then suddenly the first great disillusionment. No miracles! The cara-

[10] Esdr. 1:2-4; 2 Chr. 36:22-23; Esdr. 6:3-5.   [11] AOT 370.   [12] Agg. 1:12; Zach. 8:6; Esdr. 9:2.
[13] Is. 11:15.   [14] Is. 40:3-4.
[15] Is. 41:18; 43:15-20; 48:21; 49:10.
[16] Is. 41:19; 55:11.   [17] Is. 52:12.

van followed the usual route. Then the re-settlement. Difficulties at every step. Those had the least troubles whose inheritance lay in ruins with land uncultivated; through hard work the idle fields again produced. A half century had passed since Nabuchodonosor granted the holdings of the deportees to the poorest among those who remained, and this undoubtedly involved practically all the tillable ground. After so many years of occupation they would not willingly leave their holdings. In Jerusalem abandoned houses were soon appropriated and repairs made, or upon the ruins new dwellings were erected, to which obviously the owners had legitimate claims.

Further trouble! Good harvests had been the rule in Babylonia, and they imagined that the oracles of the prophets on the marvellous fertility of Messianic times would be fulfilled — instead crop failures and drought! [18] They had hoped to ride in triumph over the pagan Gentiles,[19] actually the Edomites had extended their borders far into Jewish territory and would not retreat. More disappointment! Ezechiel had sketched a magnificent plan for the new temple, and Cyrus had "commanded" them to rebuild their sanctuary, according to the Chronicler's free rendering of the edict. With a portion of the money brought from Babylon a fund was created.[20] Upon beginning the foundation, however, the Samaritans and the Persian officials objected,[21] and it became impossible to accomplish even this project dedicated to Yahweh's honor. Again disillusionment!

At this point a prophet arose, most probably the same one who had prophesied Israel's return under the leadership of Yahweh's Servant. He too had promised them a glorious city [22] with walls of precious stones.[23] It had not come true. Before his eyes much still lay in ruins. But he did not lose courage; his oracles were not false, for they had come to him through divine inspiration. What he had prophesied would come to pass, but the Jews must first render themselves worthy of such tremendous privileges. He observed the religious spirit and ethical conduct of his contemporaries — how deplorable. There still were many without faith in the one true God, and morality left much to be desired. Some Jews were worshipping Gad and Mani, the gods of fate and fortune.[24] They were offering sacrifices under terebinths and in gardens,[25] they immolated their children to Moloch,[26] ate swine's flesh at cultic meals [27] and practiced necromancy.[28] In brief, their religion was harlotry, apostasy from Yahweh.[29] The prophet countered with the message: Prepare now for the blessings of the Messianic age. And he

18 Agg. 1:6, 9 ; Zach. 8:10.
19 Is. 55:5.
20 Esdr. 2:69 ; Neh. 7:69-71.
21 Esdr. 4:5.

22 Is. 49:18-22 ; 51:17-22.
23 Is. 54:11-12.
24 Is. 65:11.
25 Is. 57:5-6 ; 65:1 ; 66:17.

26 Is. 57:5-9.
27 Is. 65:4 ; 66:3.
28 Is. 65:4.
29 Is. 57:7-11.

sketched a picture of the new Jerusalem, one not unrelated to the prophecy in Is. 2:2–4 but far more colorful. He addressed Jerusalem:

Isaias

60:1	Arise! shine, for your Light has come,
	and Yahweh's glory beams radiantly upon you!
60:2	For see, darkness covers the earth,
	and dense gloom the nations.
	But upon you Yahweh is shining,
	and his glory is seen upon you.
60:3	In your light the nations walk —
	kings, in the brightness of your rays.
60:4	Lift up your eyes round about, and see:
	they all are gathered together, they are coming to you —
	your sons are coming from afar,
	your daughters carried at the hip.
60:5	Upon seeing it you will become radiant,
	your heart will throb and swell.
	For the wealth of the sea will come to you,
	and the treasures of the nations will be yours.
60:6	A mass of camels will cover you,
	camel colts from Midian and Ephah.
	From Sheba they all are coming,
	carrying gold and frankincense,
	proclaiming Yahweh's praises.
60:7	All Kedar's flocks gather about you,
	Nebaioth's rams stand at your disposal.
	They mount my altar as a pleasing offering,
	indeed, I will glorify the house of my glory.
60:8	Who are these that fly as a cloud,
	as doves to their cots?
60:9	Why, the islands are gathering unto me,
	led by ships from Tarshish,
	bringing your sons from afar,
	together with their silver and gold,
	unto the Name of Yahweh, your God,
	unto the Holy One of Israel, for he is glorifying you.

In Is. 9:1 the Messiah was heralded as the Light that would rise upon the pagan nations who walk in darkness. In the present passage Yahweh Himself is the Light that rises upon Sion while the remaining world abides in densest gloom. Frequently in the Old Testament Israel is depicted as a virgin; here the Holy City is likened to a woman, a mother anxiously longing to see her children. In Is. 2:2–4 the Gentiles pilgrimage to Sion for instruction in the true religion, here they journey to the Light in order to worship Yahweh. Not only do the nations come; the caravans include the dispersed of Israel brought along by the Gentiles. The Gentiles carry along their possessions, not as people oppressed and subjugated, but willingly, joyfully they place their treasures at Jerusalem's disposal. For it is a matter of the worship of the true God, it is a matter of the erection of His temple and the performance of His sacred cult. Therefore the Gentiles bring offerings of gold, frankincense, and cattle. Included in the caravans are Arabian traders, Syrian shepherds, inhabitants of the islands and coasts of the Mediterranean, and contingents even from distant Tartessus in Spain. All have but one intention, to worship and praise the true God.

The appearance of the Magi from the East with gifts of gold, frankincense, and myrrh for the new-born King of the Jews was a fulfillment of our prophecy; and therefore the Church uses the passage as the Lesson on the feast of Epiphany.

The prophet continues with a description of the restoration of Jerusalem's walls (verse 10), which lay before his eyes in ruins. Foreigners had destroyed the city, foreigners would rebuild it; and in the era of peace which then would begin, there would be no enemies. The city's gates would remain constantly open so that the wealth of the world might flow in unhindered. Foreigners would make it their principal concern to rebuild the temple, they would worship the true God, and acknowledge the pre-eminence of Sion, His sanctuary. The sons of those who burned the temple would restore what their fathers destroyed.

Jerusalem had been forsaken by Yahweh in punishment for her misdeeds. Now she again enjoys His good favor and becomes more illustrious than before. Often she had emptied her treasury in tribute to foreign nations, often her goods had been carted off as booty. Now, however, she is rich; gold and silver are more abundant than at the time of Solomon, nor are there limits to peace and justice.

Yahweh becomes Jerusalem's everlasting light, no longer does she need the rays of sun or moon. The sun sets, the moon vanishes, but Yahweh remains eternally. The days of mourning are past. Jerusalem's citizens no longer commit sin, all are upright men. There exists no further danger of deportation and exile, and the promises God made to the patriarchs receive their fulfillment — the children of Israel become as numerous as the stars in the sky, as the grains of sand on the seashore.

When the prophet was proclaiming these blessings, the Jewish community was small and poor. The returnees felt themselves oppressed, dependent upon the good will of neighboring tribes and Persian officials. The prophet's words were intended to fill them with hope, in time the strangers about them would worship Yahweh as the only God. Nevertheless, it was a picture of Messianic blessings painted in colors that could awaken grossly materialistic expectations.

§34. THE GLORY OF THE SECOND TEMPLE
Agg. 2:6-9

Before the exile most of the Jews were convinced that the presence of the temple implied a pledge of divine protection. They were little concerned over Yahweh's insistence upon monotheism and morality, an attitude which occasioned Jeremias' prediction of the temple's destruction as early as the reign of Joakim.[30] Ezechiel's vision of the demolition of the temple includes an insight into the high degree of idolatry practiced there. In 587 city and temple fell, the regular sacrifices ceased, and thereafter offerings were made only occasionally and upon an improvised altar.[31] After the return to Palestine, one of the first projects concerned the rebuilding of the house of God. In exile its importance had been recognized, and Ezechiel had sketched a plan. Almost immediately, however, the Jews were forced to abandon the project. But when Darius I gained control of the Persian government in the year 521, political conditions seemed favorable for resuming the work. The prophet Aggeus spoke encouragingly and inspired the Jews with enthusiasm.

But it was difficult to maintain morale. At the laying of the cornerstone the elders who had seen Solomon's temple shed tears as they realized that the new structure could never match the old. At his disposal Solomon had had the money and the material David collected, he was able to levy high taxes upon the twelve tribes, he exacted free labor from subject peoples, and Hiram of Tyre was ready to make substantial loans. The new community was small and poor. In drawing the plans little attention could be given to size and style. Now, even before the work was far advanced, the inadequacy of the edifice in comparison with Solomon's came vividly to their eyes: "Who is there yet among you who saw this house in its former glory, and how are you looking upon it now? Is it not as a non-entity in your eyes?"[32] But the realization that they could erect only a very modest sanctuary must not discourage them:

Aggeus

2:6   Thus says Yahweh of hosts: Again — after only a little while — will I
2:7   shake heaven and earth, the sea and the solid ground; and I will shake all the nations, and the treasures of all the nations will come hither, and I will fill this house with glory, says Yahweh of hosts.
2:8   Mine is the silver and mine is the gold, is the oracle of Yahweh of
2:9   hosts. The glory of this present house will be greater than that of the former, says Yahweh of hosts; and to this place I will grant peace, is the oracle of Yahweh of hosts.

[30] Jer. 7; 26.   [31] Jer. 41:4f; Bar. 1:10.   [32] Agg. 2:3.

The Jews had currently witnessed a great "shaking" in the political world. Darius finally obtained the throne, and the various rebellions against his hegemony had been crushed. There was another "shaking" in store, one more violent than that they just observed. Heaven and earth will be involved, and all nations will be affected. This event will be of greatest significance for the new house of God. It may be a modest structure, it may not stand comparison with that of Solomon.

Nevertheless, it will be to this edifice that the nations will bring their treasures. All the world's wealth, in the last analysis, belongs to Yahweh; His absolute claim will be acknowledged by men, they will see Him as the true God and worship Him. Thus this unpretentious building will play the greatest possible role in the spread of true religion. In the dedicatory prayer over the first temple, Solomon had petitioned Yahweh to answer the stranger "who came from distant lands for his Name's sake and prayed in this house." [33] There will come a time when not merely a few scattered pilgrims journey to the temple, the nations will bring their gifts in official fashion. Thus the glory of the new temple will far surpass that of Solomon's, and it would only be "a little while" until the conversion of mankind would occur. The event would introduce the era of universal peace for which mankind was longing and which the prophets had long foretold; this peace would consist not merely in freedom from external foes but in the full enjoyment of Messianic blessings.

As with other prophecies, a distinction must here be made between form and content.[34] Aggeus saw how the nations accepted Yahweh, and he presented this fact under the image of caravans bringing their treasures to Jerusalem's temple. Moreover, he chose this picture in order to console the Jews who, due to faintheartedness, might very easily discontinue building operations. A great future lay in store for their temple, the Messiah would bring the blessings for which they were waiting; and this would come to pass shortly, for their structure would still be standing when he appeared. The prophet sees the completion of the temple and the advent of the Redeemer in a single glance and recognizes no time interval between the two events. Little did he surmise how his prophecy received literal fulfillment when the Son of God was presented in the temple — for Herod's structure was only an elaboration upon Zorobabel's — and later appeared there to teach. Thereby the glory of the second temple truly became greater than Solomon's.

[33] 3 Kgs. 8:41-43.
[34] Cf. p. 204ff.

§35. THE BRANCH OF YAHWEH
Zach. 3:8-10; 6:9-15

Two months, after the first appearance of Aggeus, another prophet, Zacharias, lifted up his voice to encourage the people and their leaders in the temple project. In a series of eight visions — with an angel present as commentator — Zacharias beheld the rebuilding of Jerusalem and Israel's restoration to divine favor. The fourth of these visions, Zach. 3:1f., centered upon the high priest Josue. He appeared clothed in unclean garments, accused by Satan. But an angel of Yahweh opposed Satan, and angels dressed Josue in clean garments. The message: Josue's guilt was not personal, but as high priest he bore the sins of the Levitical priesthood during past generations. As long as he was in this condition neither he nor the other priests were able to offer acceptable sacrifices in atonement for the sins of the people; for the priest is mediator between men and God. Yahweh's wrath, therefore, continued against the Jews. Now, however, silence was divinely imposed upon Satan, and Josue forgiven. This enabled him to offer sacrifices and to bring the people's prayers before God. Then the angel of Yahweh turned his gaze to a more distant event:

Zacharias

3:8   Hear now, O high priest Josue, you and your companions who sit before you: men of good omen you truly are — for, behold, I will
3:9   send my servant, the branch. Now see, the stone which I laid before Josue, upon this stone are seven eyes. See, I am making an engraving upon it, is the oracle of Yahweh of hosts, and I am removing the guilt
3:10 of this land in a single day. On that day, is the oracle of Yahweh of hosts, you will invite each other under the vine and under the fig tree.

That these verses refer to the Messianic age is shown by the promise of Israel's full and thorough liberation from sin — she becomes a holy people. One recalls the vision of the flying scroll with its message of forgiveness and the creation of a holy people in Zach. 5:1–4, and the "epha vision" in Zach. 5:5–11 indicating the removal of sin itself along with all evil inclinations. The cleansing of the high priest Josue was imperfect, the beginning and figure of Messianic purification. On that "single day" all guilt will be blotted out, the day of redemption set by Yahweh. The promise of peace is likewise Messianic; the age of Solomon will return, as the prophets had foretold.

The blessings of Messianic times will come through "my servant, the branch." Clearly the Messiah is meant. Jeremias had spoken of the Messiah as the just bud from the house of David,[35] Isaias had proclaimed

---

[35] Jer. 23:5; 33:15.

him as the twig from Jesse's root,[36] Ezechiel referred to him as a tender
shoot,[37] and the exile's greatest prophet heralded him as "a sprig, a
shoot from sterile ground."[38] In Zacharias the word "branch" becomes
a proper name for the Redeemer.[39]

As the angel of Yahweh announced the appearance of the Messiah, he
turned to Josue and his companions who were seated before him, i.e.,
the entire Jewish priesthood. The Messiah's advent would indeed effect
the completion of the work imposed upon them, the purification of the
people. The angel calls them "men of omen"; they must continue their
work of purification, but they are figures of something far more noble.
The servant, the branch, will appear and purify Israel and all mankind
through a purification which need never be repeated.

Reference is suddenly made to a stone. This stone is given to Josue.
Upon it are seven eyes, a detail reminding us of Yahweh's seven eyes in
Zach. 4:10. It is a sign that Yahweh has turned His attention to the
stone. Upon it He intends to make an engraving. Its external appearance is unpretentious, but it is a precious stone whose value will be
revealed through Yahweh's efforts. Isaias had stated that Yahweh would
"lay a cornerstone in Sion, a proven stone, a precious foundation stone.
Whoever believes will never waver."[40] This foundation stone will be
no other than the Messiah who confers solidity upon the structure of
the Messianic kingdom. The temple then under construction resembled
an uncut diamond. But Yahweh will give it His attention, and it will
undergo a glorious completion when the "branch" comes and the people
are purified by him. The message is similar to that in Agg. 2:6–9, yet
while Aggeus speaks of the conversion of the nations, Zacharias stresses
the forgiveness of sins and Israel's sanctification.

At the close of the visions Zacharias is instructed to perform a symbolic action.[41] The Jews in Babylonia had sent a delegation to Jerusalem with contributions for the construction of the temple. A portion of
the silver and gold Zacharias should use to make a crown.[42] The word
'atereth is here used for crown, a term that properly designates the royal
head gear; the headband which the high priest wore at solemn functions
is called mişnephet.[43] It may appear strange that the high priest should
wear the crown; many exegetes hold that it was not meant for Josue
but for Zorobabel, and amend the text accordingly.

Zacharias
6:12   Speak to him therefore: Thus says Yahweh of hosts: Behold, a man,
        the branch is his Name! He will branch forth from that beneath

---

[36] Is. 11:1.
[38] Is. 53:2.
[40] Is. 28:16.
[41] Zach. 6:9-15.
[42] The Hebrew text gives the plural; perhaps a crown of several tiers is meant, but the Septuagint has the singular in

[37] Ez. 17:22.
[39] Zach. 6:12.

verse 14; and Septuagint manuscripts have the singular for v. 11; likewise the Masoretic text gives the singular form of the verb in v. 14. There can be no doubt but that a single crown is meant.
[43] In the Vulgate *tiara, mitra*; cf. p. 131 on Ez. 21:30-32.

6:13   him and he will build the temple of Yahweh. Yes, he will build the temple of Yahweh, and he will bear the glory and will sit upon the throne and govern. As a priest he will sit upon the throne, and
6:14   there will be peaceful relations between the two (powers). But the crown must remain in the temple of Yahweh as the gift of and a memorial to Helem, Tobias and Isaias, and to the son of Sophonias.
6:15   People who live in distant lands will come and work on rebuilding Yahweh's temple, and you will see that Yahweh of hosts has sent me to you. This will come to pass if you willingly listen to the voice of Yahweh, your God.

Josue received the crown not as a personal favor but in view of the branch whom he foreshadowed.[44] That the branch is the Messiah in this passage is evident from the whole context. Foreigners, Gentiles come to build the temple. The branch appears at some future date, he is not to be identified with Zorobabel. The branch rules as king, he is Yahweh's representative; and for this reason he receives symbolically a royal crown. He will build another temple, for the edifice then under construction was too inadequate to serve as the sanctuary of Messianic times. Gentiles will participate in its construction; likewise in Zach. 3:8 the completion of the sanctuary will take place in Messianic times. The branch will spring forth "from that beneath him." We recall the twig from the root of Jesse [45] and the upright sprout from David.[46] The branch receives David's throne, and clothed in royal attire he reigns as king.

But why did not Zacharias apply this symbolism to Zorobabel from whom the branch, David's son, actually descended? Deference to the Persian authorities could hardly have been the reason. For they could also have looked with suspicion upon the crowning of Josue; and Zorobabel did have their confidence, otherwise they would not have installed him as governor. In any case the political authorities could hardly have interpreted the action in terms of rebellion because the crown was not intended for the one upon whom it was placed but an individual of a future age.

According to Ps. 110:3 the Messiah will be priest forever. In that the high priest Josue received the royal crown is there an indication that the Messiah will possess the double office of king and priest? Verse 13b may be translated: "And a priest will sit upon his throne," viz., alongside the branch. But a priest needs no throne for the performance of his duties. Did Zacharias wish to imply that the Messiah would be restricted in his activity by the high priest, i.e., by priestly authorities with rights alongside his? If so, why did he not say "high priest," an expression he never omits when speaking of Josue? St. Jerome most probably

---

[44] Cf. Zach. 3:8.   [45] Is. 11:1.   [46] Jer. 23:5.

had the true answer: *As priest he will sit upon the throne.* This interpretation explains more easily why Zacharias directed his symbolical action to Josue, a type of the branch.

The prophet notes that there will be friendly understanding between the two. Some petty jealousy may have existed between Zorobabel and Josue. Before the exile kings claimed authority over the high priest in so far as the Law placed no restrictions. At the moment, under wholly different circumstances, the civil and spiritual rulers were obliged to define the limits of their power. In the Messianic age no such difficulties would exist, for the royal and priestly dignity would be united in one person.

§36. THE PRINCE OF PEACE ENTERS JERUSALEM
Zach. 9:9-10

On the lips of our prophet were comminatory words against the lands and cities of the Arameans, Phoenicians, and Philistines. But their chastisement would have as sequel the cessation of idolatry. After Yahweh restores Israel's ideal boundaries,[47] the Messiah-King will appear and establish his kingdom:

Zacharias
9:9   Rejoice greatly, O daughter Sion,
                shout for joy, O daughter Jerusalem!
            See, your king is coming to you,
                he is just, he is victorious,
            humble, and he rides upon an ass,
                (and) upon a colt, the foal of an ass.
9:10   He will do away with Ephraim's chariots
                and Jerusalem's war horses.
            He will do away with the bows of war,
                and bestow peace upon the nations.
            His sway will extend from sea to sea,
                from the river (Euphrates) to the ends of the earth.

Jerusalem is the capital of the Messianic kingdom[48] and the prophet exhorts the city, i.e., its inhabitants, to shout joyously at the entrance of their king. He is "just," not only in administering justice — an important task of any prince — but in all his thought and action. He is *nosa'*, saved, because Yahweh stands at his side and gives victory over all foes. He

---

[47] 3 Kgs. 5:4.   [48] Is. 2:2.

is "humble," for he shows personal interest in the least of his subjects. And lastly, being the prince of peace, he rides upon an ass, not upon a war horse.

Illustrious persons had acted similarly. Upon David's donkey Solomon rode to the spring of Gihon to be anointed king.[49] The Lawgiver had warned Israel's kings not to retain a multitude of horses,[50] since they must not set their hearts upon military campaigns. Isaias had deplored the fact that the land was full of horses and chariots, with the result that men forgot God.[51] The word "and" in verse 9f is epexegetical; the clause that follows simply parallels the preceding. In recounting Christ's triumphal entry into Jerusalem, St. Matthew mentions two animals, an ass accompanied by her colt;[52] perhaps this was due to the influence of the Septuagint translation which he was freely citing. The other evangelists mention only one beast.[53] Mark and Luke add that no one had yet ridden the animal, hence it seems to have been reserved for the Lord; Zacharias may have alluded to this by strongly emphasizing the beast's age.

As early as the oracle of the dying Jacob, the Messiah had been heralded as the prince of peace,[54] a point resumed by prophets following Osee.[55] The marvellous productivity of the land in the Messianic era presupposes a time of peace. Because the Messiah will inaugurate an age of peace, weapons of war, war horses, chariots and bows will no longer be needed; and since hatred will cease to exist among peoples, his kingdom extends its borders to include the entire earth.[56]

That the text tells of the Messiah is evident from the fact that "Sion's king" extends his sway over all nations and bestows peace, the foremost Messianic blessing, a peace so perfect that weapons become useless. The prophecy of Zacharias received literal fulfillment, as Sts. Matthew and John expressly indicate, when Jesus on the Sunday before His bitter passion entered Jerusalem sitting upon an ass amid the jubilation of the multitude.

§37. THE PIERCED ONE
Zach. 12:9—13:1

12:9   It will come to pass on that day that I will arrange the destruction
12:10   of all nations that rise against Jerusalem. Upon the house of
        David and upon the inhabitants of Jerusalem, however, I will

---

[49] 3 Kgs. 1:33, 38.
[50] Deut. 17:16.
[51] Is. 2:7.
[52] Matth. 21:2-7.
[53] Mark 11:2-7; Luke 19:31-35; John 12:14-16.
[54] Gen. 49:10
[55] Os. 2:20.
[56] Ps. 72:8.

pour forth a spirit of compassion and mercy; they will look upon
him whom they have pierced and mourn over him as one mourns
over an only son. They will lament bitterly over him as one laments
12:11   over a first-born. On that day lamentation will be great in Jerusalem, like the lamentation for Hadad-Rimmon in the Plain of
12:12   Megiddo. The land will mourn, each family for itself: the family
12:13   of David for itself and its women for themselves; the family of
Levi's house for itself and its women for themselves; Simei's fami-
12:14   ly for itself and its women for themselves; and all the remaining
families, every family for itself and their women for themselves
13:1   On that day there will be a fountain bursting open for the house
of David and for the inhabitants of Jerusalem to undo sin and
uncleanness.

The "pierced One" is a member of God's Chosen People. With violence he is put to death, and lamentations are made over him. He dies
innocently and the populace are responsible for the murder, at least
they participated in it because now they experience bitter remorse over
their action. Nevertheless, it is only through Yahweh's favor that they
begin to realize their guilt, for He bestows upon the murderers the spirit
of sympathy and prayerful compassion. It is a question of an event in
Messianic times. This is indicated by the repetition of the formula "on
that day," by the attack of Gentile nations upon Jerusalem, by the outpouring of "spirit" (which reminds us of Joel 3:1), by the cleansing
from sin and uncleanness, and the end of idolatry.[57] In favor of a Messianic interpretation is the fact that the pierced One is spoken of in
terms so rich in mystery. The Servant of Yahweh poems throw light
upon our passage; for the Servant is condemned to death by his people
for the sins of his people.[58] St. John regarded our prophecy fulfilled
when Jesus' heart was pierced by a soldier as He hung upon the Cross.[59]

V. 10 reads in Hebrew: "They will look upon me 'elay (upon Yahweh)." But it can hardly be said that Yahweh would be pierced through.
And although the Messiah was truly God, we still are in Old Testament
times, the age of preparation; it is certain that no pre-Christian reader
would have understood the text in this manner. Rather a pause could
be made after 'elay: "They will look upon Me. Over him whom they
pierced, they will lament. . . ."[60] More probably they look upon him
over whom they are lamenting, i.e., upon the pierced One; nor does it
require much of a textual emendation to change 'elay to 'elaw, upon him.

The lamentation of the repentant people is compared to the mourning
customary at the funeral of an only son or of a first-born.[61] Then the
prophet alludes to the lamentations over Hadad-Rimmon in the Plain

[57] Zach. 13:2f.
[58] Is. 53.
[59] John 19:37 ; Apoc. 1:7.

[60] Cyril of Alexandria, van Hoonacker, Ceuppens.
[61] Am. 8:10 ; Jer. 6:26.

of Megiddo. At the beginning of a certain Philistine campaign, Saul lodged for a time under the pomegranate (*harrimmon*) near Migron; [62] and after the war of the tribes against Benjamin, the survivors fled to the Rock of Harrimmon. [63]

The text in Zacharias has been amended in the following manner: Like the mourning at Harrimmon in the Plain of Migron. [64] The dissolution of the tribe of Benjamin indeed seemed to be a great national misfortune, and the Israelites raised loud lamentations; but this occurred at Bethel, not near the above-named Rock. [65] Allusion to the lamentations over Adonis-Tammuz adds nothing toward clarification. Hadad-Rimmon was a storm-god, not a vegetation-god; no one mourned over him, and there is no evidence that in the Plain of Megiddo any notable lamentation rites occurred over a vegetation god.

Perhaps it would be best to agree with St. Jerome, who refers the incident to the death of Josias at Megiddo in the battle against Nechao of Egypt. [66] His death did occasion unusual weeping among the people. [67] To the memory of Josias, Jeremias composed a dirge, and down to the time of the Chronicler the Jews voiced sorrow over the tragic event. [68] According to St. Jerome, Hadad-Rimmon was the place where Josias was mortally wounded; during patristic times it was called Maximini-anopolis. [69]

Dirges were executed in groups, men and women separately, even as the triumphal chants in connection with great national celebrations. [70] To the house of David the nation owed its leaders, to the house of Nathan [71] its foremost families, to the house of Levi its higher priestly orders, to the house of Simei, (descended from a son of Gerson of the tribe of Levi), [72] the lower priestly orders. The "remaining families" are those who escape death in the wars preceding the Day of salvation, people who are spared the wrath of judgment. All Israel accordingly is united in the lamentation over the death of the just man for which they bear the guilt.

At the conclusion of the crucifixion account, St. John refers to our prophecy. After noting that the side of Jesus was opened with a lance but that His bones (in fulfillment of the paschal lamb prophecy [73]) were not broken as were those of the two thieves, he adds: "And further, another Biblical passage says: They will look upon him whom they pierced." [74] This stroke with the lance was the result of action taken by the Jews who delivered Jesus to Pilate demanding His death. Perhaps,

[62] 1 Sam. 14:2.
[63] Judg. 20:45.
[64] Van Hoonacker, Junker.
[65] Judg. 21:2.
[66] In 609 B.C.
[67] 4 Kgs. 23:29-30.
[68] 2 Chr. 35:25.

[69] F. M. Abel, *Géographie de la Palestine*, II, 340.
[70] Ex. 15.
[71] 2 Sam. 5:14.
[72] Ex. 6:17; Num. 3:18.
[73] Ex. 42:46; Num. 9:12.
[74] John 19:37.

however, the evangelist did not intend to refer immediately to the piercing of Christ's side when he quoted from Zacharias, but was speaking primarily of the crucifixion.

The prophet's declaration that Israel in all her component classes would lament the death of the pierced One recalls Isaias' prophecy telling how the People of God were destined for final conversion. There was a beginning to this conversion when many Jews who witnessed the crucifixion and nature's response became terrified, struck their breasts and departed with sober thoughts.[75] And later, when Peter preached on the first Pentecost, a goodly number repented and asked for baptism.[76] As Zacharias noted, the people as a whole will find the way to their Savior only at the end of time.

Because the Jews restricted their hopes to a glorious Messiah yet gave this text a Messianic interpretation, they postulated a second Messiah, the son of Joseph who would suffer and die alongside the real Messiah, the son of David.[77]

§38. THE SACRIFICE OF MESSIANIC TIMES
Mal. 1:10-11

The prophets were men of their times, men enmeshed in a specific environment. When they spoke of the Messianic era, they could not picture the worship of Yahweh in a fashion different from that to which they were accustomed at the temple in Jerusalem. Animals, therefore, would continue to be offered in sacrifice,[78] and the Gentile nations too would show their respect and reverence for Yahweh in current forms of cult.[79] They assumed that the Aaronic priesthood must continue.[80] At first Malachias directed harsh words to the consciences of the priests, but then he proclaimed how in Messianic times they would resume the worship of Yahweh with purified hearts: "He will cleanse the sons of Levi and will purify them as gold and silver; then in righteousness will they approach Yahweh with offerings. And the oblation of Judah and Jerusalem will be pleasing to Yahweh as in the days of old." [81]

But there are other themes too in Malachias. The priests used their

[75] Luke 23:48.   [76] Acts 2:17f.   [77] Strack-Billerbeck II, 294f; Ed König,
[78] Jer. 33:11-18.   Messianische Weissagungen, 291f; Bous-
[79] Is. 19:21; Soph. 3:10; Is. 56:7; 60;7. set-Gressmann, Die Religion des Juden-
[80] Jer. 33:18.   tums, 230; Ferd. Weber, Jüdische Theol-
[81] Mal. 3:3-4.   ogie, 362.

office as a means for enriching themselves at Yahweh's expense by sacrificing blind and lame and diseased animals, beasts that no one would present to a higher official when seeking a favor. With such the case, it would be better, Malachias indignantly retorted, to lock the temple and make no offerings:

Malachias

1:10   I take no pleasure in you, says Yahweh of hosts. I will accept no fur-
1:11   ther sacrifices at your hands. But from the rising of the sun unto its setting, my Name is great among the Gentiles; and in every place there will be sacrifice, an offering to my Name. It will be a pure oblation, for my Name is great among the Gentiles, says Yahweh of hosts.

The prophet speaks of a time when Yahweh will be worshipped throughout the world and by every race, a time when sacrifice will be made to Him everywhere and by all peoples. This sacrifice will be a "perfect" oblation, it will not be marked by blemishes like those presently offered by the priests in Jerusalem. And the offering will be brought by men with pure hearts and upright intentions.

In the Messianic age the Mosaic *minhah* will be replaced by another *minhah* — hence it will be a genuine sacrifice in the literal sense of the word, not an offering in the figurative sense as, for instance, that of prayer. The latter would have involved nothing new, the true God had been honored by prayer since time immemorial. It is a sacrifice that will take place throughout the whole world; accordingly there is no reference to the sacrifices offered in the sanctuary at Elephantine [82] or to the sacrifices inaugurated in the year 160 before Christ at Leontopolis in the Nile delta. These sanctuaries attained no importance, and those who worshipped there were Jews, not converted Gentiles. The worship of Yahweh by proselytes is excluded because the text treats of genuine sacrifice.

Some have claimed that Zacharias alluded to the sacrifice offered to the sky-god Ahura Mazda during the Persian period, a sacrifice that Yahweh regarded as offered to Himself. What prophet, however, would have associated Yahweh with Ahura Mazda! Nor can the Persians be identified with "all nations." Neither would any prophet have considered Gentile sacrifices as pure; in any such comparison the maimed victims of Jewish priests would have ranked immeasurably higher.

From Is. 66:21 we know that in the Messianic age there will be priests called from among Gentile nations, and consequently the descendants of Aaron will lose exclusive rights to their high privilege. The word *minhah* is a very general word for gift, a gift made primarily to God; in

---

[82] Which was destroyed by the Egyptians in 411; whether this site was rebuilt when the Jews, after long negotiations, had received permission is doubtful.

liturgical usage it refers to unbloody food and drink offerings in contradistinction to bloody oblations. Our text concerns sacrifice as shown by the terms *muqtar, muggaš* and *tehorah*. *Qatar* in the Piel and Hiphil means to bring forward (an offering to be sacrificed — Amos 5:25); *tahor,* from *tahar,* means to be pure, clean, especially with regard to Levitical cleanliness.

The accumulation of these terms points unmistakably to true sacrifice, though perhaps not so clearly to a food oblation. The death of Jesus on the Cross was a true sacrifice in Messianic times, although it occurred but once and only in Jerusalem. The prophecy is fulfilled in the sacrifice of holy Mass. Here we have a true sacrifice; the object is the purest possible — the Son of God, and the Offerer, the Savior through the hands of the priest. It is, moreover, offered in all places throughout the world. Beginning with the Didache,[83] Christian tradition applied Malachias' prophecy to the sacrifice of Mass; thus, for instance, St. Ireneus [84] and Justin Martyr.[85] This patristic interpretation was incorporated into one of the declarations of the Council of Trent.[86]

§39. THE PRECURSOR
Mal. 3:1, 22-24

At the time of Amos the Israelites, oppressed by Gentile nations, longed for "the Day of Yahweh," the Day when God would appear and vindicate His people.[87] But the prophet rebuked them: "What will the Day of Yahweh bring you? Darkness, not light!" Yahweh will come to inflict judgment, but His avenging hand will smite the Israelites first because they were so little concerned over His commandments.

Later, in the days of Malachias many were scandalized upon observing how the lukewarm and wicked lived in comfortable circumstances, and clamored for divine intervention: "Where is the God of judgment?" [88] Malachias was convinced that the evildoers deserved punishment and knew that they would not escape; accordingly he directed his gaze to Messianic times and to the great judgment introducing it:

[83] Ch. 14.
[84] Adv. Haer. 4, 17, 5.
[85] Dial. c. Tryph. 41.
[86] Sess. XXII cap. 1.
[87] Am. 5:18.
[88] Mal. 2:17.

Malachias
3:1   Behold, I am sending my angel to prepare the way before me. Then suddenly will the Lord come to his temple, (the Lord) whom you desire, the angel of the covenant whom you demand. Behold, he is coming, says Yahweh of hosts. But who will be able to endure the day of his coming, and at his appearance who will abide? For he is like refiner's fire, like fuller's lye.

At the temple, the center of the Messianic kingdom, Yahweh will indeed appear and hold judgment. But the people would have no more reason to rejoice over His advent than they had previously in the days of Amos. Yahweh comes to judge, and it will be with a strong, heavy hand. Especially from those who question His justice, will an accounting be exacted.

With Yahweh there seems to appear a third party, the "angel of the covenant." Many exegetes of the past and present apply the phrase to the Messiah. Very probably we have here another *Mal'akh-Yahweh* passage. This vexing designation is frequently used interchangeably with the divine Name, Yahweh or Elohim.[89] Yahweh's Name, i.e., His nature, is in the Mal'akh Yahweh;[90] sacrifice is made to Him;[91] He has the power to forgive sins;[92] the angels are subservient to Him.[93] In blessing Ephraim and Manasses, Jacob spoke of the angel who delivered him from all evils in parallel terms with the God before whom his fathers had walked and whose protection he enjoyed.[94] The "Angel of Yahweh" accordingly possessed the same nature as Yahweh; and yet the word *mal'akh* should underline some distinction. The Old Testament contains no answer to this problem.

Malachias calls God the "angel of the covenant" to remind us of the revelation Moses received at the burning bush where the Mal'akh-Yahweh appeared,[95] where the initial steps were taken for the Sinai covenant and for Israel's guidance to Canaan under the Mal'akh-Yahweh[96] after the ratification of the covenant.

Because Yahweh works through the "covenant angel," the prophet continues in the singular: He is coming, His appearance is certain. Yahweh's advent spells Messianic judgment upon Israel. Isaias had predicted it, had foretold how God would wash away the filth of the daughters of Sion and Jerusalem's blood-guilt through the spirit of judgment and the spirit of fire.[97] And Ezechiel indicated the same when he prophesied how Yahweh would judge "between sheep and sheep."[98]

Just as kings are preceded by heralds, so Yahweh and His "covenant angel" have their precursor. His is not to judge, still his appearance is

[89] Cf. Gen. 16:21-22, etc.   [90] Ex. 23:21.   [93] Zach. 3:4.   [96] Ex. 23:20f.
[91] Gen. 22:12; Judg. 6:21; 13:21.   [94] Gen. 48:15-16.   [97] Is. 4:4.
[92] Ex. 23:21; Zach. 3:3-4.   [95] Ex. 3:2.   [98] Ez. 34:17.

a sign of imminent judgment. Jesus identified this messenger-angel as John the Baptist: "This is he of whom it is written: Behold, I am sending my angel before your face to prepare the way before you."[99] The Baptist himself, however, pointed out how One greater than himself — whose advent he was only proclaiming — would inaugurate judgment. With winnowing fork in hand, He would separate the chaff, gather the wheat into his barns, and burn the straw in an unquenchable fire.[1]

Again in the concluding admonition Malachias speaks of the Messiah's precursor:

Malachias

3:22   Keep in mind the Law of my servant Moses. On Horeb I committed it to him for all Israel — precepts and commandments. Behold,
3:23   I am sending you the prophet Elias before the Day of Yahweh comes, that Day of dread violence. He will turn the heart of fathers
3:24   toward sons, and the heart of sons toward fathers, lest I come and inflict the ban upon the land.[2]

A mighty prophet, who would appear shortly before the Messiah's advent, would restore amity where parents and children were at odds, principally on religious grounds. Now the family, the basic unit of society, should be at peace in preparation for that peace which the Messiah brings. Only if the people give a willing ear to the words of Yahweh's "angel" can they withstand judgment and escape the ban, i.e., total annihilation.

When the angel Gabriel announced the birth of a son to Zachary, he said: "He will bring many of the sons of Israel back to the Lord their God. He will precede him in the spirit and power of Elias and turn the hearts of fathers to their sons."[3] Illumined by the Holy Spirit, Zachary prophesied of his son: "You, O child, will be called: the prophet of the Most High. For you will go before the Lord to prepare the way for him, to give his people knowledge of salvation through the forgiveness of their sins."[4] Zachary, accordingly, knew full well that Malachias' prophecy was fulfilled in his son John.

To Jewish inquiry whether he were Elias, the Baptist did indeed reply in the negative,[5] but here there was a question of the Jewish belief that Elias would appear in person, bodily. Some Jews identified Jesus with Elias, whose advent would mark the arrival of the Messianic era.[6] Jesus explained how John was the Elias "who should come," the forerunner of the kingdom of God, and that through him Elias spoke.[7] For to the remark that "according to the Scribes Elias must appear before the Messiah's advent," Jesus pointedly replied: "I say to you, Elias is al-

[99] Matth. 11:10 ; Luke 7:27.   [3] Luke 1:16-17.   [5] John 1:21.
[1] Matth. 3:7 ; Luke 3:7f.   [4] Luke 1:76-77.   [6] Matth. 16:14.
[2] In the Vulgate, 4:4-6.   [7] Matth. 11:14.

ready come and they did not know him but did to him what they wanted." As the evangelist notes, the disciples realized that He was speaking to them of John the Baptist.[8]

In commenting upon Mal. 3:22–24 many Fathers of the Church together with a number of later exegetes express the opinion that immediately before the Last Judgment Elias will appear in person; allusion is made to his assumption as recounted in 4 Kgs. 2.

§40. THE POURING OUT OF THE HOLY SPIRIT
Joel 3:1-5

Great swarms of locusts had devastated the land, had rendered it leafless. Famine followed. Even the daily sacrifices could no longer be offered for want of suitable oblations. Presently the prophet Joel rose and gave the people this message:

Current evils were a punishment for sin. Do penance. Keep a common fast day. Let the priests pray in the sanctuary while the people rouse their hearts to sorrow. Rend your hearts and not your garments. Be awakened by the visitation, turn and amend your ways. It is the Day of Yahweh.

The people listened to the prophet's voice and humbled themselves in acts of penance. In response God bade him return, announcing a speedy end of the locust plague; there *would* be a harvest. He would, moreover, give them "the teacher of justice." [9] This promise did not refer to the Messiah. The Messianic age was not imminent, and the good harvest promised was the reward for their conversion and a further preparation for Messianic times. The phrase pointed to the prophets sent to instruct the people on how to lead upright lives.

Joel

3:1   Thereupon this will come to pass:
       I will pour forth my Spirit upon all flesh.
        Your sons and your daughters will prophesy,
       Your old men will dream (meaningful) dreams,
        and your young men will see visions.

3:2   Yes, even upon servants, male and female,
       will I pour forth my Spirit in those days.

---

[8] Matth. 17:10-13.   [9] 2:23.

3:3   And I will put signs in the sky and upon the earth:
        blood and fire and pillars of smoke.

3:4   The sun will turn to darkness and the moon to blood,
        when the Day of Yahweh comes, that great and dreadful Day.

3:5   Everyone, however, who invokes Yahweh's Name will be saved.
        For him who is upon Mount Sion or in Jerusalem
          there will be deliverance, as Yahweh has spoken,
          and among those who escape will be those whom Yahweh calls.

Yahweh's spirit is responsible for all physical and spiritual life. In pre-Christian times it was bestowed in a special manner upon certain individuals, particularly the prophets; upon the Messiah, Isaias said, the spirit of Yahweh would descend in all its fullness.[10] Usually, however, only a small number of specially favored individuals received the spirit of God. An exception occurred in the days of Moses when the spirit came upon a larger group, the seventy elders, to show that the people were to obey them too.[11] This was an isolated instance. But in Messianic times the spirit of God would descend from on high to re-create all life upon the earth,[12] transforming in particular the hearts of men.[13] The whole house of Israel would be granted this privilege,[14] and the spirit would rouse the *people* to sorrow for having pierced the Lord's chosen One.[15]

Joel too had a message on "the spirit" in Messianic times. After a formal introduction, "thereupon this will come to pass" — i.e., after the good harvest he had just promised — there will follow the sending of the spirit of God in all its fullness. It will resemble a fruitful rain. The spirit will rest not only upon certain favored individuals as in times past, but upon "all flesh." Then Joel addressed his fellow men more directly: "Your sons and your daughters will prophesy." Without distinction as to sex or age all will benefit from the marvellous outpouring. Externally the spirit will manifest itself in the gift of tongues,[16] in meaningful dreams throwing light on the present and future, and in visions. Emphasizing the point, the prophet continues with *wegam*: "Indeed, *even* servants, male and female," will share in this grace! Joel's words can hardly be restricted to Israelites who had fallen into bondage for debts but were not to be excluded from Messianic blessings because of their dependent status; rather, the context tells us that the expression "all flesh" must not be limited to Israel. Gentiles too will participate in the spirit if they are somehow associated with Israel.

On the first Pentecost, Peter reminded the multitude of Joel's oracle as they stood amazed before the apostles speaking in various tongues. He assured them of its fulfillment in their very eyes.[17] The era Joel had

---

[10] Is. 11:2.
[11] Num. 11:24.
[12] Is. 32:15.
[13] Ez. 36:26-27.
[14] Ez. 39:29.
[15] Zach. 12:10.
[16] Num. 11:24.
[17] Acts 2:16-21.

foreseen was come, he declared, and through the Holy Spirit a transformation of mankind began, one that was truly effective and lasting.

Because the prophets recognized no time intervals in their pronouncements on the future, Joel could speak of the Last Judgment immediately after his remarks on the outpouring of the Spirit. That will be a "great and dreadful Day," a Day but weakly prefigured by the locust visitation. It will be inaugurated by fearful portents in the sky and upon earth. On earth war and bloodshed, and the burning of cities; in the sky the sun will become dark [18] and the moon appear bloody red. Only he will escape judgment who has faith in Yahweh and turns to Him with full trust and confidence. From Sion, the center of the Messianic kingdom, salvation beckons; and when Joel adds, "as Yahweh has spoken," he is alluding to a previous oracle in which deliverance was likewise promised at Mount Sion on the Day of judgment.[19] The prophet's final statement, "Among those who escape — those, namely, who will be spared in the judgment — will be those whom Yahweh calls," means that it is wholly due to God's grace if one survives the terrible ordeal. Man must turn to God, but God must give His grace.

St. Paul quoted v. 5 in support of his thesis that Jew and Greek without distinction were destined for salvation.[20]

§41. THE SON OF MAN
Dan. 7

In the year 605 Daniel, together with a number of other young men, was taken to Babylon by King Nabuchodonosor to be reared at court.[21] Because of his exemplary fidelity to the Law he was highly respected by faithful Jews,[22] and at the royal palace too Daniel was well received; he lived to see the dissolution of the Chaldean kingdom and the rise of Cyrus to world power.[23] Material from the pen of the prophet himself forms the principal source for the Book that bears his name. As is evident from disagreements in the present text, this material was subjected to various revisions; and some of it was later rewritten from the viewpoint of fulfillment. Final editing on the book occurred during the persecution by Antiochus Epiphanes.

---

[18] Am. 8:9 ; Soph. 1:14.   [20] Rom. 10:13.   [22] Dan. 13:45f.
[19] Abd. 17.   [21] Dan. 1:4.   [23] Dan. 10:1.

On one occasion Daniel was granted a vision which portrayed the dissolution of the world's empires upon the rise of the Messianic kingdom. Out of a storm-tossed sea came four beasts. The first resembled a lion with eagle's wings, the second a bear with three ribs in its mouth, the third a panther with bird wings and four heads, while the fourth was dreadful, fear-inspiring, and exceedingly powerful. It had teeth of iron, claws of bronze, and ten horns; then between the horns came an eleventh horn, a small one with eyes like a man's and a mouth making proud, presumptious utterances.

Exegetes are agreed that the four beasts represent four earthly kingdoms, but there is no harmony on what four are meant, apart from the first that is commonly identified as Nabuchodonosor's. Images of winged lions were common throughout Mesopotamia, and in the dream of the mighty statue in chapter 2, the head represents Nabuchodonosor. Traditional exegesis links the bear with the kingdom of the Medes and Persians; the panther with the kingdom of Alexander and his successors; the dreadful beast for which the prophet had no name, the empire of Rome. The little horn is taken to signify the Antichrist. Among those who hold that the book received its final redaction early during the Machabean period, many identify the little horn with Antiochus and consequently regard the fourth beast as the Seleucid kingdom.

It may be questioned, however, whether the inspired author was thinking of any specific kingdoms apart from Nabuchodonosor's. The numeral four stands for completion or entirety. For example, when Babylonian kings called themselves lords of the four regions of the world, they were voicing a claim to world empire. In Jeremias Yahweh caused four winds to blow upon Elam from the four ends of the heavens.[24] During Messianic times the dispersed from the four borders of the earth will be brought together.[25] The cherubim in Ezechiel's vision had four faces and four wings, and God's chariot was accompanied by four double sets of wheels. Through revelation Abraham knew that his descendants would leave the land but would return in the fourth generation.[26] In Ez. 4:12 four agents of punishment are listed, plague, famine, war, exile; and four verses later, famine, wild beasts, plague, slaughter. In the vision of the dry bones breath came from the four winds to restore life to the dead.[27]

Nabuchodonosor's four beasts, therefore, may well represent the governments of the world taken as a unit, forces that rise up against Yahweh; with the last of them as the worst.

A judgment scene follows. In the place of honor is "One of many days," Yahweh, because He is eternal. As in the visions of Isaias and

[24] Jer. 49:36.   [25] Is. 11:12.   [26] Gen. 15:16.   [27] Ez. 37:9.

Ezechiel, He sits upon a throne with fire all about; for to the ancient mind fire was the element farthest removed from matter, the finest symbol for divinity. Angels surround Him, an innumerable throng. The guilt of the little horn is established, it had spoken presumptiously against God. The fourth beast is slain, its carcass burned.

History shows how the governments of this world have their day. After a period of power, they decline and vanish. In Daniel's vision the first three beasts come to judgment and are deprived of power — they are indeed symbols. Thereupon another figure appears:

Daniel
7:13   Behold, with the clouds [28] of the heavens there came one like a (son of) man, and he advanced unto the One of many days and
7:14   was brought before him. Upon him was bestowed sovereignty and glory and kingship that all peoples, nations, and tongues should serve him. His rule was an eternal rule, one that should never pass away, and his kingship such that should never be destroyed.

The phrase "with the clouds of the heavens" shows that the action is still taking place in heaven. The words "son of man," bar 'enash, indicate "a member of the genus man," like the Hebrew ben 'adam.[29] In chapter 8 the angel Gabriel addresses Daniel himself with the words ben 'adam.[30] Ordinarily the expression is used in contexts alluding to the weaknesses of human nature, a point which is not true in the present instance; for the person in question rises immeasurably superior to the beasts preceding him in the vision. While the former rise from the sea, remain upon earth, exemplify brute power, and are destined to perish, the "son of man" enters heaven itself. He is endowed with intelligence, is accorded dominion over all peoples and a kingship that endures eternally.

Uncertain over the import of the vision, Daniel asks for clarification; and an angel comes to his assistance.[31] What the prophet had seen last is discussed first. "The saints of the Most High will receive the kingdom, a kingdom that will endure forever, yes, forever and ever." [32] Daniel then inquires regarding the fourth beast with the ten horns and the one horn that spoke presumptiously, the beast that "waged war against the saints and triumphed over them until the One of many days came and executed justice in favor of the saints of the Most High." The angel replied:

Daniel
7:23   The fourth beast, a fourth kingdom it will be upon the earth . . .
7:24   the ten horns, from this kingdom ten kings will arise, and after
7:25   them still another will come . . . he will speak words against the

[28] Septuagint: upon the clouds.   [30] Dan. 8:17.   [32] V. 18.
[29] Num. 23:19; Is. 51:12; Ez. 2:1.   [31] Vv. 15-17.

Most High and he will try to destroy the saints of the Most High. He will have the audacity to alter the sacred days and the Law, and they will be delivered into his hand for the duration of a time

7:26 and times and half a time. Then, however, judgment will be held, and rule will be taken away from him, and it will be broken to

7:27 pieces and destroyed unto the end of time. Thereupon kingship and dominion and sovereignty over the kingdoms beneath the whole heavens will be bestowed upon the saints of the Most High. Their kingdom will be an everlasting kingdom, and all rulers will serve and obey him.

It should be evident now that the little horn represented Antiochus IV Epiphanes. It was he who spoke presumptiously against Yahweh; he attempted to abolish feasts and ordinances; he tried to extirpate the People of God, leaving no means of suppression untried. The length of his sway is specified as "a time and times and half a time." This can mean a year plus two years and half a year, or three and one half years; [33] in 9:27 the period is given as a half week of years. In the Apocalypse too there is mentioned "time and times and half a time," [34] a period equivalent to 42 months a chapter later.[35] What the prophet is stressing is the temporary or ephemeral character of persecution in contrast to the everlasting triumph which follows. The destruction of the little horn signifies the triumph of God's saints, the inauguration of the Messianic era. Like other prophets, Daniel heralds the Messianic age as one soon to dawn. But since it will endure forever, the final, eschatalogical phase of the kingdom must be included; the proud persecutor of God's people becomes a type of the Antichrist at the end of the world.

These considerations point the way for a correct understanding of the phrase, son of man. According to vv. 12, 18, 22, 27 the saints of the Most High receive dominion over all nations after they have suffered. Neither Daniel nor his contemporaries could have imagined a kingdom without a king. In the vision under consideration the first beast evidently was Nabuchodonosor, the little horn on the last beast Antiochus; the ten horns (a symbolical number) upon this beast were ten kings. Likewise, in Daniel's next vision the ram with two horns are the kings of Media and Persia,[36] while the he-goat is the king of Greece.[37] Accordingly, in the case of the son of man who receives the sovereignty, there is reference not only to the People of God but also to their king, the Messiah, whom God solemnly installs in his office. The "saints of the Most High" exercise dominion but they do so through their head.

Before the exile the Messiah was presented as the great king from David's family. During the exile, after the house of David had been dethroned, the Messiah was pictured as the Man of Sorrows who offers

---

[33] Cf. 12:7.   [34] Apoc. 12:14.   [35] 13:5.   [36] Dan. 8:20.   [37] Dan. 8:21.

himself as a victim and dies. The Book of Daniel, reflecting a postexilic spirit, projects the Messiah upon the clouds of heaven — although already before the exile he had been heralded as God's son; and while the Israelites had once imagined that they would dominate the nations through the Messiah, the point now stressed is that the Messianic People of God will be a heavenly creation. As already noted, particularly by Jeremias and Ezechiel, Israel must experience a spiritual purification through God's beneficent intervention. To a greater degree emphasis is now placed upon the fact that it is God who creates a new kingdom of saints; and the Messiah descends *from heaven* to assume sway over the faithful and over all the earth when the powers hostile to God have been extirpated.

Of the Jewish interpreters who explained the passage of a personal Messiah we must limit ourselves to Rabbi Jeshua: "If Israel be clean, he will come with the clouds of heaven. If Israel does not deserve this, he will come in a humble way, riding upon an ass."[38] In the parables of the Book of Henoch,[39] especially in chapters 47–59, and in the Apocalypse of Ezra[40] our son of man is the Messiah. Jesus applied the title "son of man" in a Messianic sense to Himself, particularly when He proclaimed His second Advent: "They will see the Son of Man coming with great power and majesty upon the clouds of heaven."[41] And to the high priest's decisive question whether He was the Christ, the Son of God, He replied: "Then you will see the Son of Man sitting at the right hand of (God) Almighty, and coming upon the clouds of heaven."[42] Our Savior likewise applied Daniel's prophecy to Himself when He attributed to the Son of Man the power to forgive sins[43] and to void the Sabbath laws.[44]

The first Christian martyr, Stephen, just before his death exclaimed: "Behold, I see the heavens open and the Son of Man standing at the right of God."[45] It was the glorified Christ, Daniel's Son of Man, whom St. John beheld on the island of Patmos.[46] Because of Daniel 7, the Letter to the Hebrews[47] relates the terms "man" and "son of man" in Ps. 8:5–7 to Christ. The dominion bestowed upon the saints of the Most High is needed background for understanding Christ's description of the Last Judgment in which the saints who faithfully served God during life are assigned a share in pronouncing judgment.[48]

On one occasion a prophecy involving four world kingdoms destined for destruction in Messianic times was given in a dream to Nabuchodonosor. The king could not remember the details, but Daniel, divinely illumined on the matter, explained all its implications.[49] Nabuchodono-

[38] Bab. Sanh. 98a.
[39] Ch. 37–71.
[40] Ch. 13.
[44] Matth. 12:8; Cf. 8:20; 16:13.
[41] Matth. 24:30.
[42] Matth. 26:64.
[43] Matth. 9:6.
[45] Acts 7:55.
[46] Apoc. 1:13; 14:14.   [47] 2:6.
[48] Matth. 19:28; Luke 22:30; 1 Cor. 6:2;
Apoc. 20:4.   [49] Dan. 2.

sor had seen a great image, an image of God resembling the monuments frequently erected by Assyrian and Babylonian monarchs. The hand was of gold, breast and arms of silver, belly and loins of bronze, legs of iron and feet partly of iron and partly of clay. Then, without human intervention a stone became loose upon a mountain and broke the image into bits. But the stone itself grew into a lofty mountain and filled the whole world.

In chapter 7 of Daniel animals symbolized the kingdoms of the world; now in chapter 2 the same role is taken by lifeless matter. V. 44 gives the prophet's commentary on the stone that annihilates the glory of all earthly kingdoms: "The God of the heavens will establish a kingdom that will never be destroyed; nor will that kingdom be given to any other people. It will destroy and break all other kingdoms into pieces, but itself will endure forever." As in chapter 7, there is no doubt but that the final disposition of God's People will be all-embracing and eternal; nevertheless, Nabuchodonosor's dream makes no explicit reference to a personal ruler at the summit.

§42. THE SEVENTY WEEKS OF YEARS
Dan. 9:24-27

In various visions Daniel had been privileged to see how current suffering and oppression would cease with the advent of God's new kingdom. Thereupon he asked himself when this event would take place, and consulted the Book of the prophet Jeremias. Here he read that the great visitation by which the Israelites were punished for their sins would last seventy years.[50] In Daniel's mind these years had already run their course, but the Messianic era with its blessings had not dawned. At this juncture the angel Gabriel was sent with an instruction — Jeremias spoke of the captivity and the return from exile; but the full restoration, the advent of Messianic times, would first occur after *seventy weeks* of years:

Daniel
9:24   Seventy sevens have been allotted to your people and to your holy city to abolish evil, to make an end of sin, to atone for guilt, and to introduce everlasting justice; to place a seal upon vision and

[50] Jer. 25:11 ; 29:10.

9:25   prophecy and to consecrate a sanctuary. Know therefore and understand: From the time when the order is given to reinhabit and rebuild Jerusalem until (there comes) an anointed prince, seven sevens (will transpire); and in the sixty-second seven it will be restored, and it will be built with squares and sepulchres, even if the times

9:26   be trying. And after these sixty-two sevens, an anointed one will be struck down, one who truly was innocent, and the people of the prince who comes will destroy the city and the sanctuary; and its end will resemble a flood, and war will continue its devastation unto the end. He will make a strong alliance with many during one

9:27   seven, and during half a seven he will abolish bloody and unbloody sacrifices, and a hideous desecration will defile the temple and will continue until the destruction which has been irrevocably decreed has emptied itself upon the destroyer.

The prophet speaks of seventy sevens, *šabu 'im* instead of the usual *šabu 'oth*, to indicate that he does not mean weeks of seven days. Seven symbolizes completion, fullness, finality. If punishment is to be sevenfold,[51] it means that it must be exceptionally severe. Wars were to make such inroads on the male population of Judah that seven women would cling to one man for the purpose of obtaining a husband.[52] The same implication holds for the number seventy. The mourning over Jacob lasted seventy days.[53] Those in Jacob's family who journeyed to Egypt are given as seventy.[54] In the Sethite genealogy the number seventy is prominent, e.g., Adam lived 930 years — 1000 less 70. In the early history of Israel the seventy elders played important roles.[55] The judgment upon Tyre was destined to last seventy years.[56] Haughty and insolent Lamech believed his murder should be avenged seventy-seven times.[57] Since, then, the numbers seven and seventy frequently do have symbolical significance, it is improper to insist upon mathematical values in a particular instance.

In St. Matthew's genealogy of Jesus [58] there are numerous omissions because the evangelist intended to give three lists with fourteen (2 x 7) in each to cover the generations from Abraham to Christ. To Peter's question whether he ought to forgive his brother seven times, Jesus replied: Seventy times seven times.[59] Because of its symbolism the seventh day was to be kept holy, the seventh new moon was celebrated in a special manner, the seventh year was a year of rest, and the seventh seven or jubilee year brought liberty to the prisoner and restoration of inheritance to the dispossessed. In the time of Elias only 7000 remained faithful to Yahweh.[60] Therefore, when Jeremias sets seventy years as the duration of the exile, his figure must not be taken mathematically;

[51] Lev. 26:18, 21, 24.   [54] Gen. 46:27.   [58] Matth. 1.
[52] Is. 4:1.   [55] Ex. 24:1; Num. 11:16.   [59] Matth. 18:22.
[53] Gen. 50:3.   [56] Is. 23:15.   [57] Gen. 4:24.   [60] 3 Kgs. 19:18.

it simply means a very long time. The exile came to an end in 538. In the fourth year of King Joakim (605), Jeremias for the first time declared that Judah's punishment by the deportation of the people would last seventy years.[61]

When those who had been deported to Babylon with Joachin in 597 were dreaming of a speedy return, Jeremias wrote a letter (594) in which he admonished them to settle down in Babylonia because the exile would continue for a long period: "Only after seventy full years have passed in Babylon's favor will I be mindful of you and permit my saving words to be fulfilled in your regard and bring you back to this place."[62] For the Jews who were deported in 597 the exile lasted sixty years; for the multitude who were forced away with Sedecias in 587, it lasted fifty years. The prophet Ezechiel predicted forty years of banishment for those deported in 597.[63] Like the number seventy, forty too is a symbolic figure, the length of one generation. Egypt was destined for a forty year period of desolation.[64] In these various texts both Jeremias and Ezechiel simply intended to say that the exile would last a very, very long time, and only a very few, those who had been deported as young men, would live to see its close.[65]

Now we have an approach on how to understand Daniel's seventy weeks of years. More than a hundred systems of computation have been devised by exegetes from antiquity and the Middle Ages in an effort to correlate chronologically the death of Jesus and the destruction of Jerusalem by the Romans with this prophecy; and the number is still increasing![66] This observation is noteworthy: although the New Testament writers love to quote prophecies referring to our Savior, there is no indication — not even in St. Matthew — that any of them regarded the Messiah's advent chronologically indicated in Daniel's prophecy.

V. 24 describes the blessings of the Messianic era. In three expressions the sacred writer tells how mankind will then be reconciled with God. Evil, *peša'*, will have come to an end — the word often is used to denote apostasy from God, infidelity. Sin, *ḥattoth*, will be a thing of the past. And guilt, *'awon*, will be atoned for and forgiven. In place of infidelity the People of God will practice justice, always. Whatever had been seen in "vision and prophecy" concerning the Day of salvation will have come to pass. Lastly, a "sanctuary" will be consecrated. The word does not refer to a person but to a thing or place. In our text it is not the Holy of Holies of the temple structure because the article is lacking; neither is it the altar of holocausts erected by Judas Machabeus[67] which

---

[61] Jer. 25:1, 11. [62] Jer. 29:10.
[63] Ez. 4:6.
[64] Ez. 29:12.
[65] Cf. Esdr. 3:12.
[66] Fr. Faidl, *Die Exegese der siebzig Wochen Daniels*; a summary of the more important of these interpretations may be found in G. Hoberg, *Katechismus der messianischen Weissagungen*, 86–92.
[67] 1 Mach. 4:47, 54.

never was a token of the Messianic age. Rather, it is that sanctuary in which God will be worshipped during the Messianic era, the structure Ezechiel saw in vision,[68] and of which Aggeus [69] and Zacharias spoke.[70] Its consecration is to be understood figuratively.[71]

V. 25. The period until the advent of Messianic glory covers seventy "sevens" or weeks of years; these are divided into three sections: seven, sixty-two, and one. The *terminus a quo* is "the moment when the order is given." The edict of Cyrus is not meant, but the divine decree promulgated by Jeremias which Daniel had read. At the close of the first seven weeks an anointed prince arises. This was Cyrus who permitted the exiles to return home. The prophecy of Jeremias may be regarded as fulfilled by Cyrus' edict in the year 538.[72] Is. 44:26,28; 45:13 express the hope that Cyrus would give the command to rebuild Jerusalem, and Is. 45:1 calls Cyrus "the anointed of Yahweh." Between 587 and 538, forty-nine years elapsed, seven weeks of years. During the second period of sixty-two sevens, the rebuilding of the city is undertaken; it is not stated in the text that building operations continued throughout the entire period. "Even if the times be trying" — construction continued, although the Samaritans and neighboring tribes who had occupied a portion of the country created great difficulties for the returnees; and the Persians themselves were not always cooperative.

V. 26. At the beginning of the seventieth seven "an anointed one" [73] was put to death; he is thus distinguished from the anointed one (Cyrus) in v. 25. He dies an innocent victim, whether one restores the text with Theodotion, "justice is denied him," or assume that after *'ayin* the word *'ayen* was omitted by haplography — which would give the reading "in him there was no guilt"; or retain the Masoretic reading, "there is nothing to him," i.e., he is wholly abandoned, about to perish. The assassination of a prominent Jew, the high priest Onias III, did occur in the year 171. While he was appearing at the Syrian court at Antioch to justify himself against the false accusation of treason, Jason, his brother, was installed as high priest after sending Antiochus a considerable sum. Menelaus, a later conniver for the dignity, bribed the Syrians with money robbed from the temple; and when Onias objected, he was lured from his retreat in the sanctuary at Daphne and murdered.[74]

If one regards Onias as the anointed in v. 26, the second period would cover the years between 538 and 171, or 367 years; sixty-two weeks of years would require 434. The two periods, the seven weeks and the

[68] Ez. 43:12 ; 45:3.
[69] Agg. 2:7-9.
[70] Zach. 6:12-13.
[71] The Vulgate has *ungatur Sanctus sanctorum*, a reference to Christ. This interpretation may be accounted for by way of application; for Christ did effect the effacement of sin, He introduced justice, and is the fulfillment of prophecy.
[72] 2 Chr. 36:22-23 ; Esdr. 1:1-2.
[73] Without the article.
[74] 1 Mach. 4:23-35.

sixty-two weeks, follow upon each other and are not partially contemporaneous. Therefore one may not subtract 171 from 587 (and obtain 416 years), still less from 605, and thus obtain the required 434 (7 x 62). The prophet obtained his figure of sixty-two weeks simply by deducting the first period of seven weeks and the final one week of tribulation from a symbolic seventy.

After the assassination of the anointed one, a prince appears who destroys city and sanctuary. Whether Jerusalem would be wholly or partially destroyed, whether the temple would sink into ruins or merely be deprived of traditional cult, is not stated. "Its end" refers to the city and sanctuary. Now Antiochus IV (175–163) inaugurated a bloody persecution against Jerusalem in the year 169 and plundered the temple; in 167 he ordered the city's walls torn down, put many Jews to death, consigned women and children to prison.[75] Until and after his death in the spring or summer of 163 the Jewish rebellion under the leadership of the Machabean brothers was in full progress. But for our prophet the final days of the last week lie in the future. He divides the time of the last oppression into two sections. He gives "half a seven"[76] as the duration of greatest suffering; in 8:14 he speaks of 2300 evenings and mornings, i.e., 1150 days; in 12:7 the expression used is "a time, two times and half a time;" in 12:11 it is 1290 days; in 12:12, 1335 days. The minute differences between these figures may be due to a dissimilar computation of the beginning and end of the visitation. After the oppression has reached its climax, it still continues until divine intervention brings deliverance.

V. 27 develops v. 26. The godless prince enters into an agreement with many,[77] and this agreement continues beyond the "half seven" during which time Yahwistic cult is proscribed. During the reign of Antiochus many Jews abandoned the religion of their fathers and supported the tyrant's hellenizing efforts. To obtain the office of high priest Jason pledged himself to rear Jewish youths in Hellenistic fashion. Many priests became unconcerned about sacred cult and would rather attend the games in the gymnasium that Jason had erected. Jews who participated in the games became ashamed of circumcision, the sign of membership in the Chosen People and of obligations toward the Law, and sought to remove its traces through surgery. When the persecution took a more open and violent turn, many complied with the orders from Antioch; and the Hellenistic party among the Jews created many difficulties for those who struggled to liberate their fellow men.[78]

Moreover, royal decree sought to abolish all sacrifices, bloody and

[75] 1 Mach. 1:21-24; 2 Mach. 5:11-21.
[76] Three and a half years.
[77] MT has the article.
[78] 1 Mach. 1:10-15; 2 Mach. 4:7-17.

unbloody. Under the penalty of death, Antiochus prohibited the continuation of sacrifice,[79] and desecrated the temple by erecting an altar to Zeus Olympios upon the altar of holocausts, sacrificing upon it swine's flesh.[80] A half week is mentioned as the time during which sacrifice would cease. This would agree roughly with the 1290 days during which, according to Dan. 12:11, the daily sacrifice would be abolished and a hideous abomination erected. The first time an offering was made upon the pagan altar occurred on the 25th of Kislev in the year 167.[81] Legitimate sacrifices were discontinued until the 25th of Kislev in 165, when after the successes of the Machabees, regular temple ritual was resumed.[82]

In Dan. 11:31; 12:11 the pagan altar of sacrifice is termed a hideous desecration; hence also in 9:27. The word *šiqquṣ* often denotes the abomination of idolatry. The term *šomem* recalls Baal-samen, the Sky-Baal who stood at the head of the pantheon, the Canaanite equivalent to Zeus. The expression, "hideous desecration" in 1 Mach. 1:54, is not independent of Dan. 9:27, in fact, it presupposes the fulfillment of Daniel's message in the actions of Antiochus. For Josephus too the desecration of the temple by Antiochus was pointed to in Daniel's prophecy.[83]

Our interpretation, then, relates the literal message of v. 24 to the blessings of the Messianic era but finds the historical events of the Machabean period described in vv. 25–27, events which the sacred writer himself somehow experienced. The seventy weeks of years are symbolical. The author was concerned principally with the final week, the one of which he had immediate knowledge; the two other periods served only as an introduction about which he had little to say. He chose the number 70 not merely because of its symbolism as a figure indicating perfection and completion, but because it served well as a link with Jeremias' prophecy of the seventy-year period of exile. He saw God's people in an oppressed condition and knew that much tribulation was still awaiting them. But the tyrant causing the evil would not long triumph; he would fall, and then would come the desired blessings listed in v. 24. During the trials of persecution the Jews must not lose trust in God; the Messianic era was about to dawn, even though not so speedily as they would wish. He himself undoubtedly expected the great change with the death of Antiochus, just as the prophets before and during the exile believed that the deliverance from Babylonian bondage would herald the Messiah's appearance.

This interpretation has often been criticized in that the duration of only the first period, the seven weeks of years, can be correlated chrono-

---

[79] 1 Mach. 1:45.   [80] 2 Mach. 6:4-5.   [82] 1 Mach. 1:59.
[81] 1 Mach. 6:4-5.   [83] Jos. Ant. XII 7, 6, 322.

logically with historical events. The last week, upon which the Messianic era will dawn, cannot be correlated chronologically with the Messiah's advent; and as already noted, the sixty-two sevens served only as a phase transitional to the last week to which the author directed his principal attention.

When prophesying the destruction of Jerusalem and the temple,[84] Jesus alluded to the hideous desecration of the holy places that would occur according to Daniel's oracle. This should be the signal for His followers to flee immediately because judgment was imminent. In the great rebellion of the Jews against Rome in the years 66–70, the crimes of the Zealots, who had no respect for the temple, served as a clear warning to Christians to seek security elsewhere; and they left Jerusalem before the city was besieged. Thereupon a still greater abomination took place: the "people of a prince who came," Titus, destroyed the city and the temple. And from that moment on sacrifice ceased forever.

What had occurred at the time of Antiochus IV typified the events Jesus foretold, the destruction of Jerusalem and the temple; and these latter in turn typify conditions at the end of the world, as stated in the Gospel account. In Daniel's book the anointed one who suffered death innocently was the high priest Onias; he prefigured the One who was truly anointed, Christ, and whose spotless Blood was shed to cleanse a sin-laden world. Likewise in Yahweh's anointed prince, Cyrus, who changed the story of the Chosen People by granting freedom and enjoining the reconstruction of Jerusalem, we ought to see a type of our Savior freeing mankind from Satan's bondage and establishing God's new kingdom. Just as the first two periods came to an end with an anointed one,[85] so also the whole seventy week-year period whereupon Messianic salvation dawns, should bring an anointed One uniting in himself kingship and priesthood.

This typically Messianic message is intimately related to the literal Messianic message of v. 24. The typical sense does not demand that type and antitype [86] agree in every detail; and if v. 24 literally proclaims the blessings of Messianic times, while vv. 25–27 describe events under Antiochus which refer typically to the death of Jesus and the temple's destruction, one must remember that the prophets are not concerned primarily over sequence in time or logic when depicting the future.

The figures in Daniels' prophecy are *understood mathematically* by those exegetes who relate the slain anointed One directly with the Messiah and Titus' destruction of the temple with the hideous desecration. The objection, however, remains — the death of Jesus and the destruc-

[84] Matth. 24:15.
[85] Cyrus, Onias.
[86] Here Cyrus—Onias: Jesus; Antiochus: Titus—hideous desecration.

tion of the temple did not occur in the space of seven years; victim and food offerings only ceased with the temple's actual destruction while already with Christ's sacrificial death they had lost all significance.[87] In Daniel's prophecy these sacrifices were only discontinued for a half week and then *were resumed* again.

Patristic writers interpret v. 24 of the Messianic kingdom. There is no unanimity in the explanations given to vv. 25–27, and hence we cannot speak of a "traditional" interpretation. The Septuagint, Theodotion and the Itala translate v. 26 so as to refer to an object, not to an individual — the anointing, *chrisma*, unctio, will cease. For this reason the older Fathers of the Greek and Latin Church find no allusion to Christ's death in the passage; some do allude to the end of Jewish authority in the year 70 A.D. In explanations of this verse as well as in interpretations of the "week-years" and "the anointed," we find the greatest diversity and liberty among the Fathers of the Church. St. Jerome told his readers to hold whatever they regarded as fitting and proper.

[87] Matth. 23:28 ; 1 Cor. 5:7 ; Heb. 9:12.

The Apocrypha and Christ

During the Hellenistic period we find few expressions of Messianic expectation and hope in the canonical writings. Most of the inspired literature composed or receiving its final redaction at this time is didactic or historical in character. References to the coming Messianic kingdom, however, are not entirely absent, even though little or nothing is said of a personal Redeemer. Tobias looked forward to a new Jerusalem resplendent with unparalleled glory, the construction of a new temple, the return of the ten tribes, and the conversion of the Gentiles.[88] With allusion to Is. 66:24 Judith spoke of judgment upon the nations.[89] Jesus Sirach recalled the promises made to the patriarchs[90] and to David,[91] and was aware of prior prophecies concerning imminent judgment upon the Gentiles;[92] he prayed for the union of the tribes,[93] and noted past prophecy on Elias' return.[94] In vivid terms the author of the Book of Wisdom painted the judgment which the pious will hold over those who oppressed them.[95] After the fall of the Hasmoneans, Messianic expectation flourished among the common people. By the time of Jesus large circles of Jews, and the Samaritans too,[96] anxiously awaited the appearance of a personal Messiah.

The following pages will be devoted to a very cursory sketch of the

[88] Tob. 13:10-13; 14:5-7.
[89] Jud. 16:17.
[90] Sir. 44:21-23.
[91] Sir. 45:25; 47:1.
[92] Sir. 35:22; 36:2-3.
[93] Sir. 36:13.
[94] Sir. 48:20.
[95] Wis. 3:8; 5:1.
[96] John 4:25f.

Messianic hopes of pre-Christian Judaism. We shall see to what extent their expectations rested upon the oracles of the prophets, what development took place, and in what respects their ideas went counter to truths previously revealed.

Among the Apocrypha the most important works are the *Third Book of Sibyls* (652–793; the oldest portions date from 140 B.C.); the *Ethiopian Book of Henoch* (oldest portions from the second century before Christ; the parables in ch. 37–71 very probably date from the first century after Christ); the *Psalms of Solomon* (composed roughly between Pompey's seizure of Jerusalem in 63 B.C. and his death in 49 B.C.); the *Assumption of Moses* (written soon after the death of Herod); the *Fourth Book of Esdras* (from the reign of Domitian, 81–96); the *Syrian Apocalypse of Baruch* (after 100 A.D.). Of less importance is the *Book of Jubilees* (composed between the middle of the second century before Christ and the time of Herod); and the *Testament of the Twelve Patriarchs* (from the second or first century before Christ).

There is little unity in the portrait of the Messiah or in the expression of Messianic hopes as found in the Apocrypha. In the same book or even in sections of a book by the same author mutually contrary or contradictory statements may be found. Following are some of the main lines of emphasis.

The prophets had predicted dreadful judgment upon Israel and the nations; the apocryphal books describe a terrible visitation to come upon mankind, one, however, which is not identified with the judgment at the end of time. A preliminary judgment, called "the woes of the Messiah" by the Rabbis,[97] must precede the Messiah's birth or advent.[98] Sun and moon will become dark, the sun will shine in the night and the moon in the daytime, swords will be seen in the sky, blood will drop from the trees, full barns will become empty, springs will dry up.[99] Among men there will be general consternation and confusion: every bond will be broken, friend will rage against friend, son against father, daughter against mother. Nation will attack nation, and to the horrors of war will be added earthquakes, fire, famine — all bringing death to men.[1] On the basis of Mal. 3:23–24, Elias was expected as the Messiah's herald.[2]

After this turmoil, the Messiah appears, the Anointed One. The surname, Anointed, occurs frequently in the Apocrypha.[3] Because Daniel's "son of man"[4] was interpreted of a personal Messiah, this designation

---

[97] Cf. Matth. 24:8; Mark 13:9.
[98] Ferd. Weber, *Jüdische Theologie* 350.
[99] Sib. 3, 795–807; 4 Esdr. 5:1-13; 6:18-28.

[1] Apoc. Bar. 70:2-9; 4 Esdr. 6:24; 9:1-5; 13:29-31.
[2] Cf. Matth. 17:10; Mark 9:11.
[3] Hen. 48:10; 52:4; Ps. Sol. 17:32; 187; Apoc. Bar. 29:3; 30:1; 39:7; 40:1; 70:9; 72:2; 4 Esdr. 7:28-29; 12:32.
[4] Dan. 7:13-14.

also is found, especially in the parables of Henoch.[5] He is called "Son of Men" in Hen. 62:5; 69:29; 71:14, the "Chosen One" in Hen. 39:6; 40:5; 45:3-5; 49:2-4; 51:3, 5; 52:6, 9; 53:6; 55:4; 61:5, 8-10; 62:1, and "the King" in Sib. 5, 108; Ps. Sol. 17:42. In accord with prophetic tradition the Messiah was regarded as a descendant of David,[6] hence the title "Son of David" in Ps. Sol. 17:21; Sib. III 288. This designation became very common,[7] those Jews who regarded or suspected Jesus to be the Messiah addressed Him as "Son of David." God calls the Messiah His son in Hen. 105:2; 2 Esdr. 7:28; 13:32; 14:9. Apart from the prevailing opinion that as a son of David he would belong to the tribe of Judah,[8] we find an isolated passage declaring his descent from the family of Aaron and the tribe of Levi.[9] Because the *Testament of the Twelve Patriarchs* was written in a period when the priestly family of the Hasmoneans governed the nation, the Messiah is here heralded as a priest.[10] In the *Book of Jubilees* Levi is blessed by Isaac![11]

Pre-Christian Judaism pictured the Messiah as a ruler endowed by God with special powers. Accordingly he appears in the *Psalms of Solomon* as an earthly king,[12] yet without sin[13] and filled with power and wisdom through the operation of God's holy spirit.[14] The Sibylline literature takes the same approach; God's Messiah is simply "the holy Ruler."[15] But in later writings pre-existence is ascribed to him out of deference to Mich. 5:1: "His origins are from of old, from the days of eternity."[16] In the parables of Henoch we read: His Name[17] was mentioned in the presence of the Lord of spirits before the sun and the zodiac signs were made, before the stars of the heavens were created.[18] He was "chosen and hidden in God's sight" before the world was made.[19]

From the beginning he was hidden, and the Most High preserved him.[20] When Henoch, therefore, was led by the angel through the celestial regions, he saw "the Chosen One" under the wings of the Lord of spirits.[21] His appearance was as sweet as one of the holy angels.[22] His glory extended from eternity to eternity, his power from generation to generation. Upon him rested the spirit of wisdom and the spirit of him who bestows understanding, the spirit of doctrine and fortitude, and the spirit of those who die in righteousness.[23]

In 4 Esdras the Most High preserves the Anointed One for the end of days.[24] Esdras was promised that after his assumption into heaven, he would abide with the Messiah, the son of God, until the fullness of

[5] Hen. 46:1-6; 48:2-7; 62:5-11, 14; 63:11; 69:26-29; 70:1; 71:17; 4 Esdr. 13:3.
[6] Ps. Sol. 17:21; 4 Esdr. 12:32.
[7] Matth. 22:42.   [8] Jub. 31:18.
[9] A. Barucq, *De Messianismo in Documento Zadoquaeo* VD 16, 1936, 89-96. 123-127. 188-192. 242-245.
[10] Test. Levi 18.   [11] 31:13f.

[12] Ps. Sol. 17:23, 47.
[13] Ps. Sol. 17:41, 46.   [14] Ps. Sol. 17:42.
[15] Sib. 3, 49.   [16] Cf. Dan. 7:13-14.
[17] I.e., his being, nature.
[18] Hen. 48:3.   [19] Hen. 48:6.
[20] Hen. 62:7.   [21] Hen. 39:6.
[22] Hen. 46:1.   [23] Hen. 49:2-3.
[24] 4 Esdr. 12:32; 13:26.

time.[25] For no one on earth can see "God's son." [26] Later Judaism was satisfied with ascribing pre-existence only to the Name of the Messiah, because in arguing with Christians they emphasized his human aspects.

From his place at the throne of God, the Messiah will be sent to earth.[27] Certain texts speak of him as rising from the depths of the sea.[28] He will appear suddenly as triumphant ruler. Because a prophet had placed his birth at Bethlehem, it is assumed that he will live unknown for a time. In the discussion whether Jesus was the promised Messiah, the Jews said: "Of him (Jesus) we know whence he is (from Nazareth), but when the Christ comes, no one will know whence he is." [29] In Justin's Dialog, Trypho proposes the possibility that the Messiah was already born but had not as yet manifested himself publicly.[30]

Upon the Messiah's advent there will occur a violent uprising of the powers hostile to God.[31] But the Messiah will triumph over them.[32] The annihilation of the enemy will be effected through a mere word from his lips.[33] In Hen. 90:18 he appears after God inflicts judgment. The leader of the forces hostile to God is he who in the New Testament is called Antichrist.[34]

For the Apocrypha, too, the center of the Messianic kingdom is Jerusalem. According to the older concept, the new Jerusalem will be constructed by Gentile hands.[35] Even after the demolition of the city by the Romans, the Jews still hoped for its glorious restoration. But because of the canonical passages describing the beauty of the new Jerusalem, passages do occur in which the Jerusalem of eschatalogical times would be a heavenly one, far more magnificent than that on Sion; and presently it would descend to earth.[36] The dispersed of Israel return home to Palestine.[37] Thereby the Messianic kingdom is inaugurated, with God Himself as the supreme king.[38] This kingdom embraces the entire world, as the prophets had foretold. And the Gentile nations acknowledge Israel's God as their Lord.[39] Of the various Messianic blessings the presence of God and of the Messiah constitutes the greatest.[40] Men lead holy lives.[41] There is constant peace.[42] Even wild beasts do no more damage.[43] The deceased participate in these blessings, for all who lived virtuously will rise from their graves.[44] Some texts assume the resurrection both of the good and wicked.[45]

[25] 4 Esdr. 14:9.   [26] 4 Esdr. 13:52.
[27] Sib. 3, 286.   [28] 4 Esdr. 13:2, 25, 51.
[29] John 7:27.   [30] Dial. c. Tryph. 8.
[31] Sib. 3, 663f; Hen. 90:16; 4 Esdr. 12:32-33; 13:33.
[32] Sib. 3, 652; Hen. 46:4; Ps. Sol. 17:24f; Apoc. Bar. 39:56, 72f; 4 Esdr. 11:39f; 13:27.
[33] Ps. Sol. 17:22, 29; 4 Esdr. 13:28.
[34] 1 John 2:18, 22; 4:3; 2 John 7.
[35] Ps. Sol. 17:25, 33.
[36] Hen. 53:6; 90:28-29; 4 Esdr. 7:26; Apoc. Bar. 32:4.
[37] Ps. Sol. 11:2f; Hen. 57:4; Esdr. 13:34.

[38] Sib. 3, 704; Ps. Sol. 17:1, 38, 51.
[39] Sib. 3, 616, 698-726; Hen. 90:30, 37; 48:1; 53:1; Ps. Sol. 17:32-35; Apoc. Bar. 72:5.
[40] Hen. 45:4-5; 62:14.
[41] Ps. Sol. 17:20f; 18:8-9; Hen. 10:21-22.
[42] Sib. 3, 371-380; 751-760; Apoc. Bar. 73:4-5.
[43] Sib. 3, 788-798; Apoc. Bar. 73:6.
[44] Hen. 22:17; 91:10; Ps. Sol. 3:10f; 14:3f; Apoc. Bar. 30:1.
[45] Hen. 51:1; 61:53; Sib. 4, 180f; 4 Esdr. 5:45; 7:32; Apoc. Bar. 36:11; 42:7.

There are two opinions regarding the duration of the Messianic kingdom. According to one it is eternal, with judgment coming at its beginning.[46] This opinion prompted the retort when Jesus spoke of His death: "We know from the Law that the Messiah abides forever." [47] To live in the Messianic kingdom was regarded as the greatest of blessings, in fact it was impossible to imagine anything more desirable. Nevertheless, there were some who cherished the hope of still greater beatitude, that of heaven; and these found it necessary to restrict the duration of the Messianic kingdom. According to Apoc. Bar. 40:3, the reign of the Messiah would last until the world perished by divine decree. According to 4 Esdr. 7:28–29, the world would last for 400 years; then the Messiah dies and with him all mankind. Thereupon, in both these apocalypses, the restoration of the world takes place and the Last Judgment. The "400 years" result from reading Gen. 15:13 with its prediction of a 400 year serfdom in Egypt in association with Ps. 90:15 with its hope that the days of joy equal the days of oppression.

According to 4 Esdr. 14:11, the history of the world falls into twelve periods. At the time of the author "nine parts and half of the tenth part were already past" with but "two and one half" remaining. By allowing 400 years for each period, the world should last 4,800 years, after which it perishes only to be renewed again. According to Rabbinic computation the world must last 6,000 years, reflecting the six days of creation; an eternal Sabbath then follows — for 1,000 years are before God as a day gone by.[48] This 6,000 year period is further subdivided into 2,000 years before the Law, 2,000 years under the Law, and 2,000 years of Messianic bliss. On this theory the Messianic era should already have begun, but because of the sinfulness of the people, he is delaying his advent.[49]

It is remarkable that the Apocrypha never mention a suffering Messiah. His death after a 400 year reign in 4 Esdr. 7:28–29 involves no atonement for sin. For the Jews the Cross was a stumbling bock.[50] In Justin's Dialog, the Jew Trypho admits that the Christ must suffer as recorded in the Scriptures; [51] and reference is made to Is. 53:7. Rabbinic Judaism at times did come to the conclusion that the just Man would suffer to expiate the guilt of others.[52] But Trypho's admission was exceptional. Jewish opinion at the time of Jesus is reflected in the efforts of the apostles against the doctrine of a suffering and dying Savior.

In describing the blessings that accrue to mankind in the Messianic era, the older Apocrypha stress spiritual values, peace in God, righteousness among men. Thus we read in the Test. Levi 18: "He (the Messiah)

---

[46] Sib. 3, 49, 50, 288, 767; Ps. Sol. 17:3-4; Jub. 50:5; Hen. 45:4-5; 62:18.
[47] John 12:34.   [48] Ps. 90:4.
[49] Sanhedrin 97a, Abodah zara 9a.

[50] 1 Cor. 1:23.
[51] Dial. c. Tryph. 68. 89. 90.
[52] Ferd. Weber, *Jüdische Theologie* 326-330.

will open the gates of paradise; he will remove the sword that threatens Adam, and nourish the saints from the tree of life, and the spirit of holiness will be upon him. Beliar (the devil) will be bound by him; he will give his children the power to tread upon the evil spirits."

In this passage the Messiah appears less as a national king than as the prince of peace, the restorer of religious life. Likewise when there is question of peace in the animal world, early apocryphal literature does not contain a message different from that propounded by the prophets. But as a consequence of oppression by foreigners, the Jews showed increasingly less sympathy for a doctrine involving the conversion of Gentile nations and their reception into the Messianic kingdom, or personal purity of life. With a growing fervor they demanded the subjugation of the Gentiles, and to an ever increasing degree they imagined that the kingdom of God must bring them material benefits, even greater than paradise. The fruits of the earth would be multiplied ten thousandfold, a single vine would bear a thousand branches; a single branch a thousand clusters, a single cluster a thousand grapes, with a single grape yielding a kor of wine (about 90 gallons).[53] Manna would fall from heaven,[54] milk would bubble up from the ground.[55] From a measure of olives would flow ten baths of oil (about 360 quarts).[56] Men would live a thousand years and that without aging,[57] and would have 1,000 children.[58] Childbirth would be painless, nor would men tire in the labor of harvesting.[59] Behemoth and Leviathan would be served at banquet tables.[60]

In comparison to these utopian ideas, Philo's expectations with reference to Messianic blessings were most reserved. Like the prophets he counted on the return of fellow Jews dispersed throughout the world, peace between man and man and between man and beast. For him the most important attainment was virtue and the acceptance of God's law; descent from Abraham was not essential. But in supplying details to the picture, he could not rise above the popular approach: riches, health, power, countless descendants; and for him too the Messiah was a great warrior who conquers mighty nations.[61]

In Judaism's official literature, the Mishnah and Talmud, there are few references to the Messiah. The interest of Scribes was the Law and its application. In explaining passages from the Old Testament that refer to a personal Messiah, they agree on most essentials: the Messiah is a descendant of Judah and David, he is born at Bethlehem and is filled

---

[53] Apoc. Bar. 29:5.
[54] Apoc. Bar. 29:8.
[55] Sib. 3, 744.
[56] Hen. 11:19.
[57] Jub. 23:27-30.
[58] Hen. 10:17.
[59] Apoc. Bar. 73:2; 74:1.

[60] Apoc. Bar. 29:4; 4 Esdr. 6:19. In apocryphal literature Behemoth and Leviathan are mythical monsters created on the fifth day. In Job 40:15f the words describe the crocodile and hippopotamus.
[61] Philo, De Praem. et poen. 88f; De exsecrationibus 163f.

with the spirit of God; he rules with justice, bestows peace, subjects the Gentile nations to his Law, is victorious, enjoys the protection of the Most High. His kingdom is a glorious one and will endure; he is both king and priest, and will effect the deliverance of his people. On these points the doctrine of the Rabbis and Scribes reflected tradition. They do not agree, however, on the time of the Messiah's appearance, whether he would come humbly or in glory, whether he would be riding upon an ass or upon the clouds of heaven. To the problem whether the Messiah would suffer, the Rabbis follow an opinion advanced in the Targum: there will be two Messiahs, the one a son of Joseph (or at times Ephraim), the other a son of David. The first will struggle with enemies and suffer a violent death, the second will rule in Jerusalem and live forever. Nor is there unanimity among them on the question of the Messiah's relationship to Israel and to Gentile nations.[62]

Three times daily in the prayer *Shemone 'esre* [63] the pious Jew begged that God would "establish the kingdom of the house of David" and "hasten the budding of the shoot of David."

The Targum interprets messianically most of the passages that have been discussed above; an exception is the text concerning the Suffering Servant, which is transformed into a petition.

[62] Brierre-Narbonne 37.

[63] 18, or in later versions 19, ejaculations of praise.

Prophetic Form and Fulfillment

1. SKETCHING THE MESSIAH PICTURE. The period in which the Old Testament prophecies concerning the coming Redeemer were consigned to writing extended over many centuries. Countless millenia before Moses, who lived in the first half of the 13th century, the hope for a Savior had been placed in man's heart, shortly after the first sin in paradise. During this long primeval period, Messianic expectation had a history of its own. The first prophecies are quite obscure, and only gradually does the Messiah picture attain clarity. From the very beginning, however, it was evident that the Redeemer would not come into the world to deliver a given people, Israel, from temporal difficulties; his mission would involve the entire human race in its relationship to God. The protoevangel told of the battle each person must wage against the infernal serpent, and at his call Abraham, from whom the Chosen People would descend, heard that *all the tribes of the earth* would participate in his good fortune. In the centuries following, heralds of the Messianic message enriched the picture sketched by their predecessors with new shades and lines. The survey of Messianic prophecies made above has provided us with details.

The protoevangel showed how every person is able to ward off the serpent's enticements, and has the duty to do so; but as the New Testament teaches, it will be a certain Individual who will crush the head of the evil enemy definitively, even though He may experience something of his bite. Then from Noe's blessing we learn how salvation will be mediated to mankind through Sem's posterity.[64] The call of Abraham and the promises made to him repeatedly by God show that he was destined to preserve the heritage of the true religion for mankind. The blessing of the dying Jacob revealed that a specific person, a descendant of the tribe of Judah, had the mission of bringing salvation to the world.[65] Genealogical pointers become increasingly more definite as the ages pass. The Redeemer stems from the family of David,[66] and as proclaimed by Ezechiel during the Babylonian exile, he will be a child of Joachin.[67]

While the Southern Kingdom was passing through a period of gravest danger, we hear that a virgin will give birth to the child divinely chosen to deliver Israel.[68] He will be born in humble circumstances, at a time when the royal family of David had lost status and resembles a hut fallen and lying in ruins.[69] He is the sprout from Jesse's stump, a twig from his root.[70] And because David's family no longer reigns in Jerusalem, his birth takes place at Bethlehem.[71]

Since the Messiah has the mission to redeem mankind, he must be more than mere man. Isaias calls him "strong God, Father forever," [72] titles applied to the true God and which no Old Testament prophet ever received. He is God's Son,[73] destined to sit at Yahweh's right hand.[74] Because Jesus solemnly acknowledged that He was "the Messiah, God's Son" before the Sanhedrin, He was officially condemned to death.[75]

2. THE MESSIAH'S MISSION. In the providence of God, the Messiah was sent to deliver mankind from the misery of sin. He fulfilled this task functioning as king, as prophet, and as priest.

Jacob had heralded the Messiah as the ruler to whom belonged the sceptre and to whom the Gentile nations would tender obedience.[76] For Balaam he was the star that would rise out of Jacob; he would crush Moab, the symbol of powers hostile to God, and destroy all the sons of warmongers.[77] When the tribe of Judah attained hegemony in the person of David, the Messiah was proclaimed as the sprout of David. His sway was to embrace the whole world. The nations would seek him.[78] He would rule from sea to sea and from the river Euphrates to the ends of the earth, while all kings would do homage before him, all nations be his subjects.[79] Even as a child he governs,[80] justice is his guiding star, peace his gift to the world; [81] and he teaches men to live

---

[64] Gen. 9:24-27.
[65] Gen. 49:10.
[66] 2 Sam. 7:16 ; Ps. 89:30, 37-38.
[67] Ez. 17:22.
[68] Is. 7:14; Mich. 5:1-2.
[69] Am. 9:11.

[70] Is. 11:1.
[71] Mich. 5:1.
[72] Is. 9:5.
[73] Ps. 2:7.
[74] Ps. 110:1.
[75] Matth. 26:63-64.

[76] Gen. 49:10.
[77] Num. 24:17.
[78] Is. 11:1.
[79] Ps. 72:8-11 ; 2:6 ; 110:1.
[80] Is. 9:5.
[81] Is. 9:5-6.

virtuously.[82] He does not attain his ends through the might of arms, but as we hear in exile times, he acts toward his followers as a good shepherd.[83] He will accord preferential treatment to the oppressed, the sick, the unfortunate. Such a spirit was, of course, unintelligible to later Jewry. They demanded a political Messiah who would break the yoke of the Romans and make them world rulers. Jesus sought to lead sinners back to God; highly disillusioned the Jews accused Him of "claiming" to be "Christ the king" before the Roman governor.[84] Therefore the inscription upon the Cross: "Jesus of Nazareth, the King of the Jews." [85]

As the prophet whose task was to proclaim God's will and convert the erring, the Messiah would possess the fullness of God's holy spirit.[86] He was to address not only Israel, the Gentiles too should be recipients of his message on justice, on the true God, and on man's duties toward Him [87] — a Light to the Gentiles.[88] As the "light for the illumination of the Gentiles," the Christ-Child was greeted by Simeon.[89] Jesus was "the Light that shone in the darkness." [90] At the time of His appearance, the Jews were expecting that God would raise up a prophet, and some of them identified Him with this prophet.[91] The Samaritans cherished a like hope, relying upon the words of Deut. 18:15, 18, which promised the people prophetic guidance whenever needed.

When the Northern tribes were led into the Assyrian captivity, Isaias comforted those who remained and were living among pagans by saying: "The people who walk in darkness see a great Light; those who live in the land of the shadow of death — for them a Light has risen." [92] Assyria's yoke would be broken, and a Redeemer would come. Because Jesus preached principally in Galilee where Assyria's "rod of correction" had fallen most severely, St. Matthew saw in His action a fulfillment of the Isaian prophecy.[93] In a very true sense, the Messiah's work as prophet was not destined for success, in vain would be his efforts, "for nothing and uselessly" would he spend his energy.[94] Jesus was obliged to complain bitterly over the obstinacy of the Jews.[95]

To predict future events was not an essential part of any prophet's mission, yet many prophets were privileged to know what the future held in store; the charism served as a means of divine accreditation. Jesus foretold intimate details of His death and resurrection, revealed the vicissitudes of His Church, and directed His gaze to the end of time. Another token of divine endorsement was the power to work miracles. Now the activity of Jesus was like a chain of miracles. Accord-

[82] Jer. 30:9; Ps. 72:7.
[83] Ez. 34:23; 37:23, 25.
[84] Luke 23:2.
[85] John 19:19.
[86] Is. 11:2.
[87] Is. 42:1.
[88] Is. 42:6; 49:6.

[89] Luke 2:32.
[90] John 1:5.
[91] John 7:40-41.
[92] Is. 8:23; 9:1.
[93] Matth. 4:14-16.
[94] Is. 49:4.
[95] Matth. 23:37; 11:20-24.

ing to Malachias the Messiah's advent was to be heralded by a prophet.[96] This oracle Jesus interpreted as referring to John the Baptist.[97]

The coming Redeemer should unite in himself the royal and the priestly functions, being "a priest forever according to the order of Melchisedech."[98] To His disciples Jesus gave His flesh and blood as nourishment under the forms of bread and wine. That the Messiah would be king and priest had been expressed symbolically when the prophet Zacharias placed the royal crown upon the head of the high priest Josue.[99]

It was our Savior's task to lead men back to God through His activity as a teacher or prophet; and as the innocent "Man of Sorrows" He shed His blood for sinners. Isaias' Servant of Yahweh was mocked and spit upon, he suffered and died as an expiatory sacrifice for mankind.[1] Those responsible for his death would some day bitterly regret their deed.[2] Death at the hands of evil men did not spell the end for the Suffering Servant. The lamentation of the innocent sufferer in Ps. 22 suddenly changes into jubilation when he miraculously receives new life and escapes death; and the Servant of Yahweh rises anew after burial with evildoers. With highest confidence the psalmist looks forward to resurrection in Ps. 16. These prophecies were fulfilled in Jesus and only in Jesus.

3. The Messianic Kingdom. The great Deliverer would be an Israelite, a descendant of David; but his activity would not be restricted to his own people. Israelites would belong to his kingdom, not, however, simply because they were sons of Abraham. Yahweh would enter into another covenant with a cleansed, purified people, a people who had abandoned the ways of sin. The Messianic kingdom, accordingly, includes those of Israel who serve Yahweh in all fidelity after passing through the sea of suffering *and* the Gentile world that likewise experiences the chastisement of God to the point of annihilation. Judgment was intended to convert both God's Chosen People and the pagan nations; certain passages imply that the Gentiles will find the way to God first and then through their mediation Israel as a people will enter the kingdom of God.[3] The salvation of the world is effected through the Jews in so far as they preserved the true faith and furnished the racial background for the Redeemer.

4. Jesus and Prophetic Pronouncements. The Old Testament was a time of expectation, the New Testament one of fulfillment. The Old Testament was the shadow, the New Testament is the reality. The Old Testament was the dawn, the New Testament is the full light of day.

[96] Mal. 3:1, 22-23.
[97] Matth. 11:10, 14; 17:12-13.
[98] Ps. 110:4.　[99] Zach. 6:11-14.
[1] Is. 52:13—53:12.
[2] Zach. 12:10.
[3] Is. 11:10-12; 19:16-24.

The Old Testament heralded what was to come, the New Testament proclaims what has been done. When the sun of the new Day rose before their eyes did the Jews realize that they were privileged to witness a blessing for which their fathers had been longing through many centuries?

The teaching and miracles of Jesus did make a significant impression, and the Jews could not but ask themselves whether He was the promised Redeemer. The question was raised at the restoration to life of the youth at Naim,[4] again at the miraculous multiplication of bread.[5] To Jesus' inquiry concerning the Son of Man, Peter replied that some regarded Him as the promised prophet.[6] On occasion Jesus admitted openly that the prophecies were fulfilled in Him. "You search the Scriptures; they give testimony of me," He retorted to the Scribes and Pharisees when they sought to upbraid Him for healing the lame man and violating the Sabbath rest. On another occasion He reproached them in a similar manner: "If you believed Moses, you would believe in me, for he wrote of me."[7] When John the Baptist sent messengers from prison with the question whether He was the Messiah promised by the prophets, He simply reminded them in the prophet's words of the miracles He had worked.[8] And then He explained how the Baptist was the one whom Malachias had proclaimed as the Messiah's forerunner.[9]

On occasion He reminded the apostles of the prophecies describing His passion, death, and resurrection: "Now we go up to Jerusalem and all will be accomplished that was written by the prophets about the Son of man; for he will be handed over to the Gentiles and will be mocked and scourged and spit upon; and after they have scourged him, they will put him to death. But on the third day he will rise again."[10] While making their way to Mount Olivet, He reminded the apostles: "This text too must be fulfilled in me: With evildoers he will be counted."[11] He reproached the disciples from Emmaus: "How slow and dull of heart you are in believing all what the prophets have said! Was not the Messiah obliged to suffer, and so enter into his glory? Then he began with Moses and in each prophet through all of Scripture he explained to them the prophecies about himself."[12]

The apostles considered the Old Testament prophecies fulfilled in Jesus. When Peter appeared before the multitude on the first Christian Pentecost, he quoted Joel's oracle on the outpouring of God's spirit in Messianic times and passages from the psalms revealing Christ's resurrection and ascension.[13] Philip instructed the pagan treasurer of the

4 Luke 7:16.
5 John 6:14.
6 Matth. 16:14.
7 John 5:39, 46.
8 Matth. 11:4.
9 Matth. 11:10.
10 Luke 18:31-33.
11 Luke 22:37.
12 Luke 24:25-27.
13 Acts 2:14f.

queen of Ethiopia by showing how Isaias' words in the Ebed-Yahweh poems had come true in Christ's atoning death for the sins of mankind.[14] Paul began his richly theological letter to the Romans by noting how God had foretold the gospel through His prophets.[15] In the Letter to the Hebrews, one citation from the Old Testament follows another, all bearing upon the Lord Jesus. In his Gospel St. Matthew never wearies showing how prophecies about the coming Redeemer have been fulfilled in our blessed Savior.[16]

This difference, however, must not be overlooked between the Old Testament messages and their fulfillment. Jesus was David's son and, as such, a king. The Magi from the East came to reverence Him as the King of the Jews. But His kingship reflected nothing of earthly splendor.

The very fact that the family of David retained nothing of its former prestige after the Babylonian exile and was gradually forgotten, should have been a warning to the Jews not to associate an earthly kingdom with the Messiah. Poverty marked the life of Jesus — the foxes have holes and the birds nests while the Son of Man has nowhere to lay His head.[17] He promised those who followed Him no worldly honor or fortune, but demanded self-denial and love for the cross.[18] He praised as blessed those who willingly become poor and suffer persecution,[19] He insisted that His followers remain free from profane cares,[20] He fled from the multitude when they attempted to crown Him for having provisioned them plentifully with bread, in expectation of further material aid.[21]

Before Pilate He acknowledged: "I am a king." But He immediately added: "I was born and came into the world for this purpose: to give witness to the truth. My kingdom is not of this world." [22] Quietly His kingdom had already taken form in the midst of the Jews to whom He was preaching; [23] there was no resort to force, rather He forbade His disciples to fight.[24] His entrance into the Holy City on Palm Sunday riding upon a donkey — the only occasion on which He accepted human acclaim — shows that He came to bring peace.[25] These considerations should be sufficient to show that the prophecies on the kingship of the Messiah are to be understood spiritually according to Jeremias' dictum: "I will put my Law in their midst and write it in their heart; and I will be God to them and they will be my people." [26] The portrait of the Messiah as king must not be dissociated from that of the Suffering Servant.

---

[14] Acts 8:26f.
[15] Rom. 1:2.
[16] Cf. likewise Acts 3:18, 21; 10:43; 13:27; 26:22; 28:23; 1 Cor. 15:3; Heb. 1:1; 1 Pet. 1:11; 2 Pet. 3:2.
[17] Matth. 8:20.
[18] Matth. 16:24.
[19] Matth. 5:3, 6.
[20] Matth. 6:25f.
[21] John 6:15.
[22] John 18:37.
[23] Luke 17:21.
[24] Matth. 26:52; John 18:36.
[25] Zach. 9:9; Matth. 21:1f.
[26] Jer. 31:33.

The same holds true of the prophecies which present the Messiah as a prophet. Jesus was not only a prophet, but the consummation of prophecy. He applied to Himself the text describing the duties and the spiritual endowments of prophets.[27] Of John the Baptist, who deemed himself unworthy to loose the sandal strings of the "One greater" than himself, our Savior said, "He is more than a prophet,"[28] because he prepared the day for Him about whom all the prophets had spoken. Christ's relationship to the prophets of the Old Testament resembled that of a king's son to the royal household.[29] A distinction, therefore, is made between the prophets through whom God "in times past" had spoken and His Son.[30] And lastly, as priest He offered Himself as an atonement sacrifice for the sins of the world and with His Blood effected an eternal covenant between God and men.[31]

5. MESSIANIC BLESSINGS. a) *Modus loquendi*. In describing the Messianic kingdom, the prophets reveal themselves as artists who have more than one color on their palettes. The metaphors they use are media to convey the ideas God's spirit inspires; and they seek to edify and arouse those whom they are addressing. Now according to their oracles Israel's fields will become incomparably fruitful in Messianic times, a point already made by the patriarch Jacob.[32] Sowing and harvesting, plowing and vintage will follow upon one another without intervening delays.[33] Children will be so numerous as to defy a count — like the stars in the sky and the grains of sand on the seashore.[34] Disease will be a thing of the past, no one will die young.[35] The era of Solomon, when the wealth of the world flowed to Jerusalem, will return.[36] Precious stones will serve as building material in the Holy City.[37] The people enjoy unbroken peace.[38] Wild beasts, a plague in the days following a war, constitute no danger; the wolf tarries alongside the lamb, and the panther rests with the goat.[39] Even the heavenly bodies will change; their rays will become more intense,[40] no longer will there be the constant change of day and night.[41] God creates a new heaven and a new earth.[42]

On the basis of these and similar statements the Jews expected that the Messiah would bring them a wealth of material blessings, with Gentiles humbly standing at their service. Are the prophets responsible for such deductions? The very fact that the Messiah was depicted as the Suffering Servant should have made them cautious. Nor did material advantages ever constitute a major point in prophetic preaching; they stressed the development of a religious mentality, love of God, moral living. Their oft-repeated spiritual challenges, their exhortations to

27 Luke 4:16 ; Is. 61:1-2.
28 Matth. 11:9 ; 3:11.
29 Matth. 21:37.
30 Heb. 1:1-2.
31 Matth. 26:28.
32 Gen. 49:11-12.
33 Am. 9:13.
34 Os. 2:1 ; 14:7-8.
35 Is. 35:5-6 ; 65:20, 23.
36 Is. 23:17-18 ; 45:14 ; 60:5-17 ; 61:6.
37 Is. 54:11-12.
38 Os. 2:20; Is. 9:4-6 ; Mich. 4:3-4.
39 Is. 11:6-9 ; 35:9.
40 Is. 30:26.
41 Is. 60:20.
42 Is. 65:17; 66:22.

penance and conversion, their assurance that Israel would not escape impending judgment, were so many indications to evaluate rightly those descriptions of Messianic times which seemingly proposed material benefits.

b) *Impossibilities.* There are statements in the prophets which seem utterly impossible when coldly and deliberately considered. Could Palestine, for instance, be divided into equally large strips running from east to west without reference to the rugged terrain and the rivers when the twelve tribes re-inhabit the land in Messianic times? [43] Of the Northern tribes only remnants remained, the tribes in historical times were not equally large, long before the exile the tribe of Simeon had already been amalgamated with that of Judah. And how could precious gems serve as building material in Jerusalem, or lions change their natures to such a degree as to feed upon straw! If the heavenly bodies would emit a substantially greater amount of light, there would likewise be an increased intensity of heat — to the destruction of vegetation.

c) *Metaphor and reality.* The above considerations prompt the conclusion that in the descriptions of blessings proper to the Messianic era we are not to see a calm, prosaic recital of future eventualities, but figures of speech whose meaning is to be deduced from the context and the author's purposes. A distinction must be made between the language employed and the message intended, between the essential idea and accidental phraseology. It is the divinely revealed truth that gives prophetic pronouncement its value; the terms employed to express this truth derive from the environment; the prophets naturally used idioms proper to their day. Moreover, the literary ability of one writer differed from that of another. Divine inspiration does not modify an individual's natural talent or skill. An identical message could and often was expressed in most unlike terms by successive hagiographers. There was a continual striving for originality of expression. Old wine in new bottles.

According to Os. 2:20; Is. 9:4; Mich. 5:9–10; Zach. 9:10, all weapons of war will be broken and burned with the advent of the Messianic era; but in Is. 2:4; Mich. 4:3 they are beaten into useful tools. In Mich 5:7; Zach. 14:14 the Gentile nations are plundered, in Is. 60:5–11; 66:12; Agg. 2:7 they willingly bring their treasures to Jerusalem. The water from the spring in the temple flows into the Dead Sea (Ez. 47:1–12), or half into the Dead Sea and half into the Mediterranean (Zach. 14:8), or thirdly, it waters the valley of Shittim. [44] In Ez. 34:25 the wild beasts are extirpated, while a number of other passages make them friendly and domestic. [45] Sion is the highest of mountains in Is. 2:2. In Zach. 14:10 it is the only mountain with all the remaining land a level plain.

[43] Ez. 48.
[45] Is. 11:7-9 ; 35:9 ; 65:25.

[44] By which the Kedron valley is probably meant. Joel 4:18.

Always remember: the prophets were children of their age and their country, they were poets and cast their prophecies in *poetic* forms; they preferred an attentive audience, and common people never remain attentive to an abstract speaker.

d) *Lack of perspective.* Frequently the prophets were instructed about coming events in visions. Details remained hazy. In presenting the message received, chronological sequence was unimportant. They would juxtapose events of the immediate and most distant future alongside one another or present them in any haphazard array. Just as the eye discerns no depth dimension in the stars of the heavens and regards the rays from various stars as equidistant while the actual light distance may vary by millenia, so in spirit the prophet beheld as contemporaneous events that would take place at various times. Accordingly, the prophets before and during the exile do not distinguish sharply between preparations for the Messianic kingdom (e.g., the return from exile) and the Messianic kingdom itself. For the older prophets the advent of the Messianic age coincides with the dissolution of the Assyrian empire or with the fall of Babylon and the return from captivity. Another example: Emmanuel *is* a child when the land is devastated by Tiglath-pileser.[46] The Servant of Yahweh should lead those languishing in exile out of their prison dungeons.[47] The Messiah did not appear till centuries after the return from Babylon, but this return was in itself a preparation for the Redeemer's appearance in the Holy Land and a type of mankind's deliverance from the bondage of sin.

This typical relationship was not overlooked by the prophets. In a single tableau they beheld two events inherently related to one another, viz., the return from Babylon and the Messiah's advent. Likewise the prophets joined together the Messiah's advent or the beginning of the Messianic era with its consummation at the end of time — our Savior's coming in lowliness and His glorious parousia. Similarly the Baptist proclaimed that the Redeemer *had* put the ax to the root and with winnowing fork in hand was cleansing the threshing floor.[48] Jesus will indeed appear as judge, but meanwhile weeds and wheat grow alongside one another. Judgment did come upon Israel with the destruction of Jerusalem, and it will come upon the world at the end of time. John the Baptist paid no attention to the intervening period in his effort to show that final judgment was inevitable and imminent.

e) *Impact of history and of political conditions.* When the prophets painted the future, Israel's past history frequently served as a model. The deliverance of the people from Egyptian bondage with the miracles accompanying the wilderness journey became the background against

---

[46] Is. 7:14-15.   [47] Is. 42:7; 49:6-9.   [48] Matth. 3:10-12.

which they sketched the liberation from exile in Babylon; and the latter in turn was employed as a type for Messianic redemption. Because of a miracle Israel was enabled to cross the Reed Sea; in a similar manner Yahweh would lead His people away from Babylon in the midst of marvels.[49] David's military triumphs, by which the neighboring nations became subject to Israel, and Solomon's reign of peace and of wealth and of splendor became standard types for Messianic blessings. As enemies of God's future kingdom we meet nations that in the past had menaced the Chosen People or were currently oppressing them — Edom, Moab, Ammon, Egypt, Assyria, Babylon; and the weapons for the eschatalogical wars are the same as those with which the prophets were familiar, viz., spears, arrows, bows, swords, shields. The judgment upon God's enemies in Messianic times is depicted in terms recalling the destruction of Sodom and Gomorrha through fire and brimstone and Israel's own visitations through famine, plague, and enemy attack. Yahweh's appearance in judgment recalls descriptions of His manifestation at Sinai in the midst of lightning and thunder, tempest and earthquake. The joys of Messianic times are related in terms of the sacrificial meal associated with a Mosaic peace offering.

Current events in the social and political order also exercised an influence upon the external form of prophecy. While Israel was being oppressed by enemies, salvation was described in terms of deliverance and peace. After the exile, when the Israelites were perturbed over the "unworthiness" of the temple they were building, Aggeus consoled them, saying: This temple will surpass Solomon's in glory.[50] He was implying that the Gentiles would acknowledge as their God Yahweh who was worshipped in their temple and would subject themselves to Him; and that their temple would stand to witness the dawn of the Messianic age. While the dynasty of David was reigning gloriously in Jerusalem, the prophets spoke of the Messiah in terms of a king. After the kingdom had perished and the people had been deported to many lands, it became necessary to comfort them in their misery. Ezechiel then used the parable of the good shepherd tending his flock, and another prophet created the figure of Yahweh's Servant suffering for his fellow men — the exiles should look up to him as their model. When the Northern tribes were groaning under the bondage of an alien government, they were told that the oppressor would bring them back to the fatherland and serve them as male and female servants.[51] When they found themselves lacking the necessities of life, they were consoled by oracles telling how the Gentiles would carry their wealth to Jerusalem.[52]

We are not, however, to evaluate such prophecies in an isolated

[49] Is. 11:15.   [50] Agg. 2:6-9.   [52] Is. 23:17-18; 60:5-17; Agg. 2:7;
[51] Is. 14:2; 45:14; 49:22-23; 60:4-11.   Ps. 72:8-11.

fashion. In parallel passages, often by the same prophet, we find other oracles promising the Gentiles equal rights in the new kingdom of God.[53] In fact, there were good indications that Israel will be converted after them and through their agency. The Jews gladly accepted such predictions as made them masters and the Gentiles servants; they paid little attention to prophecies that exhorted them to humility and modesty, or demanded conversion from sin, or heralded judgment upon them, or promised God's love to the Gentiles. The prophets cannot be quoted in favor of particularistic trends. When they spoke of the Gentiles bringing the Jews back to the Promised Land and serving them, they were simply expressing how non-Jews would acknowledge Israel's mission as God's people and as the bearers of the true religion which they were now ready to accept. The incorporation of the Gentile world into the new kingdom of God on an equal basis with Israel was a point of major importance to the prophets.

f) *Paradise and the Messianic picture.* In describing the blessings of Messianic times the prophets did not hesitate to draw upon the common concept of paradise, even though no direct references are made. The Messianic paradise will not be restricted to some tiny area, to a garden in Eden; nor will its inhabitants be a few individuals especially favored. All who serve God and belong to His new kingdom will enjoy its pleasures. It must therefore extend over the entire earth. In paradise there was no sin and none of its evil consequences — no disease, no suffering, no death. This state of affairs is now resumed, since men live as saints. The desert is transformed into Eden, Sion and Canaan into the garden of Eden. In paradise the wild beasts did not injure man. They will be equally tame and harmless in Messianic times; hostility among men no longer will exist, nor among the beasts. Disharmony will disappear in God's creation, replaced by love and peace.

This is the simple message the prophets couched in figurative phraseology. In the paradise account Yahweh Himself led the animals before Adam so that he would name them. The sacred writer was simply bringing out the point how man realized the inferiority of animals because they lacked the power of reason. This animal parade in the Genesis story is a matter of literary style; the sacred author surely did not imply that all the animals upon earth filed past Adam, including polar bears and tigers, zebras and walruses. Granted that poetry enters into the description of the original paradise story, poetry should not be excluded from prophetic descriptions of the paradise of Messianic times.

g) *Cult.* In the oracles of the prophets Sion is the center of the Messianic kingdom. To Sion the nations pilgrimage, in Sion the Messiah-King

[53] Is. 56:3-7.

erects his throne. Moreover, the prophets regarded the temple as the sanctuary of the Messianic age and took for granted the continuance of the Levitical priesthood [54] as well as the continuance of bloody sacrifices.[55] The Gentile nations too will offer animal sacrifices to the true God.[56] The feasts of the Messianic era will be the Sabbath, the New Moon, Tabernacles.[57] But alongside these prophecies we find others of a different type. The Ark of the Covenant will cease to exist, in fact it will no longer be missed; [58] the Aaronic priesthood will be rejected,[59] there will be priests from among the Gentiles,[60] a new sacrifice will be offered differing from the current offerings of the Old Testament.[61] These contrary statements are an indication that temple and sacrifice are literary terms, and in the Messianic future God will be worshipped under new ritual.

h) *Material goods.* Occasionally it is a difficult task to distinguish the essential message of a prophetic pronouncement from its extrinsic form, to unravel the author's idea from the figurative language in which it is wrapped. This difficulty contributed to an interpretation of the Messianic era, its blessings, and the nature of the Redeemer's advent quite at variance with the reality. The prophets personally may have evaluated certain aspects of their prophecies in such a way that, as we know from fulfillment, was not part of the essential message. God fulfilled their pronouncements in a more perfect manner than what they subjectively imagined.

Moral reform is part of the very first prophecy, the protoevangel. Material prosperity was promised to Abraham at his call; but the essential blessing undoubtedly was the knowledge of the true God, and this constituted the good fortune that he was destined to bequeath to his descendants and to all nations. In the prophecies which heralded the Messiah as king, the principal point is the inauguration of a reign of justice, viz., a mode of living in conformity to God's holy will. The products of Canaan, grain, milk, wine were Yahweh's gifts, and therefore we find them mentioned in context with the Messiah's kingdom. But God gives His gifts as reward for faithfully serving Him — again the decisive factor is a moral one.

Jesus too promised rewards for the observance of His commandments; while the Lord's prayer itself contains a petition for daily bread. Jesus was particularly interested in the hungry, the sick, and the poor. The admonition, "Ask, it will be given to you," [62] must not be restricted to spiritual needs. Nevertheless, by clearly stating that present life must entail suffering and persecution for His followers, with the balancing of

[54] Jer. 33:18.
[55] Jer. 33:11.
[56] Is. 19:21; Soph. 3:10; Is. 56:7; 60:7; Zach. 14:20-21.
[57] Is. 66:23; Zach. 14:16, 18.
[58] Jer. 3:16.   [59] Mal. 1:10.
[60] Is. 66:21.   [61] Mal. 1:11.
[62] Matth. 7:7.

accounts following only hereafter, Jesus our Savior taught that the divine promises on material goods in the description of the Messianic kingdom are to be interpreted in a higher sense — they are symbols of spiritual values proper to the Messianic kingdom.

6. OBSCURITIES. In numerous instances the fulfillment of a prophecy is our best key to its message. Nevertheless, a survey of the various books does leave obscure passages. The fulfillment of certain oracles has not yet taken place. Some prophecies by their very nature were conditional, nor is this restricted to those comminatory in nature. "At one moment I may threaten a people and a kingdom to extirpate it and to destroy it and to annihilate it; but if this people turn from their wickedness for which reason I threatened them, I will repent of the evil that I was planning against them. At one moment I may promise a people or a kingdom to build it and to plant it solidly; but if they do what is evil in my sight by disobeying my voice, I will repent of the good that I had in store for them." [63] It is in man's power, then, to determine whether God will punish or reward. Would Jerusalem have become the center of the Church instead of Rome if Israel had listened to her Savior? Israel rejected the divine advances, and the nations she despised received the inheritance; the capital of paganism became the Holy City of Christ's kingdom on earth.

This kingdom has not yet attained its full and final perfection. Our prayer still is: "Thy kingdom come!" The true God is not yet worshipped in every place, and individuals still reject Him after an initial enthusiasm. Therefore the prophecies on the chastisement of the nations have not lost all validity. Continually judgment is being inflicted, today upon this country, tomorrow upon another; and this judgment is being carried out by modern armies although their banners may have different insignia than those of Egypt, Assyria, Babylon, Moab, Edom. Unaware of their mission, they advance according to God's designs. They are "the rod of his wrath, the staff of his fury" [64] until the Last Judgment, as was proclaimed in Ezechiel's oracle over Gog.[65] The fulfillment of the prophecies touching the end of the world still relate to the future, and until then there will be wars — the scourge of God for the sins of men. Alongside prophecies of eternal peace we meet the cry: "Prepare for war, awake the warrior, beat your plowshares into swords and your pruning hooks into spears." [66] The prophecies of eternal peace are to become a reality only after the end of the world, after the dissolution of the present world order.

A great number of prophecies were fulfilled with the advent of Jesus in lowliness, others will be fulfilled when He returns in glory. At the

[63] Jer. 18:7-10.   [64] Is. 11:5.   [65] Ez. 38—39 ; Wis. 4:20—5:14.   [66] Joel 4:9-10.

parousia we will see clearly which prophetic oracles referred to the present stage of the Messianic kingdom and which to its eschatalogical phase. The promises of peace in Messianic times, a peace like that in paradise, have not been voided by the miseries now current throughout the world. The prophets were not the only ones who foresaw a renovation of the material order.[67] For St. Paul creation "was subjected to vanity" but it will be "delivered from the servitude of corruption into the glorious liberty of God's children; for we know that all creation groans and is still in labor." [68] Concerning Christ's second advent and the end of the world, St. Peter wrote: "According to his word we await a new heaven and a new earth in which justice lives." [69] And St. John beheld "a new heaven and a new earth; for the first heaven and the first earth are passed away." [70]

These passages clearly differentiate between the first advent of our Redeemer in the flesh and His second to judge mankind. The prophets never made this distinction so precisely. How nature's transformation will be effected remains a mystery in spite of New Testament revelations.

<hr>

[67] Is. 65:17 ; 66:22.　　[68] Rom. 8:20-22.　　[69] 2 Pet. 3:13.　　[70] Apoc. 21:1.

Christ in Type

~~~~~~~~

1. LITERAL AND TYPICAL SENSES. We have seen how the Old Testament presents Jesus as the Messiah and how the Messianic picture becomes increasingly clearer and richer in the course of centuries. This was due to the efforts of the prophets, men illumined by God in a most extraordinary manner. We evaluated their pronouncements in the literal sense, viz., according to the meaning they intended to convey. The latest encyclical on Sacred Scripture, *Divino afflante Spiritu*, of September 30, 1943, again stressed the necessity of basing exegesis upon the literal sense of the text.

Nevertheless, in addition to the literal sense the Old Testament contains a second, or typical sense, in numerous passages. In His omniscience God was able to attach a significance to persons, objects, and events that remained unknown to those living in pre-Christian times. This hidden message, one related to Christ or to His kingdom, was not made known to the inspired authors themselves; it was only revealed "in the fullness of time," with the fulfillment of the literal sense of the pertinent Messianic oracle. The persons, objects, and events in question are called *types*; that to which they point forward or signify is called the *antitype*.

The New Testament sacred writers were highly aware of this relationship between the two Testaments. They regarded the Old Covenant as "the shadow of future things," [71] and while St. Paul emphasized the superiority of the New over the Old, he still interpreted the one as a

[71] Col. 2:17; Rom. 5:14; Heb. 8:5; 10:1.

212

preparation for the other. This too was the approach of the early Church. St. Augustine's classic dictum, "In the Old the New is concealed, in the New the Old lies revealed," [72] has a special relevance to the typical implications present in the Old Testament story. The passages are innumerable in which the liturgy utilizes Old Testament types. One of the more notable listing of types is found in the Sequence of the Mass on Corpus Christi:

> In figuris praesignatur:
> cum Isaac immolatur,
> agnus paschae deputatur,
> datur manna patribus.

The sacrifice of Isaac, the paschal lamb, and the manna are types of the Blessed Eucharist. The typical sense does not involve any message on the part of the inspired writer flowing immediately from his words; it is related to the persons, objects or actions which, apart from the message proper to the words and intended by the author, point to some other truth in the economy of salvation. The persons concerned actually lived, the precepts involved were obligatory, the events in question did occur at the time indicated. The typical sense, therefore, *must not be confused with figurative language or allegory* — with which it has nothing in common.

Since the typical sense is a true sense of Sacred Scripture, it was intended by the Holy Spirit and may be used as Biblical support for dogma. First, however, it must be established that the Holy Spirit actually intended the relationship between the given antitype and the person, practice, event, or object with which it is associated; this may at times be difficult. The norm or criterion is the New Testament and tradition, and only when these provide a solid basis may typical exegesis serve as theological proof. The opinion of an individual ecclesiastical writer from antiquity is not sufficient for dogmatic certitude. Nor is it sufficient simply to recognize a similarity between the Old Testament person or thing and its New Testament antitype. The primary author of Sacred Scripture, the Holy Spirit, must have willed each specific typical relationship. Some New Testament texts reveal the Holy Spirit's mind by introducing the statement as the "fulfillment" of an Old Testament passage.[73] The dignity of the antitype always surpasses that

[72] Aug. *Quaest. in Hept.*, II, 73, cf. *Sermo*, 160, 6.

[73] Matth. 2:15; John 19:36. The introductory formula, "so that it might be fulfilled what was written," could be used by the sacred writer with reference to genuinely literal or typical passages or, secondly, with reference to passages to which he was alluding by way of accommodation or association. Instances of the latter would not meet all the conditions for true types. Because scholars are debating the note to be attached to a considerable number of types, no distinction is made in the following pages between genuine types, probable types, and accommodated types. Accommodated types abound in patristic literature and in the Liturgy, some of which are mentioned in the following pages. (*Translator's note*).

which prefigured it, even as the New Covenant enjoys a far higher status before God than the Old.

2. Jesus and the New Testament Sacred Writers. On various occasions Jesus gave testimony to the existence of types in the Old Testament. "Just as Jonas was three days and three nights in the belly of the fish, so the Son of Man will be three days and three nights in the belly of the earth." [74] By his stay in the whale's belly and his subsequent deliverance, Jonas prefigured our Savior's burial and glorious resurrection. "Just as Moses lifted up the serpent in the desert, so the Son of Man must be lifted up so that every one who believes in him may not perish but may have eternal life." [75] When the Israelites murmured against Moses in the wilderness, they were bitten by serpents and many died. Directed by Yahweh, Moses placed a bronze serpent upon a stake. If one who had been bitten directed his attention to it with confidence and trust in God, he was healed. So too anyone who takes refuge in the crucified Redeemer finds an antidote for the poison of eternal death injected by the infernal serpent. The serpent, ordinarily a type of sin, is here associated with deliverance: Bearing the world's guilt of sin, Jesus was raised upon the Cross to raise up a fallen world.

Jesus applied to Himself a number of passages which, in their literal sense, cannot be regarded as directly Messianic. "The stone which the builders rejected is become the head of the corner." [76] The context treats of a festal procession in which the participants praise Yahweh for having aided His People in their needs against enemies. Arriving at the door of the temple, the worshippers reflect on how God's sanctuary rose out of ruins despite opposition and crushing difficulties. Just as masons carefully eye the stones before them and cast away those that seem unsuitable, so the hostile nations had been watching the re-establishment of the Jewish commonwealth, gazing disdainfully upon Jerusalem and the temple. Yahweh's intervention produced results quite contrary to what they had imagined. Sion was the most important stone in the structure God was building — the cornerstone that gives solidity (or the keystone that adds beauty). For the Chosen People had the unique mission to bring the true faith and with it genuine blessings to mankind. Now the Chosen People of old prefigured God's Chosen People of the new dispensation. Although rejected by the leaders of His nation, Jesus did triumph, He became the cornerstone upon which God's new kingdom rests. And He made this clear to His opponents. [77] The apostles did not forget their Master's words. Peter and John quoted our passage when they were summoned before the Sanhedrin. [78]

---

[74] Matth. 12:40; John 2:1.
[75] John 3:14-15; Num. 21:8.
[76] Ps. 118:22.

[77] Matth. 21:42.
[78] Acts 4:11; cf. 1 Pet. 2:4; Eph. 2:20-21.

While ascending the Mount of Olives on the night before He died, Jesus said to His apostles: "Strike the shepherd, and the sheep will scatter." [79] He was quoting a prophecy in which Jerusalem was threatened with divine visitation, a visitation that would finally effect the people's purification. [80]

In St. Matthew's Gospel we find a goodly number of typically Messianic references. When Herod was seeking the death of the Christ-Child, Joseph and Mary were obliged to flee to Egypt with the Infant. "And Joseph stayed there until the death of Herod, so that the Lord's word through the prophet would be fulfilled: 'Out of Egypt have I called my Son.'" [81] The passage as found in Osee 11:1 describes God's paternal love toward Israel, shown by delivering her out of Egypt. This divinely ordained event in the history of the Chosen People typified an episode in the life of the Messiah.

Concluding his account of the slaughter of Bethlehem's innocent babes, St. Matthew observes: "Then was fulfilled what was said by the prophet Jeremias: A voice was heard in Rama — lamentation and loud weeping — Rachel, weeping for her children; nor would she be comforted because they are no more." [82] A prophecy in Jeremias 31:15–17 concerns the defunct Northern Kingdom to which the prophet directed words of comfort in his own sorrow. A great number had been taken into captivity. Rachel, Joseph's mother and Ephraim's grandmother, is depicted as lamenting over the loss. Jeremias bids her be at ease: her sons will return. To the evangelist Rachel appeared as a type of those mothers who grieved over the infants slain by Herod's henchmen.

After returning from Egypt the Holy Family lived in Nazareth "in order to fulfill what was written by the prophets: He will be called a Nazarene." [83] In this text the point of reference concerns the oracles in which the Redeemer is called neṣer, sprout. [84]

After recounting a series of parables which Jesus addressed to the people but explained only to His disciples, St. Matthew notes: "All this Jesus spoke in parables to the crowds; without parables he would not address them in order to fulfill the prophet's statement: With parables I will open my mouth, I will utter things hidden from the foundation of the world." [85] The quotation comes from Ps. 78:2. In a series of examples the psalmist recalled God's gratuitous guidance of Israel, a favor so often repaid with rankest ingratitude. Just as the obstinate Israelites should have learnt a lesson from the points the psalmist had covered, so Christ's contemporaries should have taken the parables seriously.

---

[79] Matth. 26:31.
[80] Zach. 13:7.
[81] Matth. 2:15.   [82] Matth. 2:18.

[83] Matth. 2:23.
[84] Is. 11:1; Jer. 23:5; 33:15; Ez. 17:22; cf. Zach. 3:8; 6:12.   [85] Matth. 13:34-35.

With the thirty pieces of silver that had been given to Judas for the betrayal of his Master, the chief priests and elders decided to buy a plot of ground to serve as a burial site for transients. St. Matthew concludes: "Then was fulfilled what was said by the prophet Jeremias: They took the thirty pieces of silver, the price of the appraisers, a price set in favor of the sons of Israel, and gave them for the potter's field as the Lord had enjoined upon me."[86] The evangelist's commentary involves the combination of a number of Old Testament texts. Mention of thirty pieces of silver is made by Zacharias as he endeavored to show God's great love toward Israel in terms of a shepherd, and the insulting treatment he himself received from the nation's officials.[87] In the parable the prophet, representing Yahweh, is given the money. How trifling a value had the leaders put upon Yahweh's services — not more than the fine levied for causing the death of a slave.[88] And for this sum Jesus was sold. Jer. 32:7f tells about the purchasing of a field; Jer. 18:2f concerns a potter and his work.

The fourth evangelist notes that after Christ had cleansed the temple, the disciples recalled the words: "Zeal for your house has consumed me."[89] They were quoting Ps. 69:10..

At the Last Supper Jesus revealed that one of the twelve would betray Him "in order that the Scripture would be fulfilled: He who ate bread with me, will lift up his heel against me."[90] In Ps. 41:10 David complains that "his closest friend, one in whom he trusted and with whom he ate bread," had risen against him. David's trial typified the bitter suffering Jesus experienced because of the action of one from His intimate circle, an apostle.

Continuing to prepare the apostles for His death, our Redeemer spoke of those who were plotting against Him: "The word must be fulfilled that is written in their Law: They hated me without cause."[91] It was a complaint voiced centuries earlier by a psalmist who suffered innocently.[92]

After recounting how our Savior's side was opened with a lance, while His legs were not broken as were those of the two thieves, St. John comments: "This was done that the Scriptures might be fulfilled: You shall break no bone on him."[93] In the prescriptions governing the killing and preparing of the paschal lamb, the Israelites had been expressly told: "None of its bones shall you break."[94] Jesus was the true paschal Lamb, the antitype of the lamb immolated annually on the feast of Passover; and this detail must not go unheeded.

Greater use of the typical implications inherent in the Old Testament

[86] Matth. 27:9-10.
[87] Zach. 11:12.
[88] Ex. 21:32.

[89] John 2:17.
[90] John 13:18.
[91] John 15:25.

[92] Ps. 35:19; 69:5.
[93] John 19:36.
[94] Ex. 12:46.

is made in the Letter to the Hebrews than in other apostolic letters. Examples appear throughout the following pages.

Types may be divided into a) personal types; b) material types. The former pertain to Old Testament persons or human actions that fore-shadowed the Redeemer; the latter include Old Testament events, facts or objects that have been divinely associated with New Testament realities.

3. PERSONAL TYPES. As *Adam* stands at the beginning of the human race, Christ heads the race of the redeemed. St. Paul expressly calls Adam "a type of the One to come." [95] Christ is "the last Adam," [96] the "second man." [97] Adam's violation of God's command brought sin and death upon all men, Christ's redeeming work restored justice and life.[98] The first Adam had an immortal soul, the second Adam possessed divin-ity. The first Adam was mortal, formed from the dust of the earth; the second Adam descended from heaven, and uniting divinity with human-ity, would have been immortal had He not waived the privilege in order to suffer and die. From the first Adam comes death; from the second, immortal glory.[99]

Abel, who was called "just" by Jesus,[1] offered to God a pleasing and acceptable sacrifice. In the Canon of the Mass his offering is mentioned with relation to Christ's. The blood of Abel called to God for vengeance.[2] Before God Christ intercedes through His blood "better than that of Abel" [3] because it pleads for forgiveness and grace and eternal beatitude.

Noe was "a just man and walked with God." [4] After the flood God entered into a covenant with him, promising never again to destroy all flesh by means of a flood.[5] In the Letter to the Hebrews, Noe's faith is singled out as noteworthy. Through faith "he built an ark by which he condemned the world that would not take warning from the word of God." [6] Noe was a "preacher of righteousness;" [7] he warned his con-temporaries to repent of their evil ways and by building the ark, made them aware of the impending visitation. Jesus preached penance, de-nounced sin. He mediated a covenant between God and men, and through His death on the Cross brought salvation to men. The death of those who would not listen to Noe's warning typifies the final judgment.[8] The ark is a symbol of the Church; all who seek refuge within her are saved.

Melchisedech. Heb. 6:20 alludes to Ps. 110:4, "You are a priest for-ever according to the order of Melchisedech," in order to show the parallel between two personages in the following ten verses. The type

[95] Rom. 5:14.   [96] 1 Cor. 15:45.   [4] Gen. 6:9.
[97] 1 Cor. 15:47.   [98] Rom. 5:12-21.   [5] Gen. 9:9; cf. Sir. 44:17-18.
[99] 1 Cor. 15:45-49.   [6] Heb. 11:7; 1 Pet. 3:20.
[1] Matth. 23:35; cf. Heb. 11:4.   [7] 2 Pet. 2:5.
[2] Gen. 4:10.   [3] Heb. 12:24.   [8] Matth. 24:37; Luke 17:26.

bore the name Melchisedech, i.e., king of justice; he was king of Salem, i.e., king of peace. He appears abruptly in history, and disappears equally abruptly. He is without father, without mother, without genealogy; his days have no recorded beginning, his life no given end. Because mention is not made of his forefathers, Scripture likened him to our Savior. His father's name is unknown: Jesus was born of a virgin. Nor do we know his mother: as God Christ had no mother. There are no details on Melchisedech's birth: Jesus is eternal, His life will have no end. Prophecy had said of Jesus: "I will establish the throne of his kingdom solidly forever." [9]

Next in the Letter to the Hebrews that part of the Genesis account is stressed where Abraham gives tithes to Melchisedech; in this act the latter appears superior to the patriarch Abraham and priests of the Old Covenant who possessed the legal right to tithes. Moreover, we might point to Melchisedech's sacrificial gifts of bread and wine, types of the holy sacrifice of Mass; for this reason the priest-king of Salem is named after Abel and Abraham in the Canon.

Isaac. After Ismael's ejection, Abraham's only son obediently carried upon his shoulders the wood upon which he was to be sacrificed. Without complaint he ascended Mount Moria, where he patiently awaited the immolating knife. Jesus, the only-begotten Son of the eternal Father, willingly carried the wood of the Cross to Golgotha, there to lay down His life. Through the intervention of the Angel of Yahweh, Isaac escaped death. God did not spare His Son. Jesus became obedient unto death, even death upon a Cross. [10]

Joseph, the beloved, obedient, innocent son of Jacob was hated by his brothers, was envied, mistreated, sold, delivered into the hands of aliens. Repeatedly tempted to sin, he remained faithful to God. Falsely accused, he was thrown into prison. He suffered patiently, placing himself in God's hands. To one of his two fellow prisoners he foretold speedy restoration to royal favor. When the days of his suffering were completed, he was exalted and placed over all Egypt.

Jesus was obedient unto death, was tempted by the wicked, falsely accused, innocently condemned. Crucified between two thieves, He soon restored one to divine favor. After His death He was exalted as king over the whole world. Joseph was given the name *Saphanethphanee,* he who nourishes life (in the Vulgate: *Salvator mundi*), because he preserved the Egyptians from death by famine. Jesus delivered the whole world from an eternal hunger. The Egyptians hailed Joseph and genuflected before him; [11] at the Name of Jesus every knee of those in heaven, on earth, and under the earth bends in adoration. [12]

---

[9] 2 Sam. 7:16.   [10] Phil. 2:8.   [11] Gen. 41:43.   [12] Phil. 2:10.

Job. Bowed down by severest bodily and spiritual suffering, a wretched death staring him in the eyes, bereft of human comfort, Job surrendered himself humbly to God's holy will, but not without struggle. On Mount Olivet our Savior begged: Father, if it be possible!, and was strengthened to embrace the most painful of deaths. On the Cross He groaned: My God, my God, why have you forsaken Me! And then: Father, into your hands I commend My spirit.

Moses was the author of the Old Covenant, Jesus is the author of the New Covenant. As a child Moses escaped death only through a marvellous intervention by God. He forsook the luxury of Pharaoh's court in order to aid his brethren. Jesus put aside the glory of heaven in His effort to redeem mankind. In desert solitude Moses prepared himself for his mission. Then he delivered the people from bondage, performed great miracles and repeatedly pleaded for his fellow men. As Lawgiver and prophet, he proclaimed God's will as he led Israel towards the Promised Land. Jesus began His Messianic work by passing forty days fasting and praying in the wilderness. It was His task to liberate men from Satan's bondage. He worked miracles which aroused universal admiration. He gave a new law, preached God's will, and interceded for sinners to His dying breath on the Cross.

The account of the journey through the wilderness is replete with types. The passage through the Reed Sea under the protection of the pillar of cloud presaged baptism.[13] Just as all the Israelites were obliged to cross the watery depths to obtain deliverance from Egyptian slavery, so all men must be baptized in order to be freed from Satan's chains. At Mara the Israelites murmured over the water as unfit to drink; Moses threw a piece of wood into it and it became sweet.[14] This wood is a figure of the Cross which sweetens the bitterness of human life, inspires patience and shows how suffering must be borne.

When the Israelites became hungry, Moses gave them manna, "bread from heaven,"[15] a type of the Blessed Eucharist.[16] The manna came from above, from God, day after day, just as Jesus descends upon our altars daily in order to serve as sweet nourishment upon our pilgrimage through the desert of life. Jesus Himself associated the manna with the "bread of life" that He would give, the true bread from heaven that brings life everlasting to anyone who eats of it.[17] Every time Benediction with the Blessed Sacrament is given the Church prays: "You gave them Bread from heaven which contains in Itself all sweetness."

When the Israelites needed water, Moses struck a rock and water gushed out.[18] This stream prefigured the flood of graces which comes

[13] 1 Cor. 10:1-20.
[14] Ex. 15:23-25.
[15] Ex. 16:4.

[16] 1 Cor. 10:3.
[17] John 6:31f.
[18] Ex. 17:6.

to us from the opened, pierced side of our Savior.[19] "If anyone thirst, let him come to me and drink."[20] While fighting the Amalekites who had attempted to hinder Israel in the trek through the desert, Moses gave himself to prayer, with Aaron and Hur supporting his outstretched arms.[21] In this position Moses typified Christ nailed with outstretched arms to the Cross on Golgotha, praying for our redemption. By virtue of Moses' intercession, Israel conquered the Amalekites — the Church militant proceeds victorious over the enemy under Christ her head.

Moses established the Old Covenant on Sinai, Jesus sealed the New Covenant with His blood on Calvary. The Old Law involved a small group of people, the New Law embraces every nation under the sun. The Old was destined to prepare the way for the New and then to disappear, the New by nature will last to the end of time. The Old Covenant was validated with the blood of animals, the New through the Blood of Christ Jesus:[22] "This is the blood of the new covenant shed for the forgiveness of sins."[23] The Old Covenant imposed the Law, the New Covenant bestows every grace needed to fulfill God's demands, changing hearts of stone, as the prophet said, into hearts of flesh. The typical message of the bronze serpent set up by Moses was revealed by Jesus Himself.[24]

Josue led the Israelites into the Land of Promise and through a series of victorious campaigns insured their claim. Through His death and resurrection Jesus triumphed over Satan and made sure our heavenly heritage. The very name Josue makes us think of our Redeemer, for it means etymologically: "Yahweh is salvation" or "Yahweh is Savior;"[25] and our Savior, who assumed flesh from Mary, received the Name Jesus because He "was to save his people from their sins."[26] Like the passage through the Reed Sea, so too crossing the Jordan foreshadowed baptism through which men enter God's kingdom upon earth, viz., the Church.

Among Israel's judges *Gedeon* was admired in a special way because of his victory over the Midianites.[27] Little is known of Gedeon's early life. So too Jesus passed the years preceding His public ministry in little Nazareth unknown to all. With only 300 men at his command Gedeon proved victorious over the hosts of Midian. Jesus sent a dozen apostles to meet and triumph over a hostile world.

Sampson was associated typically with Christ by the earliest of the Church fathers.[28] According to Origen the point of comparison lies in the extraordinary strength both had at their disposal.[29] Ambrose observes that Sampson's fellow men did not understand his riddle; nor did

[19] 1 Cor. 10:4.   [20] John 7:37.
[21] Ex. 17:12.
[22] Heb. 9:12-22.
[23] Matth. 26:28.
[24] Num. 21:9 ; John 3:14.
[25] Jerome, *Ep. ad Paul.*, 8: *Typus Do-*

mini non solum in gestis, sed etiam in nomine.
[26] Matth. 1:21.   [27] Is. 9:4.
[28] Cf. Calmet; V. Zapletal, *Das Buch der Richter*, 252.
[29] Orig. *Com. in Matth.*, 27, 11.

Christ's disciples at the beginning understand His words.[30] In Sampson's physical strength St. Augustine saw exemplified the strength of Christ, in Sampson's weakness, the suffering Savior. In both cases an angel brought the message of birth. Sampson overcame a lion, Jesus the infernal dragon. Sampson, betrayed by kinsmen and delivered over to enemy Philistines, was mocked and abused. The Jews delivered Jesus into the hands of Gentile Romans. Sampson offered his life as he brought the house down upon the assembled Philistines, Christ offered Himself as an atonement victim for all mankind.[31] St. Jerome points out how closely Sampson's name is related to the word *shemesh*, sun — Christ is the true sun. Calmet notes that Sampson was a Nazirite and married an alien, while Jesus spent His youth in Nazareth and gave His life for a Church predominantly Gentile.

David. The prophets at times call the Messiah David because David was his forefather. In various psalms David described the suffering and the triumph of the Redeemer, but many vicissitudes of his life were likewise prophetic in character. Born at Bethlehem, he early lived a hidden life. He was victorious over Goliath with unpretentious weapons, was persecuted by Saul against whom he had not offended, patiently endured much suffering, even loved jealous foes and forgave them from the bottom of his heart. Frequently he did not know where to rest his weary head. Under attack by his own son and accompanied by only a few companions, he sadly crossed the Kedron and ascended Mount Olivet; he was destined, however, to return in triumph to the Holy City. These many points we see repeated in the life of Jesus, but far more dramatically because the antitype greatly surpasses the type. David was king and prophet. Jesus too united in Himself the royal and prophetic offices.

Solomon. While Abel, Isaac, Job, Moses, David prefigured our Savior in His sacred passion, Solomon foreshadowed His glory. The name itself, *šelomoh*, peace, points to the true "prince of peace." Solomon's own nation, and neighboring nations too, marvelled at his wisdom; in Christ are hidden all the treasures of wisdom and of knowledge.[32] The wealth of Israel's king brings to mind the treasures of grace Jesus has at His disposal. Solomon built a temple of stone and cedar, Jesus constructed a living temple, the Church. The queen of Sheba traveled a great distance to visit Solomon and bring costly presents, the Magi from the East came to the Infant with gifts of gold, incense, myrrh. Nations were subject to Solomon, before Jesus the hosts of heaven and men from every race do homage.

Elias. Distinguished by having a successor in John the Baptist, who

---

[30] Judg. 14:14; Ambros., *De Spiritu Sancto,* 2, 7f. [31] Augustine, *Sermo,* 364; *Enarratio in Ps. 83, in Ps. 88.* [32] Col. 2:3.

would, as Malachias prophesied, walk in his ways, privileged by appearing with Moses at the side of the Savior on the mount of transfiguration, Elias was further divinely favored in being selected as one of the Old Testament types of the Redeemer. Like Jesus he was a prophet and a miracle worker. He raised the son of the widow of Sarephta from the dead, Jesus did the same for the widow of Naim. Elias increased a widow's flour and oil to save her from death by starvation,[33] Jesus miraculously multiplied the loaves. Elias was hated and persecuted, became despondent to the point of death,[34] was comforted by an angel, was taken away to heaven in the presence of Eliseus his successor.[35] During His whole public ministry Jesus was persecuted. He sweat blood in agony on Olivet, was strengthened by an angel, and ascended gloriously into heaven in the presence of disciples who continued His work.

Jonas. We have already observed how Jesus applied to Himself the distinctive episode from the life of Jonas. Ancient Christian art shows Jonas as a symbol of resurrection.

Among the literary prophets *Jeremias* shows the greatest resemblance to Jesus. This point was already noted by the earliest Christians. While in the womb of his mother Jeremias was destined by God for the prophetic mission.[36] It was his task to struggle against immoral priests and false prophets, as Jesus did against chief priests, Pharisees and Scribes. The prophet's relatives and fellow men in Anathoth rose against him and plotted his death,[37] even as the inhabitants of Nazareth turned against Jesus and sought to hurl Him from a precipice.[38] The accusations of the priests and the subsequent popular assault upon the prophet[39] has a parallel in the passion account. Jeremias was persecuted because he exhorted the princes and people to repent, because he upbraided them for their sins. His denunciation of the priests for having made the temple a den of thieves was repeated by Jesus.[40] Like Jeremias, Jesus foretold the destruction of the temple.[41] No prophet before Jeremias inveighed as strenuously against externalism in religion. He renounced marriage,[42] lived a solitary life, shed bitter tears over the inevitable destruction of Jerusalem because of the obstinacy of the people,[43] while at the same time seeking to avert the catastrophe by intercessory prayer.[44] With Jesus he could say of himself: "I was like an innocent lamb that is led to slaughter."[45]

The Lamentations of Jeremias, which in the literal sense describe Jerusalem's destruction and Israel's well-merited deportation, are put on the lips of the suffering Savior in the liturgy of Holy Week.

[33] 3 Kgs. 17:14. [34] 3 Kgs. 19:4. [41] Jer. 7:14; Mark 13:2.
[35] 4 Kgs. 2:11. [36] Jer. 1:5. [42] Jer. 16:2.
[37] Jer. 11:18f. [38] Luke 4:39. [43] Jer. 8:18; 13:17.
[39] Jer. 26:1. [44] Jer. 7:16; 11:14; 14:11; 15:1; 11;
[40] Jer. 7:11; Matth. 21:13. 18:20. [45] Jer. 11:19.

In Daniel's prophecy of "the seventy week-years," the anointed one innocently put to death was the high priest *Onias*. Typically he portrayed Christ, the only Anointed One who was truly innocent and yet made to die by the hands of fellow men.

The *people of Israel* taken as a unit likewise prefigured the Redeemer. They are spoken of as the "son of God" in Exod. 4:22; Os. 11:1. Theirs was the duty of serving God in a most extraordinary manner, of preserving faith in the true God for the Gentile world. Israel also prefigured God's Chosen People in the new dispensation of grace; for when she had proven unworthy, a new "Chosen Generation" assumed her mission and in them the oracles of the prophets regarding Israel of the Messianic future are fulfilled.

This section would be incomplete without some space devoted to *the just man* of Wis. 2:12–20:

Wisdom

2:12   Let us lie in wait for the just man,
            for he is troublesome to us and opposes our actions;
          he accuses us of transgressing the Law,
            and upbraids us for violating what we have learnt.

2:13   He glories in possessing the knowledge of God,
            and calls himself a child of the Lord.

2:14   He has become a censurer of our thoughts,
            his very appearance is annoying to us

2:15   because his way of life is not like that of others,
            and his paths are wholly different.

2:16   In his eyes we are counterfeit,
            as from filth he stays distant from our acts.
          The just man's final lot he esteems as blessed,
            and boastfully calls God his Father.

2:17   Let us see whether his words are true,
            let us put it to the test as to what his end will be;

2:18   For if the just man is God's son, God will espouse his cause
            and deliver him from the power of his opponents.

2:19   With insults and mistreatment let us put him to the test
            so that we may discover his patience
            and prove his constancy.

2:20   To a shameful death we must condemn him,
            for, as indeed he claims,
            a merciful deliverance will be his portion.

Between these words of hatred against the "just man" and many of the sentiments expressed around the Cross of Jesus, there is a striking agreement. Christ's enemies mocked Him: "Save yourself. If you are the son of God, descend from the Cross. He trusted in God, let him save him if he wills; for he has said: I am the son of God." [46] Crucifixion was the

---

[46] Matth. 27:4-43.

most shameful death imaginable.[47] Christ's claim to being the Son of God was regarded as blasphemy: "Therefore the Jews made still greater effort to kill him, because he not only violated the Sabbath, but called God his Father."[48] And before Pilate His accusers angrily cried: "We have a Law and according to it he must die, because he made himself the son of God."[49] These considerations have prompted many Fathers of the Church and later Christian exegetes to see in Wis. 2:12–20 a directly Messianic prophecy.[50]

From the words introducing the passage under consideration, it is evident that the designation, *just man*, is not to be understood of some specific individual; for along with the "just (poor) man," the widow and the aged man (all in the singular) are persecuted. In 2:21–22 the author pronounces his verdict upon those who spoke in vv. 12–20. Here he uses the plural, those whom the wicked lie in wait for are "pure souls," and in 3:1f the lot of the virtuous (plural) is contrasted with that of their enemies. In 3:10 and 4:7 the plural and singular are used interchangeably. After death, the "just man" (singular) will come face to face with those who persecuted and oppressed him here on earth;[51] but the sacred writer's resolution of the case cannot be applied to the Messiah: "He will be numbered among the sons of God, and with the saints will be his portion."[52] For the Messiah infinitely outranks any of the elect in the glory of heaven. In 2:19 the just man's enemies propose to torment him, but in afterlife the just (plural) are delivered from all suffering.[53]

Moreover, those who are so fiendishly opposed to the just man are apostate Jews, now become materialists and hedonists. They have abandoned all belief in the spiritual order. According to their outlook there is no afterlife, death ends all. So they seek to enjoy life, and because the pious man by his very presence acts as a reproach, they plot his death. Such Jews would not feel out of place in the company of evil-minded Gentiles devoid of every noble ideal. They had adopted the pagan way of life, and through the influence of pagan thought had apostatized from the God of their father. They could join their Gentile neighbors singing the "Rose Song," giving vent to their joy in earthly pleasures,[54] and these friends would not have hesitated assisting degenerate Jews in persecuting a faithful believer. The Book of Wisdom was written in Alexandria, where pogroms against pious Jews were not unusual.

The Jews, however, who pursued Jesus to death were primarily

---

[47] V. 20a.
[48] John 5:18.   [49] John 19:7.
[50] Cf. F. X. Reusch, *Gehört Weish. 2:12-20 zu den messianischen Weissagungen?* ThQ 1864, 330-346, where the passages from the Fathers are gathered together and explained.
[51] Cf. 5:1.   [52] Wis. 5:5.
[53] Wis. 3:1.
[54] Wis. 2:6-9.

Pharisees, proud of their virtues, men dedicated to the strict observance of the Law, given to fasting and public prayer, avoiding every contact with the "accursed crowd," despising the unbelieving pagan, and believing not only in the immortality of the soul but likewise in retribution in afterlife. Nor were the Sadducean priests or the Scribes (who for the most part belonged to the Pharisees) atheists. It was this combination that condemned Jesus and delivered Him to Pilate. Their interests were indeed centered upon things of this world, but they retained the ancient tenets of Mosaic religion. The message therefore in the passage under consideration is simply this: faithless Jews and degenerate pagans in Alexandria, filled with hatred toward religious persons who are a standing reproach to them, determine to do them evil even to the point of death.

Conflict between the godless and the pious is ordinary experience. The just man *par excellence*, however, is Christ; and because He laid claim to a unique relationship with the Father, He met violent opposition and was finally put to death. The description of the oppressed just man in the Wis. 2:12–20 applies to Him in an eminent manner. At the time of His sacred passion hostility against God and all who belonged to God reached its climax. The similarity between the words of the Jewish free-thinkers and the expostulations of Christ's enemies as He hung upon the Cross are partly explicable from the similarity of situation; moreover, the author of the Book of Wisdom placed upon their lips words from the Messianic psalm in which the innocent sufferer laments over being unjustly mocked and persecuted: "All who see me scoff at me . . . he relied upon Yahweh. Let Yahweh save him; Yahweh will help him, if he is pleased with him." [55] The author may also have had in mind the Isaian prophecy of the Suffering Servant. Truly, Jesus is the type of all those "who suffer persecution for justice sake." Because the author, in formulating the discourse of the faithless Jews, alludes to a Messianic prophecy and because his words hold true in an eminent sense of the persecuted One who is God's only-begotten Son, this passage in the Book of Wisdom must be regarded as typically Messianic.

4. MATERIAL TYPES. The apostle Paul regarded the whole Old Testament with all its dispositions as a type of the New. In the Letter to the Hebrews Christ is the eternal high priest, with the high priest of the Old Law a weak prototype. [56] As they offered sacrifice the priests of old "served as a mere copy and shadow of things heavenly." [57] Moses constructed the tabernacle according to the model which was shown him on the mountain, [58] and Christ as high priest of the good things to come

[55] Ps. 22:8-9.
[56] Ch. 7.
[57] Heb. 8:5.
[58] Heb. 8:5.

passed through the higher and more perfect tabernacle not made with hands.[59]

The *tabernacle* with its appurtances is associated with Christ and the Church or with the life of Christians by the Fathers of the Church and ecclesiastical writers beginning with Clement of Alexandria. The table of showbread anticipated the Blessed Eucharist, and the seven lamps illuminating the Holy Place presaged the seven Gifts of the Holy Ghost.

To patristic writers the garments of the high priest prefigured Christ and the Church. For Tertullian the Church was the holy robe in which Christ the high priest was clothed; and he related the twelve precious stones in the high priest's breastplate to the twelve apostles. St. Jerome likewise associated these twelve gems with the twelve apostles which Christ the true high priest bears upon His breast, while he regarded the two precious stones on the high priest's shoulders as symbols of the sacraments of the Old and the New Covenants.

By means of material *sacrifices*, including those prescribed by Mosaic Law, man expresses visibly that he belongs to God together with all that he has, and that he owes all to God, not excepting life itself. This too was the purpose underlying the sprinkling of blood. Blood was regarded as the principle of life; now man owes his entire life to God, but in its stead presents the life-blood of an animal. To make more explicit that the sacrificed animal belonged to God, it was burned in whole or in part, the smoke ascending to heaven, God's dwelling. A holocaust more effectively than other sacrifices expressed one's whole dependence upon God because it implied the total destruction of the victim. The characteristic feature of a peace or thank offering was the sacrificial banquet at which Yahweh was host, those bringing the offering, the guests.[60] Only in the state of perfect purity could an Israelite partake of the meal;[61] he was obliged, therefore, to examine his conscience as to whether he had complied with God's moral demands. Since slaves, Levites, the poor, and strangers were to be invited to the sacrificial meal,[62] it likewise brought home the duty of loving the less fortunate and of sympathizing with those in need.

Atonement sacrifices served to reconcile the sinner with God and to ward off deserved punishment. It was a prerequisite that the sinner acknowledge his guilt and was endeavoring to make compensation for any damages. By food and drink offerings the Israelite showed his gratitude to God for preserving him alive. The showbread, renewed each Sabbath in the Holy Place, was a reminder that he owed his daily bread to divine providence. Incense offerings symbolized the ascending clouds of prayer.[63]

[59] Heb. 9:11.
[60] Ps. 23:5.
[61] Lev. 7:19-21.
[62] Deut. 12:12, 18; 16:11, 14.
[63] Ps. 141:2.

Yet in spite of all their significance and value for vitalizing religious life, Old Testament sacrifices did not in themselves have the power to efface sin. Forgiveness was an act of purest mercy on God's part: "It was impossible that the blood of bulls or goats should expiate sin." [64] The sacrifices offered by Old Testament priests "could never take away sins." [65] But these imperfect oblations did point to the one perfect sacrifice of the New Covenant, the sacrifice which the Son of God offered to His heavenly Father "for all times" [66] by shedding His Blood on the Cross for the sins of mankind. [67] In view of this future sacrifice God accepted the holocausts of old as signs of self-immolation, atonement sacrifices as means unto the forgiveness of sins, peace offerings as tangible evidence of the just man's effort to strengthen his union with God and deepen his love. The latter, in particular, was destined to attain its consummation in the Eucharistic banquet of holy Mass. [68] The sacrifice of the Cross is the greatest of holocausts because the Redeemer spilt all His Blood and consumed Himself in the fire of infinite love unto the glory of the heavenly Father. The sacrifice on Calvary is the greatest of atonement sacrifices because it effaced the sins of the world and tore up the ledger of man's guilt. It is the supreme peace offering because it reconciles heaven to earth, unites man most intimately with God, inspiring love, and requiring perfect purity of heart of all who seek to draw nigh and eat.

The oldest feast observed by God's Chosen People was the *Passover* [69] on the evening of the 14th of Nisan. Every Israelitic family was bound to slay a lamb without breaking any of its bones, and to eat it roasted in memory of the exodus from Egypt. In Goshen, where the feast was first observed, the blood of the lamb was sprinkled against the lintel and two door-posts of each house to ward off "the destroyer" that would pass through the land that night to slay every Egyptian first-born. The blood of the lamb preserved all Israel from death and opened for her the way to freedom. The paschal lamb was a sacrifice, unique in its kind, and not to be classified with other sacrifices prescribed by Mosaic Law. It had this in common with atonement sacrifices that the sprinkling of blood effected expiation of sin and reconciliation with God; and like peace offerings it was associated with a meal. Only those who by circumcision belonged to the Chosen People could partake of this meal.

The paschal lamb was a type of Christ. "Our paschal lamb, Christ, is immolated," the Church sings in her Easter preface. [70] The death of God's spotless Son upon the Cross was a true sacrifice. His Blood delivered us from the bondage of Satan and preserves us from everlasting

[64] Heb. 10:4.
[65] Heb. 10:11.
[66] Heb. 10:12.
[67] Heb. 9:28.

[68] Ps. 22:17.
[69] Ex. 12:1-14, 21-28, 43-51; Lev. 23:4-8; Deut. 16:1-8.
[70] Cf. 1 Cor. 5:7.

perdition. Only members of the Church whose souls are alive with grace may partake of the Eucharistic banquet instituted by Christ at the last celebration of the Old Testament Passover, the unbloody renewal of Calvary's bloody sacrifice. No bone of Jesus was broken on the Cross nor at the killing and preparation of the Passover lamb, as noted by St. John.[71]

Tradition is unanimous in relating the Jewish Pasch to Christ's sacrifice on the Cross.

The feast of *Tabernacles* was the annual memorial of blessings received on the journey from Egypt to Canaan, the period in which the Hebrews lived in tents or huts.[72] In postexilic times a water libation was added to the ritual to recall the marvellous manner in which water was provided in the desert wilderness. It was to this ritual that Jesus referred when on the seventh day of the feast He called Himself the fountain of living water.[73] The same sacred service has a typical relationship to the Holy Spirit because the bestowal of grace and the conferring of the Spirit in Messianic times is frequently described in terms of water.[74]

The *Day of Atonement*, the holiest feast day of the entire year, was kept in fall, on the tenth of the seventh month.[75] It was a day of penance, the day on which the people of the Old Covenant were publicly reconciled to God. Its principal service consisted in an atonement sacrifice and the confession of sin. Even the high priest appeared as a penitent; he was not permitted to wear his priestly robes at the prescribed ceremonies, but the simplest attire made of white linen. And every Israelite was bound to fast throughout the entire day. Two goats, equal in worth, were brought before the high priest; one was for Yahweh, the other for the demon Azazel. Upon the goat destined for Azazel the high priest consigned all the sins of Israel, and thereupon the goat was driven off into the desert to die of starvation or to be eaten by wild beasts. The act portrayed how the sins of the nation were taken away to the region of demons where they belonged; for the desert was regarded as the preferred habitat of evil spirits. Then a bullock and Yahweh's goat were slaughtered and the blood carried into the sanctuary, into the very Holy of Holies, to be sprinkled there. The fat of the sacrificed animals was burnt on the altar, while the flesh was consigned to flames outside the camp.

These ceremonies on the "Good Friday of the Old Testament" typified realities on the first Good Friday in the New, that great day on which atonement *did* take place, and the sins of mankind were actually washed away.[76] The agreement between figure and fulfillment embraces

---

[71] John 19:36.
[72] Ex. 23:16; Lev. 23:33-44; Num. 29:12-38.
[73] John 7:37f.

[74] Is. 44:3; 55:1; 58:11; Joel 2:22-23; 3:1, 18; Zach. 13:1; 14:8; Ez. 47:1f.
[75] Lev. 16; 23:26-32; Num. 29:1-11.
[76] Heb. 9:7, 11, 12.

even such details as the Savior's death outside Jerusalem's walls, a parallel to the burning of the flesh outside the camp of Israel.[77]

The sacrifice of the *red heifer*.[78] Certain acts pertaining to sex, whether natural or involving physical disorder or disease, were regarded as rendering the individual unclean.[79] Leprosy[80] or touching a dead animal produced a similar condition.[81] In practically all of these cases no moral guilt was involved, but the person who had become unclean was not permitted to participate in an act of divine cult. These prescriptions reflect ancient pre-Mosaic customs and attitudes. The ordinances regarding external, physical purity were not strictly differentiated from ethical, moral purity in Israel – as was generally the case in antiquity. In our Christian religion with its universal mission, such Mosaic injunctions retain no validity, but they did have importance for the Israelites and for their outlook on life.

Contact with a corpse was regarded as the greatest of defilements, whether intentional or accidental, whether the dead man had been a notorious sinner or had led the saintliest life. The wages of sin is death, and at a funeral the connection between sin and death is most easily seen. While a simple washing sufficed to remove ordinary defilements, a kind of lye prepared from a special expiatory sacrifice was required to cleanse oneself after touching a corpse. A bullock was slaughtered for the sins of the people, in this case a heifer (because the female is responsible for life – another point of contrast with death). No yoke could she have borne, being still unbred. Red, the color of blood, was to be her color – in blood was the principle of life. Slaughtering and burning took place outside the camp to forestall any possible defilement within the enclosure. The regulations ordered the blood to be sprinkled "toward the front of the tabernacle" and whatever remained was to be thrown into the fire in order that the ashes which were to be saved would have greater efficacy. This was heightened by adding cedar wood, noted for its lasting qualities; hyssop, accredited with the power to cleanse; and scarlet yarn, because of its color. With the water prepared from these ashes any man who had defiled himself by contact with a corpse must be sprinkled. According to Heb. 9:1 this purificatory water was a type of Christ's sacred Blood, the "immaculate offering which cleanses our consciences from dead works."

In the sacrifice of the red heifer slaughtered outside the camp, the Fathers saw prefigured the crucifixion taking place beyond Jerusalem's walls; and in the purificatory water, baptism which washes sins away.

By *circumcision* one became a member of the Chosen People and assumed the obligation of observing the Mosaic Law. Circumcision

---

[77] Heb. 13:11-12.
[78] Num. 19.
[79] Lev. 15.
[80] Lev. 13:14.
[81] Lev. 11.

was the abiding sign of the covenant. This external mark on the body was ordained as a constant reminder of covenant obligations, an indication of "circumcision of the heart" or "of the ear," [82] as the prophets phrased it.[83] It is this moral approach to circumcision that St. Paul refers to in Rom. 2:29 and regards as a type of baptism in Col. 2:11.

5. TYPOLOGY OF PATRISTIC WRITERS. The typical explanations given above are rooted in statements of Christ and the apostles as contained in the inspired writings of the New Testament. But typology also played a role in the allegorical interpretation of the Bible, a procedure which regarded practically everything in the sacred text as figurative. Philo, the most illustrious Jewish exegete who at the time of Christ lived in Alexandria, developed this method to perfection; and the Alexandrian exegetical schools founded by Clement of Alexandria and Origen, followed the Philonic method.[84] In their interpretations, which pay scant attention to the literal message, phantasy runs rampant. The Fathers who exemplify this type of exegesis witness to opinions current in the ancient Church, but their exegesis of Sacred Scripture cannot be followed unreservedly or claim a blind acceptance.

In the following pages we will quote repeatedly from two earliest representatives of the "allegorical-typical" school of exegesis, giving special attention to how they associated Christ and the Church with the Old Testament. Our first witness is the author of the Letter of Barnabas, the second Justin Martyr. Both were active before the establishment of the Alexandrian school.

a) *The Letter of Barnabas* [85] was written toward the end of the first century or during the first half of the second century of the Christian era. The author, himself a converted Jew who probably lived in Alexandria, addresses a congregation composed of Jewish and Gentile Christians. Like Philo he distinguishes between the literal sense and an allegorical, spiritual sense; the former is evident to every one, the latter is hidden under the husk of words. The persons mentioned and the actions narrated in the Bible were real persons and historical actions, but these persons and actions at the same time signified truths of a much higher order. Abraham was a historical person and circumcized himself, but the account must be read with Jesus in mind.[86] In seeing allegorical meanings the author of the Letter of Barnabas is far more facile than Philo. For Philo the precepts of the Old Law were ordinances that had to be obeyed as such; for Barnabas all the Old Testament precepts and ceremonies had as little validity as for those Jewish allegorists whose

---

[82] Lev. 26:41; Deut. 10:16; 30:6.
[84] P. Heinisch, *Der Einfluss Philos auf die älteste christliche Exegese — Barnabas, Justin und Clemens von Alexandrien* (AA 1, 2).

[83] Jer. 4:4; 6:10.
[85] The author, called Barnabas in our remarks, is not the Barnabas mentioned in the Acts of the Apostles.
[86] Barn. 9:7.

interpretation Philo attacked because they denied the literal sense of the Law or regarded its observance impossible and therefore not required.

The Law, says Barnabas, is not to be understood "according to the flesh," i.e., in its literal sense; it must be understood "according to the spirit," as Moses wished. Words are used solely for the embodiment of higher truths. From the very outset the Lawmaker intended only the typology, and by obeying the prescriptions in their normal meaning, the Jews showed that they did not understand what Moses had written. This grand delusion could not be accounted for unless they had been deceived by an evil spirit.[87] The Covenant which God made with Israel at Sinai was invalidated by the sins of apostasy which the Israelites committed, as Moses himself showed by breaking the tablets of the Law.[88] The whole ceremonial law, therefore, rests upon gross misunderstanding. God did not demand abstention from the flesh of certain animals, but abstention from the sins symbolized by these animals.[89] The prohibition of swine's flesh really means that we must not associate with men who resemble swine, viz., those who have a superabundance of earthly goods and forget the Lord, or when hungry begin to grunt and only quiet down upon being fed. Eating the flesh of the eagle, hawk, vulture, raven is forbidden: do not mix with men who act like these birds, who do not earn their living by toil and trouble but wickedly rob the goods of others.

Philo realized that Jewry rose or fell with the observance of the Law, he could not abandon the normal, literal sense of the Law without denying Judaism. Unlike later Christian theologians, Barnabas was not content with saying that the Law was rendered obsolete by the death of Jesus. He claimed it never possessed validity in his effort to preserve Gentile Christians from inclining toward Jewish spirit and to restrain converted Jews from making Gentile Christians observe Mosaic prescriptions.

For example, in Ex. 20:8 God commanded that the Sabbath "be kept holy with pure hearts and with pure hands" (the Masoretic and Septuagint texts have only: "to keep holy"). Now although we have been renewed by Christ, writes Barnabas, this is impossible in the present world. The commandment, therefore, cannot be understood in its literal sense. The Sabbath, which we should keep holy, is the thousand year kingdom in which we become holy.[90] Sometimes Barnabas finds several meanings in one and the same passage, e.g., "Enter into the land that flows with milk and honey." [91] This means a) the human nature of Christ, whose appearance in flesh was here predicted by Moses; b) every man

---

[87] Barn. 9:4.
[88] Barn. 4:7-8 ; cf. 14:1-5.

[89] Barn. 10.
[90] Barn. 15:6-7.

[91] Ex. 33:1.

who is re-created upon becoming a Christian; c) the Church which nourishes mankind.[92]

According to Barnabas truths proper to the Christian dispensation are implied or prefigured in every portion of the Old Testament. Thus in the account of the circumcision of Abraham's 318 servants, he sees a mystical reference to the death of Jesus on the Cross; for the figure 18 can be linked to $\iota\eta$, the initial letters of the name Jesus, and 300 to the letter τ, the form of the Cross.[93] Actually, it is in the account of Lot's deliverance[94] that the number 318 occurs, and these were only a part of Abraham's servants. According to Gen. 17:23 he circumcized *all* his servants, and to the number 318 must be added the boys, the old men, and those who remained behind to watch over the flocks. We might have imagined that Barnabas would have taken the Hebrew alphabet as the basis for his numerical evaluations, for the Hebrew letter *taw* is made like a cross in the Old Hebrew alphabet, and stands for 400, not 300. The Alexandrian Jews and Christians rested their number exegesis and etymologies exclusively upon the Septuagint which they regarded as inspired.

The Letter to the Hebrews places a typical value upon the ceremonies proper to the Day of Atonement.[95] In the Letter of Barnabas this sober beginning mushrooms, and rites are mentioned that do not occur in the Law or even in the tract "Yoma" which gives the post-biblical Jewish tradition, but upon certain Jewish customs with which he was familiar. According to his *halakah* the priests were obliged to eat the entrails of the goat slaughtered on the Day of Atonement, unwashed and *with vinegar*.[96] Here we have a type of Christ, offering Himself for the sins of mankind, as He was given a drink mixed with gall *and vinegar*. Only the priests ate of it, not the people, because the priests were guilty of Christ's death, while the people, i.e., the Christian world, fasts and is sorrowful and shares in the sacrifice on Calvary through contrition over their sins.[97]

Regarding the goat destined for Azazel, Barnabas adds the following details not contained in the Law: he was spit upon, struck,[98] cursed, and covered with a scarlet-red woolen cloth, driven out into the desert where the woolen cloth was hung upon a blackberry bush. This goat is a type of the crucified Savior whom the Jews mistreated in a like shameful fashion and led out in the wilderness dressed in scarlet.[99] The other goat, the one slaughtered as an offering to God and which resembled Azazel's, is Jesus transformed with glory, who through His self-oblation entered the heavens and will return again in judgment. The similarity

---

[92] Barn. 6:9-14.   [93] Barn. 9:8.

[94] Gen. 14:14.

[95] Heb. 9:7-12; 13:11-13.

[96] Cf. Mishnah, Menachoth 11:7.

[97] Barn. 7:3-5.   [98] Mishnah, Yoma 6:4.

[99] A detail not given in the Gospels.

of the goats prescribed by the Law [1] signifies that Jesus upon His return in royal majesty will be recognized by the Jews who scoffed at and killed Him. The crown of thorns (blackberry bush) will then become a royal crown, the red mantle (the woolen cloth) a royal robe. That the woolen cloth was placed upon a bush which bore sweet berries signifies the hardships and tribulations they must suffer who follow Christ crucified.[2]

In his commentary on the sacrifice of the red heifer, Barnabas likewise lists a number of practices given nowhere else. The ashes are cleaned away by twelve innocent children; these are the twelve apostles who proclaimed the goods news of the forgiveness of sins. Three boys sprinkle those who need cleansing with a wooden stick around which is wound a scarlet cloth and hyssop. These boys represent the patriarchs Abraham, Isaac, and Jacob. The wood used as a sprinkler typifies the Cross, the scarlet woolen prefigures Christ's royal dignity; the hyssop, because of its bitterness, foreshadows the bitter days which bring salvation to the Christian.

Esau's forefeiture of the inheritance to his younger brother Jacob [3] typified how Christians, the new People of God, are the true inheritors of the promises, not the Jews, their older brothers. The same typology is to be seen as the younger son Ephraim is preferred to the older Manasses in Jacob's blessing.[4]

b) *Justin Martyr* was born about the year 100 in Palestine and was martyred in Rome by the prefect Junius Rusticus (163–167). He is the most important apologete of the primitive Church. To him the Old Testament was one big prophecy to be read wholly in the light of New Testament revelation; no passage but bears its higher sense. The prophets are responsible for concealing the true meaning under husks of words. The phrase, "blood of the grape" in Gen. 49:11, was chosen by Moses to point out the divinity of Christ. For just as the blood of the vine is not the product of a man but of God, so the blood of Christ did not come from human seed but through divine power.[5] Likewise the phrase, "like a son of man" in Dan. 7:13, signifies that Jesus was not conceived from human seed, even though He became man and appeared as such.[6] So for Justin the particle like, ὡς, is both a prophecy of Mary's virginity and a proof of Christ's divine sonship.

Jacob married two wives in order to prefigure the work of our Savior. Lea must be linked with the Jews, for she had weak eyes — and the Jews did not recognize the Lord. Rachel is the Church, for she took along and put away Laban's gods; so too the Church, composed of Gentiles,

---

[1] More correctly: by tradition.
[2] Barn. 7:6-11.   [3] Gen. 27:27.
[4] Gen. 48:14; Barn. 13.
[5] Dial. 54.   [6] Dial. 76.

puts away idolatry. That Jacob had concubines in addition to his two wives is not without its bearing upon the work of redemption.[7] The Savior had two names, Jesus and Christ, in order to correspond with the two names of the last patriarch, viz., Jacob and Israel.[8]

In practically every passage which mentions *wood* or *tree* Justin sees prefigured the Cross. This holds for the tree of life in paradise, of the wood in Noe's ark, of the theophany Abraham had at Mamre,[9] of the ladder leading to heaven at Bethel, of the staff Jacob used in crossing the Jordan,[10] of the branches Jacob placed in the watering trough so that the flocks would breed in his favor,[11] of the staff Juda gave to Thamar the harlot,[12] of the staff of Moses [13] and Aaron,[14] the wood Moses threw in the spring at Mara,[15] the trees at Elim,[16] the wood Eliseus used to recover a fallen ax,[17] etc.

By his struggle with a higher being which resulted in a limp, Jacob prefigured the struggle, suffering, death, and triumph of Christ.[18] Zacharias' prophecy, "See, your king is coming to you . . . he rides upon an ass, (and) upon a colt, the foal of an ass," [19] and the words of the dying Jacob to Juda, "To the vine he tethers his ass, his ass's colt to the choicest vine," [20] were fulfilled at the entrance of Jesus into Jerusalem.[21] But for Justin the passages contain a higher meaning still: the young beast that had not yet been hitched to the yoke signifies the Gentiles who only upon embracing the Gospel take the yoke and halter upon themselves and become willing to bear everything for the sake of eternal reward. The asses, accustomed to the yoke, are the Jews who already had been carrying the burden of the Law and should now take on the yoke of Christ. The passages, then, in Justin's mind indicate that both Jew and Gentile should embrace Christianity.[22] The Septuagint text for Moses' blessing over Joseph reads: "Like the horns of a unicorn are his horns." [23] Here Justin finds a contradiction. The unicorn does not have several horns. Therefore, the Cross is meant, because it should always precede like a horn, and it has several arms that proceed from it like horns.[24]

Upon the outer garment [25] of the high priests pomegranates and little bells were added as adornment, but how many is not stated in the Bible. Since Justin equated the high priest with Christ, the little bells with their sweet tinkling became the apostles whose preaching fills the whole world with the praise of God and His Anointed. And because

---

[7] Cf. Dial. 134, 140.
[8] Dial. 134.
[9] Gen. 18:1 ; with the Septuagint Justin read "at the tree."
[10] Gen. 32:10.
[11] Gen. 30:37.
[12] Gen. 38:18, 25.
[13] Ex. 4:17.
[14] Num. 17:8.
[15] Ex. 15:23.
[16] Ex. 15:27.
[17] 4 Kgs. 6:6 ; Dial. 86, 138.
[18] Dial. 125; Gen. 32:25f.
[19] Zach. 9:9.
[20] Gen. 49:11 (G).
[21] Ap. I 32 ; Dial. 53.
[22] Dial. 53.
[23] Deut. 33:17 ; the Masoretic text has *re'em*, wild ox.
[24] Dial. 91.
[25] *Me'il*, tunica.

there were twelve apostles who preached the Gospel, Justin concluded that there were twelve little bells hanging on the high priest's vestment. Clement of Alexandria likewise regarded the high priest as a type of Christ, but he related the tinkling little bells to our Savior's preaching. Then, because of the passage in St. Luke, "Preach the acceptable year of the Lord," [26] he assumed that the public ministry of Jesus lasted one year. The number of bells must, therefore, have been 360, the number of days on which the Lord had preached the Gospel.[27]

In the two goats that played a role on the Day of Atonement, one of which was driven out into the desert while the other was kept at the sanctuary, Justin, like Barnabas, saw a type of Christ's twofold advent — in His suffering and in His glory.[28]

c) *Critique.* Many of the interpretations given in the Letter of Barnabas, in the Dialogues of Justin, or in the writings of the Fathers of the Alexandrian school may well be called versatile or ingenious; frequently, however, it is difficult to see even anything edifying in them. Christ is the treasure hidden in the field of the Old Testament,[29] but He does not lie under every clod; and who digs at random works in vain. There is sequence and progress in the history of God's Chosen People; revealed religion too experienced a development, the precepts of the Old Testament were extended and harmoniously applied as new circumstances arose. And who would deny that the appearance of the Son of God opened new vistas in dogma, moral, and worship? Therefore, the Old and the New Testaments may not be merged into one, the New Testament may not be read into the Old Testament against its own clear message.

The fact that the New Testament gives a typical sense to relatively few Old Testament passages should be a warning not to construe relationships arbitrarily between persons and things of the Old Covenant and New Covenant truths or realities. Typological exegesis may not be applied haphazardly to Old Testament passages without contradicting the method of the inspired authors of the New Testament books. The exegete must ask himself what each inspired writer intended to say; texts torn from context prove nothing. The Old Testament is the antechamber to the Church, but an antechamber remains an antechamber. The Old Testament is the dawn heralding the break of day; it is not the noonday sun. Old and New Testament form a unit; the same God speaks to us in both, the same Holy Spirit inspired the whole. And certain passages of the Old Testament do contain a typical message in addition to the primary message immediately inherent in the words.

[26] 4:19; Is. 61:2.   [27] Strom. V 6, 37; P. Heinisch, BZ 4,
[28] Dial. 40, 111.   [29] Iren. IV 26, 1.   1906, 402-407.

For typical exegesis the Fathers of the Antiochian School serve better as guides. Unlike the Alexandrians, they accorded attention to the text and context, but even here we will keep in mind that when these writers speak of a type, very frequently they actually mean only an association of ideas (*accommodatio sensus*); they do not imply that the Holy Spirit intended the ideas they advance. In recent years attempts have been made to give typology greater prominence. High respect is accorded the methods of Origen and the Alexandrian School, and one may note a tendency to confuse the messages of the Old and New Testaments.[30]

[30] Cf. Th. Deman, *Französische Bemühungen um eine Erneuerung der Theologie*, ThR 46, 61-82.

The Messiah's Mother

1. MARY DURING THE PUBLIC MINISTRY OF JESUS. References to our Lady are strikingly rare in the life of Jesus, apart from His infancy, early youth, and the time after the resurrection. Only three times does she appear in the Gospel account during His public ministry; but each occasion marks an important moment in the work of redemption: first, at the marriage at Cana;[31] then, as Jesus taught in a house surrounded by the people;[32] lastly, as He hung dying upon the Cross.[33]

When Jesus appeared at Cana with the disciples whom He had just invited to follow Him, Mary approached and remarked: "They have no more wine." The bridegroom certainly was not wealthy, for the wine supply was so soon exhausted. It was not necessary for Mary to inform Jesus of the situation; but a word from her would help to undo the embarrassment in which the bridal party presently found themselves. Evidently a miracle was needed. At a later date Jesus had compassion on a hungry multitude and twice gave them bread. He had compassion upon the widow of Naim and restored her son to life on the way to burial. And now His appearance with disciples had augmented difficulties among friends, or perhaps relatives of some degree. His reply to Mary seemed a refusal: "Woman, what have we in common? My hour is not yet come."

Jesus was standing before His mother not as a son but as the Redeemer who must listen to the heavenly Father. Mary bows, as once she had

[31] John 2:1-11.   [32] Matth. 12:46-50.   [33] John 19:25-27.

done upon hearing her twelve year old Child say: "Why did you seek me? Did you not know that I must be concerned with what pertains to my Father?" [34] Nevertheless, she must have understood that Jesus would answer her request because she told the servants: "Whatever it may be that he tells you, do it." Despite the reply, she was certain that Jesus would work a miracle; it was knowledge from an interior enlightenment, the reward for having humbly submitted to God and to her Child. Thus not through pleading but through a humble spirit did she move Jesus to reveal "his glory" and thereby confirm the faith of the earliest disciples. This, the beginning of miracles, came through the mediation of Mary "and his disciples believed in him."

It was during the Galilean ministry, and Jesus was preaching at a certain house. Opposition against Him was on the increase, and the crowds were wavering. Because they had Abraham as their Father, many Jews believed themselves certain of God's love. Presently the mother of Jesus appeared outside the house and His "brothers," and they demanded to speak with Him. The bystanders judged that Jesus would interrupt His teaching. He does not. Stretching a hand toward His disciples He says: "See my mother and my brothers. Whoever does the will of my Father in heaven, he is my brother, and my sister, and my mother!" Jesus was telling the Jews: blood relationship is of no value in God's new kingdom which He was establishing; nor would descent from Abraham count more. The decisive thing was accomplishing the Father's will. And the disciples learnt this lesson: the apostolic call excludes all considerations of flesh and blood, of human bonds. The mission is paramount.

The "brothers" perhaps wanted Jesus to discontinue His incessant activity for a while. Not a moment does He spare for them. We must suppose that Mary had come for her own reasons. A mother dismissed would make a far different impression both upon the bystanders and the disciples than some mere relatives. But His mother too must recede into the background, for the Messianic work is more important than deference to maternal affections. Any other mother turned away by a son in this fashion would have felt offended. Mary again bowed to God's holy will, even supposing she was aware of her duty to make the sacrifice in the interest of her Son's redemptive mission.

Again Mary steps out of the Gospel story. But when the time had come to consummate the renunciation of her Child, she rose from seclusion. On the way to Golgotha she accompanied Him in order that Simeon's prophecy might be fulfilled in all its bitterness: "A sword will pierce your very soul." [35] She is here not merely as the mother of a dying

---

[34] Luke 2:49.   [35] Luke 2:35.

Child, but as the Mother of the world's Redeemer. To the disciple whom He loved, Jesus said: "Behold your mother." And to His mother: "Behold your son." With the disciple who now becomes her son, she receives all the redeemed as her spiritual children. This was God's response to her final, perfect sacrifice. At the moment she would not have grasped the tremendous significance of the words. When her twelve year old Boy spoke of His Father's will in the temple at Jerusalem, she understood little of what He was saying. But after the resurrection and ascension, and especially after the descent of the Holy Spirit when the infant Church began to grow, then did Mary attain full understanding of the mission confided to her by her divine Child upon the Cross.

If the New Testament, the fulfillment of Messianic prophecy, devotes so little space to the Messiah's mother, we should not expect too much concerning her in the Old Testament. There are only three passages which refer to her in the literal sense: Is. 7:14; Mich. 5:2–3; Jer. 31:22. To which we ought add the venerable text, Gen. 3:15. Here, according to the literal sense, Eve is the woman and mankind as such is told to crush the serpent's head; but the protoevangel found its definitive fulfillment in one Child of Eve's, Jesus. The usual Vulgate text for the passage is: *ipsa conteret caput tuum,* she, the woman, i.e., Mary, will crush the serpent's head — testimony to the faith of the ancient Church that between Mary and the serpent abiding enmity reigns. It was Mary who gave birth to Him who crushed the serpent, Jesus. In her was fulfilled in a most unique way that primeval prophecy urging all to struggle against the devil and informing all of Satan's wiles.

Conceived without original sin and living without stain, Mary still did not escape wholly the serpent's bite. In a stable she was forced to give birth to her Child, no one could be found to provide more suitable lodging. To save her Child from Herod, there was the long, dangerous journey to Egypt. While Jesus was preaching the Gospel, the good news that now the world and Israel above all could attain salvation, she saw how opposition constantly increased. Under the Cross she stood and saw her Child crushed out like a common criminal, tortured to death with indescribable pain. She shared that suffering and that sacrifice. Not only did Mary crush the serpent's head when she gave birth to the Redeemer, but likewise through her life and through her sufferings — as *Mater dolorosa,* as *Regina Martyrum.* In this role she truly merited her heavenly crown and became a model for us.

Nevertheless, the proper or primary message of the protoevangel in the mind of the sacred writer is not pointed to Mary. The majority of the Fathers do not understand it of the Mother of God, neither Basil, nor Gregory of Nazianz, nor Chrysostom, nor Cyril of Alexandria in the

East, nor Ambrose,[36] nor Augustine, nor Jerome, nor Gregory the Great. It is found in the writings of Sts. Ireneus, Cyprian, Leo the Great, and Epiphanius.

The veneration which the Church pays to the Mother of the Redeemer finds expression in the many Biblical persons and objects regarded as types of the Messiah's mother and the many passages applied to her, *accommodatio sensus*, in the liturgy.

2. PERSONS TYPIFYING MARY. *Eve.* The typical relationship between Adam and Christ is certain.[37] From earliest times a corresponding parallel has been drawn between Eve and Mary. Eve listened to the serpent, Mary to the angel Gabriel and thereby undid the sin of Eve. Through pride Eve brought misery upon her children, through humility and obedience to God's will Mary shared in the work of our redemption: *mors per Evam, vita per Mariam.*[38] Eve's first child was a sinful man, a murderer; Mary's Child was the Savior. Eve is the mother of all men, Mary the mother of all the saved.

Miriam, or Mary, the sister of Moses, chanted a canticle of gratitude to God after the crossing of the Reed Sea, the miracle that freed her people from Egyptian servitude. Mary sang her Magnificat at the beginning of mankind's spiritual liberation.

Jael. For slaying Sisera who had grievously oppressed Israel, Jael's praises were sung by Debora: "Praised be Jael, the wife of Heber the Kenite, above all woman. In the tents may she be lauded above all women." [39] By giving birth to a Savior, Mary conquered Satan, and therefore she is ever exalted "above all women."

Jephte's daughter. When Israel was being harassed by Ammonite hordes, the judge Jephte made a vow: "If you (Yahweh) will give the Ammonites into my hand, then whoever will come out of the door of my house to meet me upon my victorious return from the Ammonites will belong to Yahweh. I will offer him as a holocaust." Jephte won the campaign and returned home. The first to come out of his house and welcome him was his dearest and only daughter. Jephte was heartbroken but felt obligated to keep his ill-considered vow. He had not excluded the possibility of a human sacrifice, but that it would be his daughter had never entered his mind. She too was heroic, she also believed her father's vow must be fulfilled. Her only request was a two months respite to sorrow over her virginity with her maidens away in the hills. When the period was over, her father "fulfilled the vow he had made." [40]

Jephte was a rude chieftain, a free-booter, before he found himself in command of the Transjordan tribes. The text leaves no doubt that he

---

[36] In spite of the *ipsa* reading found for the first time in his writings.
[37] Rom. 5:12-20; 1 Cor. 15:21-22.

[38] Jerome, *Ep. 22 ad Eustoch.*
[39] Judg. 5:24.
[40] Judg. 11:30-40.

actually did sacrifice his daughter, believing to honor God thereby. But because the observation is made that his daughter sorrowed over her *virginity* and because the account closes with the remark, "she had relations with no man," some exegetes hold that Jephte dedicated his daughter perpetually to the Lord and obligated her to live as a virgin. These interpreters, moreover, see in the maiden a type of Mary's virginity.

While Holofernes was besieging Bethulia, *Judith* rose as the savior of the city and of Israel. The despondent inhabitants on the point of surrendering, she encouraged. She made her way into the enemy's camp and seized the opportunity to behead the general. Thereupon Israel attacked and put the foe to flight. Similarly, Mary overcame the serpent and saved mankind from its power. After her husband's death Judith lived in perpetual chastity, Mary was ever the most pure virgin. At her return Judith was hailed by the officials and the populace, Elizabeth greeted Mary as "Blessed among women." In all her accomplishments Judith referred the credit to God. In the Magnificat Mary praised God for regarding the lowliness of His servant and having done great things for her. Judith had recourse to God in all her endeavors and fortified all her efforts with prayer, Mary is the "singular vessel of devotion." By her life of virtue Judith was a model for her contemporaries, Mary is *the* mirror of justice. At Vespers on the feast of the Immaculate Conception we praise Mary with words once addressed to Judith: *Tu gloria Jerusalem, tu laetitia Israel, tu honorificentia populi nostri*.[41]

Esther brought deliverance to the Jews threatened by annihilation in Persia. Because of her natural beauty Esther was chosen queen; because of her spiritual beauty Mary became the mother of the Messiah and the Queen of heaven. Esther alone was exempted from the decree forbidding approach to the king without a special call, Mary was exempted from the law of original sin. Magnificently adorned Esther came into the king's presence, in the brightness of her virtue Mary shines before God. Esther interceded for a people destined to perish, Mary intercedes for all who suffer and are oppressed.

Two characters from the Old Testament sapiential books must not be overlooked. Already in earliest times the marriage theme in Ps. 45 depicted the relationship of the Messiah to the ideal Israel, of Jesus to the Church, while the bride's role in the second strophe was applied to Mary and used on Marian feasts in Mass and Office. Mary is the queen standing at the right of her Son, gloriously attired with virtue and heavenly light. Gabriel's greeting, *Ave, gratia plena, Dominus tecum*, may well be placed parallel to the psalmist's words to the bride: "The king is desirous of your beauty, for he is your lord (the Vulgate adds: your

---

[41] Jud. 15:10.

God)."[42] The honor accorded the queen in v. 13 found its highest actualization in Mary when the angel Gabriel and Elizabeth greeted her, an honor that continues to be fulfilled after her assumption into heaven. Mary's incomparable virtue is the thought underlying the words: "Wholly magnificent is the king's daughter."[43] The phrase, "Sons will replace your fathers,"[44] has been associated with the spiritual progeny that has been Mary's since John was given to her at the foot of the Cross.

The *valiant woman*, whose worth is above pearls and who surpasses all daughters who live virtuously, may be regarded as a prototype of Mary.[45] For Mary was the ideal woman and mother, and her spiritual fortitude at the feet of her dying Son has no parallel.

3. MATERIAL TYPES. Moses, the founder of the Old Covenant, received his mission when God appeared to him in a bush enveloped by flames but not consumed by them. This *burning bush* prefigured Mary's perpetual virginity that was in no way impaired by the conception and birth of the Redeemer: *Rubum quem viderat Moyses incombustum, conservatam agnovimus tuam laudabilem virginitatem.*[46]

In the Litany to the Blessed Virgin we invoke her as "Ark of the Covenant." The *ark*, according to Mosaic Law, was made from incorruptible wood, gold-leafed within and without, and contained the tables of the Law. It represented the holiest object of the Old Dispensation. Upon it Yahweh revealed Himself in a cloud, and upon it the cherubim symbolizing God's presence were embossed. Beneath her heart Mary carried Jesus. All virtues shine resplendently in her, angels approach to do homage before her. She was overshadowed with power from the Most High.

The sign of Gedeon. In confirmation of his mission as Israel's deliverer, Gedeon, petitioned a sign. A fleece of wool should become wet with dew, with no dew falling next to it.[47] This miraculously bedewed fleece has been construed by the Church Fathers as a type of the incarnation of the Son of God. As the dew descended upon the fleece, so the Son of God assumed a human nature of Mary the Virgin. On the feast of the Circumcision, the Church prays at Vespers: *Quando natus es ineffabiliter ex Virgine, tunc impletae sunt Scripturae; sicut pluvia in vellus descendisti ut salvum faceres genus humanum.* Then Gedeon requested a second sign from God: the fleece of wool should remain dry while dew fell upon all the surrounding ground.[48] This foreshadowed Mary's Immaculate Conception; of all men she alone was preserved free from contamination by original sin.

Our final example, the vision of the new temple as seen by Ezechiel.

---

[42] Ps. 45:12.
[43] V. 14.
[44] V. 17.
[45] Prov. 31:10-31.
[46] 1 Vespers on the feast of the Circumcision.
[47] Judg. 6:37.
[48] Judg. 6:39.

After God had made His entrance into this temple, the prophet was led by an angel to its outer door toward the east and told: "This door will remain locked. It will not be opened and no one may enter through it because Yahweh, Israel's God, has entered by it. Therefore it will remain closed." [49] It was unbecoming that any creature should use the portal through which the Creator had solemnly made His entrance. To a much greater degree was it fitting that the womb of the Virgin, sanctified by the Lord of the world, should remain untouched after His birth; that Mary should live as a virgin until the heavenly Father had assumed His daughter, the Son His mother, and the Holy Spirit His purest Bride into heaven. For these reasons many patristic writers associated the passage from Ezechiel with the Virgin whose womb remained pure from all defilement after the Holy Spirit had overshadowed her. The passage is used as the Lesson for Sext in the Office of the Feast of the Immaculate Conception.

4. POETICAL BOOKS. a) *The Canticle of Canticles* is a collection of songs which expresses the love of a bride for her lover and of a lover for his bride. In the literal sense this relationship showed God's love for His Chosen People, a type of the intimate union between the ideal Messianic Israel and her God. The earliest prophets described the bond between God and Israel under the figure of a marriage divinely contracted at Sinai, a union resting upon Israel's free choice and decision. Now the Old Covenant was a preparation for the New Israel, God's people of old portrayed the Church, God's people in Messianic times. When the prophets gazed into the future and described the blessings in store for purified Israel, they actually meant the baptized of the Christian era.

Jesus too used the figure of marriage. When the Baptist's disciples asked Him, "Why don't your disciples fast?," He answered, "Can the wedding guests be sad while the bridegroom is still with them? Surely the days will come when the bridegroom will be taken from them; then they will fast." [50] The Savior was comparing Himself to a bridegroom, His disciples to wedding guests. And when the followers of John the Baptist became envious over the great numbers being baptized by Jesus and interpreted the turn as a lessening of their master's status, he upbraided them for their petty spirit and stated his relationship to Jesus in a figure suggested by the Canticle of Canticles: "He who has the bride is the bridegroom. The friend of the bridegroom, however, who is present and hears him, rejoices greatly over the bridegroom's voice." [51] The bridegroom was Jesus, and John was the bridegroom's friend who was happy over the honor accorded Him on the day of the bride's be-

---

[49] Ez. 44:2.   [50] Matth. 9:15.   [51] John 3:29.

trothal, the day when Jesus was joined to the nascent Church procured for Him through the "friend's" preachments of penance. The apostle Paul used the same picture when he told the Corinthians: "I have espoused you to one man, as a pure virgin to belong to Christ." [52] And the last book of the New Testament, the Apocalypse, concludes by hymning the marriage of the Lamb — Christ espousing forever His bride, the redeemed of the New Covenant. [53]

Thus does the Canticle of Canticles portray the love of Christ towards His Church and the Church's love towards Christ. Nevertheless, the espousal of Christ with His Church takes place within the souls of individual persons who give themselves to God. Now what union was more intimate than that between the mother of God and the Son of God? What creature was endowed with greater grace than Mary? Whom did God love more dearly than the bride of the Holy Spirit? And, on the other hand, what soul responded to grace with greater enthusiasm, what soul produced richer fruits than the soul of the immaculately conceived? In her the covenant of love between God and mankind, the covenant of love between Christ and the Church attained its highest consummation. Beginning with Hippolyt, Ephraem, and Ambrose, spiritual writers have applied the praises of the bride in the Canticle to the mother of God. In the Breviary on feasts of the Blessed Virgin and in the liturgy of holy Mass, texts very frequently are culled from this Book of the Old Testament.

To list only a few of the passages that have been applied to our Blessed Mother. The Book's opening sentence, in which the bride voices her longing for the bridegroom, may well come from Mary's lips: "Kiss me with kisses from your mouth; for your love is better than wine." [54] These are words that tell her inmost sentiments toward God whose love meant more than all earth's goods. And when the angel came to announce that she should be the Messiah's mother, she could pray with the bride: "Lead me, O king, into your chamber; we want to exult and rejoice in you." [55] Our thoughts may well dwell upon the jubilation to which she gave expression in the Magnificat. And when the bride continues to pray, "Tell me, you whom my soul loves, where do you pasture (your flock), and where do you rest at noon?," [56] our thoughts may turn to the prayers that Mary sent up to God during her pilgrimages to the temple or in her ardent petitions for the advent of the Messiah.

The bride's prayer, "Black (from the sun) am I, yet beautiful," [57] afford us the opportunity of seeing Mary working zealously to obtain daily bread in the poverty of her environment, even after she had found a support in Joseph. The lover in the Canticle is very conscious of the

[52] 2 Cor. 11:2.
[53] Apoc. 19:7 ; 21:9.
[54] Cant. 1:2.
[55] Cant. 1:3.
[56] Cant. 1:7.
[57] Cant. 1:5.

bride's beauty; he calls her the most beautiful of women.[58] How God treasured Mary's beauty! He flooded her with graces to make her a worthy dwelling for His Son, and she accepted every grace gratefully, with fullest cooperation: "Full of grace, the Lord is with thee."

The lover tells his bride: "My love, you are beautiful; ah, so charming." [59] Mary knew that God is the source of all beauty and that she herself owed all her privileges to His bounty. Humbly she compared herself to a simple flower, to a crocus on Sharon's meadows, to a lily in the valley.[60] Did not Mary pass her youth in quiet retirement, blushing at the suggestion of becoming a carpenter's bride? And what humility and holy simplicity did she not show when her Son became the famous teacher, the great miracle worker! The bridegroom muses on the bride's reflections; he takes her comparison to the lily and gives it a startling turn: "As a lily among thorns, so is my beloved among daughters." [61] To what mortal do these words of praise apply better than to Mary! She is the only one who remained unstained by the pollution of original sin, nor did she offend God through the least personal sin. She is not only pure as an angel, she is the Queen of angels.

To such a bride does the divine Bridegroom protest His love: "My dove in the clefts of the rocks, in the cliff's recesses! Let me see your face, let me hear your voice." [62] The heavenly Father is here seeking to effect in Mary the mystery of His Son's incarnation, the divine Word is seeking to become her Child, the Holy Spirit is seeking to overshadow her as His bride. She is to become God's mother, she who as a dove passed her life quietly in the clefts of rocks, humbly in the cliff's recesses. The bride responds: "My beloved is mine, and I belong to him . . . And Mary said: I am a handmaid of the Lord, be it done to me according to your word!" [63]

Enraptured over the beauty of his bride, the lover exclaimed: "Who is she that rises as the dawn, fair as the moon, brilliant as the sun, majestic as an army in array!" [64] Just as the moon beams forth a mildly light through the hours of night with no star to contest its glory, so in virtue does Mary excel every saint in the skies of heaven. Born in holiness and grace, she turned to virtue as easily as dawn turns to day. Like an army advancing formidably, she put to flight and continues to scatter the enemies of her divine Son. With the Church we pray: "You alone have overcome all false teaching throughout the entire world."

In the Litany we invoke Mary as the "Tower of David" [65] that cannot be shaken by enemy attack, a true guarantee of security. We also hail her as the "Tower of Ivory" [66] resplendent in virginal purity; as a garden enclosed [67] because she remained virginal and produced the choicest

---

[58] Cant. 1:8 ; 5:9 ; 6:1. [60] Cant. 2:1. [62] Cant. 2:14. [64] Cant. 6:10. [66] Cant. 7:4.
[59] Cant. 1:16. [61] Cant. 2:2. [63] Cant. 2:16. [65] Cant. 4:4. [67] Cant. 4:12.

Fruit; as a sealed fountain [68] because the celestial waters of grace flow through her mediation.

But love is not love until it has been proven, love is not love until guaranteed by suffering and sacrifice. The Church meets this objection in her application of Canticle texts to the mother of God on the feast of the Seven Sorrows. In one part of the Canticle the bridegroom becomes separated from the bride. Thereupon in deepest sorrow she wanders through the city searching for him. Mary was granted heavenly joys, but at what price! The angel Gabriel had said to her: "He will be great." Was her Infant great in Bethlehem's stable? Was He great as His parents were forced to flee with Him before a ruthless tyrant into Egypt? Was He great in the eyes of the people while sweating in the workshop at Nazareth? In human estimation was He great when He had no place whereon to lay His head while going about preaching?

The angel Gabriel had also told Mary: "He will be called the Son of the Most High." But how did those for whose salvation He had come speak of Him? "Is this not the carpenter's son!" [69] Did they not accuse Him of having a devil? [70] The angel said: "God will give him the throne of David his Father." Was the crib a throne? or the Cross upon which He was raised? "He will rule in the house of Jacob forever." But when the multitude sought to make Him a king, He withdrew; and the accusation that destroyed Him was that He had made Himself king of the Jews. What suffering all this meant for Mary, what testing of her faith and of her spirit of sacrifice. What pangs tore that mother's heart when vainly she sought her twelve year old boy, when she saw how the people were abandoning Him who was their Redeemer, when she finally sensed His dreadful, inevitable death on Calvary. As she stood beneath the Cross, how ironical would those words of the Canticle have sounded: "Come, daughters of Jerusalem, and see King Solomon with the crown his mother placed on him on the day of his nuptials, on the day of the joy of his heart." [71] The bride in the Canticle could find high delight in the costly robes her beloved had provided for their marriage day. Mary experienced bitterest grief as she witnessed her Son ascending the wood of the Cross with a crown of thorns pressed upon His head by that unnatural mother, the Synagogue, on her day of unholy glee.

Mary proved true to her sublime calling in spite of severest trials and suffering. The bride's plea could well be hers: "Place me as a seal upon your heart, as a seal upon your arm. For love is strong as death, its zeal obstinate as sheol. Floods of water cannot quench love, nor rivers sweep it away." [72] As the impression of a seal leaves a true indication of the seal itself, so Mary reflected the divine image to the highest

[68] Cant. 4:12.   [69] Matth. 13:55.   [70] John 8:48.   [71] Cant. 3:11.   [72] Cant. 8:6-7.

degree possible for any person; and as cylinder seals were carried about on one's person in the ancient Orient, so Mary was attached wholly to God, ever in closest intimacy with Him.

The path of tears leads to happiness. Mary's beatitude far surpasses that of any saint. At her assumption the angels and saints could greet her with the words spoken by the populace in the Canticle as they watched the bride's train approach, words which the Church uses on the feast of the Assumption: "Who is this now coming up from the desert like a column of smoke, perfumed with myrrh and frankincense?" [73] Up from the wilderness of this world Mary ascended to her eternal homeland. Because of its acrid, pungent odor, myrrh has always been associated with suffering — an appropriate symbol for her life of tears and sacrifice; but she likewise was "perfumed with frankincense" in token of the galaxy of virtues adorning her, that array of good works she had performed. These ascended to God like the clouds of smoke from a pleasing incense offering. The bridegroom's words are also appropriately applied to Mary: "I will go to the mountain of myrrh, and to the hill of frankincense." [74] Upon her assumption into heaven, Mary can say with the bride: "I have found him whom my soul loves! I will cling to him and never leave him!" [75]

b) In the *Books of Proverbs, Sirach, and Wisdom* the inspired poets sang the glories of divine wisdom. Wisdom created the universe, wisdom loved all men, particularly the children of Israel. As the time for Messiah's appearance approached, the sacred writers personified wisdom in an increasingly striking manner. But their descriptions never transcended figurative language, their speculation did not attain the definite conclusion: Wisdom proceeding from God is a distinct, divine Person. It was reserved for the incarnate Son of God to reveal this mystery to mankind.

The highest and most perfect of God's creatures was none other than the maiden destined to be the mother of His only Son. When God created the world, redemption was part of His plan, and therefore she was not excluded who was to become the Redeemer's mother. If God rejoiced over His creation, it was not without reference to His crowning achievement. Divine Wisdom cannot escort men to their eternal goal without the mother of Wisdom playing a role. So it is not strange if the Church, on Mary's feast day, culls texts from the sapiential books which treat the attribute of divine wisdom and applies them to the mother of Wisdom — for, in the light of the New Testament, Jesus her Son appears as Wisdom incarnate. Who except Mary can truly say: "My home is with prudence, at my disposal I have knowledge and in-

[73] Cant. 3:6.   [74] Cant. 4:6.   [75] Cant. 3:4.

sight"? [76] For she was that wisest of virgins who made God the object of her every effort. It was she whom Elizabeth praised as the "one who had believed," [77] it was she who remained heroically humble under the loftiest exaltation possible for any human being — that of becoming the mother of God.

Mary was "the first fruit of his ways," [78] the most perfect of God's creatures through her sinless conception and her *fiat* to the angel's message. It is Mary who may say, "I am enraptured over the children of men," [79] because she is perpetually interceding for them, guarding them from dangers of body and soul, and striving to gather them as her children into heavenly mansions. From her lips too comes a motherly warning: "My sons, listen to me. Accept instruction so that you may become wise." [80] Her lessons are given not by words but example; and one who imitates her will experience the truth of the statement: "Whoever finds me, finds life, and he will obtain grace from the Lord." [81] In union with eternal Wisdom, to whom she gave birth, Mary can say: "Like the cedar on Lebanon grew I tall, like the cypress on the hills of Hermon. Like the palm at Kadesh did I thrive, like the rosebush at Jericho." [82] For she made spiritual progress day by day, her whole life a steady growth in grace; while her virtues resembled the sweet scent of roses.

With uncreated Wisdom Mary could say: "Like the vine I bore sweet-smelling, luscious fruit." [83] The vine is not a noble tree, nor does it lift its branches to lofty heights; still it was Palestine's most valuable plant. Its fruit refreshed the weak and restored strength to the sick. How modestly did Mary conduct herself, and yet how precious the fruit of her good works, a glory that will endure forever. Her most precious fruit, for which we must be eternally grateful, was the "blessed fruit of her womb." As mother of the Redeemer, Mary may say of herself: "I am the mother of fair love and of fear, of knowledge and holy hope . . . [84] Come to me, all you who desire me, and fill yourselves with my fruits . . . [85] Anyone who listens to me will not be put to shame, and those who work in my behalf will never sin." [86]

c) The *Lamentations* of the prophet Jeremias give expression to the grief experienced by those who remained in the ruins of Jerusalem, smitten witnesses to the judgment God had brought upon the sinful city. Jerusalem is compared to a mother who lost all her children and now weeps and groans under her sorry lot. In the liturgy portions of the Lamentations are applied to the Blessed Virgin, our Mother who 600 years after Jerusalem's destruction stood upon a hill outside that city, where her only Child was slowly dying. It is not a question of the

[76] Prov. 8:12.　　[79] Prov. 8:31.　　[82] Sir. 24:13-14.　　[85] Sir. 24:18.
[77] Luke 1:45.　　[80] Prov. 8:32-33.　　[83] Sir. 24:17.　　[86] Sir. 24:21.
[78] Prov. 8:22.　　[81] Prov. 8:35.　　[84] Sir. 24:24 Vg.

whole book pointing to Mary. For the disaster that struck the city was a just punishment for sin, and Jerusalem acknowledged her guilt. Jerusalem lamented because her youths were forced into slavery, her virgins deflowered, her children dying of hunger; and she called down God's punishment upon the oppressor. Mary was without stain of sin. In unison with her Son she prayed: "Father, forgive them!" However, some of Israel's cries of sorrow and pain the Church can apply to Mary, to make more vivid the depths of her grief and sorrow — our *Mater dolorosa.*

"She weeps, she weeps through the night. Tears wet her cheeks. No one is near to comfort her, none from all who loved her. All her friends have forsaken her, unfaithful, they have become her enemies." [87] Our thoughts easily recall how the apostles vanished when Jesus was apprehended — all except John, and he needed comforting. The people who but a few days previously had acclaimed the Savior with loud *Hosannas* now despised Him, and looked with ridicule and contempt upon His mother. "See, Lord, how terrified I am! What pain sears my soul! My heart churns within my breast, for I am sated with bitterness." [88] Her ears were pierced by the cry, "My God, my God, why have you forsaken me!," a dereliction that enveloped Son and mother. With the desolate City of old she could say: "All you who pass along the way, look and see whether there is any sorrow like unto my sorrow." [89] Her condition was well expressed in the words Jeremias addressed to Jersualem: "To what can I compare you, with what can I liken you, O daughter Jerusalem? To what can I compare you, so as to comfort you, O virgin daughter Sion? For great as the sea is your wound — who can heal you!" [90]

Jerusalem's fate occasioned ridicule and scornful jeering. A similar lot was Mary's beneath the Cross: "All who pass along the road clap their hands at you; they hiss, they wag their heads at the daughter Jerusalem. All your enemies open their mouths jeeringly at you, they hiss and gnash their teeth and say: We have destroyed her!" [91] At Jerusalem's plight the enemy rejoiced; they were Gentiles. At the plight of the world's Redeemer there was boisterous rejoicing on the part of the high priests and Scribes who had opposed Him during His whole public ministry. Now they had attained their goal, and for the pain-laden, apparently helpless form on the Cross they had nought but mockery and ridicule: "We have destroyed him!" "If you are Israel's king," Mary heard them say, "come down from the Cross!" Every word a dagger's wound through that Mother's loving heart! The prophet's words again held true: "Cry loudly to the Lord, O virgin daughter Sion! Let your

[87] Lam. 1:2.   [88] Lam. 1:20.   [89] Lam. 1:12.   [90] Lam. 2:13.   [91] Lam. 2:15-16.

tears stream torrent-like through the day and through the night. Give yourself no respite, your eyes no rest." [92] And Simeon's prophecy was fulfilled: "A sword will pierce your soul." Yet one final parallel. Under the mighty stroke of judgment Jerusalem did turn to God; purified, she became worthy to rise to new life. And Mary, by conforming her will perfectly with God's and remaining close to the Cross of her Son, worthied herself for the heavenly crown of Queen of Martyrs.

[92] Lam. 2:18.

Biblical Messianism— a Unique Phenomenon

In God's plan the whole Old Testament was meant to prepare mankind for redemption from sin. For this purpose there were the sacrifices, in which individuals and the people as a whole surrendered themselves to God or begged His forgiveness; for this purpose various purifications were enjoined upon those who had defiled themselves (physical uncleanness being a reminder of spiritual uncleanness that must be sloughed off); for this purpose the feasts were instituted, on which the Israelites thanked God, petitioned aid, or begged forgiveness; for this purpose God intervened visibly in the history of His people, whether to bring assistance in times of need or to chastise in order to effect a conversion of morals; for this purpose God raised up Israel's great leaders, particularly the prophets who reminded the people of their sinfulness and admonished repentance; for his purpose there were priests and wisdom teachers. And last but not least, this was why oracles were given concerning the coming Redeemer, oracles that buoyed up the people during difficult days with the promise of aid, oracles that told of the judgment preceding the Messiah's appearance and that revealed man's reconciliation with God and the remission of sins.

Old Testament Messianic hope is founded on faith in a just and loving God, the one Father of all men who wills that His children should not perish after falling into sin but rather find their way back to His loving embrace. Now just as Old Testament religion with its monotheism and ethical ideals rests upon revelation, so too the origin and development of Biblical Messianism was due to special divine illumination which brought to maturity the seed divinely planted in the human heart in paradise.

In times of turmoil and trouble men spontaneously hope for an amelioration of conditions, the dawn of happier days. Israel's desire for the "Day of Yahweh," that moment when God intervenes to restore the fortunes of His People, is a not uncommon wish.[93] But such natural, human longing is wholly insufficient to explain the origin and flowering of Biblical Messianism. Messianic hope existed before the time of the literary prophets, it is older even than Israel as a nation; it dates to the protoevangel in paradise. That first sin occasioned hope for forgiveness and deliverance from evil, for God did not will to abandon men to their fate but sought to instill confidence and a desire of again attaining His love.

The Messiah is presented as a deliverer. Was this approach occasioned by some extraordinary political crisis? True, when the horizon was darkened by Assyrian war clouds, reliance upon Yahweh's aid became more alive and various prophecies on the Messiah and his activity were proclaimed. Messianic hope as such, however, was nothing new; and moreover, it flourished during the exile and after the exile when Israel no longer enjoyed political status as a people; and precisely during this later period was the Messianic movement enriched with many new features. Deliverance was indeed proclaimed at the time of the Assyrian crisis, but deliverance from Assyrian tyranny was not predicted as the work of the Messiah; he would only appear *after* Assyria had perished. God would allay the present danger with reference to the Messiah. Would it have been humanly possible for any prophet to propose such a resolution of political conditions on his own initiative, or must such insight rather be ascribed to divine enlightenment?

The prophecy concerning the Redeemer's virgin birth [94] was pointed against the king then in power, Achaz. About the same time Israel was told that the Savior would behold the light of day in Bethlehem.[95] Could these pronouncements have been devised by the prophets or be derived from outside sources? The Messiah would deliver men from their sins, but this deliverance was to be achieved only through his own suffering and death. Although the doctrine of vicarious atonement through suffering dates to the exile, the exile offers no explanation why the Messiah should be harassed by his own people and be put to death by them. The Savior rises from the dead, a marvel responsible for the world's conversion, affecting deeply not only the Jews but the Gentiles too. Can this prediction be adequately accounted for on the basis of

---

[93] Cf. Am. 5:18.   [94] Is. 7:14.   [95] Mich. 5:1.

subjective self-scrutiny or any literary borrowing? No one has adduced even the vaguest parallel to this doctrine from the whole, huge body of Oriental literature, nor will any be discovered because a conversion of all men to the one true God and the cessation of idol worship was too lofty a dream to have been entertained by any Oriental.

Some writers have claimed that Israel's Messianic hopes were prompted by an "enthronement feast" in Yahweh's honor observed in Israel on New Year's Day. The festivity is said to have its precedent in the Babylonian New Year's celebration at which Marduk annually assumed anew his duties as sovereign ruler of the four corners of the earth.[96] Now neither the historical Books of the Old Testament nor the Books of the Prophets betray any indication of such a ritual; there are absolutely no references to Israelites preparing for gaudy parades. The psalm texts that speak of Yahweh as Israel's king and are quoted as "proof" actually are utterly beside the point.[97] For their every pronouncement on the future, Israel's prophets relied wholly upon divine illumination — koh 'amar Yahweh, "Thus saith the Lord!" They would never have projected a passing spectacle into the future. Moreover, Yahweh's kingship had no beginning and will have no end. Marduk's reign, however, did begin at the very historical moment when Hammurabi installed him as the nation's foremost god. And why did not the Babylonians themselves ever light upon the idea to extract from their festivity hopes for a blessed future era? Year after year they had repeated Marduk's enthronement with all pomp and splendor.

Nor could the "experience at Sinai" have produced Old Testament Messianism.[98] Messianic hope antedates Moses, and moreover, there would have been little reason for Israel to look forward to someone to bring them deliverance at a future date at the very time when Yahweh was espousing their cause in so many marvellous ways and had provided them with the most gifted of leaders, Moses. Nor is the statement so often found in the prophets and the psalms concerning Yahweh's appearance to inaugurate world rule and judgment adequate as an explanation for scriptural Messianic hope; for the Messiah was heralded not only as king, but also as priest, as prophet, and as the Man of Sorrows.

It is a rich, full, and deeply etched picture the prophets have given us of the Messiah. None of these divinely inspired men, however, left a complete portrait peculiarly his own; rather, each added new lines to the picture inherited from predecessors according to his own natural genius

---

[96] S. Mowinckel, Psalmenstudien, II: Das Thronbesteigungsfest Jahwäs und der Ursprung der Eschatologie. H. Schmidt, Die Thronfahrt Jahwes. F. Böhl, Nieuwjaarsfeest en Koningsdag.

[97] A. Schulz, Kritisches zum Psalter, 48f.

[98] E. Sellin, Der alttestamentliche Prophetismus, 103-193.

and the supernatural enlightenment granted him. Emphasis and approach could and did vary, even to the extent of seemingly contradictory assertions, e.g., the Messiah is man and God; a glorious king and a man of sorrows; sovereign ruler of the world and despised by his fellow men, persecuted and put to death; the son of David and born of a virgin; warrior and prince of peace. He dies yet lives forever; he floods the earth with blessings while demanding self-abnegation; he redeems from sin while shattering all in his paths; he is desired by the very nations upon which he inflicts judgment. Nevertheless, these many points made by various prophets did harmonize to form a unified picture, one destined to fill the people with trust in God's mercy and goodness and with longing for the day when they could worship under the sceptre of the Messiah-King, without sin; the day when guilt had been expiated through the self-immolation of Yahweh's Servant and all were united in a single faith. Of course, only in the light of fulfillment do all the seemingly discordant notes blend perfectly together in symphonic unison — to the astonishment and amazement of every age and race.

Non-Jewish Messianic Hopes

1. THE PROPHETS AND PROFANE LITERATURE. Are there parallels to the Old Testament prophecies on redemption in pagan literature?

Awareness of sin and its evil consequences cannot be restricted to Israel. The pagans too felt indebted to the gods, for they had atonement sacrifices and purificatory rites; and their myths witness to the desire to live on friendly terms with the spirit world. Did they also look forward to and hope for a spiritual reconciliation of mankind with the Powers on High? Did they long for a redeemer and deliverance from sin? We must remember that they had no prophets to proclaim the future in God's Name — their "prophets" could rely on nothing except their own ingenuity. Nor did they have a correct concept of sin, an impossible attainment under polytheism and demon worship. And still their desire would some day be satisfied, the desire implied in Jacob's oracle, "Till he comes whom the nations will obey," [99] or which the prophet of the exile clearly stated as he spoke of the Suffering Servant: "The islands are awaiting his teaching." [1] When called to the office of prophet, Ezechiel heard Yahweh say: "If I would send a prophet to the nations, they would listen to him," [2] and when Jonas preached to the

[99] Or more clearly in G S V: "whom the nations are awaiting."

[1] Is. 42:4.
[2] Ez. 3:6.

255

Ninevites, they obeyed his admonition to do penance. Eventually the time came when He whom the prophets had proclaimed as the Redeemer from sin commissioned a tiny band of apostles: "Go into all the world and teach every nation." [3]

In the effort to deny the revealed character of Old Testament religion and to explain "naturally" its greatest glory, monotheism with its moral demands, writers have argued for an evolution from lower forms, viz., from totemism to fetishism, animism, ancestor worship. Others have tried to discover the source for Israel's theology among other Oriental peoples from whom Israel borrowed. No exception is made for the Bible's doctrine on the Redeemer. In matters of cult Israel did not, of course, stand wholly isolated from environment. God's Chosen People had altars and sacrifices like their neighbors; their purification rites and cleanliness code are pre-Mosaic, and the tabernacle itself was not wholly free from Egyptian artistic lines.

Did environment color the Messianic picture? No one would be surprised if this were proven in the pronouncements of the false prophets. For the false prophets spoke of Yahweh's intervention in favor of the people, granting them aid at once to meet any danger. They never insisted on the prerequisites for obtaining divine assistance, viz., penance and conversion. They never heralded judgment, it was always peace and prosperity; and they accorded no consideration to a personal Redeemer, one whose mission was to expiate sin. The prophets, however, who were truly enlightened by God and to whom we owe Biblical Messianism, did proclaim judgment upon king and people. They derided the gods of the Gentiles as "non-entities" [4] and their cult as a passing illusion.[5] They knew the day was coming when Bel and Nebo would sink prostrate to earth.[6] They ridiculed the idols that could proffer no aid to their devotees in the time of distress.[7] The true prophets used the fact of the fulfillment of their oracles on the destruction of the kingdom and the exile as proof for Yahweh's wisdom and power, while the gods were "things of nought," utterly unable to give their clients any insight into the future.[8] There were, moreover, countless oracles on the punishment to be inflicted on the Gentile nations because of their godlessness and immorality, a visitation that would occasion their conversion. The attitude of the prophets toward the pagans and their pantheons is a most sobering consideration when treating the question whether Israel's Messianism arose under the influence of neighbor nations.

2. PERSIA. Noblest among the religions of the ancient Orient was that of Zarathustra — excluding, of course, Israel's revealed religion. There

---

[3] Matth. 28:19-20.
[4] Is. 2:8. 18 ; 10:10 ; 19:3.
[5] Is. 2:18 ; Soph. 2:11.

[6] Is. 46:1-2.
[7] Hab. 2:18; Jer. 10:3-15 ; Is. 44:10-17.
[8] Ez. 6:10,14 ; 7:9 ; Is. 41:21-29 ; 43:9-11.

was no contact, however, between the Hebrews and Persians until the Old Testament Messianic picture had long been sketched in its principal lines. The claim that prophecies pertaining to a Redeemer first arose in postexilic times rests upon a preconceived literary critique, and falls with it. This does not imply, however, that Persian religion had no effect on the subsequent development of prophetic ideas as found in the Apocrypha.[9]

3. EGYPT. Egyptian literature contains a goodly number of oracles concerning periods of national calamity terminated by eras of prosperity. The new king inevitably inaugurates an age of plenty! [10] In a papyrus document dating to the eighteenth dynasty (1580–1320),[11] a priest predicts an incursion of Asiatics into the Nile country in addition to the current evils of civil war and famine. Then a king comes from the south who expels the foe and rebuilds the capital, Amen-em-het, the founder of the twelfth dynasty (2000–1970).[12] Under King Bokchoris (c. 720 B.C.), we find a prophecy of enemy attack; the country is oppressed and the idols are carried off. Soon the Egyptians take heart, they drive out the enemy (the Assyrians), bring back the gods, and an era of prosperity dawns. At the time of a certain Amenophis a potter predicted how evil times would precede a good Pharaoh upon the throne.

All these "prophecies" follow the same pattern: Times are bad; there is war and civil turmoil; enemies enter the country; false rumors, lies; temples are desecrated, crops fail; the Nile, Egypt's principal source of wealth, is low, women are sterile. Then appears the savior-king! He conquers the foreigner, brings back the sacred idols, the Nile rises, everywhere there is abundance.

These texts do not predict the future. They simply describe current conditions in oracular form. This is evident in the above "potter's prophecy," since he gives the length of the savior-king's reign as 55 years. These predictions were made to glorify the reigning monarch, and therefore the time previous must be painted in darkest hues. Misfortune strikes only the Egyptians, it is not a punishment inflicted for sin as in the Old Testament comminations against Israel and the Gentiles; and when prosperity returns, it is restricted to Egypt. A Savior whose "kingdom is not of this world" and whose advent would not take place for centuries finds no mention in Egyptian oracles.

Egyptian mythology describes how Osiris was slain by the wicked god Set, then came to life again and lives forever. His lot was regarded as typical of what is in store for every mortal. Osiris could hardly have served as the protoytpe for the Servant of Yahweh in his death and

---

[9] Bousset-Gressmann, *Die Religion des Judentums*, 506f; Schürer, *Geschichte des jüdischen Volkes*, II, 413, 578.

[10] AOT 46-51.
[11] Cf. Drioton-Vandier, *L'Egypte*, 170.
[12] Cf. *Ibid.*, 246-251.

resurrection. Osiris was a mythical figure of the past, Yahweh's Servant would be an historical person in the future. Osiris remained in the underworld as its ruler, the Servant of Yahweh returns to real life on earth. All men were destined to descend into the shades with Osiris, but through death the Suffering Servant blots out sin and reconciles mankind with God.[13]

4. BABYLON. Those who claim Babylon contributed significantly to the development of Israel's Messianic theology place great stress on the fact that Israel's Messiah was hailed as a king from earliest times. For the Babylonian gods were royal personages. Anu was king over the Igigi and the Anunnaki. Ea was king of the watery deep. Marduk won supreme kingship by triumphing over Tiamat. Earthly kings reign as representatives of the divinities, and become divinized in time. The proud boastfulness of Babylon's king was immortalized by one of Israel's prophets: "To the heavens will I ascend, above the stars of God I will set my throne. In the farthest north on the mountain where they gather will I be seated; I will scale the clouds of heaven and match the (Lord) Most High."[14] Tyre's king was not ashamed to say: "I am a god."[15] An even greater arrogance characterized the Pharaohs, since they claimed to be the incarnation of the god Re. In his celebrated *Hymn to the Sun,* Amenophis IV, who abolished the Egyptian pantheon, wrote conceitedly: "No one else knows you except your son Ikhnaton who proceeds from you."[16]

Babylon's king, from whom all good fortune was awaited, was closely associated with the gods from time immemorial and regarded as the nation's savior. With every new ruler an era of prosperity began, while previously conditions were anything but pleasant. This was true already of Sumerian monarchs; then of Hammurabi, who at the beginning and end of his famous Code sketches the picture of the king flooding his people with benefits; then of Ashurhaddon, Ashurbanipal, Merodach-Baladan, Cyrus, and the princes of Hellenistic times like Antiochus I who took the surname *Soter,* savior. All this reflects the flattery and adulation of court attachés who seek to glorify their king as the ideal sovereign, the one who grants whatever his subjects may desire. But it was always the reigning king who was the benefactor, never one projected to an indefinite future date.

In one anthology of Babylonian "prophecies," lean years alternate with fat years. Under a given ruler, who reigns eighteen years, the citizens prosper. Under his successor, who rules thirteen years, foreign hordes enter the country, the temple is destroyed, and all suffer the

---

[13] Thirty years ago H. Gressmann argued strongly in favor of Egyptian influences upon Israel's Messianic concepts, a position he later abandoned; see P.   Volz, OrLz, 1931, 543.
[14] Is. 14:13.
[15] Ez. 28:2.
[16] Cf. ANET 369.

ravages of famine. Thereupon conditions improve; a capable ruler appears, the sacrifices are resumed, and the land produces abundant crops. Again under subsequent rulers who remain in power "briefly," three years, then eight years, then three years, then eight years again, there is the alternation of good and hard times. The exact figures for each prince's rule would hardly be given if genuine prophecies had been intended. Such literary productions witness to the universal longing for social and economic improvement. An era of spiritual beatitude that never ends is nowhere mentioned. Promises and predictions touch only material goods; only current regimes are praised, never some future king. It is the monarch on the throne who surpasses previous occupants. Nor is there ever any reference to a religious or moral betterment — always the essential point for a Biblical prophet.

The evils from which the Babylonian wished to be freed consisted in deliverance from temporal misfortune, from sickness, human contempt, death. At times he may have associated misfortune with sin, but his cloudy concept of sin prevented any use of suffering as a means to appease an offended divinity; much less would he have arrived at the knowledge of a redeemer who at some future date would come to bring all men forgiveness from sin. This point likewise holds true of the Messianic expectations of other peoples. Caesar Augustus, for instance, was not Rome's only savior; he merely effected an interval of peace after decades of bloody civil wars. And no one hoped he would remain in power forever.

There is no proof for the assertion that legitimate exponents of revealed religion relied on stories about Adonis and Tammuz when they spoke of the Messiah as dying and rising again. The salvation to be effected by the Redeemer promised by God's prophets was not material in nature; it consisted in the reconciliation of mankind with God, and only those individuals who reform themselves morally will share its blessings. And this holds true both for Jew and Gentile. The judgment God or His Messiah holds may indeed be marked by the most extraordinary natural phenomena: the sea dries up; the hills quake; the mountains leap; the rocks split open; [17] men and cattle, the birds of the heavens and the fish are snatched up; [18] the stars cease to shine; sun and moon become dark; the earth turns into a desert [19] as the stars fall from the sky like withered leaves from a tree.[20] It is a judgment, however, that does not merely destroy; through it mankind is cleansed and prepared for Messianic blessings.

Although the hypothesis deriving Israel's theology from Egypt or Babylon must be rejected, it does not follow that the prophets, in de-

[17] Nah. 1:4.
[18] Soph. 1:3.
[19] Hab. 3:1-10 ; Is. 13:6-11.
[20] Is. 34:4.

lineating the Messiah picture, worked in utter isolation from their environment or that the literary form of their message contains no lines resembling the royal annals found along the Nile and Euphrates. As in the Biblical descriptions of Messianic glory,[21] we must distinguish between the message and its dress. Here prudence and caution is required. Where parallels seem to exist, first investigate whether it may simply be an instance of some common Semitic idiom. Hebrew belongs to the Semitic family of languages, and many turns of speech which seem peculiar in Indo-European usage, were common throughout the Semitic world. Examples could begin with the very names or expressions used for God throughout the Fertile Crescent: *'el 'elyon*, Highest God; *ba'al*, Lord; *melekh*, King. The Israelites, moreover, could have used words current among other nations in an entirely different sense — there are numerous examples of loan words assuming meanings quite unlike that originally proper to them. Milk and honey may have been regarded as food for the gods among some Oriental peoples, but the expression as found in Ex. 3:8,17; 13:5; Num. 13:27; 16:13–14 only implies the fertility of the land; an analogous phrase in the Ras Shamra texts describes a rich, well-watered land producing luxuriant vegetation.[22] But in the Isaian passage on the Virgin birth, milk and honey are the products of a land *devastated* by invading armies.

There is nothing mythological in the Biblical descriptions of the Messianic era as a time of greatest productivity and constant peace, when even the wild animals become tame. We might think of the happy state in paradise when there was no sin, and therefore the consequences and punishment for sin did not exist. Peace was desired by the Israelites, especially during periods marked by suffering from the plagues of war. There was no need to consult foreign sources to desire the Messianic gift of peace. The text proclaiming the deliverer as "ruling from sea to sea and from the River (Euphrates) to the ends of the earth," [23] did not originate in Babylon. Under David and Solomon, Israel dominated the region northeast of Canaan to the Euphrates.[24] As the "sprout of David," the Messiah would extend his influence still farther, to the very ends of the earth. The Euphrates is regarded as Canaan's ideal border as early as Gen. 15:18; Ex. 23:31. To the ancient mind the earth was wholly surrounded by water, over all of which the Messiah-King must rule.

In Israel as in neighboring nations, the king was hailed as the source of all material blessings. When the prophets heralded the coming savior as king, David's great descendant, they employed expressions and phraseology in common usage. But their audience would interpret the

---

[21] Cf. Heinisch-Heidt, *Theology of the Old Testament*, pp. 324-336.
[23] Ps. 72:8; Zach. 9-10.

[22] R. Dussaud, *Les découvertes de Ras Shamra*, 79.
[24] 3 Kgs. 5:4.

terms differently than an audience in Egypt or Babylon. Under divine enlightenment the prophets consciously proclaimed a Redeemer from sin, while to the people at large he was a ruler to whom foreigners would do homage. Into language in vogue at the courts of kings, Yahweh's seers did not hesitate to inject new and subtler ideas.

In the ancient Orient, kings were praised as "righteous rulers" and were expected to espouse the cause of the poor and the oppressed. In the introduction to his Code, Hammurabi glories in his allotted destiny of destroying the wicked and evildoers to prevent the powerful from injuring the weak. With him justice came to Babylon, under him all peoples were treated rightly; and his laws would be the source of countless blessings. At the end of the decrees he repeats his plan to make the country prosperous, the citizens happy. He will take pains that no one frightens them, he will prevent the strong from oppressing the weak, and will give to orphans and widows their full rights. Justice was the sun-god Shamash's characteristic attribute, for the sun sheds its light everywhere and scatters darkness. He was one judge who could not be bribed; he destroyed the wicked, unmasked the liar, punished the judge who accepted bribes. To him the weak, the needy, the oppressed, the downtrodden could hopefully appeal. It ought cause no alarm if the Israelites too expected their king to rule justly and give due assistance to those in need; nor should their Messiah lack these basic virtues.

No people but wish their king would never die. In Israel we find the exclamation: "May the king live forever." [25] Solomon assumed that his dynasty would continue "forever." [26] In the Bible the word 'olam, for-ever, often denotes nothing more than a long period of time. It could have been applied to the Messiah without any deeper connotation. But in Nathan's oracle the word was used in its absolute sense, as we know from subsequent passages.

Divine honors were accorded kings in the ancient Orient, and Pharaoh claimed physical descent from the god Re. That the Messiah is called "God" and divine attributes are ascribed to him does not, however, have its origin in non-Jewish literature with its polytheistic presuppositions. For the names of the Messiah, "Wonderful-Counsellor, Mighty-God, Father-Forever," [27] we may find parallels in Babylon, but it must always be remembered that in Israel the message came unmistakably from God. The Sumerian King Gudea of Larsa may have prayed to the goddess Gatumdug: "A mother I do not have, you are my mother; a father I do not have, you are my father. You took my seed into your heart and gave birth to me in the Unu (sanctuary)." [28] But he was, by

---

[25] 3 Kgs. 1:31; Dan. 2:4; Neh. 2:3; Ps. 21:5.
[26] 3 Kgs. 2:45.

[27] Is. 9:5.
[28] Cyl. A3, 6-8; M. Witzel, *Keilinschriftl. Studien*, 99, 113.

no means, insinuating a virginal birth, rather that the goddess had adopted him when he had been quite helpless; he therefore mentions no god as his father.

As noted in our explanation of Balaam's oracle, nothing obscure was involved in calling the deliverer a star.[29] A similar usage of the word occurs in the Isaian passage in which Babylon's king likens himself to God: "How have you fallen from heaven, you morning star, son of the dawn." [30] Yahweh Himself was described in terms of light. The New Testament calls Christ the "bright morning star," [31] while the early Church honored Him as the rising sun.[32]

Sumerian, Babylonian, and Assyrian rulers loved to call themselves "shepherds," and the Pharaohs too. We find the same practice in Israel. David was a shepherd over his people,[33] and likewise the princes.[34] Yahweh was Israel's good shepherd.[35] So if the Messiah is presented as a shepherd deeply attached to his flock,[36] particularly to those most in need of his loving care, it simply reflects a commonplace analogy from everyday life.

The Babylonian and Assyrian kings are sometimes referred to as "royal sprigs." The phrase was used to indicate a legitimate claim to the throne; they did not wish to be regarded as usurpers. The Messiah was called the "bud of David" [37] or simply "bud." [38] The term occurs for the first time in Is. 11:1 and carries the message that the Redeemer would be born only after the Davidic dynasty had been deeply humbled and had lost the throne.

The concept of a suffering, dying, and rising Servant of God was not imported from Mesopotamia, it was not occasioned by the Babylonian penitential psalms or by the New Year ceremony in which the king acquiesced to a ritual humiliation. Had the prophet, who was awaiting Babylon's doom momentarily, recalled that ceremony while describing the functions of Yahweh's Servant, it would have served no other purpose than that of contrast, showing how God's Servant far excelled the Babylonian monarch.

5. The Poet Vergil cherished hopes for deliverance from the turmoil of his day and associated his yearning with the birth of a child. In the year 40 b.c. the Consul Asinius Pollio effected a rapprochement between Octavian and Antony. It was believed that the dreadful period of civil strife with its terror, bloodshed and proscriptions had come to an end, and Vergil hailed a child soon to be born [39] as the omen of good

---

[29] Num. 24:17.   [30] Is. 14:12.   [31] Apoc. 22:10.
[32] F. J. Dölger, *Sol Salutis*, 336f.   [36] Ez. 34:23; 37:24.
[33] 2 Sam. 5:2.   [37] Jer. 23:5; 33:15.
[34] Jer. 2:8; 10:21; 22:22; 23:1-4; Is.   [38] Zach. 3:5; 6:12.
56:41.   [39] Very probably a son of Pollio, his
[35] Ez. 34:12; Mich. 4:6; Soph. 3:19; Jer.   patron; according to others a son of Au-
31:10; Ps. 23:1.   gustus.

fortune. With his birth a golden age for the whole, wide world would dawn. The child would be divinely endowed, and momentous changes were imminent. His father would witness them and contribute his services. It would be a time of exceptional productivity, the means for human livelihood no longer need be brought from distant regions with all the concomitant danger and difficulty. Honey drops from oaks, grapes ripen on thornbushes. Wild animals no longer do damage, the cow no longer fears the lion. Poisonous reptiles and plants cease to exist. There is no need for dyes, for sheep bear purple and saffron wool.[40]

This description of the future cannot be classed as a true prophecy. The poet was simply voicing the popular hope for speedy improvement in economic and political conditions. The "expected child" does not cause the change, he is only a symbol of it. The form, however, in which Vergil clothes his hopes leads one to think of Oriental influences, and it is this consideration that justifies the present discussion. At the beginning of his description of the golden age, Vergil refers to the Sibylline books. After the capitol with its various collections of oracles had been destroyed by fire in the year 76, a senatorial commission was sent to Asia Minor to obtain a new one. It is probable that some Jewish Sibylline literature was included; a passage in the Third Book of Sibylls, 652–660, comes easily to mind: Then God will send a king from the land of the rising sun; he will put an end to wicked war all over the world, slaying some and making firm covenants with others. He will not do this according to his own counsel, but in accord with the beneficent decrees of God most High. The temple of the great God will be his, abounding in riches, in gold and silver and purple adornment. The earth will produce its fruits, and the sea will be full of treasures.

Thereupon, however, will follow further bloodshed, and even Vergil expected occasional wars and revolutions. His deference to the Sibyll of Cumae does not exclude culling from Jewish Sibylline literature. Nor was it impossible that Jews should have placed genuine Old Testament prophecies into the hands of the Roman commission, for example, Is. 11, and that in this manner Vergil became aware of Jewish Messianic hopes. The Jews, at least those in the Diaspora, were eager to spread their religious heritage. Some patristic writers have regarded Vergil's words as a true prophecy of Christ's birth, e.g., Augustine,[41] Lactantius,[42] Eusebius.[43] St. Jerome, however, protested against such interpretation of the passage, asserting that Vergil could not be made a Christian without Christ.[44]

Human longing for "better times" expresses itself in many ways. Some

[40] Ecl. IV.
[41] De civ. Dei, 10, 27.
[42] Inst. div., 7, 24.
[43] Vita Const., 5, 19.
[44] Ep. 53, ad Paulinum.

similarities in phraseology, however, should be expected. Nevertheless, the passages from Oriental literature produced as parallels to the prophecies in Sacred Scripture do not prove that hope in a personal Redeemer arose in Israel or that it developed as the prophetic oracles indicate. That familiarity with the royal annals of neighboring kingdoms influenced the external form of the Messianic message need not be denied. Even today, when we are able to understand the religion and history of Israel much better because of modern progress in Oriental studies, Justin's observation still remains valid: The Messianic prophecies constitute the "greatest and most convincing proof" for the divinity of Christ and the supernatural nature of Christianity.[45]

CONCLUSION

The intimate relationship between the Old and the New Covenants was shown upon the Mount of the Transfiguration when Moses and Elias, representing the Law and the prophets, appeared speaking with Jesus. Through Moses as a mediator, God entered into a covenant with Israel and gave them a Law that remained in force for over 1,000 years, a Law that served as the "pedagogue unto Christ"[46] and kept Israel from being engulfed by her pagan environment, a Law that enjoined self-mastery and preserved alive the consciousness of sin and the desire for redemption.

Elias labored in the Northern Kingdom during her darkest years. With the support of the royal family, Baal was officially worshipped. Only 7,000 remained loyal to Yahweh in the face of persecution, and Yahweh's prophets were put to death. By fiery preaching Elias roused the people and through the contest on Carmel proved Baal's impotence. He blazed the way for later prophets, showing them how to "prepare the way for the Lord" by penitential and comminatory discourses as well as by prophecies on the Messiah and his kingdom. On the mountain of transfiguration Moses and Elias spoke with Jesus about His imminent death, the crowning act in His work of redemption.[47]

When Jesus appeared, the Jews should have realized that He was the Redeemer whom the prophets had foretold. The fulfillment of the

---

[45] *Ap.*, I, 30.   [46] Gal. 3:24.   [47] Matth. 17:3 ; Luke 9:30-31.

Messianic prophecies should have motivated them to hail Him as the long-awaited Savior. On occasion Jesus Himself quoted the prophets.[48]

The Redeemer did "come to his own," even though His own would not receive Him.[49] There were, we must not forget, some pious persons in Israel. Enlightened by God, Zachary realized that with the birth of his son the Messianic age had dawned, that his child was destined to "go before the Lord to prepare his ways."[50] Elizabeth hailed Mary as the "mother of her God," the one in whom the Virgin birth prophecies were being fulfilled.[51] Simeon was numbered among those who were longing for the consolation of Israel, the advent of the promised Redeemer; and he greeted the Child presented in the temple as the Light God had prepared unto the illumination of the Gentiles and the glory of His people Israel.[52] The prophetess Anna spoke of the Infant to all who were desiring redemption.[53] And there were Gentiles too who came to worship, as we read in the second chapter of St. Matthew's Gospel.

Heralded as the Messiah by John the Baptist and miraculously attested by His heavenly Father,[54] our Redeemer found His first followers among the fishermen of Galilee — Andrew and Simon Peter; James and John; Philip (who exclaimed: "We have found him of whom Moses and the prophets wrote!"[55]) and Nathaniel-Bartholomew (whose guileless heart quickly responded: "You are the Son of God, you are the King of Israel!"[56]). However, it was not long before the stage was set for the fulfillment of Simeon's prophecy: "He is destined for the fall and for the resurrection of many in Israel and for a sign that will be contradicted."[57] Christ's miracles awakened popular astonishment, the crowds listened with enthusiasm to His words, and the Jews observed His every move. But as soon as there appeared the first sign that the people regarded the miracle-worker and teacher as the promised son of David, the leaders of the people, the Pharisees and Scribes, plotted feverishly to thwart Him. And finally they moved the mob to demand the crucifixion of the One on whose account God had chosen them as His people. As Jesus hung naked on the Cross between two thieves, the Pharisees and Scribes mocked him as cursed by God.

The great mass of the people had formed for themselves a picture of the Redeemer that did not harmonize with Christ's spirit and teaching. A deliverer from sin, One who would judge Israel, One who is poor, who demands self-denial and the renunciation of sinful ways, One whose kingdom has no show of power at its disposal and which lacks all pomp and splendor — such a Messiah had not been the object of Israel's longing already in pre-exilic days. David's great descendant was expected

---

48 John 5:39, 46; Matth. 11:4-5, 13.
49 John 1:11.
50 Luke 1:76.
51 Luke 1:42-45.
52 Luke 2:25-32.
53 Luke 2:38.
54 Matth. 3:13.
55 John 1:45.
56 John 1:49.
57 Luke 2:34.

to break the yoke of Rome and make Israel foremost among the nations. Israel listened to the Sadducean priests and followed the Pharisees who would have accorded salvation to the Gentiles only on condition that they subjected themselves to the multitudinous details of scribal law. They would not consider the prophetic message in its entirety but stressed unessentials that flattered selfish, earthly ambitions and disregarded its primary message that went counter to personal inclinations. For the Messiah their interpretation spelt death.

The prophecies that assured Israel of eternal blessings under the sceptre of the Messiah-King were indeed fulfilled. "If some (Jews) became unfaithful, should their infidelity render null the fidelity of God?," the apostle Paul asked rhetorically, and immediately answered: "By no means. God will be true, even though all men are liars." [58] Then he proposed another question: "Does it imply God's rejection of his people?," and again he replied: "Not at all." [59] The prophetic pronouncements were fulfilled differently than Israel in her blindness had imagined. From the wicked caretakers who did not hesitate to murder His Son, God took the vineyard and gave it to those who would render Him its fruits.[60] Gentiles entered into the inheritance Judaism had contemned, they became the new Israel. Still Paul could conclude, in harmony with a long series of prophets: "Blindness has come upon a part of Israel until the full number of the Gentiles enter (Christ's kingdom) and then all Israel will be saved." [61] The Messianic kingdom is a kingdom of grace, it is not a kingdom of external show and pomp and political maneuvering. And at some future day the one-time People of God, a nation so highly privileged, will likewise accept the Savior.

At first only a few gave themselves unreservedly to Jesus, the apostles. They saw in Him One greater than any of the ancient prophets, God's only-begotten Son. They acknowledged Him as such, in contrast to the people who could not bring themselves to make this act of faith.[62] Nevertheless, their Messianic ideas contained much earthly alloy. Their picture of the kingdom Jesus was endeavoring to establish, followed too closely the external coloring once used by the prophets. Jesus did not come to rule over a kingdom in any earthly-political sense; His mission was to conquer sin and Satan, and this end He could achieve only by suffering and dying. Much education was needed before the apostles grasped this. However, after the resurrection of their Master and the descent of the Holy Spirit, they stood up fearlessly and preached Christ crucified. They withstood the temple officials who forbade them to teach [63] and when scourged for witnessing to the truth, "they went away rejoicing from the Sanhedrin because they had been found worthy

[58] Rom. 3:3-4.   [60] Matth. 21:33f.   [62] Matth. 16:13-20.
[59] Rom. 11:1.   [61] Rom. 11:25-26.   [63] Acts 4:15f.

to suffer contempt for the Name (of Jesus)."[64] It had finally become clear that the kingdom of God upon earth does not consist in ease and glory but in suffering and sacrifice.

The King of the Jews died upon a Cross. To Him who arose from the dead all power was given in heaven and upon earth.[65] He sent out His apostles not as the head of an earthly principality but as the sovereign ruler of the universe. They were to preach the good news of His Gospel to Gentile nations, as the prophets had foretold. The Church they were establishing should embrace the entire world and continue to the end of time. The world was not destined to remain pagan, it was to be transformed in Christ.

Nevertheless, the kingdom of God heralded by the prophets, founded by Jesus and proclaimed by His apostles does not immediately bestow the beatitude of heaven. During the first centuries thousands offered their blood in testimony to their faith in Christ and His Gospel. Down to this very day Jesus is preached as the Crucified, and men accept and obey the despised and persecuted Son of God. Opposition to God continues, as once upon the mount where Jesus was tempted. Bread, fame, and power are promised Christians if they but fall down and adore. Princes and people continue to rise against God and against His Anointed. Again and again it appears as if victory was theirs. But Christ remains King of the world. He shatters His foes as a potter's vessel,[66] and on the Last Day will return, as the prophet said,[67] upon the clouds of heaven.

[64] Acts 5:41.
[65] Matth. 28:28.
[66] Ps. 2.
[67] Dan. 7 ; Matth. 24:30.

ABBREVIATIONS

AA — Alttestamentliche Abhandlungen

AfO — Archiv für Orientforschung

ANET — Ancient Near Eastern Texts (edit. by J. B. Pritchard)

AOB — H. Gressmann, Altorientalische Bilder zum Alten Testament, 1927

AOT — H. Gressmann, Altorientalische Texte zum Alten Testament, 1926

Bb — Biblica

BZ — Biblische Zeitschrift

BZF — Biblische Zeitfragen

G (LXX) — Septuagint

It — Old Latin translation

M (MT) — Masoretic Text

OrLz — Orientalistische Literaturzeitung

Rb — Revue biblique

S — Syrian Version

Sam — Samaritan Pentateuch

StZ — Stimmen der Zeit

Targ — Aramaic versions (Targums)

ThQ — Tübinger theologische Quartalschrift

ThR — Theologische Rundschau

V — Vulgate

VD — Verbum Domini

ZatW — Zeitschrift für alttestamentliche Wissenschaft

ZdmG — Zeitschrift der Deutschen Morgenländischen Gesellschaft

INDEX